QuickBooks® 2016

The Best Guide for Small Business

QuickBooks® 2016
The Best Guide for Small Business

BOBBI SANDBERG
LESLIE CAPACHIETTI

New York   Chicago   San Francisco
Athens   London   Madrid   Mexico City
Milan   New Delhi   Singapore   Sydney   Toronto

Cataloging-in-Publication Data is on file with the Library of Congress

McGraw-Hill Education books are available at special quantity discounts to use as premiums and sales promotions, or for use in corporate training programs. To contact a representative, please visit the Contact Us pages at www.mhprofessional.com.

QuickBooks® 2016: The Best Guide for Small Business

1 2 3 4 5 6 7 8 9 0   DOC DOC   1 0 9 8 7 6 5

ISBN   978-1-25-958544-9
MHID   1-25-958544-1

Sponsoring Editor
Wendy Rinaldi

Editorial Supervisor
Janet Walden

Project Editor
Howie Severson,
Fortuitous Publishing

Copy Editor
Lisa McCoy

Proofreader
Claire Splan

Indexer
Jack Lewis

Production Supervisor
James Kussow

Technical Editors
Anne Bobinac,
Michael Olney, CPA

Composition
Cenveo® Publisher Services

Illustration
Cenveo Publisher Services

Art Director, Cover
Jeff Weeks

About the Authors

Bobbi Sandberg is a consulting accountant and retired CPA who has been a trainer, instructor, and teacher of QuickBooks in the Pacific Northwest for more than 40 years. Specializing in "making numbers your friend," Bobbi has helped small businesses succeed by both teaching and supporting QuickBooks, from installation to complex accounting issues. Through her small business–focused community college classes, she helps small business owners understand and use the many features in QuickBooks. Bobbi has authored and co-authored nearly two dozen computer- and accounting-related books, including *QuickBooks 2015: The Best Guide for Small Business* and *Quicken 2016: The Official Guide* (McGraw-Hill Professional, 2016).

Leslie Capachietti, MBA, is an Advanced Certified QuickBooks ProAdvisor, Authorized Intuit Reseller, and a member of Intuit's Accountant Training Network. As a national speaker and trainer, she has taught thousands of accounting professionals on best practices to employ when supporting their QuickBooks clients. Her firm, Automated Financial Solutions, has been recognized by Intuit as a Top Performer for outstanding achievement in supporting QuickBooks users. Leslie has written several books about QuickBooks, including *QuickBooks 2013: The Guide* (McGraw-Hill Professional, 2012).

For Sharie M.—the best administrative coordinator
on the planet—thank you for always being wonderful,
dependable, supportive, and fun! And, always
and ever, to Sandy.

Contents at a Glance

Part Four

Using QuickBooks Reports, Planning Tools, and Budgets

Part Five

Work with Inventory and Personalize QuickBooks

Part Six

Additional Tasks in QuickBooks

Contents

Part One
Getting Started Using the Desktop Version of QuickBooks

Part Two
Daily Operations Using QuickBooks

Part Three
Payroll

Part Four
Using QuickBooks Reports, Planning Tools, and Budgets

Part Five
Work with Inventory and Personalize QuickBooks

Part Six
Additional Tasks in QuickBooks

Acknowledgments

It took a team of dedicated and talented professionals to deliver this book to you.

This book is due to the hard work of Wendy Rinaldi and her great team at McGraw-Hill Education and their attention to detail and always supportive suggestions and advice. This team is a joy with which to work, and more professional, capable, and amazing people would be extremely hard to find! New to the project this year is Howie Severson, a delightful addition. His experienced, practiced, and expert eye has made this endeavor shine. (His sense of humor is top-notch as well!) And the best copy editor in the business, Lisa McCoy, found typos, grammar errors, and other faux pas with her capable proficiency. She really is the best! More new team members this year are Anne Bobinac and Michael Olney, our technical editors. They worked hard, using their vast experience and QuickBooks knowledge to ensure that this book gives as much information as possible about the QuickBooks Desktop versions. Their combined decades of experience makes my job easier! This team has worked very hard to make this book helpful to you and your business and we wish you every success!

Introduction

Use This Book to Get the Most from QuickBooks

Whether you're a novice or an experienced QuickBooks Desktop version user, the information in this book is organized and presented in a way that can benefit you. If you're brand new to QuickBooks Desktop, the chapters that make up Parts One and Two are required reading. Following the advice and detailed steps outlined in these chapters will help ensure that your QuickBooks file is set up correctly from the start. You'll also learn about all the day-to-day bookkeeping chores you'll be performing in QuickBooks. If you're already a more experienced QuickBooks user or you've mastered the basics, you'll find the information in Parts Three through Six relevant. You can refer to these chapters to confirm that you're on the right track or to learn how to use some of the more advanced features QuickBooks offers.

When you have an immediate need to know how to do something, both the table of contents and the index are designed to make it easy for you to identify quickly where in the book a specific task or feature is covered.

You and Your Accountant

In a number of places throughout this book, you are reminded to talk to your accountant before making a decision about the best way to enter a beginning balance or handle a particular transaction in QuickBooks. We encourage you to heed this advice. Although QuickBooks gives you the tools you need to manage your business's financial operations, your accountant can play a vital role in helping you maintain a healthy and viable business by providing valuable tax and strategic business-planning advice. In addition, to help *your accountant* better assist *you,* throughout the book we identify information that we think you should share with your accountant because it tells him or her how QuickBooks handles certain accounting functions—for example, payroll and inventory.

If you don't have an accountant and want to connect with one, there are accountants in your area who are certified by Intuit as QuickBooks experts. They often provide on-site assistance with setup and troubleshooting and are a great resource if you get "stuck" while setting up your QuickBooks file—or just want to have an expert review the information you've entered in your system. To locate a Certified QuickBooks ProAdvisor in your area, select Find A Local QuickBooks Expert from the QuickBooks Help menu.

Getting Started Using the Desktop Version of QuickBooks

Welcome to QuickBooks! Whether this is your first version or you've used the program for years, this guide is for you. QuickBooks is, at its base, a bookkeeping program. However, when it is properly set up and maintained, it may become one of your company's most valuable assets. Not only will you use it to track your bank balances and what your customers owe you, but you'll also refer to it as you make important decisions such as hiring more employees, making a price change, or even selling your business.

In Part One you'll learn how to gather the information you need to get started so you can create and start using your company file. You'll learn what steps are critical, what you may need to ask someone else, and what you can do on your own. Part One also includes chapters containing instructions and hints when you enter all of the important information for your company into QuickBooks, such as customers, vendors, and the other lists that contain data to help you track your finances more accurately.

Preparing Your QuickBooks Company

In this chapter:

- Preparing for QuickBooks
- Installing the software
- Getting around in QuickBooks
- QuickBooks administration
- Setting up accounts

Chapter 1

The first time you open the desktop version of QuickBooks, the QuickBooks Setup window launches. From here, you can begin the process of either creating a brand-new company file or working with an existing file. The focus of this chapter is on ensuring that you have what you need to set up your new QuickBooks company file and to help you get familiar with basic navigation so that you can begin to work in the program right away. You'll learn how to set up those who will be entering data into your program (called Users) and how to create the foundation of your financial data, the chart of accounts.

What to Do Ahead of Time

Before you purchase software, you need to decide which desktop version of QuickBooks is best suited for your needs. Once the software is in your hands, you need to gather the required information so the program has the proper beginning balances, and finally, determine the best time to start using the software.

Choose Your Version

As you consider moving to QuickBooks 2016, you'll notice several desktop versions for small business from which you can choose. In a Windows environment, you can select QuickBooks Pro, QuickBooks Premier, or QuickBooks Enterprise Solutions. For those companies using an Apple iOS, Intuit provides QuickBooks for Mac. The QuickBooks Online version is also available, but not covered in this book.

> **Note** An additional version is QuickBooks Desktop Accountant, a special version designed for accounting professionals.

Table 1-1 shows just some of the features available in the various versions.

Gather Information

After you have decided which version of QuickBooks Desktop to use as your bookkeeping program, it is a good time to get out that shoebox, binder, or spreadsheet you've been using to keep track of your business so far, because you'll need to have the following handy:

- Your last tax return for the business
- Your bank register and statements for the year
- Loan statements and terms
- A list of the customers that owe you money and how much they owe as of the date you want to start using QuickBooks

Feature	QuickBooks Pro	QuickBooks Premier	QuickBooks for Mac	QuickBooks Enterprise Solutions
Track sales, customers, and taxes	X	X	X	X
Pay bills, track expenses, print checks	X	X	X	X
Use e-mail to send estimates, invoices, and reports	X	X	X	X
Use an Inventory Center		X		X
Download from banks and credit card companies	X	X	X	X
Import data from Excel and Quicken	X	X	X	X
Track international transactions in multiple currencies	X	X		X
Use classes (departments), create forecasts and business plans		X		X
Use bar coding and other inventory tracking, FIFO (first in, first out) costing, and multiple location inventory				X

TABLE 1-1   Features of QuickBooks 2016 Desktop Versions

- A list of the suppliers that you owe money to and how much you owe them as of the date you want to start using QuickBooks
- A list of any special equipment, machinery, or computers you own, including their current value and amounts previously depreciated
- A written tally of the money you've put into your business

You need this information because you want the most accurate and complete information you have about your business to make its way into your new QuickBooks file. It's not that you can't change things in QuickBooks later on; it's just that if you start with incorrect or even incomplete data, you sometimes won't be able to figure out what was wrong to begin with. Moreover, if you can't find the problem's source, you run the risk of the problem becoming permanent.

Decide on the Start Date

Your start date is the date that you begin tracking your business in QuickBooks. Even though activities may have occurred before this date, you enter transactions into your new file starting on this date.

Choosing a start date is an important decision, because the date you choose can affect how much work it will take to set up your QuickBooks file. As you are deciding on your start date, consider the following.

Do you want every detail since the beginning of the current year to be available in QuickBooks? If so, you will need to enter every invoice you sent to customers and all the payments you've received on them, every check you wrote to vendors, every payroll check issued to an employee, and so on.

If you are not as concerned about each transaction, you can enter summary totals for each of your company's transaction types up until the day before your QuickBooks start date. Entering monthly summary totals will allow you to run valuable reports (such as the Profit & Loss statement and Balance Sheet) with month-to-month comparisons.

As you can see, the start date and the entry method you choose make a difference in the reports you can generate with QuickBooks.

Gather Additional Information

Whatever method you choose for entering your information, it's a good idea to have all the information together and in one place rather than trying to locate each piece of information during the setup. You'll learn how to enter customer and vendor information and their beginning balances in Chapter 2, so have that data handy along with your last tax return, bank registers, and the items mentioned in the previous section.

Cash Balances

QuickBooks needs to know the reconciled balance for each of your business bank accounts, so verify the balances as of your start date. If you haven't balanced your checkbooks against the bank statements for a while, do so before you enter data into QuickBooks. In addition to the reconciled balance and the statement itself, you need to have a list of the dates and the amounts (both deposits in transit and checks) of the transactions that haven't yet cleared.

Customer and Vendor Balances

If any customer owes you money as of your start date, you have to tell QuickBooks about it. Enter each unpaid customer invoice, using the actual, original dates. Those dates must be earlier than your QuickBooks start date. This means you have to assemble all the information about unpaid customer invoices, including such details as how much of each invoice was for services, items sold, shipping, and sales tax. You'll learn how to set up a customer in Chapter 2. As you enter the information about each invoice, QuickBooks automatically creates the accounts receivable balance for you.

The money you owe as of your start date makes up your accounts payable. Similar to the way you enter your accounts receivable, enter each unpaid bill into QuickBooks using the bill's original date. As with your customer information, you'll learn how to do this in Chapter 2.

Asset and Liability Balances

In addition to knowing your bank account balances, you have to know the balances of the rest of your business's assets. For example, you'll need to know the cost basis of your fixed assets (such as equipment and furniture) and any accumulated depreciation on those assets. Ask your tax preparer for this information.

Gather all the information about your company's liabilities (dollars you owe to others). If you have not paid your current payroll liabilities, for example, you must enter those unpaid amounts. Although the open vendor bills you enter determine your accounts payable balance automatically, you'll need to know the current balance of any loans or mortgages as well. Check with your lender or tax preparer if you're unsure of this information.

Payroll Information

If you do the payroll yourself instead of using a payroll service, you'll need to know everything about each employee: social security number, all the information that goes into determining tax status (federal, state, and local), and which deductions are taken for health or pensions. Double-check the information on each employee's current W-4 form.

You also need to know which payroll items you have to track: salary, wages, federal deductions, state deductions (tax, state unemployment insurance (SUI), state disability insurance SDI), local income tax deductions, benefits, pension, and any other deductions (garnishments, for example). You also need the name and your account number for each government department to whom you send these withheld amounts—some examples are government tax agencies, insurance companies, and so on. You'll learn to create payroll in Chapter 9.

Inventory Information

If you maintain an inventory, you will need to decide on the names you want to assign to every inventory item you carry and, most importantly, how much you paid for each item and how many of each you have in stock as of the start date. QuickBooks needs these last two key pieces of information to keep an accurate inventory valuation for you. It is a good time to be thinking about any other information you want to track for each of the items you carry in inventory. For example, what description do you want your customers to see on their invoices? Do you have a preferred vendor from which you purchase an item? Learn more about setting up your inventory in Chapter 13.

You're now ready to set up and configure your QuickBooks company file! Let's get started.

Install and Launch the Software

Whether you're installing QuickBooks from a CD or using a download link from the Intuit website, the installation process is quite straightforward. Simply follow the installation instructions to where you'll read and accept the software license agreement, and select where on your computer you want to install the program. Once the installation of the program is complete, you'll see a QuickBooks 2016 icon on the desktop in either Windows 10 or Windows 7. Also in Windows 10, you can find a link in the Apps Center (look for "All Apps") under "Q" for QuickBooks. In either operating system, you can pin QuickBooks to the taskbar (right-click the icon and select Pin To Taskbar).

Depending on whether you have existing QuickBooks files, you may see the No Company Open window, as shown next. You see the following options:

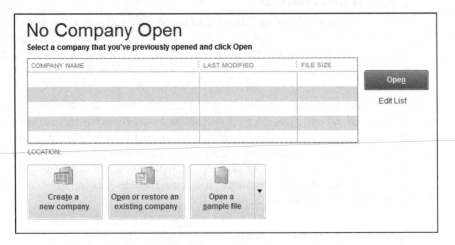

- **Create A New Company**   Select this option to begin the process of creating a company file. See all of the steps involved in this task in the next section.
- **Open Or Restore An Existing Company**   Select this option if you're upgrading from a previous version of QuickBooks. Go through the windows in the Open Or Restore Company Wizard to select your company file. QuickBooks offers to upgrade the file to your new version. Place a check mark in the I Understand That My Company File Will Be Updated To This New Version Of QuickBooks box to accept the offer. QuickBooks then requires that you make a backup of your file in its current version. When the backup is complete, you see a message reminding you that the file is being converted to a newer version. Click OK to begin working in your updated file.
- **Open A Sample File**   Click this option to display a list of sample companies you can use to explore QuickBooks. Depending on your QuickBooks version, you may see two or more sample companies.

If you choose the Create A New Company option, the QuickBooks Setup window opens, as shown next. This window provides links to help you get started by using either the Express Start or Detailed Start. You can also create a new company file based on an existing file.

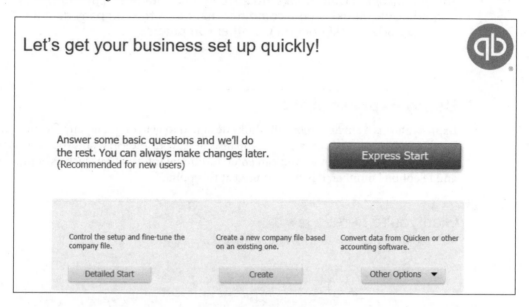

Let's get your business set up quickly!

Answer some basic questions and we'll do the rest. You can always make changes later. (Recommended for new users)

Express Start

Control the setup and fine-tune the company file.

Detailed Start

Create a new company file based on an existing one.

Create

Convert data from Quicken or other accounting software.

Other Options ▼

Small Business Tip As seen in the earlier illustration, QuickBooks Accountant offers the option of creating a new QuickBooks file based on an existing one. When this option is selected, QuickBooks creates a new company file using the existing company's chart of accounts, items, preferences, and sales tax items.

Create Your Company File

Use the following options to create your new company file:

- **Express Start** Asks for some very basic information about your business, such as its name, the type of industry, and how your business is organized. For each required entry, you see an asterisk and a link to help you make a choice.
- **Detailed Start** When you use this option, you will move through several screens, answering questions and providing information so that QuickBooks can fine-tune your company.
- **Create** Helps you create a new company based on information from an existing company.
- **Other Options** Enables you to create a new file from an existing Quicken file or from other accounting software information. Select the Convert Other Accounting Software Data option and follow the onscreen directions to launch the QuickBooks Conversion Tool.

> **Small Business Tip** If you're working in a network environment and you installed QuickBooks Pro 2016 as an upgrade to a previous version, upgrade QuickBooks on the computer that holds the company data file *first*. Then upgrade QuickBooks on the other computers.

Using Express Start

Express Start is a single screen with links designed to get your company file created quickly. As shown next, only your company name, your industry, and your company type are required. Although you can enter additional information, such as your address and telephone number, it is not required at this point.

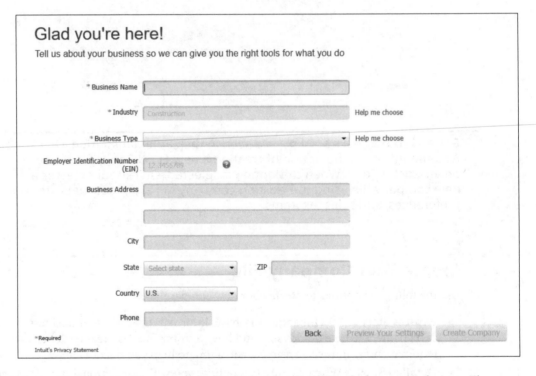

Click Preview Your Settings to review what QuickBooks has set up for you. There are three tabs of information. Do take the time to check what appears in each tab. Although you can make changes later, verifying this preliminary information can save time. Click OK to return to the previous window.

Click Create Company. You will see another screen asking if you want to add customers, vendors, or other information. If you choose to add these later, click Start Working to begin using your new company file.

Using Detailed Start

The Detailed Start option opens the EasyStep Interview Wizard, as seen in Figure 1-1. This gives a step-by-step approach to creating your company file. Click Next to move through the windows.

Entering Company Information

In the first screen of the interview, you enter basic information about your company. Notice that the information about your company name has two entry fields. The first field is for the real company name, the one by which you do business. The second field, for your company's legal name, is optional and is used only if the legal name of your company differs from the company name you use for doing business. For instance, your company may do business as Win Contracting, but your legal or corporate name might be Winchester Contracting, Inc.

Enter the company tax ID number. Your federal employer ID number (EIN) is a nine-digit number in the format $XX\text{-}YYYYYYY$. You need a tax ID number if you have employees. If you don't have an EIN, enter your social security number.

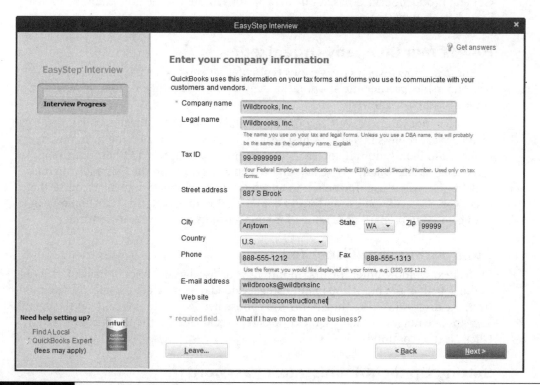

FIGURE 1-1   Use the EasyStep Interview Wizard to enter details about your company.

Small Business Tip If you are a sole proprietor using your social security number for business purposes, consider applying for a federal ID number. This can help you separate your business and personal finances by using the T/EIN (Taxpayer/Employer Identification Number) for business transactions and maintaining a separate bank account in your business name. As your business grows and you hire subcontractors, consultants, or employees, you'll eventually need an EIN to pay these folks.

Enter the contact information (address, telephone number, and so on). QuickBooks uses this on the transactions you print (such as invoices), so enter this information as you want it to appear on printed documents. After you have entered the information on this screen, click Next to continue.

Selecting the Industry

In the next window, select the industry that matches the type of business you have. Scroll up or down to see the options. If you don't see an exact match for your business type, choose one that comes close. Alternatively, you can simply select either of the General Product/Service-based Business options located at the bottom of the industry list. Click Next to continue.

How Is Your Company Organized?

The next window displays the various types of legal entities for businesses, such as proprietorship, partnership, corporation, and so on. Select the one that matches the way your business is organized.

If you're not sure, ask your accountant or find a copy of the business income tax you filed last year (unless this is your first year in business) and match the form number to the list in the window. If you can't find the information, select Other/None. You can change it later via the My Company screen accessed from the Company menu. QuickBooks uses this information to attach tax-line information to all accounts that affect your taxes. If you use an Intuit tax preparation program, this information can then be used to prepare a tax return for your business. Click Next to continue.

Configuring Your Fiscal Year

In the next window, enter the first month of your fiscal year. QuickBooks enters January as the default entry, but if you're not using a calendar year, select the appropriate month from the drop-down list. The month you choose here will automatically set the default year-to-date ranges for many QuickBooks reports, including the Profit & Loss report. Click Next to continue.

Setting Up the Administrator Password

The next window asks you for an administrator password. It's a good idea to create a password to limit access to your company file and to prevent unauthorized access to your business's financial information, especially if you plan on storing customer credit card information. PCI DSS (Payment Card Industry Data Security Standard) compliance standards also require a complex password if you are storing customer credit card information in QuickBooks.

Creating user logins and passwords lets you place restrictions on what users can do and see in QuickBooks. See "Setting Up Users and Permissions" later in this chapter. Click Next to continue.

Creating Your Company File

The next window explains that you're about to save your company file. Click Next to see the Filename For New Company dialog, as seen next. This saves the company information using a filename based on the company name you've entered. Just click Save to use that filename. If you prefer, you can change the name of the file. It takes a few seconds for QuickBooks to save the company file and set up all the files for the company. By default, QuickBooks saves your company file in a subfolder under the Documents folder.

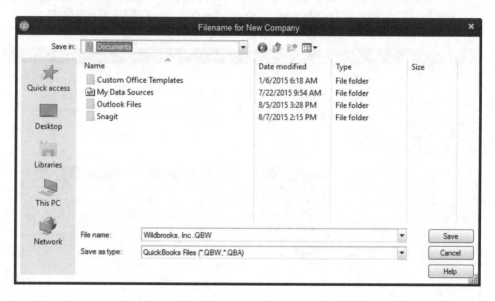

S m a l l   B u s i n e s s   T i p   Consider creating a folder on your hard drive for your QuickBooks data (for instance, C:\QBDataFiles). This makes it easier to find and back up your data.

Customizing QuickBooks for Your Business

The remaining EasyStep Interview windows provide a series of choices and options about the way you do business. For example, you're asked what you sell (services, products, or both), whether you charge sales tax, whether you use estimates, and so on. The questions are clearly stated and easy to answer, and you won't necessarily have to perform any setup tasks right away if you answer Yes. For example, if you answer Yes when you're asked if you have employees, you don't have to create employee information immediately—you can do all of that later.

Essentially, QuickBooks is setting configuration options for you, but you can set any of those options for yourself at any time. Find information about the options you need to perform certain tasks in the appropriate chapters throughout this book.

Selecting a Start Date and Creating the Chart of Accounts

Before you begin creating your chart of accounts, you'll be asked to choose a QuickBooks start date. Before filling in your answer, be sure to read the section "Decide on the Start Date," earlier in this chapter. Click Next after you've completed this page to review the income and expense accounts that QuickBooks suggests you use.

QuickBooks displays the income and expense accounts it has established for your company, based on your responses to the interview question regarding your type of business. Figure 1-2 shows the review page for your chart of accounts.

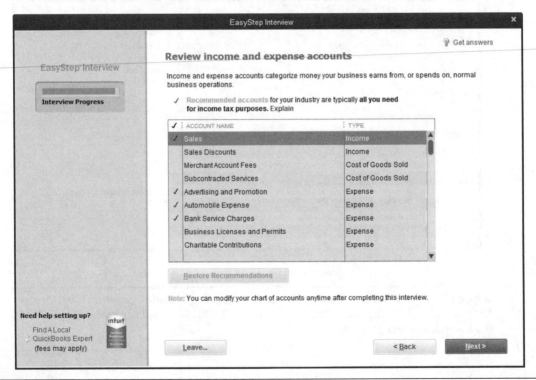

FIGURE 1-2   You can select or deselect items for your chart of accounts on this screen, or wait until you begin using QuickBooks.

You can select or deselect specific accounts if you know you need or don't need any of them. However, it may be easier to go through that process later. You'll likely need additional accounts in your chart of accounts, but it's easier to add them after you've finished this company setup task. Learn more about setting up your chart of accounts in the section "Create Your Company's Chart of Accounts" later in this chapter.

Click Next to finish with the basics of creating your QuickBooks company file. You can now continue building your file by clicking the Go To Setup button and launching the QuickBooks Setup window.

The QuickBooks Setup Wizard

The QuickBooks Setup Wizard (which launches after either a Detailed or Express Startup) gives you three important options designed to help simplify the task of getting information into your new company file, as shown in the following illustration.

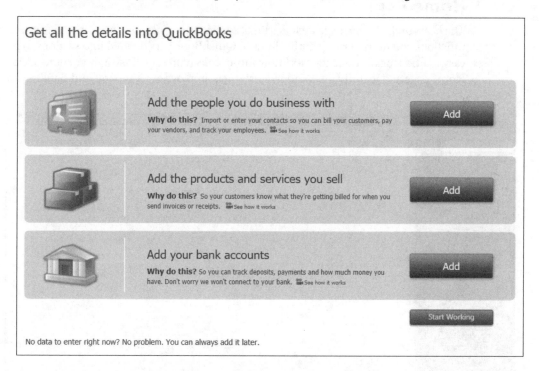

Click the Add button next to the list type that you want to enter. You may enter the information manually or import the data from Excel and even several e-mail applications. QuickBooks will tell you any fixes that need to be made to the information prior to importing it.

If you prefer to start exploring your file now and work on your lists later, click the Start Working button at the bottom of the window to open the QuickBooks Home page.

Navigate in QuickBooks

With your new file created, let's take a look at how you get around in the software.

The Home page, as seen in Figure 1-3, shows the following elements:

- **Title Bar**   Located at the top of the QuickBooks window, this displays the name of your QuickBooks company file.
- **Menu Bar**   Gives you access to all areas in QuickBooks.
- **Icon Bar**   Contains buttons for quick access to frequently used functions. By default, it appears at the left side of the Home page. Learn how to change the location and functions on the Icon Bar in the section "Customize the Icon Bar," later in this chapter.

Home Page

The heart of the Home page includes links and icons you can use to access the features and functions you need to run your business in QuickBooks. It's divided into sections to make it easy to find icons and see the workflow those icons represent. Take a moment to review the Home page and identify the Vendor, Customer, Employees, Company, and Banking areas.

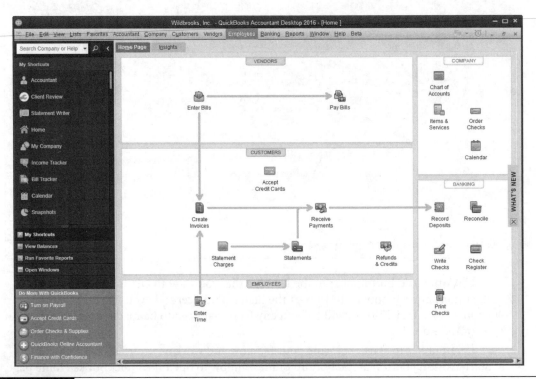

FIGURE 1-3   The QuickBooks Home page makes navigation easy.

The Home page is dynamic—that is, the icons and workflow arrows it contains change as you enable the various features available in QuickBooks. For example, if you enable inventory tracking, QuickBooks adds icons in the Vendors section for inventory-related tasks

QuickBooks Centers

QuickBooks centers are windows in which information is displayed about specific areas of your company. Most centers have a dedicated button on the Icon Bar or directly in the middle of the Home page; other centers are accessible from the menu bar. You can see current data, analyze that data, and perform tasks. QuickBooks centers are shown in Table 1-2.

Center	What It Contains
Customer Center	Open the Customer Center by selecting it from the Customers menu at the top of the QuickBooks window. Here you find everything you'd ever need to know about your customers, including your list of customers and all the information about each. You can also perform routine customer-related tasks using the buttons at the top of the Customer Center window. Information about using and customizing the Customer Center is in Chapter 2.
Vendor Center	The Vendor Center makes it easy to view detailed information about your vendors and to enter transactions into QuickBooks related to them. Select Vendor Center from the Vendors menu on the menu bar to open this center. Learn how to use and customize the Vendor Center in Chapter 2.
Employee Center	Whether you process your own payroll or use a QuickBooks payroll service, you can find detailed information about each employee, your payroll liabilities, and the payroll transactions for each employee in the Employee Center, accessed from the Employees menu. Refer to Chapter 9 to learn more about the ways you can process payroll in QuickBooks.
Report Center	The Report Center can be opened directly from the Icon Bar and includes three views: Carousel view, List view, and Grid view. For each view, the major category of reports displays in the left pane. Learn more about reports in Chapter 11.
Bank Feeds Center	From the Icon Bar, you can also launch the Bank Feeds Center, where you can go to download and enter transactions directly from your credit card and bank accounts into QuickBooks. Do consider taking advantage of this useful and time-saving feature. Learn more in Chapter 8.
Docs Center	The Docs Center holds documents and files on your computer that you can then "attach" to or associate with a specific transaction or record in QuickBooks. Learn how in Chapter 14.
App Center	The App Center shows other software programs that interface with QuickBooks.
Lead Center	Unlike the other centers, the (Customer) Lead Center doesn't have a button of its own on the Icon Bar (although you can add it if you want by customizing the Icon Bar, as explained in the next section). Access the Lead Center from the Customers menu.
Calendar	Although not a "center" per se, the QuickBooks Calendar can give you a unique view of all the important transactions and reminders you need to monitor to keep your business running smoothly. Click the Calendar button on the Icon Bar to open your calendar for the first time. If you haven't yet entered any transactions into your QuickBooks file, your calendar will be empty. Check back in once you've entered some bills or invoices, and your calendar will show the dates that these bills or invoices were created and are due.

TABLE 1-2   QuickBooks Centers

Customize the Icon Bar

To customize the Icon Bar, choose View from the menu. You'll see options that let you move the default location of the Icon Bar from the left side of the window to the top of the window, or you can hide it altogether.

QuickBooks put icons on the Icon Bar, but the icons QuickBooks includes may not match the features you use most frequently. Choose View | Customize Icon Bar to display a list of the icons currently occupying your Icon Bar, as shown next. From here, you can add, remove, or reorder the icons to suit you.

Small Business Tip When you log into QuickBooks with your own login name, the Icon Bar settings you establish are linked to your login name only. You are not changing the Icon Bar for other users.

Changing the Order of Icons and Their Display

You can change the order in which icons appear on the Icon Bar. To move an icon, click the small diamond to the left of the icon's listing, hold down the left mouse button, and drag the listing to a new position.

You can also change the way the icons display:

- **Display icons without title text** By default, icons and text display on the Icon Bar when it's positioned at the top of the window. You can select Show Icons Only to remove the title text under the icons. As a result, the icons are much smaller (and you can fit more icons on the Icon Bar). Positioning your mouse pointer over a small icon displays the icon's description as a Tool Tip.
- **Change the icon's graphic, text, or description** To change an individual icon's appearance, select the icon's listing and click Edit. Then choose a different graphic (the currently selected graphic is enclosed in a box), change the Label (the title), or change the Description (the Tool Tip text).
- **Separate icons** You can insert a separator between two icons, which is an effective way to create groups of icons after you move icons into logical groups. The separator is a black vertical line. In the Customize Icon Bar dialog, select the icon that should appear to the left of the separator bar and click Add Separator. QuickBooks inserts the separator on the Icon Bar and "(space)" in the listing to indicate the location of the separator.

Adding and Removing Icons

You can remove any icons you never use or use infrequently and fill the space they took up with icons representing features you use a lot. Select the unwanted icon in the Customize Icon Bar dialog and click Delete. QuickBooks does not ask you to confirm the deletion; the icon is just removed from the Icon Bar. The icon is not gone for good, though. You can add it back at any time from the Customize Icon Bar dialog.

If you're currently working in a QuickBooks window and it strikes you that it would be handy to have an icon for fast access to this window, while the window is active, choose View | Add "*Name Of Window*" To Icon Bar. A dialog appears so you can choose a graphic, name, and description for the new icon.

You can add an icon to the Icon Bar in either of two ways:

- Choose Add in the Customize Icon Bar dialog.
- Automatically add an icon for a window (transaction or report) you're currently using.

To add an icon from the Customize Icon Bar dialog, follow these steps:

1. Click Add to display the Add Icon Bar Item dialog.
2. Scroll through the list and select the task you want to add to the Icon Bar.
3. Choose a graphic to represent the new icon.
4. If you want, change the label and/or the description (the text that appears in the Tool Tip when you hold your mouse pointer over the icon).
5. Click OK to close this dialog when you're done.

The Favorites Menu

The Favorites menu (located on the menu bar) gives you the flexibility to list up to 30 of the QuickBooks tasks and lists that you use most often, saving you from having to navigate to other areas of the program to complete your most common QuickBooks tasks. To add menu items to your Favorites menu, do the following:

1. Select Favorites | Customize Favorites from the menu bar. The Customize Your Menus window opens, as shown next.

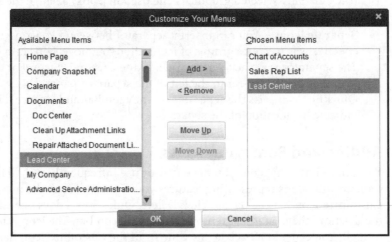

2. Select a menu item, and then click the Add button to add it to your Favorites menu.
3. Click OK when you're finished.

Closing QuickBooks

To exit QuickBooks, click the X in the top-right corner of the QuickBooks window, or choose File | Exit from the menu bar. QuickBooks will ask you if you're sure you want to exit. If you choose Yes, the company file open at the time you exit the software is the file that opens the next time you launch QuickBooks.

Setting Up Users and Permissions

If several users access your QuickBooks file, either at different times or at the same time, each user should have an individual user name and password. In this way, you can track who is making what changes to your company file. Even if you're the only one using QuickBooks, you should make sure that you log in with a password to ensure the security of the company file.

When multiple users can access a company file from other computers on the network, QuickBooks requires user logins. Although it is tempting to avoid the extra step of logging in and remembering a password, don't yield to that temptation. If anyone else wanders into your office and accesses your computer, without passwords, it is possible for him or her to open QuickBooks and view your financial information.

User names are linked to permission levels. This means if you choose, you can limit the parts of QuickBooks that certain users can access to create or view transactions and reports. For example, you can keep users from seeing payroll information or sensitive reports that contain information about your company's profits, debts, and so on.

The QuickBooks Audit Trail report tracks activities with a time and date stamp and displays the name of the logged-in user for every transaction it tracks, but if you and your staff are all using "Admin" as the login name each time you use QuickBooks, the practice diminishes the value of this report. Learn more about the Audit Trail report in Chapter 11.

Working with User Names and Passwords

Most of us who use computers and the Internet on a regular basis know that passwords are very important when it comes to protecting our personal and business information. Remember not to use passwords that are based on information that someone else may know, such as your child's name, your dog's name, your nickname, your license plate, or your birth date, because many computers are attacked by hackers who have successfully guessed such passwords.

If you've enabled the credit card protection feature in QuickBooks (covered in Chapter 2), you must create a complex password (also sometimes called a strong password) if you're the Admin user or a user who has permission to view customer credit card information. A complex password contains a minimum of eight characters, comprising uppercase and lowercase letters, numbers, and symbols. Even if you do not use the credit card protection feature, you should still consider using a complex password.

Of course, the longer the password and the more complicated it is, the harder it is for someone else to guess; but complicated passwords can also be difficult to remember. For example, Xyyu86RDa is a great password, but it would be very difficult to remember. Try to strike a balance between complexity and your ability to remember the password.

Small Business Tip   Whatever your password, do not affix it to your computer monitor on a sticky note.

The QuickBooks Admin

The first person to open the company file (usually the person who creates it) becomes the Admin (administrator) user automatically. The Admin user is in charge of all QuickBooks users and is the only user who can set up additional users, set period closing dates, and complete other sensitive activities in the company file. QuickBooks lets you change the name "Admin" to any other name without losing the administrator power.

As previously mentioned, it is never a good idea to use QuickBooks without the security of having users log in to a company file with a unique user name and a password. Even if you are the only person who works in QuickBooks, and therefore you are automatically the administrator, be sure the user named Admin has a password.

Small Business Tip The administrator's (Admin) privileges in QuickBooks are totally unrelated to your Windows login name and privileges. Even if you're an ordinary user in Windows and can't install software or manage users on the computer, you can be the QuickBooks administrator.

You can create the Admin password when you first create a QuickBooks file or at any time later. If you did create a password and you think someone else may have discovered it, you can create a new password.

To add or change the password for the user named Admin, follow these steps:

1. Log in to QuickBooks as Admin and choose Company | Set Up Users And Passwords | Change Your Password to open the Change QuickBooks Password dialog shown in Figure 1-4.
2. If the Admin account is already password-protected and you're merely changing the password, you'll need to enter the current password to complete the process.
3. Enter the new password, enter it again in the Confirm New Password field, and select a challenge question and the answer. You cannot see what you're typing in the Answer field, so type carefully. QuickBooks treats this the same way it treats password entry; you see bullet characters instead of the characters you're typing. (Keep reading for more information about this question and answer.)
4. Click OK when you're finished.

If you don't remember your Admin password, you can't get into your company file. If Admin is the only user, that means you can't use QuickBooks. If there are other users, they can open the company file, but they can't perform administrative tasks in the file (many QuickBooks functions can be performed only by the Admin user). Essentially, forgetting your Admin password brings your QuickBooks work to a screeching halt.

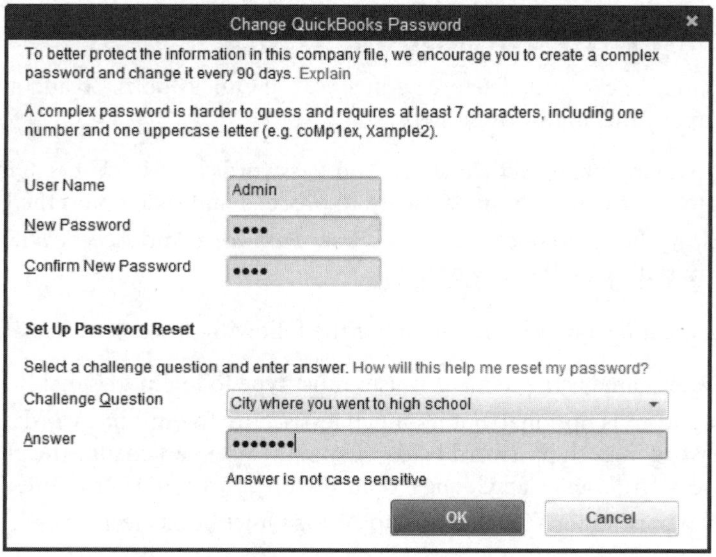

FIGURE 1-4   You can easily add or change the Admin password.

To prevent this inconvenience, QuickBooks gives the Admin user the opportunity to create a reminder about the password. Select a question from the drop-down list in the Challenge Question field and then enter the answer to that question in the Answer field. If you forget your Admin password, you can reset it using the challenge question you created. In the QuickBooks Login dialog, click the I Forgot My Password link. The challenge question shows in the Reset QuickBooks Administrator Password dialog. Enter the answer you recorded in the Answer field (this time you can see what you're typing). When you answer the question correctly, all of your password information is removed from the company file and you can start all over with a new password (and a new challenge question and answer).

If you can't remember your challenge question, click the I Forgot My Answer link. The Reset QuickBooks Administrator Password window opens, where you'll have to enter your QuickBooks license number, your name, address, and e-mail address. Once this information is completely filled in, click OK. The Reset QuickBooks Administrator Password window opens, notifying you that a password reset code was sent to the e-mail address provided. Enter the reset code sent to you and click OK. In the next window, you'll be asked to enter and confirm your new password and create a challenge question with the appropriate answer. Click OK, and your password will be reset.

Working with QuickBooks Users

The Admin user can add, delete, or edit a user in QuickBooks. To add a new user to your company file, follow these steps:

1. Choose Company | Set Up Users And Passwords | Set Up Users. QuickBooks asks you to enter your Admin password to proceed and then opens the User List dialog.
2. Click Add User to open the Set Up User Password And Access Wizard that assists you in setting up the new user.

When creating a new user, remember the following:

- The user name is the name this user must type to log in to QuickBooks.
- A password is optional, but it's much less secure to omit passwords. Enter the same password in both password fields. (Later, the user can change the password—see the section "Users Can Change Their Own Passwords" later in the chapter.)
- Assign permissions for this user to access QuickBooks features.

Deleting a User

To remove a user from the User list, select the user name and then click the Delete User button. QuickBooks asks you to confirm your decision. Note that you are not able to delete the Admin user.

Editing User Information

To change the user settings for any user, select the user name in the User List window and click Edit User. You see a screen similar to the Set Up User Password And Access Wizard, with which you can change the user name, password, and permissions.

The Edit User feature is handy when one of your QuickBooks users comes to you because he cannot remember his password—and you don't have it handy either. You can create a new password for the user, who then has the option to change the password to something of his own liking. See "Users Can Change Their Own Passwords" later in this chapter for more details.

Setting User Permissions

When you're adding a new user or editing an existing user, the wizard walks you through the steps for configuring the user's permissions. Click Next on each wizard window after you've supplied the necessary information.

The first permissions window, shown next, asks if you want this user to have access to selected areas of QuickBooks or all areas. If you give the user access to all areas of QuickBooks, or you select the option to make this user an External Accountant, when you click Next you're asked to confirm your decision, and there's no further work to do in the wizard. Click Finish to return to the User List window. (See Chapter 11 to learn about the External Accountant user type.)

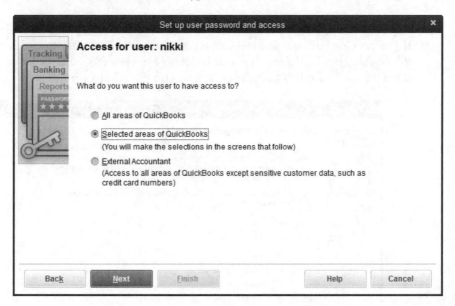

If you want to limit the user's access to selected areas of QuickBooks, select that option and click Next. The windows that follow take you through all the QuickBooks features (Sales And Accounts Receivable, Check Writing, Payroll, and so on) so you can establish permissions on a feature-by-feature basis for this user. You should configure permissions for every component of QuickBooks. Any component not configured is set as No Access for this user (which means the user cannot work in that part of QuickBooks). For each QuickBooks component, you can select one of the following permission options:

- **No Access** The user is denied permission to open any windows in that section of QuickBooks.
- **Full Access** The user can open all windows and perform all tasks in that section of QuickBooks.
- **Selective Access** The user will be permitted to perform the tasks that you choose.

If you choose to give selective access permissions, you're asked to specify what tasks this user can perform. Those rights vary slightly from component to component, but generally you're asked to choose one of these permission levels:

- Create transactions only
- Create and print transactions
- Create transactions and create reports

You can select only one of the three levels, so if you need to give the user rights to more than one of these choices, you must select Full Access instead of Selective Access.

Special Permissions Needed for Customer Credit Card Data

If you provide Full or Selective Access permissions to a user for the Sales And Accounts Receivable area, by default, the user is not able to view customer credit card data. A separate option for this permission appears on the wizard window.

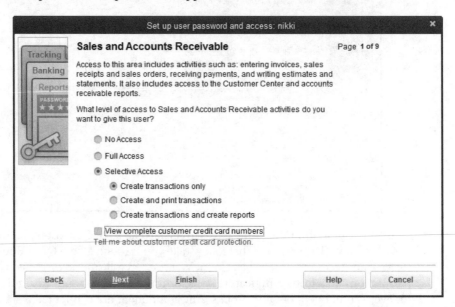

- If you've enabled the Customer Credit Card Security feature (explained in Chapter 2), the next time this user logs in to the company file, he or she will be asked to create a strong password.
- If you haven't enabled the Customer Credit Card Security feature, this user, and any other user you configure to have access to customer credit card information, does *not* have to set up a strong password and can view credit card numbers you store in your customers' records.

Configuring Special Areas of QuickBooks

You'll use two wizard windows for setting permissions that are not directly related to any specific area of the software: sensitive accounting activities and sensitive accounting reports.

Sensitive accounting activities are tasks that aren't directly related to QuickBooks transactions, and *sensitive financial reporting* provides important financial information about your company, such as those described in Table 1-3.

Sensitive Accounting Activities	Sensitive Financial Reporting
Making changes to the chart of accounts	Financial statements, such as the Profit & Loss reports and the Balance Sheet
Manipulating the register for any balance sheet account	Budget reports
Using online banking and transferring funds between banks or accounts	Cash flow reports
Reconciling bank accounts	Trial balance reports
Creating journal entries	Income tax reports
Working with budgets	Audit Trail reports

TABLE 1-3   Sensitive Areas in QuickBooks

Configuring Rights for Existing Transactions

You can limit a user's ability to delete or change existing transactions, even in areas for which the user has been granted permissions and for a user that originally created the transaction.

When you have finished configuring user permissions, the last wizard page presents a list of the permissions you've granted and refused. If everything is correct, click Finish. If there's something you want to change, click the Back button to return to the appropriate page.

Users Can Change Their Own Passwords

Any user can change his or her own password by choosing Company | Set Up Users And Passwords | Change Your Password to open the Change QuickBooks Password dialog. The dialog opens with the name of the currently logged-in user in the User Name field, and that text cannot be changed.

To change the password, the user must enter the old password and then enter the new password twice. That's an excellent security device, because it prevents other users from changing a user's password (which can happen if a user leaves the computer without logging out of QuickBooks).

Small Business Tip   Although theoretically it's a good idea for the QuickBooks administrator to know all user passwords and to ask users to notify the administrator when a password is changed, tracking passwords can be burdensome if more than one or two users are involved. It is perfectly acceptable to decide that you don't want to know user passwords, because if a user forgets a password, you can edit the user's record to create a new one (as described earlier in this chapter) and tell the user his or her new password.

Create Your Company's Chart of Accounts

QuickBooks uses accounts to categorize the many different transactions that occur as you operate your business, and the list where all these accounts live is called the *chart of accounts*. In addition, these accounts are further categorized by type. Assets, liabilities, income, and expenses, for example, are the account types most frequently used. (See Table 1-4 for more explanation of each account type.) As you enter a transaction, QuickBooks takes care of all the "behind-the-scenes" entries needed for the affected accounts.

Assets	Liabilities	Equity	Income	Expenses	
Something your company owns	Something your company owes to someone else	Net worth of your business	Also called revenue	Funds you spend to operate your business. Generally, expenses are divided into two main categories: *cost of goods sold (COGS)* and *general and administrative expenses*.	
				Cost of Goods Sold	**General and Administrative Expenses**
Money in your bank accounts (sometimes called *cash on hand*)	Money you owe your vendors and suppliers (QuickBooks account type: *Accounts Payable*)	Capital invested in your business (called *capital*)	Money you collect when you sell products	Cost of raw materials for manufacturing	Overhead (utilities, rent, insurance, office supplies, and so on)
Money owed to you by your customers (called *accounts receivable*)	Sales tax you have collected and must turn over to the state (QuickBooks account type: *Current Liability*)	Capital you've withdrawn from the business (if your business isn't a corporation)	Fees you collect for services	Cost of goods you resell in a wholesale or retail business	Services you purchase
Equipment, furniture, and so on (called *fixed assets*)	Money withheld from employees' pay that you must turn over to government agencies (QuickBooks account type: *Current Liability*)	Profit (or loss), including accumulated earnings in prior years (called *retained earnings*)	Income derived from interest	Cost of materials consumed/ sold in a service business	Payroll
Inventory you stock for resale if you are a distributor or manufacturer (called *inventory assets*)	Outstanding loan balances (QuickBooks account type: *Long Term Liability*)				Taxes

TABLE 1-4   Account Types in QuickBooks

For example, when you sell goods or services to a customer and send them an invoice, you enter the name of the customer, the product or service you sold, and the amount you charge. QuickBooks posts the amounts related to the transaction to the accounts you specify and records that transaction in the customer's account. Later, when the customer pays the invoice, QuickBooks shows that the invoice has been paid and increases your Undeposited Funds account by the amount of the payment When you deposit the funds, the Undeposited Funds account is decreased by the amount of the payment and the bank account is increased. QuickBooks created some accounts for you during the initial setup of your company, but you'll likely need to create additional accounts to ensure that your chart of accounts reflects your unique business. You create the chart of accounts first because some of the other QuickBooks lists you create require you to link the items in those lists to your accounts.

Use Account Numbers

By default, the chart of accounts in QuickBooks uses account names only. However, you can change this setting so that your accounts show numbers in addition to the names.

The advantage of using numbers is that you can arrange each section of the chart of accounts by category and subcategory because within each type of account, QuickBooks displays your chart of accounts in alphanumeric order. Without numbers, QuickBooks displays each section of your chart of accounts in alphabetical order, which can cause confusion when running reports. You can also use numbered subaccounts (see the section "Use Subaccounts" later in this chapter) to provide subtotals for accounts on many QuickBooks reports and to make it easier to enter transactions.

To switch to a number format for your accounts, you have to enable the account number feature. Choose Edit | Preferences from the menu bar to open the Preferences dialog, and select the Accounting icon in the left pane. Click the Company Preferences tab, and select the Use Account Numbers check box as shown in Figure 1-5. (Learn more about Preferences in Chapter 14.)

➡ Small Business Recommendation

As convenient as it is for you (and your accountant) to have numbered accounts so you can track your finances by category and subcategory, you may have to produce reports for an outside stakeholder (such as your bank). They may have certain financial categories that they'll want to look at first, and sometimes it is easier for them if your accounts, especially your expenses, are in alphabetical order.

To produce reports without account numbers, putting each account type list back into alphabetical order, turn off the account number feature by deselecting the option in Accounting Preferences (Edit | Preferences | Accounting). Print the reports, and then turn the feature on again. QuickBooks stores account numbers as part of the account name, so when you re-enable account numbers, all your numbers appear exactly as you created them.

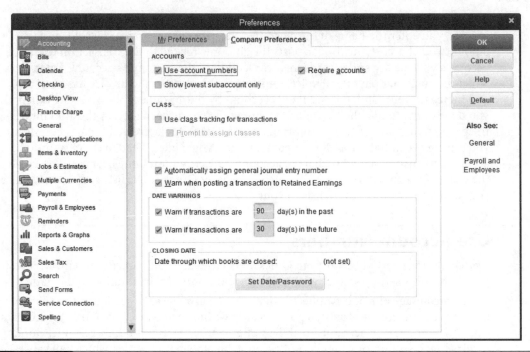

FIGURE1-5 Use QuickBooks Preferences to enable numbers for your chart of accounts.

When you set up your company file and chose a preset chart of accounts, those accounts were switched to numbered accounts automatically. However, the QuickBooks numbering scheme is designed to keep accounts in alphabetical order, especially in the Expenses section. This costs you some of the advantages and efficiencies that well-planned numbers bring, but all you have to do is create your own plan and then edit the accounts to change the numbers (see "Edit and Delete Accounts" later in this chapter).

Small Business Tip Accounts you added to the preset accounts set up when you created your company file have to be edited to add numbers. QuickBooks doesn't automatically number them.

When you select the option to use account numbers, the option Show Lowest Subaccount Only (refer to Figure 1-5) becomes accessible. This option tells QuickBooks to display only the subaccount on transaction windows instead of both the parent account and the subaccount, making it easier for you to see precisely which account is receiving the posting.

Creating a Numbering System

After you've set up numbered accounts, you have a more efficient chart of accounts, so you, your bookkeeper, and your accountant will have an easier time managing your chart of accounts. Numbers give you a quick clue about the type and category of the account you're working with. As you create accounts, be sure to maintain the logic of your numbering system, assigning ranges of numbers to account types. The example shown next, a common approach to account numbering, uses five-digit numbers because QuickBooks uses five-digit account numbers. QuickBooks permits account numbers of up to seven digits, so you're not going to run out of numbers no matter how many accounts you need for your business.

- 1xxxx Assets
- 2xxxx Liabilities
- 3xxxx Equity
- 4xxxx Income
- 5xxxx Expenses
- 6xxxx Expenses
- 7xxxx Expenses
- 8xxxx Non-operating Income
- 9xxxx Non-operating Expenses

Creating Ranges of Numbers

Account types have subtypes, and you need to assign ranges of account numbers to match those subtypes. The starting number of each range has to be the same as the starting number for the account type. That means that if you use numbers starting with a 1 for assets, all of the number ranges for different subtypes of assets must start with a 1.

When numbering assets, you can use 10000 through 10999 for bank accounts, 11000 through 11999 for receivables and other current assets, and 12000 through 12999 for tracking fixed assets such as equipment, furniture, and so on. Follow the same pattern for liabilities, starting with current liabilities and moving to long term. It's also a good idea to keep all payroll withholding liability accounts together.

If you have inventory and you track cost of goods, you can reserve a section of the chart of accounts for those account types. Some businesses dedicate the numbers in the 5*xxxx* range to that purpose.

Usually, you should create new accounts by increasing the previous account number by 10 or 20 (or even 100 if you don't have a lot of accounts), so you have room to insert more accounts that belong in the same general area of your chart of accounts when needed.

▶▶ Small Business Recommendation

When you first set up your chart of accounts, your accounts are sorted by type and then by number. Because the order of these accounts can be changed manually, you may, over time, find it more difficult to find and work with some accounts in your list. You can fix this by re-sorting the list. Open your chart of accounts, click the Account button, and select the Re-Sort List command to return the list to its original order.

Name Conventions

Whether or not you choose to enable account numbers, you have to give each account a name. What's more, you should take steps to ensure that your account naming convention is consistent. Why is this important? Because it's not uncommon to find accounts with names such as these:

- Telephone Exp
- Exps-Telephone
- Tele Expense
- Telephone
- Tele

The problem here is that every one of those accounts had amounts posted to them. That's because users "guess" at account names when they see a drop-down list, and they point and click whatever they see that seems remotely related. If they don't find an account named the way they would have entered the name, they create a new account using a name that is logical to them. You can avoid all of those errors by establishing rules about creating account names, limiting which users have authority to create new accounts, and then making sure your users search the account list before applying an account to a transaction.

Here are a few suggestions. You can adjust them to meet your own needs or create different rules with which you are more comfortable. However, the important thing is consistency!

- Avoid apostrophes and quotes.
- Set the number of characters for abbreviations. For example, if you permit four characters, telephone is abbreviated "tele"; a three-character rule produces "tel".
- Make a rule about whether spaces are allowed. For example, would you rather have "Repairs & Maintenance" or "Repairs&Maintenance"?

Create Accounts

After you've done your homework and decided on a naming and numbering scheme, creating accounts is a piece of cake:

1. Press CTRL-A to open the Chart Of Accounts window.
2. Press CTRL-N to enter a new account.
3. In the Add New Account: Choose Account Type dialog, as shown next, select the type of account you're creating. If the account type you need doesn't appear in the major category list on the dialog, select Other Account Types and choose an account type from the drop-down list.
4. Click Continue to create the account.

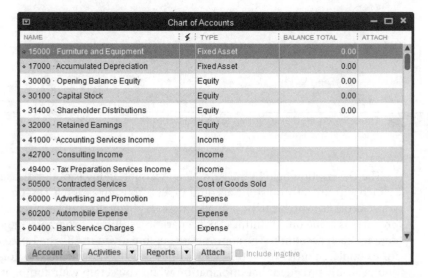

The dialog you see when you fill out account information varies depending on the account type you chose because different types of accounts require different information. In addition, if you've opted to use numbers for your accounts, there's a field for the account number. Figure 1-6 shows a blank Add New Account dialog for an Expense account.

Small Business Tip   If you created your company file in QuickBooks 2016 and you selected an industry type during the setup, a button labeled Select From Examples in the Add New Account dialog will display for certain account types. Clicking the button produces a list of accounts that QuickBooks thinks you might want to consider adding to your chart of accounts. The list of accounts matches the account type you selected when you started the process of adding an account.

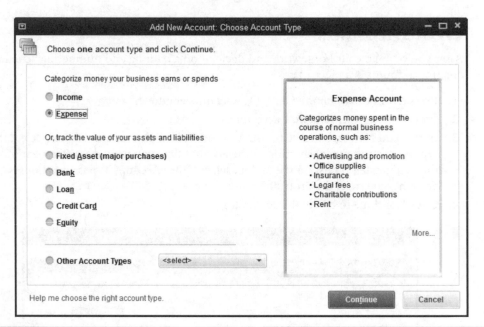

FIGURE 1-6 The only required entry for an account is a name.

The Description field in the Add New Account dialog is optional, as is the Note field (which appears only on some account types). You can assign a Tax-Line Mapping to your accounts, which can be a huge timesaver if you do your own taxes or if your tax preparer is using one of Intuit's tax preparation software programs. QuickBooks exports data for each account to the appropriate tax line if you use TurboTax to do your taxes, for example. In order to do this, QuickBooks has to know which tax form you use, and you probably provided that information when you set up your company file. In fact, if you selected a tax form when you set up the company file, QuickBooks automatically inserts a tax-line assignment for Income, Cost of Goods Sold, and Expense Accounts.

If you didn't select a tax form, the Tax-Line Mapping field doesn't appear. But you can add the tax-line information in the Company Information window. You get to this window by opening the Company menu, selecting My Company, and then clicking the Edit icon (the small pencil) on the top-right side of the My Company window. You'll find the Income Tax Form Used drop-down list located on the Report Information tab.

Small Business Tip   You can use QuickBooks without assigning a tax line. Knowing which tax line to assign to an account is not always apparent, so if you're unsure about assigning a tax-line mapping, consult with your accountant or a tax professional first.

As you finish creating each account, click Save & New to move to another blank Add New Account dialog. By default, the new dialog is configured for the same account type as the account you just created, but you can change the account type by selecting another type from the drop-down list at the top of the dialog.

When you're finished creating accounts, click Save & Close, and then close the Chart Of Accounts window by clicking the X in the upper-right corner.

➡ Small Business Recommendation

Unless you start your business the day you start using QuickBooks, many of your accounts already have an existing balance. For example, you probably have money in your business bank account, either because your business has been operating for a long time and you're just getting around to using QuickBooks, or because you provided startup money for your new business.

It is best not to enter any figures in the Opening Balance field of any account that has this option, because QuickBooks (which is a true double-entry accounting application) needs to make an entry of the same amount you entered into an offsetting account. Of course, QuickBooks has no way of knowing the source of that money, so the offsetting account it uses is called Opening Bal Equity, which is an account QuickBooks invented for just this purpose. In actuality, the money in your bank account may be the result of a loan you made to your business, capital you invested in your business, or sales you made before you started keeping records in QuickBooks.

Chapter 3 details the easy-to-follow process you can use to enter opening balances and historical data correctly and efficiently. Be sure to ask your accountant to help you create the transactions that provide the details behind the opening balances for your accounts.

Use Subaccounts

Subaccounts provide a way to post transactions more precisely by using subcategories for main account categories, while also giving you the ability to view key reports at both the subaccount and parent account levels. To create a subaccount, you must first create the parent account.

For example, suppose you have the following parent account:

- 60100 Automobile

You can create the following subaccounts:

- :60110 Fuel
- :60120 Insurance
- :60130 Repairs and Maintenance

(The colon in the account names listed here is added automatically by QuickBooks on some reports to indicate a parent account:subaccount relationship.)

Creating Subaccounts

To create a subaccount, you must have already created the parent account. Then take these steps:

1. Open the Chart of Accounts list and press CTRL-N to create a new account.
2. Select the appropriate account type and click Continue.
3. Enter a number (if you're using numbered accounts).
4. Name the account.
5. Click the Subaccount Of check box to place a check mark in it.
6. In the drop-down box next to the check box, select the parent account.
7. Click Save & New to create another account or Save & Close if you're finished creating accounts.

Small Business Tip To get the most out of using subaccounts when viewing reports, once you create subaccounts, ensure you post transactions to the correct subaccount. When you post directly to a parent account that has subaccounts attached to it, reports that include transactions to this account will appear as if they were posted to a subaccount called "Other."

Viewing Subaccounts

When you have subaccounts, the Chart Of Accounts window displays them indented under their parent accounts, as seen next, when you've configured the window to display accounts in Hierarchical view.

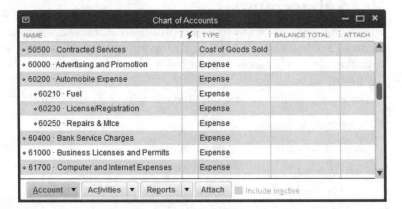

If you know you created subaccounts but you don't see any indented listings, your Chart Of Accounts window has been configured to display accounts in Flat view, which is a simple listing of accounts. To remedy this, click the Account button at the bottom of the window and select Hierarchical View.

Showing Lowest Subaccounts Only

When you view accounts in the Chart Of Accounts window, subaccounts appear under their parent accounts, and they're indented. However, when you view a subaccount in the drop-down list of a transaction window, it appears in this format: *ParentAccount:Subaccount*. (If you're using three levels, the list appears as *ParentAccount:Subaccount:Sub-subaccount*.)

For example, if you create a parent account named Income with a subaccount Consulting, the Account field drop-down list in transaction windows shows Income:Consulting. If you've used numbers, remember that the number is part of the account name, so the Account field shows something like the following: 40000-Income:40010-Consulting.

Because many of the fields or columns in transaction windows are narrow, you may not be able to see the subaccount names without scrolling through each account. This can be annoying, and it's much easier to work if only the subaccount name is displayed. That's the point of enabling the preference Show Lowest Subaccount Only, discussed earlier in this chapter. When you enable that option, you see only the subaccounts in the drop-down list when you're working in a transaction window, which makes it much easier to select the account you need.

Edit and Delete Accounts

If you need to make changes to any account information (including adding a number after you enable numbered accounts), select the account's listing in the Chart Of Accounts window and press CTRL-E. (You can also right-click on the name of the account and choose Edit Account from the resulting context menu.) In either case, the Edit Account dialog appears, which looks like the account card you just filled out. Make your changes and click Save & Close to save them.

To delete an account, right-click its listing in the Chart Of Accounts window, and choose Delete Account or press CTRL-D. QuickBooks asks you to confirm the fact that you want to delete the account. Click OK to remove it.

You can delete any account that is not in use, which means the account has never been used in a transaction or linked to a sales or payroll item. You don't have to search all your transactions to find out whether an account has been used in your system; you can just try to delete it, and if it's been assigned to a transaction or item, QuickBooks issues an error message explaining why you can't delete it.

Also, you cannot delete an account that has subaccounts unless you first delete the subaccounts, which can be accomplished only if the subaccounts have never been used in a transaction. However, a workaround for saving the subaccounts and getting rid of the parent account is first to turn the subaccounts into parent accounts. To accomplish this, either drag the subaccount listing to the left in the Chart Of Accounts window (be sure the window is displaying accounts in Hierarchical view and the list is in its original sort order), or edit the subaccount to remove the check mark in the Subaccount Of check box.

If you can't delete an account but you don't want anyone to use it, you can hide it—QuickBooks calls this making it *inactive*. If you have a duplicate account, you can merge it with the other account. Those topics are covered next.

Make Accounts Inactive (Hiding Accounts)

When you make an account inactive, you're hiding it from users. When an account is inactive, it doesn't appear in drop-down lists in transaction windows, so it can't be selected. The account continues to exist "behind the scenes" and its history remains in the system; it just doesn't appear in drop-down lists during transaction entry.

To make an account inactive, right-click its listing in the Chart Of Accounts window and select Make Account Inactive. QuickBooks doesn't ask you to confirm your action. You can also make an account inactive by selecting it and pressing CTRL-E to open the account record in Edit mode; then select the check box labeled Account Is Inactive to enter a check mark.

By default, inactive accounts aren't displayed in the Chart Of Accounts window, but if you've made any accounts inactive, the Include Inactive check box at the bottom of the window becomes accessible (if it's grayed out that means no inactive accounts exist). Select the check box to insert a check mark, and you can see your inactive accounts, which are displayed with an "X" to the left of the listing.

To return an inactive account to active status, be sure that the Chart Of Accounts window is displaying inactive accounts, and then click the "X" to toggle the account's status to Active.

Merge Accounts

Sometimes you see two accounts that should be one. For instance, you may have accidentally created two accounts for the same purpose, such as Telephone and Tele, with transactions posted to both accounts. Those accounts are definitely candidates for merging. You can merge accounts only when the following conditions exist:

- Both accounts are of the same account type (for example, you cannot merge an Expense account with an Other Expense account).
- Both accounts are at the same level (you cannot merge a subaccount with a parent account).

Take the following steps to merge two accounts:

1. Open the Chart Of Accounts window and select the account that has the name you do not want to use.
2. Press CTRL-E to open the Edit Account dialog.
3. Change the account name to match the account you want to keep.
4. Click Save & Close.
5. QuickBooks displays a dialog telling you that the account number or name you've entered already exists for another account and asks if you want to merge the accounts. Click Yes to confirm that you want to merge the two accounts.

Remember, the way to do this is to start with the "bad" account and rename it to match the "good" account—the one you want to keep.

Entering Customers and Vendors

In this chapter:

- Entering customer information

- Working with customers in the Customer Center

- Using custom fields

- Ensuring credit card security

- Entering vendor information

- Working with the Vendor Center

- Learning about 1099s in QuickBooks

Chapter 2

Two groups help your company succeed: your customers who provide the income, and vendors, those from whom you purchase goods and services. With QuickBooks, it is easiest to enter the names of both groups before you start entering transactions. For both, you can store basic information such as addresses, phone numbers, and e-mail addresses, but you can also track and manage nearly everything and anything you need to know about your customers and your vendors in their respective centers. Let's start with your customers. Note the small icons at the right of each customer and vendor data window. The small paper clip is used to attach information, the small pencil to edit information, and the pushpin shows notes pertaining to that customer or vendor, as seen here.

📌 NOTE

Build Your Customer List

You can add your customers to QuickBooks in several ways. You can add them one by one, you can use the Add/Edit Multiple List Entries window, or, if you've stored this information in an Excel sheet or a comma-separated values (.csv) file, consider using a special QuickBooks utility designed to import this information. This import utility offers a step-by-step wizard you access by choosing File | Utilities | Import | Excel Files. Use the utility to import your vendors, inventory items, and your chart of accounts.

To create a new customer manually, click the Customers button on either the Icon Bar or the Home page to open the Customer Center. Next, click the New Customer & Job drop-down arrow at the top of the Customer Center window and select New Customer from the submenu. This action opens the New Customer window with the Address Info tab in the foreground, as shown in Figure 2-1. Fill in the appropriate information.

Customer Information

Start with the Customer Name field at the top. The text you enter here doesn't appear on printed transactions. You could consider this as an internal code, because what you enter in the Company Name/Full Name fields appears as the customer name in printed sales transactions.

Create a customer name system so that you'll enter every customer in the same way and avoid the risk of entering the same customer multiple times. For example, if your customer is a business, you can simply enter the name of the business; if your customer is an individual, it's good practice to enter the last name first in the Customer Name field for sorting purposes. Use the name by which you and your employees refer to the customer.

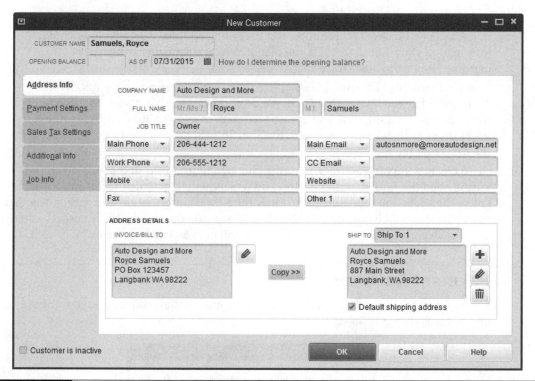

Use the New Customer window to enter basic customer information.

Small Business Tip   Each entry in the Customer Name field must be unique. For example, if you have several customers named Johnson, be sure to enter them so it is easy to determine which Johnson each listing represents. Since this field can contain up to 41 characters, you should be able to create a workable naming scheme.

➡ Small Business Recommendation

Although QuickBooks makes an Opening Balance field available in the New Customer setup using today's date, it's best not to use the Opening Balance field. When you enter an amount here, it may include the balance from more than one outstanding invoice, and you'll have no detailed records for what makes up that balance. This makes it difficult to match payments against specific invoices. Since QuickBooks posts the amount you enter in this field to Accounts Receivable and makes an offsetting entry into an account named Opening Balance Equity, at some point you will need to zero-out the balance in Opening Balance Equity. Entering individual transactions that total the beginning balance is far more accurate than entering a total using the Opening Balance field.

In the Company Name, Full Name, and Address Details fields, enter the company name, a contact name if you choose, and the billing address. Add any other contact information you want to track. If you plan to e-mail statements or invoices to this customer, be sure to enter the e-mail address.

If your customer has multiple shipping addresses, choose a name for each Ship To address that you'll later choose from a drop-down list when you're entering sales transactions. If the shipping address isn't different from the billing address (or if you never ship products), you can ignore the Ship To field or click the Copy button to copy the data from the Bill To field.

To create a shipping address, click the plus sign button next to the Ship To address area to open the Add Shipping Address Information dialog. QuickBooks automatically enters the address name "Ship To 1." Enter the address information and specify whether this address should be the default Ship To address, and then click OK. If needed, enter another Ship To address for this customer; it will have a default name of "Ship To 2."

Payment Settings

The Payment Settings tab puts all the important information about customer finances in one place, as shown in Table 2-1.

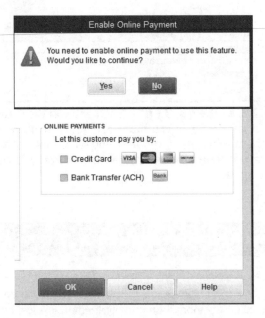

Sales Tax Settings

If you collect sales tax, complete the fields on this tab. Select the appropriate sales tax code and item for this customer, or create a new sales tax item or code here if needed.

Payment Setting Field	What to Enter
Account No.	Use this field if you assign account numbers to your customers.
Credit Limit	Set a "credit limit" to establish the total amount a customer can owe you for purchases. When a new order, combined with any unpaid invoices, exceeds the limit, QuickBooks displays a warning. Although the warning doesn't prevent you from selling to the customer, consider shipping the order COD (cash on delivery). Also, leaving the Credit Limit field blank is not the same as entering a zero. Zero indicates you do not want to sell to this customer on credit.
Payment Terms	Click the arrow to the right of the Payment Terms field to see the list of predefined QuickBooks terms, or choose <Add New> to define a new one. The terms in the Payment Terms List are for both customers and vendors, and you may need additional terms to meet your needs. See Chapter 3 to learn how to create different types of terms.
Price Level	Use Price Levels to customize your prices on a customer level. Select an existing price level, or create a new one.
Preferred Delivery Method	This field stores the default value for the way you want to send sales transaction information to this customer, not how you send products. Choose None for no special method, E-Mail, or Mail.
Preferred Payment Method	Choose from the drop-down list to indicate how this customer prefers to pay, or add a new method.
Credit Card Information	Record this customer's credit card information in these fields. If you opt to store this information, be sure to enable QuickBooks Customer Credit Card Protection as discussed in the section "Secure Customer Credit Card Information" later in this chapter.
Online Payments	In the Online Payments option shown at the right side of the Payment Settings window, click either Credit Card or Bank Transfer to see the Enable Online Payment dialog, shown in the illustration. Click Yes to subscribe to this for-fee service, as seen in Figure 2-2.

TABLE 2-1 Customer Payment Settings Options

If the customer does not pay sales tax, select Non from the Tax Code drop-down list, and enter the customer's resale certificate number in the Resale No. field. See Chapter 3 to learn about setting up sales tax codes.

Additional Info

Use the Additional Info tab to enter more information about your customers, as shown in the following list. Here, you can use the available fields or create custom fields of your own to design reports based on the data captured in these fields.

- **Customer Type**   Use this field to sort your customers by a type you choose, such as wholesale and retail customers. Click the arrow to select a type from the list, or create a new type.
- **Rep**   This field is the place to track a sales representative. Sales reps can be employees, vendors, or "other names" as entered in the Other Names list. Select a rep from the list of reps, or add a new rep by choosing <Add New> from the drop-down list.

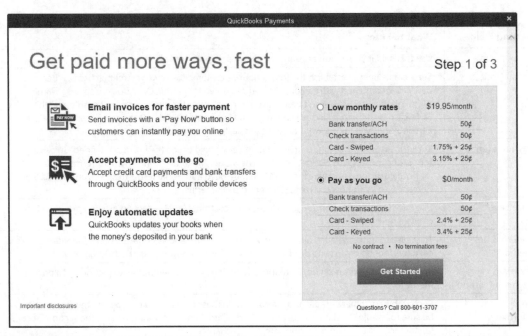

FIGURE 2-2 QuickBooks offers several methods by which you can accept online payments from your customers.

- **Custom Fields** Custom fields enable you to create fields for tracking special information about your customers (such as contract renewal date, for example). See how to use these fields in "Use Custom Fields" later in this chapter.

Job Info Tab

You can enter jobs for this customer by selecting the Job Info tab at the left of the New Customer information window. Use the fields on this tab to help you keep track of the status of your work with this customer. See the "Use Jobs" section later in this chapter. When you have finished filling out the fields, click OK.

Adding Multiple Customer Records

Use the Add/Edit Multiple List Entries window to add multiple customers at once (or to make changes to the information for existing customer records). From the Customer Center, from the New Customer & Job drop-down menu, choose Add Multiple Customer:Jobs.

The Add/Edit Multiple List Entries window opens with the Customers list already selected. As shown in Figure 2-3, you can add new customers and jobs, change customer information, or fill in additional data. You can even copy and paste customers from an Excel sheet into the Add/Edit Multiple List Entries window.

To get the most benefit from using the Add/Edit Multiple List Entries window, notice the following important features and functions:

- **List and View filters**   Select the List or View drop-down arrow to display only those records with which you want to work.
- **Find field**   Use this field to quickly locate and work with a specific customer record.
- **Customize Columns button**   Click to open the Customize Columns window, where you can add columns for the fields within the customer record that you want to modify.
- **Copy Down**   Right-click within any field, except the Name field, and select Copy Down to copy the contents of a selected field to all the remaining records in the list.
- **Duplicate Row**   Place your cursor on any row in the table, right-click, and from the resulting menu, select Duplicate Row to duplicate the selected record in the row below. The new duplicate record name will start with "DUP."

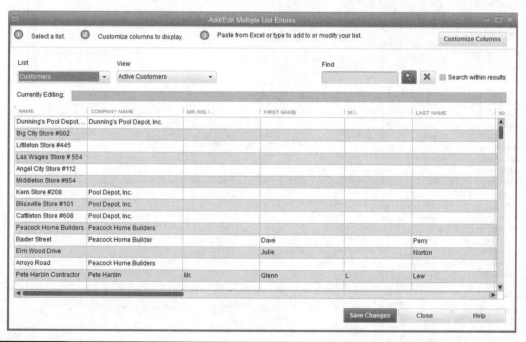

FIGURE 2-3   The Add/Edit Multiple List Entries window can save you time when entering more than one item.

The Customer Center

QuickBooks stores all of your customer detail information in the QuickBooks Customer Center. From here, you can create, edit, and get reports about customers and jobs. Click the Customers button on either the Icon Bar or the Home page to open the Customer Center.

Shown in Figure 2-4, the left pane of the Customer Center has two tabs: Customers & Jobs and Transactions. The list opens to a customer in the Customers & Jobs List, and the right pane of the Customer Center displays information about that selected customer or job.

All of your customer transactions are shown by transaction type in the Transactions tab. Selecting a transaction type displays the current transactions of that type in the right pane. You can manipulate and filter the display by choosing categories and sorting by column.

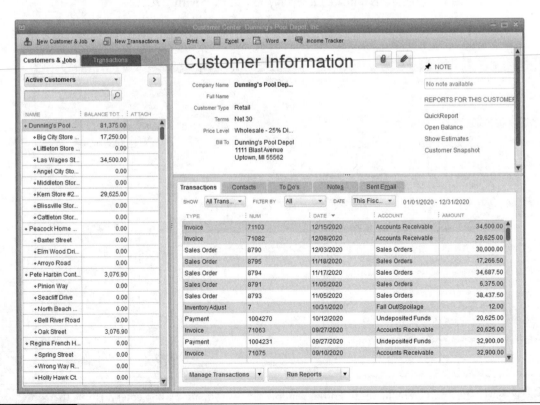

FIGURE 2-4 Use the Customer Center to perform many tasks.

Customizing the Customers & Jobs List

You can customize the information shown in the Customers & Jobs List. By default, the list has three columns: Name, Balance Total, and Attach. (Learn about attaching documents in Chapter 14). Customer balances display next to their names. If you have enabled the multiple currencies feature, the Currency column will also be visible.

To add more columns to the Customers & Jobs List, right-click anywhere in the list and choose Customize Columns to open the Customize Columns dialog, seen next. To add a column, select its label in the left pane and click Add. Alternatively, if you want to eliminate a column from your list, highlight its label in the right pane and click Remove.

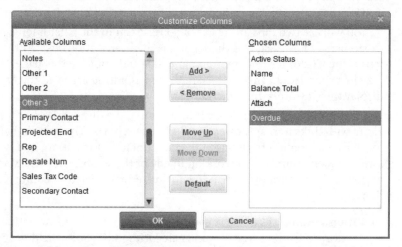

Some users add an Overdue column so they know which customers have an overdue or almost due invoice. Learn more about this feature and the Collections Center in Chapter 5.

To rearrange the left-to-right order of the columns, select a column you want to move, and then choose Move Up to move a column to the left or Move Down to move it to the right. The order of columns displayed in the Chosen Columns pane of the dialog translates as top to bottom = left to right.

If you add columns to the Customers & Jobs List, you won't be able to see all the information unless you widen the list's pane and widen each column. To maximize this pane, click the Show Full List Only button, the right-pointing arrow located on the top-right corner of the Customers & Jobs List.

Small Business Tip   Use the Manage Notes to add a note about a customer or job. You can pin any note to your customer record, and that pinned note becomes the default note on any report about that customer and will appear in the Customer Information pane in the Customers list.

Working in the Customer Information Pane

The Customer Information pane is where QuickBooks keeps all of the customer information you've entered, as well as each sales-related transaction. You can quickly see the details behind a customer's past due balance, add or update important notes or To Do's that relate to a specific job, and even run key customer reports.

You will see two tabs at the left of your screen in the Customer Center. One is the Customers & Jobs List, and the second is the Transactions list. At the right of these two tabs is the Customer Information pane. If you do not see this pane, the Customer list may be expanded. In this case, click the left-pointing arrow at the far right of the list to display the Customer Information pane.

The top half of the Customer Information pane displays basic contact information, along with links to maps, directions, and key reports. The bottom half of the pane has five tabs that contain transaction details, contact information, To Do's, notes, and sent e-mail information. When working in any of these tabs, click the Manage *<tab name>* button at the bottom of the window to add, edit, or delete the information contained therein.

- **Transactions**   Use the Transactions tab to filter for information about a particular customer. Choose from several categories in the Show field drop-down lists. You can add and remove columns of information by right-clicking anywhere on or below the column headings and choosing Customize Columns.
- **Contacts**   Use the Contacts tab to store all the ways that you can keep in touch with your customers. Click the drop-down arrows in the available fields, and you'll see that there's a place for several types of phone and e-mail information and even for social media sites.
- **To Do's**   From the To Do's tab, click the Manage To Do's button and select Create New to compose a specific reminder for this customer. This can be very useful, because you get to specify the date on which you want to be reminded (the Due field) and categorize your new To Do as a call or meeting in the Type field, for example. You can then view your To Do note in the calendar or directly in the Customer Center. When the task is complete, open the reminder and change its status to Done. Click the Run Reports button on the To Do's tab to see a detailed listing of all your To Do's, including those for vendors and employees.
- **Notes**   From the Notes tab, click the Manage Notes button to add, edit, or delete a note. The Date/Time Stamp button inserts the current date and time automatically when you add text to the notepad.

- **Sent Email**   This is the best way to keep track of all the sales transactions you've e-mailed to a customer. In a single list, you can see the e-mail addressee, the date it was sent, and the form that was sent, including the reference number and amount.

➡ Small Business Recommendation

If you want to edit a customer record individually, use the Customer Center. Locate and double-click the customer's listing in the Customers & Jobs List to open the customer record in Edit mode to change or add any information.

Take care when making changes to the Customer Name field, as it may result in some unintended consequences, such as changing the order in which that name appears in the Customers list and customer reports and causing a retroactive change to the customer's name on all past transactions. Also, changes in the Customer Name field do not automatically change the name as it appears in the Bill To or Ship To address field—you need to update that manually.

Small Business Tip   You can add a purchase order number column (or several other columns) to the options in the Transactions tab. Right-click anywhere in the Transactions list (at the right side of the Customers & Jobs tab), choose Customize Columns, and select P.O. Number. You can add additional columns in both the Transactions list and in the Transactions section of either the Job Information or Customer Information sections.

Use Jobs

QuickBooks handles customers and jobs together so you have the option of creating a single customer and posting all the invoices to that customer, or creating multiple jobs for that customer and job-level invoices. Some businesses track only the customer, but if you're a building contractor or subcontractor, or a service provider who sends invoices based on a project, you should track jobs. Jobs don't stand alone; they are always attached to customers, and you can attach as many jobs to a single customer as you need.

When you track jobs, you can enter any current jobs during your QuickBooks setup phase or as you start them. Because jobs are attached to the customer, the customer has to exist in your QuickBooks Customers & Jobs List before you can create a job. Once the job is created, you can track its progress and keep an eye on the promised end date. If you think this will be the only job you perform for this customer, you can do the same thing for a customer without creating a job, because the customer record also has a Job Info tab. When you get another project from the customer, you can always add that new job.

Creating Jobs

To create a job, open the Customer Center and right-click the listing of the customer for whom you're creating a job. Choose Add Job to open the New Job window. Create a name for the job (you can use up to 41 characters) and make it descriptive enough for both you and your customer to understand. Make any appropriate changes in the job's Address Info tab. QuickBooks maintains this information only for this job and won't change the original shipping address in the customer record. Update the Payment Settings and Additional Info tabs as required. The sales tax settings relate to the customer rather than the job, so you won't see the Sales Tax Setting tab.

Fill in the details of this job in the Job Info tab. All of the information on the Job Info tab is optional. The Job Status drop-down list offers choices that you can change as the progress of the job moves along. You can change the default text to reflect the way you refer to each progress level, but the changes you make for the text are system-wide and affect every job. To change the text you use to track job status, follow these steps:

1. Choose Edit | Preferences to open the Preferences dialog.
2. Click the Jobs & Estimates icon in the left pane, and then open the Company Preferences tab in the right pane to see the current descriptive text for each status level.
3. Change the text of any status levels if you have a descriptive phrase you like better, such as "Working" instead of "In Progress."
4. Click OK to save your changes, and this new text is used on every existing and new job in your system.
5. When you finish entering all the data about this job, click OK to close the New Job window and return to the Customers & Jobs List. The jobs you create for a customer become part of the customer listing.

Deleting and Hiding Customers and Jobs

From time to time, you may need to delete a customer or a job that you've created. Deleting a job is a bit more common than deleting customers, because sometimes QuickBooks users add a job when they prepare an estimate for a client for a new project and then delete the job if the project doesn't materialize.

You can delete a customer (or a job) only if it has never been used in a transaction. Although many users complain that they can't remove a customer that is essentially "dead wood" on their Customers & Jobs List, unfortunately, a zero balance doesn't matter; the rule in QuickBooks is that you can delete a customer or a job only if it has never been used in a transaction. Moreover, you cannot delete a customer that has at least one job attached to it. Instead, you must first delete the jobs (if they can be deleted) and then delete the customer.

To delete a customer or job, select it on the Customers & Jobs List and press CTRL-D. QuickBooks asks you to confirm that you want to delete this customer or job. Click OK to remove the customer or job.

If you have a customer that can't be deleted but is no longer active, you can prevent users from selecting it in transaction windows by making the customer inactive (hiding the customer so it doesn't appear in drop-down lists). To make a customer or job inactive, right-click its listing in the Customers & Jobs List and choose Make Customer: Job Inactive. If you make a customer inactive, all of the jobs associated with that customer are automatically made inactive. You cannot hide a customer without hiding all the jobs associated with it.

Active and Inactive Customers and Jobs

Your Customers & Jobs List is configured to show Active Customers (the default view), so inactive customers and jobs don't appear on the list. To see which customers and jobs are inactive, select All Customers from the drop-down list at the top of the Customers & Jobs List, shown next. Inactive customers and jobs will appear with an "X" to the left of their name in the listing of All Customers.

To make a customer or job active again, select All Customers as the view, and click the "X" next to the hidden customer or job to toggle the setting back to active. If you're reactivating a customer with jobs, QuickBooks asks if you also want to make all the jobs active. If you click Yes, the customer and all jobs are activated. If you click No, the customer is activated and all the jobs remain inactive; you can activate any of the jobs individually.

Merging Customers or Jobs

Suppose you create a customer or job and enter at least one transaction before you realize it's a duplicate of an existing customer or an existing job for the same customer. The best thing to do in this case is to merge the two customer entries or two job entries and move all the transaction history into one customer record. Follow these steps to do this:

1. Double-click the listing of the customer or job you do not want to keep to put it in Edit mode.
2. Change the customer or job name to match the name of the customer or job you want to keep.
3. Click OK. QuickBooks displays a message telling you that the name is in use and asks if you want to merge the names. Click Yes to complete the merge.

Merging customers works only when neither customer entry has any jobs associated with it or when the customer name you want to delete has no jobs attached (it's OK if the customer name you want to keep has jobs). Merging jobs works only when both jobs are linked to the same customer.

Use Custom Fields

You can add your own fields to the Customer, Vendor, Employee, and Item records. Custom fields are useful if you want to track particular information but QuickBooks doesn't provide a field for it. For example, if you want to track customer birthdays or annual renewals for a contract, you can add fields to track that information. Custom fields for names are added to all Names lists, but you can configure each field you create to limit its appearance to specific lists. For example, you might create a custom field that you want to use in only the Customers & Jobs List or in both the Customers & Jobs and Vendors lists.

Adding a Custom Field

Do the following to add one or more custom fields to names:

1. Open a center (Customers & Jobs, Vendors, or Employees) and double-click any name on the list to put the record in Edit mode.
2. Move to the Additional Info tab.
3. Click the Define Fields button to open the Set Up Custom Fields For Names dialog, where you can name the field and indicate the list(s) in which you want to use the new field.
4. Click OK to save the information. QuickBooks displays a message indicating that you can add these fields to any customized templates. (See Chapter 16 for more information about templates.)

As with other fields, be sure you enter data in a consistent manner, or the information you retrieve might not be useful to you when you customize a report to include this information.

Secure Customer Credit Card Information

If you store customer credit card data, QuickBooks provides security features. These features are designed to help you meet the requirements set by the payment card industry that are known as the *Payment Card Industry Data Security Standard* (PCI DSS). When you log in to your company file as Admin, you may see a reminder about enabling credit card protection when you open the file. The first chore you face is changing your own Admin password so it matches the standards for complex passwords required by the credit card protection feature.

If you store customer credit card data, enable the credit card protection feature as soon as possible. You can perform the task by choosing Company | Customer Credit Card Protection and selecting Enable Protection as long as you are logged in as the user named Admin.

The Challenge Question section is mandatory. If you forget your password, you can click the Reset Password button on the Login dialog. When you answer the challenge question correctly, QuickBooks lets you change your password to a new complex password. When you complete the dialog and click OK, QuickBooks confirms the fact that you've changed your password and informs you that you'll have to repeat this task every 90 days.

Although you can disable the customer credit card protection feature, it is not recommended that you do so if you store *any* customer credit card information. To disable this feature, reopen the Customer Credit Card Protection window, select Disable Protection, and answer Yes to the dialog asking if you want to disable it.

QuickBooks Customer Credit Card Protection

Here are some important points to keep in mind when you enable Credit Card Protection:

- All users who have permission to view full credit card detail in the customer record must set up a *complex password*.
- The password must be changed every 90 days. Users who don't change their passwords cannot open the file. If, as the Admin user, you fail to change your password, the credit card protection feature is disabled and you see messages about your failure to comply with the rules set for businesses that accept credit cards.
- You cannot reuse any of your last four passwords.
- If a user enters an incorrect password three times (users sometimes guess different passwords when they can't remember their passwords), the company file closes for that user.
- Only the Admin user can configure the functions in this feature.
- The QuickBooks credit card security audit log tracks all actions that involve credit cards (including viewing customer credit card information).

▸▸ Small Business Recommendation

Complex passwords (sometimes called *strong passwords*) are passwords not easily discovered by hacker software that uses permutations and combinations of letters and numbers to break into password-protected files. The more complex a password is, the higher the odds are against breaking it. For example, a password that contains eight characters and includes one uppercase letter and several lowercase letters, symbols, and numbers is harder to break than a password that is entirely uppercase or lowercase (the odds are somewhere in the range of one in many millions).

User Permissions for Viewing Credit Card Information

With credit card protection enabled, when you set up users and give them full access to the Sales and Accounts Receivable area, those users are not given permission to view customer credit card information unless you specifically select that option. Users who do not have permission to view credit card information see only the last four numbers of the customer's credit card when they open the Payment Info tab of a customer's record. Users who have permission to view customer information are also forced to create a complex password during their next login.

When you set up new users and give them permission to access customer information, it's not necessary to set up a complex password for them. Provide an easy- to-enter password, and QuickBooks will force a password change when they first log in.

Viewing the Security Log

When credit card protection is enabled, QuickBooks maintains a security log called the Customer Credit Card Audit Trail. This is a special report that can be viewed only by the QuickBooks Admin user. To open the report, choose Reports | Accountant & Taxes | Customer Credit Card Audit Trail. This report is updated each time a customer's credit card information is entered, displayed, edited, or deleted. The most recent activity always shows at the top of the report.

Create Your Vendors List

You have the same options when building your list of vendors in QuickBooks that you have when creating your Customers list. To create a vendor, open the Vendor Center from the Vendors menu or the Home page. Click the New Vendor icon above the Vendors list and select New Vendor. As you saw when entering your customers, the New Vendor dialog opens to the Address Info tab.

Vendor Information

Start by filling in the Vendor Name field at the top of the window, and fill in as much information as you think you'll need, including contacts, telephone numbers, and so on. The Billed From address block is important if you plan to print and mail checks, as this is the mailing address. If you use window envelopes, when you insert the check in the envelope, the vendor name and address block is located to show through the window. Use the Shipped From address if your vendor ships from a place different from their billing location.

As with the Customer Center, don't enter anything in the Opening Balance field. Instead, separately enter the existing open vendor bills that represent the current open (unpaid) balances. See Chapter 6 to learn how to enter vendor history.

Payment Settings

Use the Payment Settings tab to store useful information:

- **Account No.**   If you have an account number with this vendor, enter it here. The number appears in the memo field of printed checks.
- **Payment Terms**   The terms you enter here apply to all bills entered for this vendor.
- **Credit Limit**   QuickBooks warns you if you enter a bill that, when added to your existing balance, exceeds your credit limit with this vendor.
- **Billing Rate Level**   (Available only in the Premier and Enterprise versions.) If you plan on billing your customers for the work performed by this vendor, you can enter either a standard hourly or custom rate here. Each time you create an invoice with billable time, QuickBooks fills in the correct rate for each service item based on the vendor that did the work.
- **Print Name On Check As**   Fill in this field if the Payee name is different from the Vendor name you entered. For example, the Vendor name for Greater State Electric may be "GSE."

Small Business Tip   If you reimburse employees for expenses they incur on your behalf, create a Vendor Name for those employees to use reimbursements. Since QuickBooks does not allow duplicate names, you'll have to change the name you use in the Employee list slightly to create the Vendor Name listing (for instance, you might add a "-V" to the end of their names). Even though QuickBooks allows it, reimbursing employee expenses through payroll is not a good practice.

Tax Settings

If you send this vendor a Form 1099 at the end of the year, enter the tax ID number for this vendor and select the Vendor Eligible For 1099 check box. You'll learn more about the 1099 tracking feature later in this chapter and in Chapter 17.

Account Settings

When you select accounts in this window for this vendor, they'll appear automatically when you enter a bill or a check for the vendor. You can always change the pre-filled account before saving the bill or check, if necessary. You can pre-fill up to three accounts for a vendor, as shown next. This feature can be very useful for making loan payments, which require postings to principal and interest.

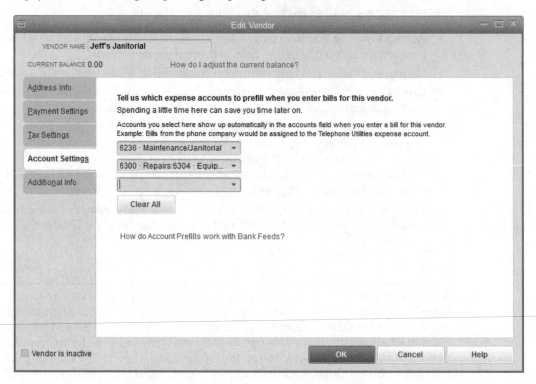

Additional Info

Use the Additional Info tab to record other details about your vendor for enhanced tracking and reporting:

- **Vendor Type** Select a vendor type or create one. This field is handy if you want to sort vendors by type, which makes reports more efficient.
- **Custom Fields** You can create custom fields for vendors just as you can for customers.

Adding and Editing Multiple Vendor Records

If you want to add information to many or all of your vendor records at once, or you want to find an easy way to enter new vendors in a more streamlined way, use the Add/Edit Multiple List Entries window.

From the Vendor Center, select New Vendor | Add Multiple Vendors. (You can also access this window by selecting Lists | Add/Edit Multiple List Entries and selecting Vendors as the list type.) The Add/Edit Multiple List Entries window opens, and you can add new vendors, update key information, or fill in data you perhaps didn't have when you first created the vendor. You can even copy and paste vendor information from an Excel worksheet into the Add/Edit Multiple List Entries window to create a new vendor record quickly.

Here are some of the important features and functions in the Add/Edit Multiple List Entries window:

- **List and view filters**   Select the List or View drop-down arrow to display only those records in your list with which you want to work.
- **Customize Columns button**   Use this button to open the Customize Columns window. Here, you can add the columns to the vendor record that you want to modify or add columns to match those in a spreadsheet that you want to copy and paste from into QuickBooks.
- **Copy Down**   Right-click any field in the table, except the Name field, and select the Copy Down command to copy the contents of the selected field to all the remaining records in the list.
- **Duplicate Row**   Right-click any row in the table and choose Duplicate Row from the context menu that appears to duplicate the selected record in the row below. The new duplicate record name will start with "DUP."

The Vendor Center

Your list of vendors is stored in the Vendor Center, along with information about each vendor's transactions. To open the Vendor Center, choose Vendors | Vendor Center from the menu bar or click the Vendors icon on the Icon Bar. The Vendor Center displays your Vendors list, gives you quick access to key reports, and makes it easy to enter vendor transactions.

As with the Customer Center, the left pane of the Vendor Center has two tabs: Vendors (your Vendors list) and Transactions. A vendor is always selected in the list (by default, the first vendor in the list when you first open the Vendor Center), and the right pane of the Vendor Center displays both the details and transactions for the selected vendor. See Figure 2-5 for an example of the Vendor Center with the Vendor Information pane.

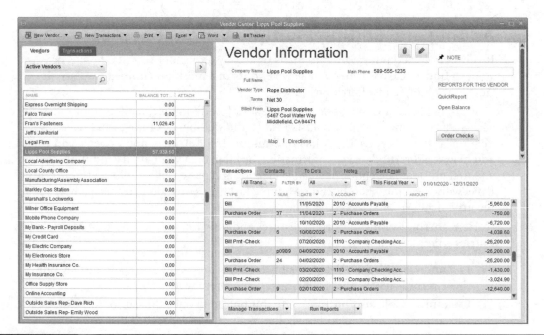

FIGURE 2-5   Use the Vendor Center to see information about an individual vendor.

Customizing the Vendors List

You can customize the information displayed in the Vendors list (the left pane shown in Figure 2-5) as well as the Vendor Information pane on the right side of the window. By default, the Vendors list has three columns: Name, Balance Total, and Attach. The Attach column displays a paper clip icon next to the vendor name if you've attached a scanned or other document to that record using the Doc Center. Use the scroll bar to find the vendor you want to see.

Small Business Tip   Use your TWAIN-compliant scanner to add documents to the Doc Center. Click the Docs icon on the Icon Bar and click Scan. Follow the onscreen directions. See more about attaching documents in Chapter 14. (TWAIN is the system used by your computer to communicate with scanners and other digital devices.)

Use the drop-down list at the top of the Vendors tab to display your vendors in any of following ways:

- All Vendors
- Active Vendors
- Vendors With Open Balances
- Custom Filter

Use Custom Filter to display only vendors that match the criteria you set in the Custom Filter dialog. The options in the dialog are easy to understand and use.

Add more columns to the list by right-clicking anywhere in the list and choosing Customize Columns to open the Customize Columns dialog. To add a column, select its label in the left pane and click Add. The information the column describes displays for each vendor in the list. As long as the vendor you're interested in is displayed on the portion of the list that's visible, the information is available—you don't have to select the listing or open the record.

You can rearrange the left-to-right order of the columns by opening the Customize Columns dialog and selecting a column you want to move. Choose Move Up to move a column to the left or Move Down to move it to the right. The order of columns displayed in the Chosen Columns pane of the dialog translates as top to bottom = left to right.

If you add columns to the Vendors list, you won't be able to see all the information unless you widen the list's pane and adjust the width of each column. To maximize this pane, click the Show Full List Only button as shown here

Working in the Vendor Information Pane

You can view all the information you've entered for each vendor as well as every purchasing-related transaction. Figure 2-5 shows five tabs in the middle of the Vendor Information pane. Each of these tabs contains detailed information about this vendor. Use the Manage *<tab name>* button at the bottom of the window to create a new entry, edit, or delete the information on any tab. If you do *not* see the Vendor Information Pane, click the Show List And Details arrow (the small right-pointing arrow) at the side of the vendor pane as shown here:

Using the Tabs and the Filters

Most of the five tabs have one or more filters by which you can view your data:

- **Transactions**   The Transactions tab lists all types of vendor transactions. There are three filters by which you can organize the information. You can sort by any of the five columns by clicking the small arrow to the right of the column heading. Add, remove, or change columns by right-clicking anywhere on or below the column headings and choosing Customize Columns.

  - Use the Show filter to see All Transactions, Balance Details, and several other choices.
  - Depending on your choice in the Show filter, you can use the Filter By option to narrow down the results that are displayed. For example, in following illustration, Bills was chosen in the Show Filter, and you can choose from All Bills, Open Bills, or Overdue Bills.

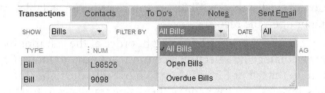

  - The Date filter lets you choose the time period for the selected information,
- **Contacts**   Use this tab to add more detail about who to contact. There are no filters for this option.
- **To Do's**   Click the Manage To Do's button and select Create New to compose a reminder for a specific vendor in the Add To Do dialog. View your To Do note in the calendar or directly in the Vendor Center, or click the Run Reports button to see a detailed listing of all your To Do's. There are three filters for this tab: Type, Status, and Date.
- **Notes**   Click the Manage Notes button to add, edit, or delete a note in the Notepad dialog. Click the Date/Time Stamp button to insert the current date automatically when you're adding text to the notepad. The only available filter is Date.
- **Sent Email**   Use the Sent Email tab to view and keep track of the purchase orders that you've e-mailed a vendor. As with the Notes option, the only available filter is Date.

Edit Vendor Information

Edit a vendor's information by double-clicking the vendor's listing in the Vendors list to open the vendor's record in Edit mode or click the small pencil icon in the Vendor Information pane. Fill in any additional data details you need. You can change any data you've previously entered. Be careful about changes in the Vendor Name field, however, since any changes will change the way the name appears in your Vendors list and vendor reports. Changing the Vendor Name field can also change the name associated with past transactions that you have cleared in QuickBooks. For example, if your phone company changes from AT&T to Verizon and you change the vendor name, all past checks and bill payments written to AT&T will show as having been written to Verizon.

To open a menu of actions you can take in the Vendors list, right-click anywhere within the list to open the menu shown here.

Delete or Inactivate a Vendor

You can remove a vendor from the list only if that vendor has never been involved in a transaction. To delete a vendor, select its listing in the Vendors tab of the Vendor Center and press CTRL-D, or right-click its listing to choose Delete Vendor from the context menu. QuickBooks asks you to confirm that you want to delete the vendor; just click OK to finish the task. If the vendor has ever been involved in a transaction, QuickBooks issues an error message saying you can't delete this vendor.

If you can't delete a vendor but you don't want this vendor used in transactions, you can hide the vendor's listing by making it inactive. To do this, right-click its listing in the Vendors list and choose Make Vendor Inactive.

If your Vendors list is configured to show Active Vendors (the default view), inactive vendors don't appear on the list. To see which vendors are inactive, click the small down arrow to the right of the View field at the top of the list and select All Vendors from the drop-down list. Inactive vendors have an "X" to the left of their listings. To make a vendor active again, select All Vendors as the view and click the "X" next to the hidden vendor or job to toggle the setting back to active. Inactive vendors are included in reports, so you can continue to get accurate reports on purchases and other vendor activity.

Merge Vendors

If you have inadvertently created a duplicate vendor and entered a transaction, you can merge the two vendors and move all the transaction history into one vendor record. Follow these steps:

1. Double-click the listing of the vendor you do not want to keep, which opens its record in Edit mode.
2. Change the data in the Vendor Name field to match exactly the name of the vendor you want to keep.
3. Click OK. QuickBooks displays a message telling you that the name is in use and asks if you want to merge the names. Click Yes.

Remember that the trick to merging is to start with the vendor name you *don't* want and merge into the vendor name you *do* want.

Use Custom Fields in Vendor Records

As with the Customers list, QuickBooks has the ability to create custom fields for only the Vendors list. For example, you might create a custom field that you want to use in only the Vendors list or in both the Customers & Jobs and Vendors lists.

Adding a Custom Field for Vendors

To add one or more custom fields to the Vendors list, follow these steps:

1. Open the Vendor Center, select any name on the Vendors list, and then press CTRL-E to put the record in Edit mode.
2. Move to the Additional Info tab.
3. Click the Define Fields button to open the Set Up Custom Fields For Names dialog, where you can create a field name and choose the list(s) that will use this new field.
4. Click OK to save the information. You'll see a message reminding you that you can add this new field to any customized templates.
5. The Additional Info tab for every name in the list(s) you selected shows the field, and you can add data to any name for which the field has relevance. Enter data in a consistent manner so you get accurate information when you customize reports that include this information.

Create 1099 Vendors

QuickBooks supports only the 1099-MISC form. If any vendors are eligible for 1099 reporting, enter that information when setting them up. See Chapter 17 for the process of verifying and filing 1099 forms in QuickBooks.

Ensure that your QuickBooks file is set up to track and process 1099 forms. Choose Edit | Preferences, click the Tax: 1099 icon, and move to the Company Preferences tab to see your settings. Click Yes next to the question Do You File 1099-MISC Forms? You are required to issue Form 1099-MISC at the end of the calendar year for a vendor to whom you've paid $600 or more for services and whose business operates as an individual or partnership.

To issue Form 1099, you must have the vendor's federal Tax Identification Number (TIN), which can be a social security number or an employer identification number (EIN). Open each appropriate vendor listing and open the Sales Tax Settings tab. Select the option labeled Vendor Eligible For 1099, and fill in the Vendor Tax ID number.

Small Business Tip Because 1099 reporting rules are becoming more complex each year, check in with your tax professional about the latest IRS rules regarding 1099s.

Creating Items, Other Lists, and Your Beginning Balances

Chapter 3

This chapter introduces you to additional lists and items you may use in your transactions. QuickBooks uses *items* to list the things you sell in sales-related transactions. You can also use items on a bill to tell QuickBooks about the things you buy from a vendor. An item can be a product (that you may or may not be tracking as inventory), a service, or any necessary entry on a sales or purchase transaction. You'll learn about many of the different items you can use in QuickBooks, except for payroll items (covered in Chapter 9) and inventory items (covered in Chapter 13).

In addition, in earlier chapters, you learned how to set up the chart of accounts and the Customers and Vendors lists used in nearly every QuickBooks transaction. In this chapter, you'll learn about additional lists that don't require extensive amounts of data or time to set up, but that can help make your work in QuickBooks more efficient and make it easier to generate more meaningful reports.

Understand How Items Are Used

What other items do you use in a transaction besides products and services? Well, think about all the different elements you see on an invoice. If you charge sales tax, that's an item. If you accept prepayments or give discounts, both are items. If you subtotal sections of your invoices to apply discounts or taxes, that subtotal is also an item. If you charge for shipping or restocking fees, these, too, are items.

QuickBooks uses items in sales-related transactions. Each line in an invoice, for example, includes an item that represents a product or service that you sell. Every item you create is linked to an income account in your chart of accounts. When you're creating a transaction, you don't have to worry about the account to which any individual line item on an invoice or sales receipt is posted—your item takes care of all that behind-the-scenes accounting for you.

Most items are linked to an income account because items are often things you're selling to the customer. You can link all of your items to one income account in your chart of accounts (called "Income" or "Sales"), or you can track different types of items by linking them to different income accounts. For example, you might want to link all product sales to an income account named Product Sales and link the services you sell to an income account named Service Sales. The advantage of linking certain types of items to certain income accounts is that when you look at a standard Profit & Loss report, you can tell at a glance what your sales totals are for each group of item types. QuickBooks also offers several item reports that give you insight into details such as your best sellers and your most profitable and least profitable items.

Some items are not linked to income accounts because they're not considered income. For example, sales tax isn't income to you; it's money you collect for a government agency, and you have to turn that money over to them. Because these funds are someone else's money, sales tax items link to a liability account.

Discounts you give your customers are also items, and you should link them to accounts designed for that purpose to help you see in your reports the savings and incentives that you've passed on to your customers. Items are a bit more varied than you may have thought, but creating and configuring them is not complicated when you follow the steps outlined here.

Understand Item Types

QuickBooks needs to categorize the items that you add to your Item List, and it does this by using *item types*. Because it sometimes may not be obvious which type you should use, the following item examples may help you make the right choices:

- **Service**   You can charge service items by the job or by the hour for services performed by either employees or outside contractors.
- **Inventory Part**   This item type is a product you buy to resell. Learn more in Chapter 13.
- **Non-inventory Part**   This item type is a product you buy and sell but don't track as inventory, such as merchandise drop-shipped to a customer or products you buy.
- **Other Charge**   This is used for shipping charges or other line items that don't fit as a Service or Inventory item.
- **Subtotal**   This item type automatically adds up the line items that come immediately before it on a sales transaction. It provides a subtotal before you add other charges or subtract discounts.
- **Group**   Group items save time because you can enter a group of individual items that you typically sell together. Each item that you want to make a Group item must first exist separately in your Item List.
- **Discount**   Discount items apply either a percentage or dollar discount to the item immediately preceding it. You can create more than one, such as a discount percentage for wholesale customers and a discount amount for a volume purchase.
- **Payment**   This item type shows on an invoice when you receive either advance payments or deposits.
- **Sales Tax**   Create one of these item types for each sales tax authority for which you collect sales tax. This item type is available only if you have enabled sales tax in Preferences.
- **Sales Tax Group**   This item enables you to create one sales tax rate out of several sales tax items.

Build Your Item List

The information that QuickBooks needs to create an item depends on the type of item you create. Service items are relatively simple to create, but inventory items require a bit more planning, which is why Chapter 14 goes into more detail.

Create a Service Item

The process of building your item starts by choosing Lists | Item List from the menu bar and selecting New (as shown next to the word "New," the keyboard shortcut is CTRL-N) to open the New Item window. The Type field at the top has a drop-down menu that displays a list of available item types, as shown here. Select Service as the type.

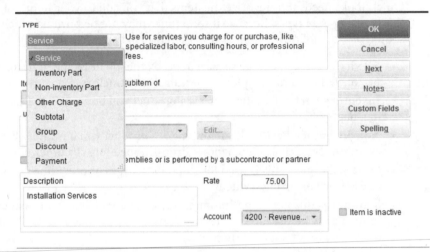

Insert a unique identifying code in the Item Name/Number field. This Item Name/Number can simply be the service that's being offered. When you fill out sales or purchase transactions, you see this name or number in the drop-down list.

If you want to make your item a subitem of another item, check the Subitem Of check box. Subitems enable you to track the sales and purchases of an item at either a summary or detail level. Use subitems to organize a complex Item List and to create lists in a way that makes sense to you and others in your company.

> **Small Business Tip** Most QuickBooks Premier editions and all QuickBooks Enterprise editions offer the option to define the unit of measure for an item. This option is not available in QuickBooks Pro.

Next, you see the check box option to tell QuickBooks whether this service is used in assemblies (only QuickBooks Premier and Enterprise Editions offer the assembly feature) or is performed by a subcontractor or partner. When you check this box, the item record expands (as shown next) to include fields that allow you to link both the expense side of this item and the income side to different accounts in your chart of accounts. If you use this feature, use the drop-down arrow next to the Expense Account field to select an appropriate expense account from your chart of accounts.

You can fill in the Cost field here or leave it at zero if you pay more than one rate for that service to different subcontractors. Later, when you pay the vendor you've hired as a subcontractor for this service, you'll select this item (using the Items tab in either the Write Checks or Enter Bills window) and fill in a cost.

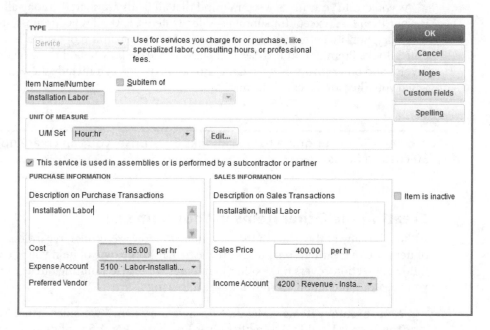

In the Sales Price field, enter the amount or hourly rate you charge for this service. You can leave this field at zero if you don't have a standard rate for this service and you want to fill in the price when you create a sales transaction. Be sure to use the Tax Code drop-down arrow to indicate whether this service is taxable, and then choose the income account to which it is linked. Click the Notes button to open a notepad to record and store any special information that you want to keep track of about this item. When you're done, click OK to return to the Item List or click Next to create another new item.

Create Custom Fields for Items

Using custom fields, you can record unique information about the products and services you sell, such as information about the size or color of an item you stock or noting the location in your warehouse where a particular part is stored. You can create up to five fields in Items:

1. Open the Item List, select an item, and choose Edit Item. (Alternatively, press CTRL-E to edit the item.)
2. Click the Custom Fields button. (The first time you create a custom field, a message appears telling you that there are no custom fields yet defined; click Define Fields to create a new custom field.)

3. In the Set Up Custom Fields For Items dialog, enter a name for each field you want to add.

4. Place a check mark in the Use column to use the field, and click OK.

As you create your fields, keep in mind that all fields are shared among all the items in your Item List (except for subtotals, sale tax items, and sales tax groups), including inventory, non-inventory, or service items. There is a maximum of five fields available in QuickBooks Premier and Pro. See Chapter 14 to learn how to add these fields to your invoice and other forms. New in QuickBooks 2016, you can include these custom fields when you filter for specific information.

> **Note** If you upgrade to QuickBooks Enterprise, you can create up to 30 custom fields.

Creating the Other Items in Your Item List

Although many of the fields in the New Item window are similar, regardless of the type of item you're creating, some fields are particular to the type of item you're creating. The following section covers these other item types while also pointing out any unique fields you need to understand, as shown in the following list:

- **Non-inventory items**   Make a Non-inventory item "two-sided" (that is, check the This Item Is Used In Assemblies Or Is Purchased For A Specific Customer:Job box) to designate both an income and expense account. If you purchase an item from a vendor that references this non-inventory part using their own unique number, use the unique number in the Manufacturer's Part Number field so it is available when you make purchases from that vendor.

- **Other Charge items**   Use this item type for shipping or other charges that you want to show on a sales transaction.

- **Subtotal items**   This useful item type enables you to add and total groups of items within the body of an invoice or sales receipt. Simply list the subtotal item immediately after the list of items for which you want to show a subtotal.

- **Discount items**   A Discount item affects the line item immediately before it. Indicate either a flat dollar rate or a percentage discount when you create this item type.

- **Payment items**   Use a Payment item to record the receipt of a partial payment. When listed on an invoice, a Payment item reduces the balance due.

Group Items

Use a Group item to list items that you typically sell together on an invoice or sales receipt. Before you create a Group item, be sure you have entered each of the individual items into your Item List. Then follow these steps:

1. From the Item List, select New (or press CTRL-N) to open the New Item window, and select Group from the Type drop-down list.
2. Create a name for the new group in the Group Name/Number field.
3. Enter a description if you choose. Note that whether or not you select the Print Items In Group option (which ensures that individual items in the group will appear in the transaction), your entry in the Description field appears on the printed sales transaction unless you decide to change it.
4. Select each item that is to be part of this group and enter the quantity (if applicable) for each item. Click OK when you are finished.

Changing Item Prices

If you want to create a price increase or decrease for one or more of the services or products you sell, use the Change Item Prices window.

1. From the Customers menu, select Change Item Prices.
2. In the Change Item Prices window, use the Item Type filter to list only those items of a particular type (Service, Inventory Part, Inventory Assembly, Non-inventory Part, or Other Charge).
3. Place a check mark next to the items subject to a price change, and tell QuickBooks if the price change should be calculated as an amount or as a percentage of the item's cost or its current price.
4. If you'd like QuickBooks to round up the adjustment, use the Round Up To Nearest drop-down menu to choose a rounding option. Otherwise, you can leave this option at its default of No Rounding.
5. Click the Adjust button to effect the change, and then click OK.

Using Sales Tax Items

If you collect and remit sales tax, you need to configure your Sales Tax Preferences and set up tax codes to link to your customers so you know whether a customer is liable for sales tax. You also need to set up tax items for the sales tax to be collected and link the item(s) to the taxing authority to which you remit the collected sales tax.

Start your sales tax setup by choosing Edit | Preferences from the menu bar. Click the Sales Tax icon in the left pane and select the Company Preferences tab. Select Yes for the option Do You Charge Sales Tax?

Sales Tax Items

A sales tax item is really just a collection of data about a sales tax, including the rate and the agency to which the sales tax is remitted. QuickBooks uses sales tax items to calculate the Tax field at the bottom of sales forms and to prepare reports you can send to your local taxing authority. You can create your first sales tax item in the Sales Tax Preferences or directly in your Item List.

Note: If you do not see Sales Tax Item or Sales Tax Group on your list of available items, select Edit | Preferences | Sales Tax | Company Preferences and answer Yes to Do You Charge Sales Tax? The Sales Tax Company Preferences dialog includes a field named Your Most Common Sales Tax Item, and you must enter a sales tax item in that field. To do that, you must first create at least one sales tax item. This item becomes the default sales tax item for any customers you create hereafter, but you can change any customer's default sales tax item at any time.

Creating Sales Tax Items in the Item List

Once you've set the Sales Tax Preference, follow these steps to create an item in your Item List:

1. Select Lists | Item List from the main menu to open the Item List.
2. Press CTRL-N to open the New Item dialog, and select Sales Tax Item as the item type.
3. Enter a name for the item. You can use the state's code for the specific sales tax rate and taxing authority. You can also enter an optional description.
4. Enter the tax rate.
5. Select the tax agency (a vendor) to which you pay the tax from the drop-down list, or add a new vendor by choosing <Add New>.
6. Click OK.

Create and Use Tax Groups

A *tax group* is a collection of two or more individual tax items that are displayed as one tax to a customer on a sales transaction. For example, you might be required to collect 7.2 percent state sales tax in addition to 4.2 percent county sales tax because of the county your business operates from or the location at which you perform your services or deliver your products. This is especially important in some states where city, county/parish, and state portions are paid to different tax entities. When you use a sales tax group, QuickBooks keeps track behind the scenes of each taxing authority to whom the tax is due, as shown next. The customer sees only the total sales tax rate.

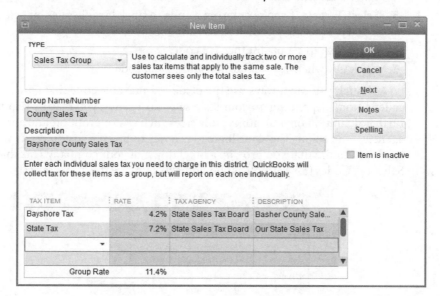

To create a tax group, first create the individual tax items and then add those items to the group item. Follow these steps to create a tax group:

1. Open the Item List by choosing Lists | Item List, and press CTRL-N to open the New Item dialog.
2. Select Sales Tax Group as the Type, and enter a name for the group.
3. Enter a Description that will appear on your sales forms.
4. In the Tax Item column, choose the individual tax code items you need to create this group. (QuickBooks fills in the rate, tax agency, and description of each tax you already selected.) Notice that the calculated total (the group rate) appears at the bottom of the dialog.
5. When all the required tax code items have been added, click OK.

Sales Tax Codes

QuickBooks uses sales tax codes to designate an item as taxable or nontaxable on a sales transaction. You can create codes to track sales tax status with more detail than taxable and nontaxable. To do so, just add new sales tax codes to fit your needs. To add a new sales tax code, follow these steps:

1. Select Lists | Sales Tax Code List.
2. Press CTRL-N to open the New Sales Tax Code window.

3. Enter the name of the new code (up to three characters in length).
4. Enter a description.
5. Select Taxable if you're entering a code to track taxable sales, or select Non-taxable if you're entering a code to track nontaxable sales.
6. Click Next to set up another tax code.
7. Click OK when you've finished adding tax codes.

Although you can always use the default nontaxable code that QuickBooks provides, called "Non," depending on your state sales tax agency, you may be required to provide further definition of your nontaxable sales such as nonprofit organizations, government agencies, and so on. The same logic may apply to taxable customers as well; some agencies require that you provide a breakdown of your company's taxable sales. Use the Sales Tax Codes (an example is shown next) to make this process easier.

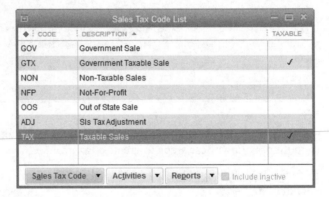

Small Business Tip   Check your local taxing authority or your tax professional before setting up your sales tax codes and items to ensure that you're recording the correct sales tax amounts and that the sales tax reports you run in QuickBooks are accurate.

Sales Tax Payments

There are two ways to remit sales tax to the taxing authorities, and they're listed in the When Do You Owe Sales Tax section of the Sales Tax Preferences dialog:

- As Of Invoice Date, which is accrual-based tax reporting
- Upon Receipt Of Payment, which is cash-based tax reporting

Check with your accountant and the local taxing authority to determine the method you need to select. Each state has its own reporting rules. You must indicate the frequency of your remittance to the taxing authority in the When Do You Pay Sales Tax section of the Preferences dialog using the schedule set by your sales tax agency.

Assigning Sales Tax Codes and Items to Customers

When you turn on the Sales Tax preference and create your first Sales Tax item, QuickBooks asks if you want to make all of your customers as well as your inventory and non-inventory parts taxable. If you do not deselect either of these options, QuickBooks will apply the "taxable" tax code to all customers and inventory parts. You can modify this setting at the customer level in the Sales Tax Settings tab of a customer's record.

If your Customers list is large, opening several records one at a time to make this change can be time consuming. Instead, use the Add/Edit Multiple List Entries window to edit the tax items or codes for multiple customers in a single view. From the Customer Center, point your mouse anywhere on the Customers & Jobs list and right-click. Select Add/Edit Multiple Customers: Jobs to open the Add/Edit Multiple List Entries window. You may have to customize the columns in this window to bring these fields into view.

You can use the Add/Edit Multiple List Entries window to modify the tax code setting for your items as well. With your Item List open, right-click anywhere in the list and select Add/Edit Multiple Items to open this window.

Use the Other QuickBooks Lists

Click Lists from your menu bar to see the other lists available to you, as shown next. Depending on your company and the options you have chosen, the list you see may be different from the one shown here. Although you may not use all (or any) of these lists, review them to see if they might be of use to you and your company.

Lists Favorites Company Customers Ven	
Chart of Accounts	Ctrl+A
Item List	
Fixed Asset Item List	
Price Level List	
Sales Tax Code List	
Payroll Item List	
Payroll Schedule List	
Class List	
Other Names List	
Customer & Vendor Profile Lists	▶
Templates	
Memorized Transaction List	Ctrl+T
Add/Edit Multiple List Entries	

Fixed Asset Item List

Use the Fixed Asset Item list to store information about the fixed assets your business owns. Choose Lists | Fixed Asset Item List to open the list that provides a way to track data about the assets you purchase and depreciate. Remember that this is not like your Item List in that it doesn't provide links to any financial data in your QuickBooks company file, nor does it interact with the chart of accounts, so any values you enter in this list have to be entered in your Fixed Asset accounts separately. This list is intended to be a way to use QuickBooks to catalog your fixed assets instead of the list you're keeping elsewhere.

➡ Small Business Recommendation

Items added to the Fixed Asset Item list are visible in the drop-down list you see when you create a transaction that involves your regular items such as an invoice, a cash sale, or a purchase order. If you accidentally select a Fixed Asset item while creating a sales transaction, for example, your financial records can become confusing. If you use the Fixed Asset Item list, consider making all the items in the list inactive to suppress their display in drop-down lists.

However, using the Fixed Asset Item list to track your businesses assets can assist your accountant in the year-end tax-related chores he or she performs for you. If your accountant uses the Premier Accountant Edition version of QuickBooks, he or she can open your company file and read from your Fixed Asset Item list using a program call the Fixed Asset Manager (FAM). FAM works by pulling the information it needs from your QuickBooks company file to calculate the depreciation for a given period and then posting a journal entry back to your company file.

U/M Set List

If you are using QuickBooks Enterprise or QuickBooks Premier (other than QuickBooks Premier Retail), you can designate different units of measure (U/M) to price services or items you sell. Once you have established units of measure, this list shows each different option you have set for selling your products, as shown in Figure 3-1. To enable this option:

1. Choose Edit | Preferences | Items & Inventory | Company Preferences.
2. In the Unit of Measure section, click Enable. (If the option is greyed out, you'll see a "Learn More" link that explains your QuickBooks version does not support units of measure.) After the option is selected, you can select one of two options:
   a. Multiple U/M Per Item to have more than one type of measurement for an item you sell
   b. Single U/M Per Item to use one unit of measurement per single item
3. If, in the future, you want to make this option unavailable, follow the same steps and choose Disable.

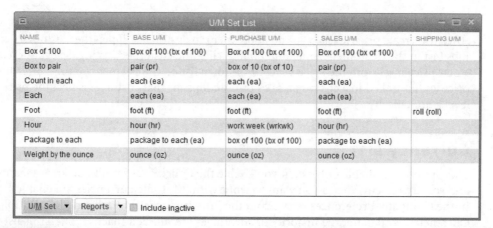

NAME	BASE U/M	PURCHASE U/M	SALES U/M	SHIPPING U/M
Box of 100	Box of 100 (bx of 100)	Box of 100 (bx of 100)	Box of 100 (bx of 100)	
Box to pair	pair (pr)	box of 10 (bx of 10)	pair (pr)	
Count in each	each (ea)	each (ea)	each (ea)	
Each	each (ea)	each (ea)	each (ea)	
Foot	foot (ft)	foot (ft)	foot (ft)	roll (roll)
Hour	hour (hr)	work week (wrkwk)	hour (hr)	
Package to each	package to each (ea)	box of 100 (bx of 100)	package to each (ea)	
Weight by the ounce	ounce (oz)	ounce (oz)	ounce (oz)	

FIGURE 3-1   The U/M Set List displays all of the various measurements that apply to the products you sell.

Small Business Tip   If you are using QuickBooks Pro, consider setting up items as a group to designate units of measure. For example, if you sell a group of items such as a pack of six, create two items on your Item List: one "Bracket" and the second "BracketPack(6)."

Price Level List

Use the Price Level list to apply special pricing to customers and jobs. This list is available after you enable price levels in the Sales & Customers section of your Preferences. Do the following to turn on this feature:

1. Choose Edit | Preferences and select the Sales & Customers category in the left pane.
2. Move to the Company Preferences tab and select the Enable Price Levels option.
3. Click OK.

Creating a Price Level

To create a price level, open the Price Level list from the Lists menu. Press CTRL-N to open the New Price Level dialog. Each price level has two components: a name and a formula. The name can be anything you wish, and the formula is a percentage of the price you entered for the items in your Item List (the formula increases or reduces the price by the percentage you specify). You can use price levels to set a price above the standard price, too.

Assigning Price Levels to Customers

After you create price levels, you can apply them to customers. Open the Customers & Jobs List in the Customer Center and double-click the customer's listing. Select or create a new price level from the Price Level drop-down list on the Payment Settings tab. Once a price level is linked to a customer, sales transactions for that customer reflect the price level automatically.

Currency List

This option is available only when you enable the QuickBooks multicurrencies feature and specify the currencies you want to work with. Multiple currencies are enabled in the Company Preferences area. From the Edit menu, select Preferences | Multiple Currencies. By default, the majority of currencies are marked Inactive; open this list to activate the currencies you need so they appear in drop-down lists.

> **Small Business Tip**   Be sure to make a backup copy of your company file before turning on the multiple currencies feature in your company file. Once enabled, it cannot be turned off.

> **Note**   Payroll Item List and Payroll Schedule List are discussed in Chapter 9.

Work with Classes

Classes provide a method of organizing your company's income and expense transactions by division or department, enabling you to filter many of the standard QuickBooks reports by class. You might choose to use classes, for example, to track expenses and profitability by location when you have more than one location, or you may need to organize financial reporting by business type, such as when your company has both retail and wholesale divisions.

The Class list appears in the Lists menu only when you enable the Use Class Tracking feature. From the Edit menu, select Preferences | Accounting | Company Preferences | Use Class Tracking For Transactions. Click Prompt To Assign Classes to ensure that each transaction has a class assigned. Otherwise, your reports will include "Unclassified Transactions." For each transaction or each line of any transaction, you can assign one of the classes you created.

Use classes for a single purpose; otherwise, the feature does not work properly. For example, you can use classes to separate your business into locations or by type of business, but not both. If you need to define a class or narrow its definition further, you can use subclasses.

When you enable classes, QuickBooks adds a Class field to transaction forms so that you can associate a class with a particular transaction. Classes are assigned only to a specific transaction, not a customer or vendor. For customers or vendors, you can assign a *type*. (See "Customer and Vendor Type Lists" later in this chapter.)

Small Business Tip   In QuickBooks Pro, you can use classes only in income and expense accounts. If you need to run a Balance Sheet report by class or other reports that show totals by class for an asset or liability account (such as a bank or loan account), consider upgrading to the Premier or Enterprise version of QuickBooks.

Create a Class

To create a class, choose Lists | Class List from the QuickBooks menu bar to display the Class List window, and choose New to open the New Class dialog. Fill in the name of the class, and then click Next to add another class, or click OK if you are finished.

If you decide to use classes, it's a good idea to create a class for general overhead expenses. You can then allocate the amounts accumulated in this overhead class to other classes with a journal entry later if you wish. Learn to use journal entries in Chapter 17.

Creating a Subclass

Subclasses let you post transactions to specific subcategories of classes, and they work similarly to subaccounts in your chart of accounts. If you set up a subclass, you must post transactions only to the subclass, never to the parent class. However, unlike the chart of accounts, classes have no option to force the display of only the subclass when you're working in a transaction window. As a result, when using subclasses, keep the name of the parent class short to lessen the need to scroll through the field to see the entire class name.

Create a subclass using the same steps you use to create a class. After you enter a name for the subclass in the Class Name field, click the check box next to the option Subclass Of to insert a check mark. Then select the appropriate parent class from the drop-down list.

Other Names List

The Other Names list is a list of people whose names are used when you write checks, but who don't fit the definition of vendor because you don't need to track payables and transactions as you do for a vendor. The names in the Other Names list appear in the drop-down list when you write checks but are unavailable when you're entering vendor bills, vendor credits, bill payments, purchase orders, or sales transactions.

One of the most common reasons to add a name to the Other Names list is to write checks to owners and partners if they are not employees. To open the Other Names list, choose Lists | Other Names List. To create a new name for the list, select New to open a New Name window. The New Name window provides fields for the address (handy for printing checks you're going to place into window envelopes), telephone numbers, and other contact information.

Customer & Vendor Profile Lists

Profile lists appear in the submenu you see when you choose Customer & Vendor Profile Lists. This list is shown next. Most of the lists in the submenu are designed to help you categorize and refine the information you keep about your customers and vendors. Other lists can contain data that is available when you create transactions.

Sales Rep List

By definition, a *sales rep* is a salesperson connected to a customer, usually because he or she receives a commission on sales to that customer. However, it's quite common to track sales reps who are not necessarily paid commissions as a way to determine who is the primary contact for a customer (some people call this a *service rep*).

To create a sales rep, the rep's name has to exist in your QuickBooks system as a vendor, employee, or a member of the Other Names list.

To create a new sales rep from an existing name, from the QuickBooks menu bar, select Lists | Customer & Vendor Profile Lists | Sales Rep List. Click Sales Rep at the bottom left of the screen or press CTRL-N to open a New Sales Rep dialog, shown next. Select the person's name from the drop-down list. QuickBooks automatically fills in the Sales Rep Initials field, which is used in reports and transaction windows with a

Sales Rep field, and the Sales Rep Type. You can modify the Sales Rep Initials field if you wish.

Customer and Vendor Type Lists

When you create your Customers and Vendors lists, you may decide to use the type field as a way to categorize your customers, vendors, and suppliers. This gives you the opportunity to sort and select customers and vendors in reports.

Job Type List

Use the Job Type list to set up categories for jobs. For example, if you're a plumber, you may want to separate new construction from repair work.

Terms List

QuickBooks keeps both customer and vendor payment terms in one list, so the terms you need are all available whether you're creating an invoice, entering a vendor bill, or creating a purchase order. To create a terms listing, from the Customer & Vendor Profits Lists menu, select Terms List. Choose the Terms drop-down menu at the bottom left of the window. Select New or press CTRL-N to open the New Terms dialog. Use the Standard section, as seen next, to create terms that are due at some elapsed time after the invoice date:

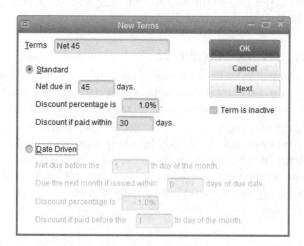

- Net Due In is the number of days allowed for payment after the invoice date.
- To create a discount for early payment, enter the discount percentage and the number of days after the invoice date that the discount is in effect. For example, if 45 days are allowed for payment, enter a discount percentage that is in effect for 30 days after the invoice date (such terms are usually referred to as "X percent 1, net 30," substituting the amount of the discount for X).

Use the Date Driven section to describe terms that are due on a particular date, regardless of the invoice date, as shown here:

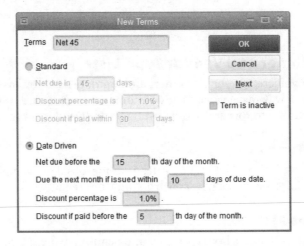

- Enter the day of the month the invoice payment is due.
- Enter the number of days before the due date that invoices are considered payable on the following month.
- To create a discount for early payment, enter the discount percentage and the day of the month at which the discount period ends. For example, if the standard due date is the 15th of the month, you may want to extend a discount to any customer who pays by the 8th of the month.

Customer Message List

Many companies write messages to customers when creating a sales transaction. If you choose, you can enter several appropriate messages ahead of time and then just select the one you want to use, such as "Thanks for your business" or "Happy Holidays!"

From the Customers & Vendor Profile Lists menu, select Customer Message List. Click New or press CTRL-N to enter a new message to add to the list. The text can be no more than 101 characters, including spaces. Keep in mind that once a message is used in a transaction, you can't delete it. However, if it becomes obsolete, you can make it inactive to remove it from your message choices.

Payment Method List

You can accept and track payments from customers in multiple ways. QuickBooks prepopulates the Payment Method list with the most common payment types (such as credit card, check, and cash). If you have a payment method that isn't listed, you can add that method to the list. To do so, select Lists | Customer & Vendor Profile Lists | Payment Method List, and select New to open the New Payment Method window. Name the payment method and select the appropriate payment type.

This list provides some detail about the payments you receive, but also allows you to print reports on payments that are subtotaled by the method of payment, such as credit card, check, cash, and so on. In addition, your bank may use the same subtotaling method on your monthly statement, which makes it easier to reconcile the bank account.

Ship Via List

Use the Ship Via list to add a description of your shipping method to your invoices (in the Via field). QuickBooks prepopulates the list with a variety of shipment methods, but you may need to add a shipping method. To do so, select Lists | Customer & Vendor Profile Lists | Ship Via List, and then press CTRL-N to add a new Shipping Method entry to the list. Then enter the name—for example, Our Truck or Sam's Delivery Service.

If you use one shipping method more than any other, you can select a default Ship Via entry, which appears automatically on your invoices (you can change it on any invoice if the shipping method is different). The default entry is in the Sales & Customers category of the Preferences dialog, where you can select the Usual Shipping Method entry you want to appear by default on your sales transactions. You can also enter the FOB site you want to appear on invoices, if you want to display this information. *FOB* (Free or Freight On Board) is the site from which an order is shipped and is also the point at which transportation and other costs are the buyer's responsibility.

Vehicle List

Use the Vehicle list to create vehicle records in which you track mileage for vehicles used in your business. You can use the mileage information for tax deductions for your vehicles and to bill customers for mileage expenses. However, even if you don't bill customers for mileage or your accountant uses a formula for tax deductions, the Vehicle list is a handy way to track information about the vehicles you use for business purposes.

To add a vehicle to the list, select Lists | Customer & Vendor Profile Lists | Vehicle List | New to open the New Vehicle dialog. The record has two fields, as seen here:

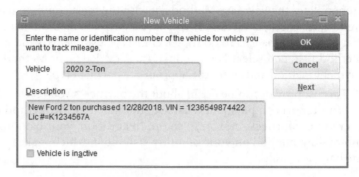

- **Vehicle** Enter a name or code for a specific vehicle. You could, for example, enter "BlueTruck" or any other recognizable name.
- **Description** Enter descriptive information about the vehicle. Take advantage of the field by entering information you really need, such as the vehicle identification number (VIN), the license plate number, the expiration date for the plate, the insurance policy number, or other "official" pieces of information. You can use 256 characters in the Description field.

Templates List

In this list, QuickBooks stores the many forms (QuickBooks calls them templates) you'll use when creating transactions. Learn more about customizing templates in Chapter 14.

Memorized Transaction List

The Memorize Transaction feature in QuickBooks eliminates having to enter the same transaction multiple times. With few exceptions, QuickBooks can memorize the transactions you enter and post them automatically on the day and with the frequency you need. The memorized transactions are stored in the Memorized Transaction List.

To view or edit a memorized transaction, choose Lists | Memorized Transaction List to open the list. Highlight a transaction name, click the Memorized Transaction button at the bottom of the window, and then choose Edit Memorized Transaction.

Your Beginning Balances

After you've created your lists and all the other setup-related activities, you've built about 80 percent of your new QuickBooks file. The last 20 percent of the setup process involves entering your beginning balances and the historical transactions (if any) needed to ensure that your data file accurately reflects your business's financial position on the day you start using your QuickBooks software. Entering accurate beginning balances and the detail behind these balances is perhaps the most important part of the setup process because if you start with inaccurate or incomplete starting balances, you'll compromise reliance on the key reports QuickBooks creates to help manage your business.

What Is an Opening Trial Balance?

Your opening trial balance is simply a detailed listing of the cost (or basis) of your company's assets, liabilities, and equity. If you have questions, consult your accountant or tax professional for more information.

If your QuickBooks start date is the beginning of the year (which is the most common start date), your opening trial balance for the first day of the year has no income or expenses to report. It will, however, contain the balances that have accumulated in your Asset, Liability, and Equity accounts since you've been in business. With the help of your accountant, prepare a "pre-QuickBooks opening trial balance." Much of the information needed for the pre-QuickBooks trial balance comes directly from the balance sheet your accountant prepared for you the previous year end. The pre-QuickBooks opening trial balance doesn't have to be fancy, just accurate. A typical pre-QuickBooks opening trial balance for a business with a QuickBooks start date of January 1, 2016, might look something like the one in Table 3-1. You then need to enter these beginning balances into your QuickBooks file.

Steps to an Accurate Opening Trial Balance

Although there's certainly more than one way to get your beginning balances into your new QuickBooks data file, many small businesses have had the least stress and most success when they follow these steps.

Account Type	Account	Debit	Credit
Assets	Checking	$25,000	
Assets	Accounts Receivable	$15,000	
Assets	Inventory	$30,000	
Assets	Fixed Assets	$15,000	
Assets	Accumulated Depreciation		$2,500
Liabilities	Accounts Payable		$7,500
Liabilities	Bank Loan		$20,000
Equity	Equity		$55,000

TABLE 3-1   "Pre-QuickBooks" Balances as of December 31, 2015

Gather All the Information You Need

In Chapter 1, you saw a detailed list of the information you should have at your fingertips before entering your beginning balances. If you haven't already organized these essential records and numbers, return to Chapter 1 to refresh your memory.

Enter Beginning Balances for Simple Balance Sheet Accounts

For this step, you use a journal entry to enter the beginning balances for accounts except bank accounts, accounts receivable, accounts payable, inventory, and sales tax payable. Those balances will be created later when you enter outstanding individual transactions and other adjustments. So what accounts are left to enter? Your fixed assets (including any accumulated depreciation) such as vehicles, furniture, and equipment, as well as any loans payable. You'll want to check in with your accountant for other balances that should also be entered as part of this first step, such as prepaid expenses, unpaid payroll taxes, or employee advances. Your journal entry should be dated as of the closing date of the prior fiscal year. In this example, the fiscal and calendar year are the same.

From the Company menu, select Make General Journal Entries to open the Make General Journal Entries window. Using the trial balance figures in Table 3-1, your journal entry should look like the one shown in Figure 3-2.

You'll see that after the balances for Fixed Assets (in this case, Furniture and Equipment), Accumulated Depreciation, and the Bank Loan have been entered, there's a debit balance of $7,500.00 that needs to be assigned to an account in order for the entry to be in balance. QuickBooks has a special account reserved for that purpose called Opening Balance Equity. Using this account to balance the entry will require that you (or your accountant) zero-out this balance (and any other balances posted to this account during the setup) to a retained earnings account in order to complete the setup. That adds another, often overlooked, journal entry requirement in the setup process. Alternatively, you can post this offsetting balance directly to a retained earnings or owner's equity account (as shown in Figure 3-2). Check with your accountant on the method that works best in your situation.

If you choose this alternative method, QuickBooks may warn you that you're posting to an account that's intended to track profits from earlier periods. Clicking OK allows you to continue with the posting. Then click Save & Close to save this entry.

Enter Bank Account Balances

The next step is to create the bank balance. Use the bank account register to do this. Select Banking | Use Register to open the register for your bank account. Enter the ending balance as it appears on the bank statement from the last month of the previous year in the Deposit side of the register. Be sure to put a note in the Memo field that will help remind you what this entry was for later on. Again, you can choose to post the offsetting balance to the Opening Balance Equity Account or directly to a retained earnings account. Click the Record button to save your entry.

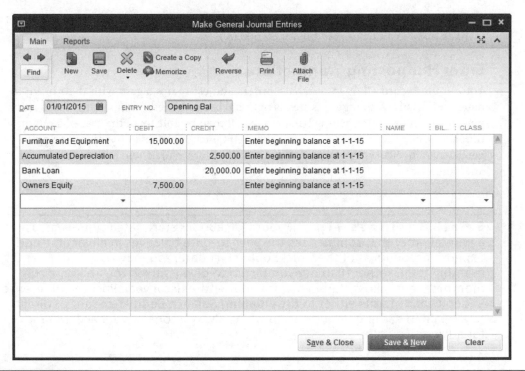

FIGURE 3-2   Establish some of your beginning balances with a journal entry.

Enter Outstanding Checks and Deposits

With your register still open, enter all outstanding transactions—checks and deposits—that occurred prior to the QuickBooks start date. This step ensures that these items will appear in the first bank reconciliation you perform in QuickBooks. Be sure to use the *original* transaction date to post these outstanding transactions.

Enter Unpaid Accounts Receivable and Accounts Payable Transactions

To establish your accounts receivable balance, create an invoice for each customer invoice that was still open as of the end of the previous fiscal year using the original transaction date and all other invoice details—customer name, item(s) purchased, terms, and so on. Don't forget to enter any unused customer credits as well. In our example, the total Accounts Receivable balance (refer to Table 3-1) is made up of two outstanding customer invoices that together total $15,000.00. Learn how create an invoice in Chapter 4.

Likewise, to establish your accounts payable balance, create a bill for each unpaid vendor bill as well as any unused vendor credits. Use the original transaction date and all other bill details. In our example, the total Accounts Payable balance (refer to Table 3-1) is made up of just one unpaid bill for $7,500.00.

Enter Nonposting Transactions

You should record all open purchase orders and estimates, again with their original dates and details. Although this step is optional because these "nonposting" transactions have no effect on your opening balances, you'll then be able to, in the case of a purchase order, for example, receive these items through QuickBooks or, in the case of an estimate, generate an invoice when you're awarded the job. Learn more about estimates in Chapter 4 and purchase orders in Chapter 13.

Small Business Tip If your QuickBooks start date is mid-year, use a journal entry that summarizes the year-to-date balances in all income and expense accounts as of the QuickBooks start date. You may also want to enter monthly totals rather than one lump sum to give yourself the ability to run monthly Profit & Loss statements for your entire fiscal year. Post the difference in debits and credits either to the Opening Balance Equity Account or directly to a retained earnings/equity account. As always, consult your accountant for advice.

Adjust Sales Tax Payable

If you collect sales tax, you may need to adjust the Sales Tax Payable account to be sure that it is in sync with the amount (if any) listed on your pre-QuickBooks opening trial balance. Make this adjustment after all open invoices are entered, since recording open invoices can affect the Sales Tax Payable account in QuickBooks. Use the Sales Tax Adjustment window to do this: select Vendors | Sales Tax | Adjust Sales Tax Due. Learn more about this window in Chapter 6.

Establish Inventory Balances

If you have inventory, you have to tell QuickBooks about the on-hand quantities of each of your inventory items as of your QuickBooks start date. This step assumes that you've already entered your Item List (minus any on-hand quantity information) and that each item has a cost associated with it. If this is not the case, you'll want to update your inventory list with that information before completing this step. Chapter 13 covers the details of how to set up an inventory item.

On-hand quantities are added using the Adjust Quantity/Value On Hand window. Select Vendors | Inventory Activities | Adjust Quantity/Value On Hand. Be sure that Quantity appears in the Adjustment Type drop-down menu field. Note that QuickBooks requires you to select an offsetting Adjustment Account to add the on-hand quantities to inventory. Like the other beginning balance entries, you can choose to post the offsetting balance that the software requires either to Opening Balance Equity or directly to a retained earnings /equity account. You may see a message telling you that QuickBooks is expecting you to use an expense account as the adjustment account.

This statement is true for most of your future adjustments—when you'll be using the Adjust Quantity/Value On Hand window to record obsolescence and shrinkage, for example. But in this instance, go ahead and post to one of your equity accounts.

Small Business Tip   Using the Adjust Quantity/Value On Hand (aka Inventory Adjustment) window to establish beginning on-hand inventory quantities is an acceptable method for a business with an existing inventory that has been paid for as of the business's QuickBooks start date. For all other situations, you should "receive" items as normal into your inventory.

Zero-Out the Opening Balance Equity Account

If you chose to use the Opening Balance Equity account to establish your opening balances, you'll need to zero-out this account to complete your setup. Use a journal entry dated with the QuickBooks start date and an offsetting entry to a retained earnings account (or another account chosen by your accountant).

Run Your QuickBooks Trial Balance Report as of Your Start Date

Run your QuickBooks Opening trial balance to be sure that it's in sync with your pre-QuickBooks opening trial balance. If you follow the steps outlined in this chapter and work closely with your accountant, establishing accurate opening balances can be a surprisingly straightforward process.

Part Two

Daily Operations Using QuickBooks

The chapters in Part Two cover day-to-day bookkeeping chores you perform in QuickBooks. They contain instructions and tips that will help you complete your routine tasks in QuickBooks efficiently and accurately. From time to time, there will also be information presented that you can pass along to your accountant, who may want to know how QuickBooks is handling the tasks you're performing.

Specifically, in Chapters 4 and 5 you'll learn what you need to know about sending invoices to your customers, recording the payments you receive from them, and creating transactions for job-costing data. Chapter 6 covers how to track and pay the bills you receive from vendors. Then, in Chapters 7 and 8, you'll gain an understanding of how to manage your bank and credit card accounts using QuickBooks.

Invoicing and Other Sales Transactions

n this chapter:

- Entering basic information in invoices

- Voiding, deleting, and pending invoicing

- Working with packing slips

- Memorizing and batching invoices

- Working with credit memos and estimates

- Understanding progress billing

- Reimbursable expenses in QuickBooks

- Printing forms with QuickBooks

- Bulk "Clear" forms

Usually, you need to send an invoice to a customer and get paid for that invoice before you can put money into your business account. Creating an invoice in QuickBooks is easy once you understand what all the parts of the invoice do and how to modify them to reflect the way you do business.

In addition to invoices, you may have to issue credits, print packing slips, and create estimates. This chapter covers these and other sales-related transactions.

Create Invoices

You can open the Create Invoices window in QuickBooks in several ways:

- Select Customers | Create Invoices from the menu bar.
- Press CTRL-I.
- Click the Create Invoices icon in the Customers section of the Home page.

A blank invoice form opens. At the top of the window (under the Create Invoices title bar) are four tabs: Main, Formatting, Send/Ship, and Reports as discussed next. Clicking the Maximize Your Work Area icon at the top right of the Create Invoices window hides these buttons (as well as the Icon Bar), making the Invoice template larger and easier to work with.

The Create Invoices window, shown in Figure 4-1, displays an informational panel that is blank at first. When you select a customer for invoicing, this panel shows

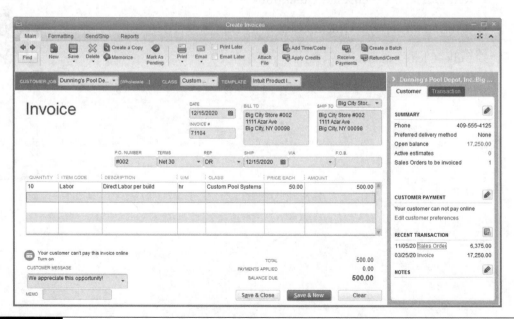

FIGURE 4-1 Create an invoice using the tools in the Create Invoices window in QuickBooks Premier or Pro Desktop.

information about the customer, such as open balance, recent transactions, or notes, if any exist. To close this panel, simply click the Hide History arrowhead to the immediate left of the customer's name. Clicking the Full Screen icon will also close the panel.

Tabs Found in the Create Invoices Window

If you take a moment to open each tab and review its contents, you'll see that each shows a set of buttons on the Icon Bar that enable you to complete any task when you're creating and working with an invoice. We will discuss the Main tab after you are introduced to the other three tabs. It is from the Main tab that you create your invoice. You have several options on the Icon Bar for the Main tab, as seen next.

The Formatting Tab

The Formatting tab has several options with which you can work with this invoice, as shown here.

- **Preview**   This option shows you how the completed invoice will look when printed. A small message may appear explaining that you can print Shipping Labels to go with your invoice. If you do not want to see this message again, click Do Not Display This Message In The Future and click OK to close the message.
- **Manage Templates**   From here, you can decide whether any of the available templates suits your needs. Remember that the prebuilt templates available to you may vary depending on your version of QuickBooks and the industry you chose during the QuickBooks setup. Take the time to look at each of the templates in your version before settling on the one you want to use. (You can also click the arrow next to the Template field at the top of the Invoice and select another invoice template from the drop-down list.).

QuickBooks has several built-in invoice templates. These are some of the most common templates included in QuickBooks:

- **Intuit Packing Slip**   This is a basic packing slip template. See "Print Packing Slips," later in this chapter for more information.
- **Intuit Product Invoice**   This template is designed for product sales, including inventory items.
- **Intuit Professional and Service Invoice**   These two templates are nearly identical, except for a difference in the order of the columns, and the Service template includes a purchase order number field.
- **Progress Invoice**   Designed specifically for progress billing against a job estimate, this doesn't appear in the Template list unless you have specified Progress Invoicing in the Company Preferences tab of the Jobs & Estimates category of the Preferences dialog.

Small Business Tip   Depending on your business and your QuickBooks desktop version, you may also see other specific invoice types. If you don't see a template you want on the list, edit an existing template or create your own. See Chapter 14 for more information about modifying templates in QuickBooks.

- **Download Templates**   With your Internet connection, this option connects you to Intuit QuickBooks Support from which you can download additional invoice templates.
- **Customize Data Layout**   This link allows you to copy the current standard invoice form and make changes. Chapter 14 discusses this in depth.
- **Spelling**   If you sometimes make typing errors, this option will help!
- **Insert/Delete/Copy/Paste Line**   Without creating a customized template, use these options to add, delete, copy, and paste lines within this invoice.
- **Customize Design**   Using the tools in this link, you can make changes on your invoice. Chapter 14 explains how.

The Send/Ship Tab

Click the Send/Ship tab to determine how the invoice and the products will be sent to the customers. You can also prepare a letter to your customer.

➡ Small Business Recommendation

New in QuickBooks Premier, Accountant, and Enterprise Desktop 2016 editions is the ability to create a custom ship-to address based on a purchase order. When you have completed an estimate or sales order, click the Create Purchase order icon. A message appears on which you can choose to drop ship the items directly to the customer, as shown here.

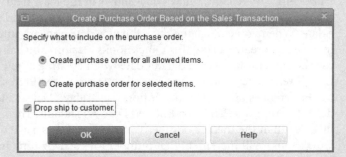

The purchase order will reflect your customer's ship-to address, as shown here, and your material will be shipped to your customer's job site rather than your warehouse, saving you the extra step of manually entering the ship-to address. QuickBooks will even remember if you repeat the order and default to these settings.

The Reports Tab

From the Reports tab, you can quickly access reports and information about the current customer and the customer's history.

The Main Tab

For this section, we're using the Intuit Product invoice template, but you'll still be able to follow along even if your version's invoice form lacks some of the fields related to products. The top portion of the invoice is called the *invoice header*, into which you enter basic information. The middle section, where you place the billing items, is called the *line item* section. The bottom section, called the *footer*, holds the totals and other details (such as customer messages). You enter data into the fields in each invoice section.

Entering Basic Information in the Invoice Header

To create an invoice, start with the customer or the job. Click the arrow to the right of the Customer:Job field to see a list of all your customers. If you've attached jobs to any customers, those jobs are listed under the customer name. Select the customer or job for this invoice. If the customer isn't in the system, choose <Add New> to open a new customer window and enter all the data required for setting up a customer:

- **Date field** By default, today's date shows in the Date field. To change it, either type in a new date or click the calendar icon at the right side of the field to select a date. When you change the date, the new date appears automatically in each invoice you create during this QuickBooks session. You can tell QuickBooks to use the current date as the default date when creating a new invoice by choosing Edit | Preferences, and in the General category of the Preferences window (in the My Preferences tab), select the option Use Today's Date As Default instead of the default option, Use The Last Entered Date As Default. The first time you enter an invoice, fill in the invoice number you want to use as a starting point. Hereafter, QuickBooks will increment that number for each ensuing invoice.

- **Bill To and Ship To addresses** These are taken from the customer record. You can select another Ship To address from the drop-down list or add a new Ship To address by choosing <Add New> from the list. If you enter or change any information about a customer while creating an invoice, QuickBooks offers to add the information to the customer record when you save the invoice. If the change is permanent, click Yes to eliminate having to go to the customer record to make the changes. If the change is for this invoice only, click No. If you never make permanent changes, tell QuickBooks to turn off this feature by changing the option: click Edit | Preferences | General | Company Preferences. Then select the option Never Update Name Information When Saving Transactions.

- **P.O. Number** Enter the customer's purchase order number (if any) in this field. You can also click the Attach File icon, located at the top of the Invoice window, to scan and store an online copy of the customer's purchase order.

- **Terms** This field fills in automatically with the terms you entered for this customer, but you can change the terms for this invoice. If terms don't automatically appear, it means you didn't enter that information in the customer record. If you enter it now, when you save the invoice, QuickBooks offers to make the entry the new default for this customer by adding it to the customer record.

- **Rep** The Rep field (available by default in the Product template, but it can be added to any template) will automatically fill in the salesperson attached to this customer. If you didn't link a salesperson when you filled out the customer record, you can click the arrow next to the field and choose a name from the drop-down list. If the rep you want to use doesn't exist in the list, you can select <Add New> to add the rep on the fly.

The following fields are available only in the Product and Packing Slip templates:

- **Ship** This is for the ship date, which defaults to the invoice date, but it can be changed if you're not shipping until a later date.
- **Via** This is for the shipping method. Click the arrow next to the field to see the available shipping choices or select <Add New>.
- **F.O.B.** Some companies use this field to indicate the point at which the shipping costs are transferred to the buyer and the assumption of a completed sale takes place. If you use Free On Board (FOB), you can enter the applicable data in the field; it has no impact on your QuickBooks financial records and is there for your convenience only.

➡ Small Business Recommendation

QuickBooks works well with alphanumeric invoice numbers. For example, if the previously saved invoice number is R-0001, the next invoice number will be R-0002. But suppose, for example, that you run a contracting business and you'd like your residential invoices to have the numbering scheme "R-0001" and your commercial invoices to use "C-0001," and you don't want to change the numbering scheme manually each time. Consider creating a second accounts receivable (A/R) account to enable you to maintain the different numbering schemes easily when creating an invoice. If this is your choice, the top of the Invoice window has a field to select the A/R account you want to use for this transaction. Remember that you must select the same A/R account when it comes time to receive payment for the invoice.

Entering Line Items

Click in the first column of the line item section. If you're using the Product invoice template, this column is Quantity. If you're using the Professional or Service invoice template, the first column is Item. Enter the quantity of the first item you're invoicing.

An arrow appears on the right edge of the Item Code column. Click it to see a list of your items and select the one you need. The description and price fill in automatically using the item information. If you didn't include description and/or price information when you created the item, enter it manually now. QuickBooks does the math, and the Amount column displays the total of the quantity times the price. If the item and the customer are both liable for tax, the Tax column displays "Tax." Repeat this process to add all the items that should appear on this invoice. You can add as many rows of items as you need; if you run out of room, QuickBooks automatically adds pages to your invoice.

QuickBooks checks the quantity on hand (QOH) for inventory line items and warns you if you don't have enough inventory to fill the sale. It's a warning only; QuickBooks lets you complete the sale anyway. It's never a good idea to sell into negative QOH, however, as doing so can affect the average cost of that item.

Applying Price Levels

If you've enabled price levels in Preferences and created entries in your Price Level list, you can change the amount of any line item by applying a price level. Most of the time, your price levels are a percentage by which to lower (discount) the price, but you may also have created price levels that increase the price. If you have already assigned a price level to this customer, the appropriate price shows up automatically.

If not, to assign a price level, click within the Price Each column to display an arrow. Click the arrow to see a drop-down list of price level items, and select the one you want to apply to this item. QuickBooks performs the math, so you not only see the name of your price level, but you also see the resulting item price for each price level. After you select a price level, QuickBooks changes the amount you're charging the customer for the item and adjusts the amount of the total for this item. The customer sees only the price on the invoice; there's no indication that you've adjusted the price. This is different from applying a discount to a price, where a line item exists to identify the discount.

Using Discounts

You can also adjust the invoice by applying discounts. Discounts are entered as line items, so the discount item has to first exist in your Item List. When you enter a discount, its amount (usually a percentage) is applied to the line item *immediately* preceding it. For example, suppose you have already entered the following line items:

- Line 1: Qty of 1 for an item with a price of $100.00 for a total line item price of $100.00
- Line 2: Qty of 2 for another item with a price of $40.00 for a total line item price of $80.00

Now you want to give the customer a 10 percent discount, so you've created a 10 percent discount item in your Item List. When you enter the discount item on the line immediately after line 2, QuickBooks will calculate the discount value as 10 percent of the *last* line you entered, in this case the $80.00, for an $8.00 discount.

Using Subtotals

You can apply a discount against multiple (or all) line items; however, you must first enter a line item that creates a subtotal of items you want to discount. To do this, use a Subtotal item type that you've created in your Item List. Then enter the discount item as the next line item *after the subtotal*, and the discount is then applied to the subtotal.

Subtotals work by adding up all the line items that have been entered after the last Subtotal item (the first Subtotal item adds up all line items starting at the first line item on the invoice). This gives you the added benefit of offering a discount to some line items but not others and the ability to apply a different discount rate to each group of subtotaled items. Because discounts display on the invoice, your "generosity" is communicated to the customer!

The Footer Section

When you're finished entering all the line items and any discounts, you'll see that QuickBooks keeps a running total of the invoice, including taxes, in the footer section of the invoice.

Adding a Message

To add a message to the invoice, click the arrow in the Customer Message field to see the messages you created in the Customer Message list. You can create a new message if you don't want to use any of the existing text by choosing <Add New> from the message drop-down list and entering your text in the New Customer Message window. Click OK to enter the message in the invoice. QuickBooks saves the message in the Customer Message list so you can use it again. You can also type the message directly in the Customer Message field and press the TAB key, which opens a Customer Message Not Found dialog that offers you the chance to do a Quick Add to put your new message in the Customer Message list.

Adding a Memo

You can add text to the Memo field at the bottom of the invoice. This text does not print on the invoice. It appears only on the screen, but you'll see it if you reopen this invoice to view or edit it. However, the memo text *does* appear on statements next to the listing for this invoice. Therefore, be careful about the text you use, and don't enter anything you wouldn't want the customer to see unless you never send statements.

Saving an Invoice

Click Save & New to save this invoice and move on to the next blank invoice form. If this is the last invoice you're creating, click Save & Close to save this invoice and close the Create Invoices window.

Small Business Tip   Consider taking the time to create a custom invoice (see how in Chapter 14), that includes your logo. If you have the in-house capability to print in color, consider using color to enhance your forms.

Choosing the Method of Sending the Invoice

There are several ways to get an invoice into the hands of your customer, as shown in Table 4-1.

Method	Process
Print each invoice as it's completed.	Click the Print button on the Main tab of the Create Invoices window to open the Print One Invoice window from which you can select your printer, set additional print options, and print a single invoice.
E-mail each invoice as it's completed.	Click the Email button on the Main tab of the Create Invoices window. The way your invoice is sent will depend on the send method and template you selected in Company Preferences.
Print your invoices later.	Select the Print Later option to print this invoice in a batch along with other invoices marked Print Later. When you're ready to print the batch, click the down arrow below the Print button on the Main tab of the Create Invoices window and select Batch.
E-mail your invoices later.	Select the Email Later option to add this invoice to a batch of other invoices to send by e-mail. When you're ready to e-mail the batch, click the down arrow below the Email button and select Batch. The Send Forms window opens, where you can also edit the e-mail to go with your invoices.

TABLE 4-1   Invoice Delivery Options

Small Business Tip   In the General section of the Preferences window is a default setting that automatically saves a transaction (such as an invoice or check) before printing. It's best not to turn off this default setting. It's a good business practice to save a transaction before you print it.

Edit an Invoice

To edit or correct an invoice, open the Create Invoices window and click the left-pointing blue arrow button located on the Main tab to move back through all the previous invoices in your file. If you have a large number of invoices to sort through, it's faster to click the Find button located just below the blue arrows. In the Find Invoices window, you can search by the customer, date, invoice number, or amount. When you're editing a previously entered invoice, keep the following in mind:

- Don't change anything if an invoice has been paid or mailed, unless you want to edit the text in the Memo field.
- If the invoice has not yet been sent, you can make any changes you want.

When you click Save & Close, QuickBooks displays a message dialog asking whether you want to save the changes you made. Click Yes.

Mark an Invoice as Pending

Marking an invoice as "pending" makes it *nonposting*, which means that it does not affect your account balances or reports. Some companies require approval before invoices are sent to customers. If so, marking them as pending is a great way to make them available to the appropriate person for review, editing, and final approval.

To mark an invoice as pending, click the Mark As Pending button on the Main tab in the Create Invoices window. A watermark appears indicating that the invoice is now Pending/Non-Posting. Similarly, to mark an invoice as final, click the Mark As Final button. The Pending Sales report lists all invoices currently marked as pending as well as the accounts that will be affected once the pending status is removed and the invoice is considered final. To run this report from the Reports menu, choose Sales | Pending Sales.

Void and Delete Invoices

There's an important difference between voiding and deleting an invoice. Voiding an invoice makes it nonexistent to your accounting and customer balances. However, the invoice number continues to exist (it's marked "VOID" on reports) so you can account for it. To void an invoice, open it, and on the Main tab in the Create Invoices window, select the Void option from the drop-down arrow below the Delete button. Then click Save. When QuickBooks asks if you want to record your change, click Yes.

Deleting an invoice, on the other hand, removes all traces of it from your transaction registers and most reports (with the exception of the Audit Trail report). To delete an invoice, open it and click the Delete button on the Main tab in the Create Invoices window. Then click Save. When QuickBooks asks if you want to record your change, click Yes.

Small Business Tip   QuickBooks tracks transactions that you void, unvoid (a voided transaction that you decide to re-enter into QuickBooks), or delete, and it displays them in two reports: the Voided/Deleted Transactions Summary report and the Voided/Deleted Transactions Detail reports. You can access these reports by selecting Reports | Accountant & Taxes | Voided/Deleted Transactions Summary (or Detail).

Print Packing Slips

QuickBooks provides a template for a packing slip, which is basically an invoice that doesn't display prices. To print the default packing slip, complete the invoice. Then click the arrow below the Print icon at the top of the Create Invoices window and select Packing Slip from the drop-down list. The Print Packing Slip dialog opens so you can select your printing options.

Changing the Default Packing Slip

If you create your own customized packing slip template, you can select it each time you print a packing slip, or you can make that new form the default packing slip by choosing Edit | Preferences to open the Preferences dialog.

Go to the Sales & Customers category and click the Company Preferences tab. In the Choose Template For Invoice Packing Slip field, select your new packing slip form from the drop-down list and click OK. If you have multiple packing slips, you can choose any of them for printing. Instead of selecting Print Packing Slip from the Print button's drop-down list in the Create Invoices window, select a packing slip template from the drop-down list in the Template field. The Create Invoices window changes to display the packing slip. To see what the printed version of the packing slip looks like, click the arrow below the Print icon on the Create Invoices window toolbar and choose Preview. Close the Preview window and return to the Create Invoices window to print the packing slip.

Batch and Memorize Invoices

If your company charges the same monthly fee to several of your customers, batch invoicing gives you an easy way to create and send the same invoice to these customers. You can also choose to create a billing group and add customer names to that group if those customers will need to be invoiced for a similar service in the future.

To batch invoices, follow these steps:

1. From the Main tab on the Create Invoices window, or from the Customers menu, click the Create A Batch button. You'll see a reminder about updating your customer information. Review and click OK.

2. From the Batch Invoice window, select the names of customers for whom you want to create an invoice (you can also hold down the SHIFT key and select multiple, contiguous customer names), and then click the Add button to include them in this batch. Alternatively, you can create a billing group (by selecting <Add New> from the Billing Group drop-down list) to which you can add customers in the same manner. Click Next.

3. Select the items for your batch invoice, add a customer message, and update the invoice date and template if necessary. Click Next.

4. Review the list of batch invoices to be created. You can deselect a customer to prevent them from receiving an invoice in this batch by clicking the check mark next to their name in the Select column. Click the Create Invoices button.

5. Review the Batch Invoice Summary window to confirm and execute the send methods (either Print or Email) of the invoices in the batch. Click Close when finished or to send any unmarked (meaning there's no send method in the customer record) invoices later.

Use Memorized (Recurring) Invoices

If you have a recurring invoice, such as rent from tenants, you can automate the process of creating it. Create the first invoice, filling out all the fields. If there are any fields that will change, leave those fields blank and fill them out each time you send the invoice. Then press CTRL-M to open the Memorize Transaction dialog.

Fill in the fields using the following guidelines:

- **Name**   Change the title in the Name box to reflect what you've done. It's easiest to add a word or phrase to the default title, such as "Retainer." You can enter up to 31 characters, including spaces.
- **Add To My Reminders List**   Choose this option, and then specify how and when you want to be reminded in the How Often and Next Date fields. The reminder appears in the QuickBooks Reminder window. Choose Do Not Remind Me if you have a great memory, or if you use this memorized invoice only for special occasions.
- **Automate Transaction Entry**   Choose this option if you want QuickBooks to issue this invoice automatically. If you opt for automatic issuing of this invoice, you must fill in the fields so that QuickBooks performs the task accurately, as follows:

  - **How Often**   Specify the interval for this invoice. Click the arrow to see the drop-down list and choose the option you need.
  - **Next Date**   Note the next instance of this invoice.
  - **Number Remaining**   Start a countdown for a specified number of invoices.
  - **Days In Advance To Enter**   Specify the number of days in advance of the Next Date field you want QuickBooks to create the invoice.

Click OK when you have finished filling out the dialog. Then click Save & Close in the Invoice window to save the transaction. If you want to view, edit, or remove the transaction, you can select it from the Memorized Transaction List, which you open by pressing CTRL-T.

Creating Memorized Invoice Groups

If you have several memorized invoices that need to go out on a particular day of the month, you can create a separate Memorized Transaction group, and QuickBooks automatically takes action on every invoice in the list on the day that you specify. To use this feature, follow these steps:

1. From any location within QuickBooks, press CTRL-T to display the Memorized Transaction List. Right-click any blank spot in the Memorized Transaction window and choose New Group from the shortcut menu.
2. In the New Memorized Transaction Group window, give this group a name (such as 1st Of Month or 15th Of Month).
3. Fill out the fields to specify the way you want the invoices in this group to be handled and click OK to save this group.

After you create the group, you can add memorized transactions to it as follows:

1. In the Memorized Transaction List window, select the first memorized invoice transaction you want to add to the group.
2. Right-click and choose Edit Memorized Transaction from the shortcut menu.
3. When the Schedule Memorized Transaction window opens with this transaction displayed, select the option named Add To Group.
4. Select the group from the list that appears when you click the arrow next to the Group Name field and click OK.

Repeat this process for each invoice you want to add to the group. As you create future memorized invoices, just select the Add To Group option to add each invoice to the appropriate group.

➨ Small Business Recommendation

If your company accepts retainers or deposit from clients for future work, ensure you track them correctly. It is also important to create a distinct job for each different prepayment or retainer.

1. Create an Other Current Liability account named Retainers or Customer Deposits.
2. Create an Other Charge item and in the Income field, enter the appropriate liability name (Retainer, Customer Deposit, etc.).
3. Create a custom invoice containing only item, description, and amount columns. You can even rename this template "Retainer" or "Customer Prepayment." Use this template as acknowledgement of the funds that the customer prepaid.
4. Then, when you have completed the job for which the customer paid in advance, create an invoice. Then create a credit memo in the amount of the retainer. Apply this credit memo to the regular invoice. When you complete the invoice, the customer will see the retainer applied.

Issue Credits and Refunds

You can return funds to a customer in the form of a credit against current or future balances, or you can write a check to refund money you received from the customer. Creating a credit memo is similar to creating an invoice. You can use the credit memo either to reduce a customer's balance or issue a cash refund to them. What's more, QuickBooks makes it easy for you to issue a credit against a particular invoice or retain it as an available credit to be used on a future date.

Creating a Credit Memo Against an Invoice

If you've sold merchandise to a customer on an invoice and later they return some or all of the items, you can issue a credit memo directly from the original invoice. This feature also saves you from having to re-enter the item information a second time on the credit memo.

To issue a credit memo, locate and open the original invoice. Click the Refund /Credit button on the Main tab to create a return receipt for this invoice. All items from the invoice are listed on the newly created credit memo. From here, you can edit the line items as needed. When you save the credit memo, QuickBooks asks you to specify the way you want to apply the credit amount.

Creating a Credit Memo Without a Previous Invoice

To create a credit memo (also referred to as a return receipt) that is not attached to a particular invoice, choose Customers | Create Credit Memos/Refunds from the menu bar to open a blank Create Credit Memos/Refunds window. Select the appropriate customer or job, and then fill out the rest of the heading. Move to the line item section and enter the item, the quantity, and the rate for each item in this credit memo. Do *not* use a minus sign, as you have already indicated this is a credit.

On the Main tab, you can use one of two buttons to designate how to use this credit— Use Credit To Give Refund or Use Credit To Apply To Invoice. Alternatively, when you click Save & Close to save the credit memo, QuickBooks asks you to specify the way you want to apply the credit amount.

Applying Credit Memos

When you save the credit memo, QuickBooks displays an Available Credit dialog, where you can choose the way you want to apply this credit:

- **Retaining the credit**   Choose Retain As An Available Credit to let the credit amount stay with the customer. You can apply the credit to a future invoice or apply it to a current open invoice later if the customer sends a payment that deducts the credit.
- **Applying the credit to an invoice**   Choose Apply To An Invoice to apply the credit to a current invoice. When you click OK, QuickBooks displays a list of open invoices for this customer or job and automatically applies the credit against the oldest invoice. Click Done to save the transaction.
- **Giving a refund for the credit**   Choose Give A Refund to give money back to the customer. When you click OK, the Issue A Refund window opens. Use the following guidelines to configure the Issue A Refund window:
  - In the Issue This Refund Via field, select the method for the refund from the drop-down list (Cash, Check, or Credit Card). If you choose Cash or Check, be sure to select the appropriate bank account in the Account field.

- If you choose Check, the dialog adds an option labeled To Be Printed, which is selected by default. If you print checks, leave the check mark in the check box, and click OK. The check is added to the list of checks to be printed when you choose File | Print Forms | Checks. (The check also appears in the bank account register with the notation "To Print.")

- If you write checks manually, deselect the check mark in the To Be Printed check box, enter the check number you'll be using, and click OK. The check is added to your bank account register, using the next available check number.

- If you choose Credit Card, follow the usual procedure for creating a credit card transaction.

Using Estimates

If you create estimates for some of your customers, they can be used as the basis for an invoice (or multiple invoices if you choose to send invoices as the job progresses). Estimates are also a great way for you to create a "budget" for the job on which you're bidding, since there are some comprehensive job reports in QuickBooks that help you keep track of actual job income and costs versus what was initially estimated. Estimates are available only if you enable them in the Jobs & Estimates section of the Preferences dialog (Edit | Preferences).

Creating an Estimate

The first and most important thing to understand is that creating an estimate doesn't affect your financial records. No amounts in the estimate post to income, accounts receivable, or any other general ledger account.

To create an estimate, choose Customers | Create Estimates from the menu bar. The Create Estimates transaction window has nearly the same navigation and task buttons as the Create Invoices window, including an informational panel to the right. Clicking the Full Screen icon at the top-right of the window closes the panel. Fill out the fields the same way you would for invoices.

Some estimate templates permit you to invoice customers with a markup over cost (such as the built-in Custom Estimate template). This is often the approach used for time and materials on bids. Just enter the cost and indicate the markup in dollars or percentage. If you decide to change the total of the item, QuickBooks will change the markup to make sure the math is correct.

If the item you use has been set up with both a cost and price, the Custom Estimate template displays both the cost and the price and automatically calculates the markup percentage for you. You can change the markup (as either a percentage or dollar amount) if you wish and the new price will appear in the Total column. If the item you use has only a price associated with it, the estimate uses that price as the cost on which the markup is calculated.

The Markup field is displayed only on the screen version of the estimate; this column doesn't appear on the printed version. And if you've created price levels, they'll appear in the Markup field for easy selection.

Creating Multiple Estimates for a Job

You can create multiple estimates for a customer or a job. You can create an estimate for each phase of the job or create multiple estimates with different prices. Of course, that means each estimate has different contents. When you create multiple estimates for the same job, they remain active (or open) by default. If a customer rejects any estimates, you can either delete them or click the Mark As Inactive button on the Main tab of the Create Estimates window—effectively closing the estimate.

Copying and Memorizing Estimates

A quick way to create multiple estimates with slightly different contents is to make copies of the original. Click the Create A Copy button on the Main tab while the estimate you want to copy is displayed in your QuickBooks window. You can also right-click in the estimate header and choose Duplicate Estimate from the shortcut menu to accomplish the same thing. The Estimate # field changes to the next number, while everything else remains the same. Make the required changes, and then click Save & Close.

If you frequently present the same estimated items to multiple customers, you can use the Memorized Transaction feature to create boilerplate estimates for future use. QuickBooks removes the name when memorizing the document so you can easily use it for other jobs. First, create an estimate, filling in the items that belong in it. Don't fill in amounts that usually change (such as quantities, or even prices). Then click the Memorize button on the Main tab (or press CTRL-M) to memorize the estimate. To fill out the Memorize Transaction dialog, give the estimate a name that reminds you of its contents, select the option Do Not Remind Me, and click OK to close the dialog.

To use this boilerplate estimate, press CTRL-T or choose Lists | Memorized Transaction List to open the Memorized Transaction List. Double-click the estimate, fill in the Customer:Job information and any pricing information that's not automatically included, and then save it. The memorized estimate isn't changed; only the new estimate is saved.

Create Progress Billing Invoices

If you've enabled estimates and progress billing in the Jobs & Estimates category of the Preferences dialog (reached by choosing Edit | Preferences), you can use the Progress Invoice template to invoice your customers as each invoicing milestone arrives.

Choosing the Estimated Job

Progress invoices are connected to an estimate for a customer or job. Open the Create Invoices window, select Progress Invoice from the Template drop-down list, and choose the customer or job for which you're creating the progress invoice. Because you've enabled estimates in Preferences, the system checks the customer record to see if any estimates for this customer or job exist and, if so, presents them.

Select the estimate you're invoicing against and click OK. QuickBooks then asks you to specify what to include on the invoice. Fill out the dialog using the following guidelines:

- You can create an invoice for the whole job, 100 percent of the estimate, or for a specific percentage. The percentage usually depends upon the agreement you have with your customer. When the line items appear, you can edit individual items.
- You can create an invoice that covers only certain items on the estimate, or you can create an invoice that has a different percentage for each item on the estimate. This is the approach to use if you're billing for completed work on a job that involves a number of distinct tasks. Some of the work listed on the estimate may be finished and other work not started, and the various items listed on the estimate may be at different points of completion.

After you've created the first progress billing invoice for an estimate, a new option is available for subsequent invoices. That option is to bill for all remaining amounts in the estimate (it replaces the 100 percent option). This is generally reserved for your last invoice, and it saves you the trouble of figuring out which percentages of which items have already been invoiced.

The items and prices in the estimate can be changed as can any other amounts or quantities while you're creating the invoice. Ultimately, however, your ability to invoice for amounts that differ from the estimate depends on your agreement with the customer.

Entering Progress Invoice Line Items

After you choose your progress billing method and click OK, QuickBooks automatically fills in the line item section of the invoice based on the method you selected. If you chose to invoice a percentage of the estimate's total, the amount of every line item on the estimate reflects that percentage. This doesn't work very well for lines that have products (it's hard to sell a percentage of a physical product). You can leave the invoice as is because the customer will probably understand that this is a progress invoice, or you can make changes to the invoice.

In addition, the line items for services rendered may not be totally accurate. For example, some of the line items may contain service categories that aren't at the same percentage of completion as others.

To change the invoice and keep a history of the changes against the estimate, don't just make changes to the line items on the invoice. Instead, click the Progress icon on the Main tab of the Create Invoices window. This opens a dialog in which you can change the line items. You can change the quantity, rate, or percentage of completion for any individual line item.

Click OK when you have finished making your adjustments. You return to the invoice form, where the amounts on the line items have changed to match the adjustments you made. Click Save & New to save this invoice and move on to the next invoice, or click Save & Close to save this invoice and close the Create Invoices window. Using this method to change a line item keeps the history of your estimate and invoices intact, as opposed to making changes in the amounts directly on the invoice form, which does not create a good audit trail.

Invoice Customers for Reimbursable Expenses

When you pay vendors, some purchases may be made on behalf of a customer, or they may be purchases needed to complete a job. When you create a vendor bill or write a check to a vendor, you can specify expenses as reimbursable and link those expenses to a specific customer or job. You can automatically invoice customers for those expenses. In addition, you can link mileage costs and time costs (for employees or subcontractors) to customers and automatically invoice customers for those expenses.

Any amounts you link to a customer are saved in the customer record, and you can collect the money by adding those amounts to the next invoice you create for that customer or create an invoice specifically to collect these reimbursable expenses.

Configuring Reimbursement Settings

In addition to enabling the option to track reimbursable costs when entering vendor transactions, QuickBooks gives you options for invoicing customers when you want to recover your reimbursable expenses. To set your own preference, choose Edit | Preferences and select the Sales & Customers category in the left pane. In the My Preferences tab, select one of the following options:

- **Prompt For Time/Costs To Add** Choose this option to open the Choose Billable Time And Costs dialog. Select this option if you always (or almost always) collect reimbursable costs from customers.
- **Don't Add Any** This option prevents the automatic display of the Choose Billable Time And Costs dialog. Choose this option if you collect reimbursable expenses periodically on separate invoices.
- **Ask What To Do** Select this option to tell QuickBooks to ask you what you want to do whenever you create a sales transaction for a customer with outstanding reimbursable costs.

Creating a Transaction for Reimbursable Expenses

When you're creating a sales transaction for a customer that has outstanding reimbursable costs, QuickBooks uses the preference you set to determine how to manage those costs. If you selected the preference Prompt For Time/Costs To Add, when you select the customer, QuickBooks displays the current reimbursable expenses so you can select those you want to include in the current transaction. If you selected the preference Don't Add Any, the invoice or sales receipt transaction window opens as usual. If you want to check for reimbursable costs for this customer and then decide whether you want to recover any of them, click the Add Time/Costs button on the Main tab above the transaction form. When the Choose Billable Time And Costs dialog opens, you can see if there are any reimbursable expenses you want to collect from your customer.

If you selected the preference Ask What To Do, when you select a customer that has unpaid reimbursable costs in the transaction window, QuickBooks displays a dialog asking how you want to handle those amounts. Your response determines whether the Choose Billable Time And Costs dialog opens automatically.

Adding Expenses to the Sales Transaction

To collect expenses, also called reimbursable costs, from a customer, select those costs from the Choose Billable Time And Costs dialog. Each type of expense is displayed in its own tab, and you'll need to review each tab to see if any amounts exist. Unfortunately, the amount displayed on each tab doesn't help you head for the appropriate tab; all the amounts are set at $0.00 until you actually select amounts to add to the sales transaction. So start clicking each tab to find reimbursable expenses to transfer to the transaction. When you find a tab that has contents, click in the leftmost column to place a check mark next to the expense(s) you want to include.

Click OK to move the item(s) to the transaction window to join any other items you're entering in that transaction. You may find reimbursable expenses on more than one tab, so you have to check each tab. QuickBooks automatically transfers the selected reimbursable costs to the invoice. The description of the reimbursable expenses that appears on the invoice is taken from the text you entered in the Memo column when you entered a bill or created a check for this vendor. If you didn't use the Memo column on the Enter Bills or Write Check window, you'll have to enter text manually in the Description column of the invoice. Otherwise, the customer sees only an amount and no explanation of what it's for. (The description of mileage or item costs is taken from the Description field of the item you configured.)

Adding Taxes to Reimbursable Expenses   If an expense is taxable and the customer is not tax exempt, choose the option Selected Expenses Are Taxable. When the expenses are passed to the invoice, the appropriate taxes are applied. If you select the taxable option and the customer is tax exempt, QuickBooks won't add the sales tax to the invoice. If some expenses are taxable and others aren't, you have to separate the process of moving items to the invoice. First, deselect each nontaxable expense by clicking its check mark to remove it (it's a toggle). Click OK to put those expenses on the invoice. Then return to the Choose Billable Time And Costs window, put a check mark next to each nontaxable expense, deselect the Selected Expenses Are Taxable option, and click OK.

Omitting the Details on the Invoice   Each of the tabs has the option Print Selected Time And Costs As One Invoice Item. When you click OK and view the results in the invoice, you still see each individual item. You're not imagining things. The screen version of the invoice continues to display the individual items. However, when you print the invoice, you'll see a single line item with the correct total in the Amount column. QuickBooks changes the format of the printed invoice to eliminate the details but doesn't change the data in the onscreen version of the invoice. This means you can open the invoice later and see the detailed items, which is handy when the customer calls to ask, "What's this reimbursable expense item on my bill?"

Excluding a Reimbursable Expense   If you have some reason to exclude one or more expenses from the current invoice, just avoid putting a check mark in the column. The item remains in the system and shows up on the Choose Billable Time And Costs window the next time you open it. You can add the item to the customer's invoice in the future.

Changing the Amount of a Reimbursable Expense   To change the amount of a reimbursable expense, select the amount in the Amount column of the Choose Billable Time And Costs window on the Expenses tab, and enter the new figure. If you reduce the amount, QuickBooks does not keep the remaining amount on the Choose Billable Time And Costs window. You won't see it again, because QuickBooks assumes that you're not planning to pass the remaining amount to your customer in the future.

Small Business Tip   If you void or delete a saved sales transaction that contains reimbursable expenses, these expenses are not automatically made "billable" again. You'll need to go to the original expense transaction and click the Invoice icon in the Billable column to make it available to invoice again.

QuickBooks Printer Setup

The transactions that you create in QuickBooks need to be delivered to your customers, vendors, or employees. In some cases, the delivery method is in the form of a printed document; in other cases, transactions are sent electronically. This section covers your options for both sending and storing these business-critical forms and documents.

If you choose to send printed versions of your documents, you have to link each type of document you print to a specific printer and then configure the way the printer processes each document type. Choose File | Printer Setup to begin. The Printer Setup dialog opens with the drop-down list of the Form Name field displayed. Select the form you want to print.

The form type you select determines the contents of the Printer Setup dialog; the tabs, fields, and options vary depending on the form. Many of the forms you print come out of the printer perfectly with little or no adjustment; however, you'll need to tweak some forms (such as checks) to make sure the output is what you want it to be. If you use multiple printers, you can assign specific printers to specific types of forms, and QuickBooks will always select the appropriate printer when you print those forms.

Choose Form Printing Settings

This section covers setting up forms for printing, with the exception of checks. See Chapter 6 to learn how to set up check printing. You must assign a printer and assign settings for the forms you print. Start by selecting the appropriate form in the Form Name field at the top of the Printer Setup dialog; the fields in the dialog change to match the needs of the form you selected:

- **Choosing a printer for a form**   The drop-down list in the Printer Name field displays the printers installed on your computer. Select the appropriate printer for this form.
- **Selecting the paper for printing a form**   For transaction forms, the setup offers three types of paper: Intuit preprinted forms, blank paper, and letterhead.
  - **Intuit preprinted forms**   You can order these forms from Intuit or your favorite supplier that carries QuickBooks forms. All the fields are preprinted and aligned to match the way QuickBooks prints the form. When you print, only the data prints, not the field names.
    - **Blank paper**   If you use blank paper to print transaction forms, QuickBooks prints your company name and address at the top of the paper and prints the field names in addition to the data. Lines to separate fields and columns are also printed.
    - **Letterhead**   This setting is the same as the Blank Paper setting, except QuickBooks does not print the company name and address information at the top, and the top of the form begins printing two inches below the top of the paper to make sure the data doesn't print over your preprinted letterhead text.

Fine-Tuning the Alignment for Printing Forms

To make sure that everything prints in the right place or to change the position of the printed output, you can fine-tune the alignment of text. Although it's important to do this if you're using preprinted forms, it doesn't hurt to check the way the printout looks on blank paper or letterhead.

Click Align to open the Align Printer dialog. Choose the template that you want to work with and click OK. This opens the Fine Alignment dialog, in which you can print a sample and then move text up, down, left, or right to make adjustments to the sample printout. Continue to print a sample and make adjustments until the printout looks the way you want it to. Adjustments affect all the text as a block. You cannot adjust individual fields, rows, or other elements in the printed form. So if you adjust the alignment by moving a field up 14/100th of an inch, for example, everything that prints on the form moves up 14/100th of an inch.

Printing Forms as PDF Files

QuickBooks automatically installs a PDF printer driver when you install the software. The printer driver is used by QuickBooks when, for example, you send an invoice or purchase order via e-mail to customers or vendors. If you want to print your forms as PDF documents, with the form open, choose File | Save As PDF.

Printer Settings vs. Printer Options

When you assign a printer to a specific form and customize the printing setup for that form, QuickBooks memorizes that selection. If you change printers when you're ready to print, the next time you print the same form, QuickBooks returns to the original printer and printer settings linked to that form type, unless you reconfigure the setup to change printers.

Every printer has its own set of options to control the way printing occurs. And when you're ready to print a document, such as an invoice, you can set the printing options when you print. On the Print dialog, shown in Figure 4-2, is an Options button that you can click to open an additional dialog with more options for the selected

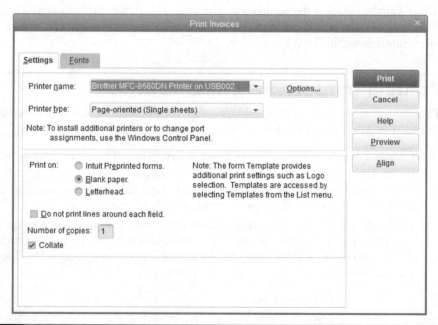

FIGURE 4-2   When you tell QuickBooks to print an invoice, it opens the Print dialog.

printer. You can change the tray (or select manual feed), change the resolution of the printing, and perform other tweaks.

QuickBooks does not memorize these options; it uses the printer's defaults the next time you print the form type. If you want to make printer options permanent, you must change the printer configuration in the Windows Printers folder.

Ways to Print Transaction Forms

All of the forms that you create in QuickBooks (such as invoices and checks, for example) can be printed one at a time, as you create them, or together in a batch. For your security and the integrity of your QuickBooks file, it's best to save the transaction before printing; that way, you have a record of the transaction in your QuickBooks file. QuickBooks has a default Preference setting that will automatically save the transaction for you before printing. You can find this option by selecting Edit | Preferences | General. On the Company Preferences tab, select the Save Transactions Before Printing option. You can deselect this option setting if you want the ability to print the current transaction before saving it.

To print the current transaction, click the Print button at the top of the transaction window. QuickBooks opens the Print dialog. Click Print to send the transaction form to the selected printer.

Previewing Form Printouts

If you want to see what the printed document will look like, click the arrow below the Print icon at the top of the document window and select Preview; often, the printed form differs from the form shown onscreen.

Printing Transaction Forms in Batches

To print transactions in batches, make sure the Print Later check box is selected on each transaction you create. Then follow these steps to batch-print the documents:

1. Choose File | Print Forms | <Transaction Type> (substitute your transaction type).
2. In the Select <Transaction Type> To Print window, all your unprinted transaction forms are selected with a check mark. Click the check marks to remove them from any forms you don't want to print at this time (it's a toggle).
3. Click OK to print. A Print <Transaction Type> dialog appears, where you can change or select printing options. Click Print to begin printing. After sending the documents to the printer, QuickBooks asks you to confirm that all the documents printed properly.

4. If everything printed properly, click OK; if not, in the Confirmation dialog, select the forms that need to be reprinted and click OK. Then return to the Print Forms <Transaction Type> dialog, where the forms you selected for reprinting are listed, so you can continue printing your batch. Of course, before taking this step, you'll need to unjam the printer, put in a new ink cartridge, or correct any other problem that caused the original print job to fail.

Small Business Tip Another new feature in QuickBooks Pro, Premier, Accountant, and Desktop 2016 editions is the ability to clear several selected forms at once from the Send Forms window. Although this does not yet work from the Print Forms window, it is a fix from previous years. To use this feature, from the menu bar, click File | Send Forms. Select Remove and then Remove Email as seen here. This removes the Email Later choice from each invoice at the same time and removes all the selected items from the Send Forms queue.

Select the email(s) you want to send and click **Send Now**

5 of 5 Selected   5 email(s) to Send

SEND TO	TYPE	NUM	DATE	AMOUNT
Project #15	INV	71047	06/01/2019	$150.00
Project #11	INV	71065	09/28/2019	$7,803.20
Project #07	INV	71087	12/15/2019	$43.20
Project #02	INV	71092	12/15/2019	$263.28
Project #12	INV	71075	12/31/2019	$9,583.10

QuickBooks Email Forms

Are you sure you want to remove the selected email?

This could take several minutes if you're removing a lot of email.

Remove Email   Cancel

Remove

Help

Managing Accounts Receivable

n this chapter:

- Recording and depositing customer payments
- Using e-invoicing
- Entering and handling cash sales in QuickBooks
- Working with a cash drawer
- Banking Accounts Receivable payments
- Using the Income tracker
- Using the Accounts Receivable reports
- Customer statements in QuickBooks

Chapter 5

Once you have sent invoices to your customers, you hope money will quickly arrive to pay those invoices. In fact, for most businesses, the most rewarding QuickBooks task is receiving payments from a customer. QuickBooks gives you the tools you need to make sure that you apply payments the way your customer intended so that you both have the same information in your records.

Your Options for Receiving Customer Payments

In QuickBooks, payments are applied to specific invoices, not to a general balance forward. You can change how QuickBooks applies payments with just a mouse click or two, using the following steps:

1. Choose Edit | Preferences and click the Payments icon in the left pane.
2. Move to the Company Preferences tab.
3. In the Receive Payments section, select or deselect options to match your needs:

   - **Automatically Apply Payments** This means that when you enter the amount you've received from the customer, QuickBooks will automatically pay off matching invoices, first by amount, and then by the oldest due date.
   - **Automatically Calculate Payments** This tells QuickBooks to let you omit the amount of the customer's payment in the transaction window and select invoices to pay off. QuickBooks adds up the invoice amounts and applies the total as the customer's payment. (This assumes the customer has sent a payment that matches the total.)
   - **Use Undeposited Funds As A Default Deposit To Account** This automatically posts the payments you receive to the Undeposited Funds account, and from there you deposit the funds into a bank account. In this way, the deposit amount shown in the check register matches the total deposit found on your bank statement.

When a payment arrives from a customer, choose Customers | Receive Payments to open a Receive Payments window, as shown in Figure 5-1. Note the ribbon bar at the top of the window that contains three tabs: Main, Reports, and Payments. Each of these tabs contains buttons that give you easy access to important payment-related tasks (such as processing credit payments) as well as reports where you can find customer balance information.

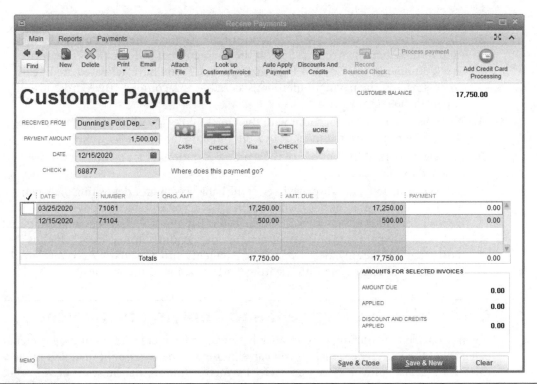

FIGURE 5-1   Enter customer payments in the Receive Payments window.

Main Tab in Receive Payments Window

This tab has several icons with which you can find previous payments, enter or delete a payment, look up invoices, and so on, as seen next.

To record a payment, follow these steps:

1. Click the arrow to the right of the Received From field and select the customer or job from the drop-down list.

   If you select a customer, the details for the open invoice balance(s) for this customer display. If the payment is for a job, select the job. The details display for the open invoice balance(s) for this specific job. If the payment covers multiple jobs, select the main customer name to see the invoices for all jobs. The details for the open invoice balance(s) for this customer and jobs display.

2. In the Payment Amount field, enter the amount of this payment.

3. To select the payment method, click one of the payment method buttons to the right of the Payment Amount field. If the payment method is a check, enter the check number in the Check # field that appears. If you have activated credit card processing and the payment method is a credit card, complete the Card No. and Exp. Date fields for your records.

4. If you have a merchant account with the QuickBooks Merchant Account Service, check the Process Payment check box on the Main tab on the Icon Bar.

5. The Memo field at the bottom of the window is optional for any note you'd like attached to this payment.

6. If the Deposit To field is displayed, select the bank account for depositing the payment, or select Undeposited Funds if you're using that account to receive payments. If the Deposit To field is not displayed, it means your Payments Preferences are configured to deposit payments to the Undeposited Funds account automatically, which is the most often used setting. See "Depositing Payments into Your Bank Account" later in this chapter to determine which setting works best for your company.

Calculating the Payment and Applying to Invoices

If you've enabled the (default) Automatically Calculate Payments option in the Payments category of the Preferences dialog, you can skip the Payment Amount field and move directly to the list of invoices in the Receive Payments window. As you select each invoice for payment, QuickBooks calculates the total and places it in the Applied [Amount] field.

If you *haven't* enabled the option to calculate payments automatically and you select an invoice listing without entering the amount of the payment first, QuickBooks issues an error message, telling you that the amount of the payment you're applying is higher than the amount you entered in the Payment Amount field. In that case, enter the amount of the payment in the Payment Amount field at the top of the Receive Payments window.

If the customer's intention isn't clear, the smart thing to do is contact the customer to ask how the payment should be applied. You must apply the entire amount of the customer's payment. If you are not tracking the customer balance by invoice and are instead using a balance forward system, just let QuickBooks continue to apply payments against the oldest invoices.

If the customer payment doesn't match the amount of any invoice, check to see whether the customer indicated a specific invoice number for the payment. If a number is specified, apply the payment against that invoice; if not, let the automatic selection of the oldest invoice stand.

Depositing Payments into Your Bank Account

If you don't see the Deposit To field in the Receive Payments window when recording payments from customers, it means your Payments Preferences setting is set to post payments automatically to the Undeposited Funds account. To confirm this, select Edit | Preferences | Payments and look on the Company Preferences tab.

If you decide to change this setting, use the Deposit To field in the Receive Payments window to select an account for depositing the payments. You can select a bank account or select the Undeposited Funds account as seen here.

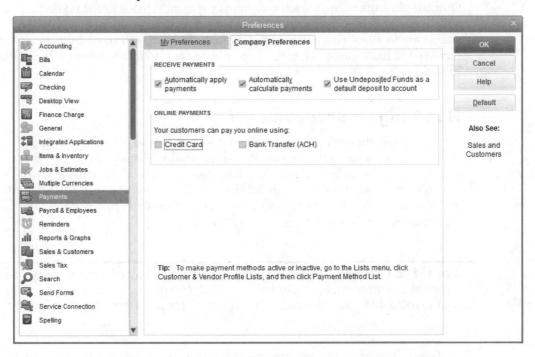

Depositing Cash Receipts into the Undeposited Funds Account

When you enable the automatic use of the Undeposited Funds account (or manually select that account in the transaction window), each payment you receive is entered into the account named Undeposited Funds that QuickBooks establishes automatically.

When you finish applying customer payments in QuickBooks and you're ready to make your bank deposit, you move the money from the Undeposited Funds account into a bank account by choosing Banking | Make Deposits from the menu bar. Because the bank statement shows only the total amount of each bank deposit (the payments you selected for transfer to the bank from the Undeposited Funds account), the Undeposited Funds account shows each individual payment you received. This matches the monthly bank statement, making it easier for you to reconcile the account.

Depositing Each Payment Directly into a Bank Account

Depositing each payment directly to the bank means you don't have to take the extra step of moving cash receipts from the Undeposited Funds account into the bank account. However, each payment you receive appears as a separate entry when you reconcile your bank account.

For instance, if you receive six payments totaling $10,450.25 and take the checks to the bank that day, your bank statement shows that amount as one deposit. When it's time to reconcile your account and you compare your bank statement to your QuickBooks bank register, each individual payment is listed in the register. When added together, these payments should all equal that same amount of $10,450.25, but you'll have to select each payment individually, mark it as cleared, and make sure it matches the bank statement. (See Chapter 7 for detailed instructions on reconciling bank accounts.)

Handling Underpayments

After you apply the customer's payment, if it isn't enough to pay off an existing invoice, the lower-left corner of the Receive Payments window displays a message that asks whether you want to leave the underpaid amount as an underpayment or write it off. To make it easy for you to contact the customer to ask about the reason for the underpayment, QuickBooks adds a button labeled View Customer Contact Information that opens to the customer record when clicked.

> **Small Business Tip** If the payment pays all of a current invoice and a partial payment on an older invoice, click the newer invoice first to clear that invoice and then the older invoice to enter the amount being paid for it.

If you opt to retain the underpayment, the invoice you selected for payment remains as a receivable, with a new balance (the original balance minus the payment you applied). When you click Save & Close (or Save & New), QuickBooks makes the appropriate postings.

If you select the option to write off the underpayment, when you click Save & Close or Save & New, QuickBooks opens the Write Off Amount dialog so you can choose the posting account and, if applicable, apply a class to the transaction, as shown next. Discuss the account to use for a write-off with your accountant. You can create an Income or Expense account for this purpose, depending on the way your accountant wants to track receivables you've decided to forgive.

Applying Credits to Invoices

You can apply any existing credits to an open invoice, in addition to applying the payment that arrived. If credits exist, customers may let you know how they want credits applied, and it's not unusual to find a note written on the copy of the invoice that the customer sent along with the check that probably represents the net due when the credit is applied.

When credits exist for the customer or job you select in the Receive Payments transaction window, QuickBooks displays the credit balance in the Available Credits field at the bottom of the window. To apply a credit balance to an invoice, click the Discount And Credits button at the top of the Receive Payments window, which opens the Discount And Credits dialog. Select the credit(s) you want to apply and click Done. Depending on the circumstances, QuickBooks handles the credits in several ways:

- *The credit total is equal to or less than the unpaid amount of the oldest invoice.* This reduces the balance due on that invoice. If the customer sent a payment that reflects his net balance due (balance minus unused credits), the invoice has no remaining balance. If applying the existing credit along with the payment doesn't pay off the invoice, the balance due on the invoice is reduced by the total of the payment and the credit. The amount of the credit is added to the postings for the invoice. This change affects only the invoice balance and the accounts receivable posting; it doesn't change the amount of the payment that's posted to your bank account.

- *The credit total is larger than the amount required to pay off an invoice.* If the customer payment is smaller than the amount of the invoice, but the amount of credit is larger than the amount needed to pay off the invoice, the balance of the credit remains available for posting to another invoice. To apply the unapplied credit balance to another invoice, click Done and select the next invoice in the Receive Payments window. Then click the Discount And Credits button and apply the credit balance (or as much of it as you need) against the invoice. Any unused credits remain for the future.

You should send a statement to the customer to reflect the current new invoice balances after you have applied the payments and the credits to make sure your records and your customer's records match.

Applying Credits to a Different Job

You may encounter a situation in which a customer has already paid the invoices for a job when the credit is created or has paid for part of the job, exceeding the amount of the credit. If the customer tells you to apply the entire credit balance to another job or to float the credit and apply it against the next job, open the credit transaction and change the job (because a credit can be applied to an invoice for that same job only). Then apply the credit to an invoice for the job you specified, or tell QuickBooks to retain it as an available credit that you'll apply when payment arrives.

Applying Discounts for Payments

If you offer your customers terms that include a discount if they pay their bills promptly (for instance, 2%10 Net30), you should apply the discount to the payment if it's applicable. QuickBooks doesn't apply the discount automatically. Instead, you must select the invoice (unless QuickBooks automatically selected it in order to apply the payment) and click the Discount And Credits button to see the Discount And Credits dialog connected to this invoice.

If the payment arrived by the discount date, QuickBooks inserts the amount of the discount to use. Accept the amount of the discount and enter a Discount Account. (See "Posting Discounts to a Sales Discount Account" later in this chapter.) If the payment did not arrive by the discount date, QuickBooks displays "0.00" as the discount amount, which can be changed at your discretion. Click Done to return to the Receive Payments window. You'll see that QuickBooks has added a discount column and displayed the discount amount in that column. If the net amount and the customer payment amount are the same, the invoice is now paid.

Applying Discounts for Untimely Payments

Sometimes customers expect to take the discount even if the payment arrives after the discount date. You can apply the payment to the invoice and leave a balance due for the discount amount deducted by the customer, or you can give the customer the discount even though the payment is late. When you click the Discount And Credits button in that case, QuickBooks does not automatically fill in the discount amount because the discount period has now passed. To preserve your goodwill with that customer, simply enter the amount of the discount manually, select the posting account, and then click Done to apply the discount to the invoice.

Posting Discounts to a Sales Discount Account

You should create a specific account in your chart of accounts to track the discount amounts you allow your customers to take. You could post the amounts taken to your regular sales account, which would have the effect of reducing the total sales reported in that account. A better approach would be to create a separate account, such as "Discounts on Sales" (account type should be Income), so you can easily track the discounts you allow your customers.

Reports and Payment Tabs in the Receive Payments Window

From these tabs, you can create a quick report, see both the history of this transaction and its underlying journal entries, and view the receipt for a payment that has been processed by the QuickBooks service. The Reports tab Icon Bar displays the choices shown here.

The Payments tab offers the option of subscribing to the credit card processing service. See "Using E-Invoicing" next for more information.

Using E-Invoicing

Today, many businesses want to use the Internet to both send invoices and receive payments. With your subscription, this fee-based service allows your company the option to do just that. You can opt to use this service by setting the option in Preferences or on the invoice itself. Again, you must subscribe to the service first. See the link at http://quickbooks.intuit.com/payments to sign up. (You can still simply e-mail invoices without using the e-pay service.)

After you have subscribed, you can send invoices using your Outlook or QuickBooks web mail. The customer will click a link in the e-mail to display your invoice. The invoice has a Pay Now link with which your customer can pay using the QuickBooks Payment service if you have a Merchant Agreement with QuickBooks. This fee-based service allows the customer to pay with Visa, MasterCard, Discover, or American Express. They can also use an ACH bank transfer from their bank.

Handling Cash Sales

In QuickBooks, a *cash sale* is handled via a transaction called a sales receipt. When entering a sale using a sales receipt, the payment you take can be in the form of cash or check. If you use a merchant service, such as the one available through QuickBooks, you can also accept an e-check or credit/debit card. This means you have no accounts receivable for this transaction. Most restaurants and retail businesses that use QuickBooks use sales receipts to record their sales.

There are two methods for handling cash sales in QuickBooks:

- *Record each cash sale as a separate record.* This provides a way to maintain historical records about those customers in addition to tracking income and inventory.
- *Record sales in batches (usually one batch for each business day).* This method tracks income and inventory when you have no desire to maintain historical information about each customer that pays cash.

To record a cash sale, choose Customers | Enter Sales Receipts from the menu bar, which opens the Enter Sales Receipts window.

Entering Cash Sale Data

If you want to track customer information, enter a name in the Customer:Job field or select the name from the drop-down list. If a customer record doesn't exist, you can add a new customer by choosing <Add New>.

If you don't want to track customers, create a customer for cash sales, such as "Cash Customer." Even if you use a generic customer name, you can still type in the actual customer name and address in the Sold To field. (You'll have to add this field to the default Sales Receipt template.) In the future, you can run the Sales by Ship to Address report (Reports | Sales | Sales By Ship To Address) to view a report that shows the transactions for this generic "cash sale" customer that includes the information you've entered in the Sold To field.

Use the payment buttons on the Sales Receipt form to indicate the type of payment being received. From there, the Enter Sales Receipts window works exactly the way it does for invoices and payments: just fill in the information. To save the record, click the Save button on the Main tab of the Enter Sales Receipts ribbon bar. You can also click Save & New to open a new blank record or click Save & Close if you're finished.

Handling Batches of Cash Sales

If you operate a cash business, such as a restaurant, you can batch and enter your cash transactions on a daily basis. This works only if you don't care about maintaining information on the customers and no customer expects a printed receipt from QuickBooks. This technique also works if you have a business in which sales and service personnel return to the office each day with customer payments in hand. Create a customized template using the steps described in Chapter 14, with the following guidelines:

- Name the template, for example, "Batch Sales."
- On the Header tab, keep only the Date and Sale Number fields in the header part of the template.
- On the Columns tab, deselect all the optional fields, leaving only the Item, Description, and Amount columns selected.
- On the Footer tab, remove the Message field.

To batch-process cash sales, use the new template with the following procedures:

- Use a customer named "Cash" or "Daily Sales."
- Create a Service type or Other Charge type item called "Daily Sales."
- In the line item section of the sales receipt, you can either use a separate line for each sale that day or enter the item once to capture the total for the day.
- Click the Save & Close button at the end of the day. If you need to close the window during the day, you can reopen the Sales Receipt window and click the Previous button to find that day's receipt and add to it as needed.

Tracking Your Cash Drawer in QuickBooks

If you deal in real cash, have a cash register, and are not using QuickBooks Point of Sale, consider these steps for keeping track of your cash drawer. (There are two basic ways to track receipts from cash sales separate from customer payments; choose the one that best suits your needs).

- Post the cash receipts to the Undeposited Funds account, but deposit those funds separately from noncash payments when you work in the QuickBooks Payments To Deposit window.
- Post the cash receipts directly to a new bank account called "Cash in Drawer" (or something similar). Then, when you empty the drawer and deposit the cash into your bank account, you can record it in QuickBooks by making a transfer (Banking | Transfer Funds) from the cash drawer account into the appropriate bank account.

The advantage of having a Cash in Drawer account is that you can match the contents of the physical till of your cash register to an account in QuickBooks. In a perfect world, you'll open the register for the Cash in Drawer account in QuickBooks and see that it matches your actual drawer count. The world isn't perfect, however, and sometimes the two amounts will not be equal. To resolve this, refer to the next section, "Handling the Over and Short Problem."

Handling the Over and Short Problem

If you literally take cash for cash sales, when you count the money in the till at the end of the day, you may find that the recorded sales total doesn't match the cash you expected to find in the till. Or you may find that the money you posted to deposit to the bank doesn't match the amount of money you put into the little blue bag you took to the bank. One of the problems you face is how to handle this in QuickBooks. If you post $100.00 in cash sales but have only $99.50 in cash to take to the bank, how do you handle the missing 50 cents? You can't just post $100.00 to your bank account (well, you could, but your bank account won't reconcile).

You can easily account for the over/short dilemma in your bookkeeping procedures. In many cases, by the way, the overs and shorts balance out: short one day, over another.

Creating Over and Short Accounts

To track over/short, you need to have some place to post the discrepancies, which means you have to create some new accounts in your chart of accounts. Because many shortages one day become overages the next, you could create just one income account, "Over/Short," to track this trend. Or you could create two income accounts, one called Over and the other called Short. Or you could make an over/short account a parent account with two subaccounts, Over and Short.

Creating Over and Short Items

If you track cash sales by tracking batches of sales in a sales receipt transaction, you need items for your overages and shortages (in QuickBooks, you need items for everything that's connected with entering sales data in a transaction window). Create items for overages and shortages as follows:

- Create two Other Charge items, "Overage" and "Shortage."
- Don't assign a price, and make the items nontaxable.
- Link each item to the appropriate account (or subaccount) that you just created for Over/Short.

Now that you have the necessary accounts and items, use the Over and Short items right in the Enter Sales Receipts window to adjust the difference between the amount of money you've accumulated in the cash-sale transactions and the amount of money you're actually depositing to the bank. It's your last transaction of the day. Remember to use a minus sign before the figure when you use the Short item.

Recording Bank Deposits

When you receive a customer payment or save a sales receipt, by default, QuickBooks posts the offsetting total on that receipt to the Undeposited Funds account. As you've been completing the receive payments and cash sales information, QuickBooks has been keeping a list of these transactions in the Undeposited Funds account. These transactions remain in Undeposited Funds until you clear them by depositing them into your bank account.

The Payments to Deposit Window

To tell QuickBooks about the details of your bank deposit, choose Banking | Make Deposits from the menu bar, which opens the Payments To Deposit window. This window has several columns:

- **Check Mark**   Use this column to indicate the payments that will be deposited in this transaction.
- **Date/Time**   These columns indicate the date and time you entered the payment or cash sale.
- **Type**   PMT is for payment of an invoice, whereas RCPT indicates a cash sale.
- **No**   If you received a check, the check number shows in this column.
- **Payment Method**   The method used to pay: cash, check, credit card, and so on.
- **Name**   The name of the customer who paid you.
- **Amount**   Total amount received.

When you create a deposit from this window, indicate which items are being deposited together. For example, if you have four checks and two cash receipts that add up to $567.22, each item will be part of your deposit, and $567.22 will be the total showing on your bank statement.

If you have only a few transactions to deposit, select the items you will take to the bank by clicking their listings to place a check mark in the left column. Click Select All if you will take all of these payments to the bank for deposit.

Most banks list credit card deposits separately from the deposit total for cash and checks because credit card deposits are usually made directly to your bank account by your merchant account bank.

- **Separate deposits by bank account**   If you're depositing money into multiple bank accounts, select only the transactions that go into the first account. After you complete the deposit, start this process again and deposit the remaining transactions into the other account(s).
- **Credit card deposits**   Don't "deposit" credit card payments to QuickBooks until your merchant bank notifies you that the funds have been placed in your account or the transfer appears on your bank's website or your paper statement.

Small Business Tip   If your merchant bank deducts fees before transferring funds, learn how to deposit the net amount in the section "Calculating Merchant Card Fees," later in this chapter.

Working in the Make Deposits Window

After you select the appropriate payments (or select all payments), click OK in the Payments To Deposit window to open the Make Deposits window, shown in Figure 5-2. Select the bank account you're using for this deposit. Then make sure the date matches the day you physically deposit the money.

Adding Items to the Deposit

If you want to add deposited items that weren't in the Payments To Deposit window, click anywhere in the Received From column to make it accessible and select an existing name by clicking the arrow, or click <Add New> to enter a name that isn't in your system. If the source of the check is any entity that isn't a customer or vendor, you can either skip the Received From column or add the name to the Other Names list. If you don't need to track the entity as a customer or vendor, it's fine to skip the name.

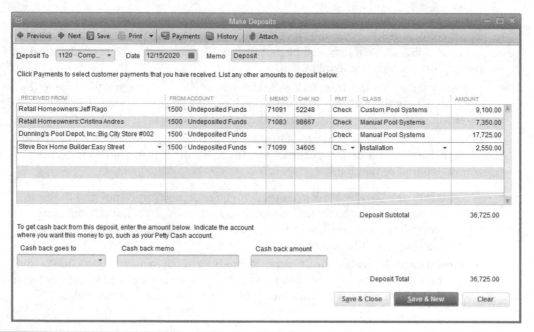

FIGURE 5-2 Create deposits in the QuickBooks Make Deposits window.

Press TAB to move to the From Account column and enter the account to which you're posting this transaction. Table 5-1 shows how to handle some noncustomer deposits. Use the TAB key to move through the rest of the columns, which are self-explanatory.

Calculating Merchant Card Fees

If your merchant card bank deposits the gross amount of each transaction and charges your bank account for the total fees due at the end of the month, you don't have to do anything special to deposit credit card payments. You can deal with the fees when your

Type of Deposit	Account to Use
Bank loan proceeds	The liability account for that bank loan. (You can create it here by choosing <Add New> if the account is not yet set up.) The bank should be in your Vendors list because you have to write checks to repay the loan.
Money you are putting into the company	Use the owner's capital account in the Equity section of your chart of accounts.
Refund	If a refund for an expense, use the vendor's name and post the deposit to the same expense account you used for the original transaction.
Rebate	If this deposit is a rebate from a manufacturer instead of a vendor, post the amount to the original expense account you used when you purchased the item.

TABLE 5-1 Noncustomer Deposit Accounts

bank statement arrives by entering the fee directly in the bank account register, posting the amount to the merchant card fee expense account.

If your merchant card bank deducts fees from transactions and deposits the net proceeds to your account, you'll need to take a few extra steps to track credit card transactions and deposit the correct amount:

1. Select the credit card transactions in the Payments To Deposit window—these are gross amounts, representing the sales price you charged (and the customer paid). Then click OK to move the payments to the Make Deposits window.

2. In the first empty line below the transactions that were transferred to the Make Deposits window, click the From Account column and select the account to which you post merchant card fees.

3. Move to the Amount column and enter the fee as a negative number. Now the net matches the amount that the merchant card company deposited in your bank account, and your merchant card expense is posted to the general ledger.

> **Small Business Tip** If you're getting cash back from your deposit, tell QuickBooks about it directly on the Make Deposits window using the Cash Back boxes rather than making a journal entry to adjust the total of collected payments against the total of the bank deposit.

Printing Deposit Slips

To print a deposit slip or a deposit summary, click the Print button at the top of the Make Deposits window. QuickBooks asks whether you want to print a deposit slip and summary or just a deposit summary.

If you want to print a deposit slip that your bank will accept, you must order printable deposit slips. If you order directly from QuickBooks, the QuickBooks deposit slips are guaranteed to be acceptable to your bank. You must have a laser printer or inkjet printer to use them. When you print the deposit slip, a tear-off section at the bottom of the page has a deposit summary. Keep that section for your own records and take the rest of the page to the bank along with your money.

If you don't use QuickBooks deposit slips, select Deposit Summary Only and fill out your bank deposit slip manually. Be sure to fill out the payment method field (cash or check), or QuickBooks won't print the deposit slip.

Keeping Track of Accounts Receivable

Collecting the money owed to you is likely one of your most important tasks when running a business. You have to track how much is due to you and from whom and then devote time and effort to collect it. QuickBooks offers several tools and reports that give you what you need to manage your accounts receivable efficiently.

Getting the Most from the Customer Center

In addition to detailed customer information, the Customer Center contains links that give you quick access to accounts receivable reports and the Income Tracker, a tool that will help you keep your client balances in check.

The Income Tracker

The Income Tracker shows all the customer-related transactions in your QuickBooks file. From this list, shown in Figure 5-3, you can review the details of any transaction by double-clicking it. Use the Income Tracker to take follow-up action on past-due transactions or outstanding estimates, or just to send an e-mail to stay in touch with a valued customer.

To access the Income Tracker, follow these steps:

1. Choose Customers | Customer Center or click the Customers icon on the Icon Bar.
2. Click the Income Tracker button at the top of the window to open the Income Tracker.

At the top of the Income Tracker window are totals for unbilled (open) estimates, unpaid invoices, overdue invoices, and paid receipts received in the last 30 days. Clicking the boxes containing these totals quickly filters the list of transactions displayed below.

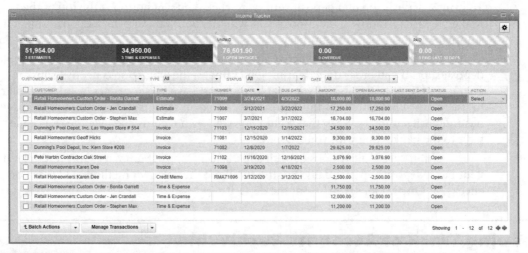

FIGURE 5-3 The Income Tracker shows the status of all open customer transactions.

Control which transactions appear in the list by using one or all of the Customer:Job, Type, Status, or Date filters located at the top of the Income Tracker window. In addition, the list of transactions displayed can be re-sorted by clicking any one of the column headings.

Use the Select drop-down menu in the Action column to take an action on a specific transaction. To create a new sales-related transaction while working in the Income Tracker, click the Manage Transactions button at the bottom of the window.

The Collections Center

An optional feature you can activate is the Collections Center. Once enabled, it's located within the Customer Center. It is designed to help you track past-due and almost past-due customer balances while giving you an easy way to send e-mail reminders to the customers listed there.

To enable the Collection Center feature, choose Edit | Preferences | Sales & Customers | Company Preferences | Enable Collections Center. A Collections Center button appears at the top of the Customer Center to the left of the Income Tracker, as seen next. When you click the Collections Center button, the Collections Center opens to the Overdue tab.

From this list, you can review the details of individual invoices in question by double-clicking an invoice. You can sort the list by balance or days overdue by clicking the appropriate column heading. If you've entered an e-mail address in the customer's record, you can also send a reminder e-mail to one or all of the customers on this list. Just click Select And Send Email at the top of the Overdue tab window. You'll see a yellow alert icon in the Notes/Warnings column if an e-mail address is missing. Clicking this icon allows you to add an e-mail address to a customer's record if you choose.

The Notes icon next to the customer name lets you document your collections activities or view previous entries. To see a list of customers that have upcoming invoices due, select the Almost Due tab.

Running Accounts Receivable Reports

A/R reports are lists of the money owed you by your customers, and they're available in quite a few formats. These reports are designed for you, not for your customers, and you can run them whenever you need to know the extent of your receivables. Many companies run an aging report every morning, just to keep an eye on the amount of money due them on a particular day.

You can run some key reports on individual customers directly from the Customer Center. Simply highlight the customer or job. Note the Reports for this Customer (or Job if you're looking at a specific job) section at the right of the Customer Information pane.

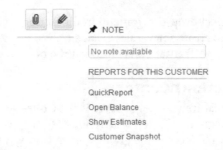

The following reports are available:

- **QuickReport**   Displays all transactions related to the customer within a specified date range.
- **Open Balance**   Displays the transactions (invoices, payments, and credit memos) that make up a customer's current balance.
- **Show Estimates**   Displays all estimates created for the customer within a specified date range.
- **Customer Snapshot**   Displays a dashboard-like view of a customer's relationship with you (including what they buy, how they pay, and how long they've been doing business with you).

A/R Aging Reports

QuickBooks has a couple of built-in A/R aging reports, and you can customize any built-in reports so they report data exactly the way you want. To see an aging report, choose Reports | Customers & Receivables, and then choose either A/R Aging Summary or A/R Aging Detail.

The quickest way to see how much of the money owed to you is current or past due is to run the A/R Aging Summary, which lists customer balances by aging period (such as 31–60 or 61–90 days), as shown in Figure 5-4.

If you choose Aging Detail from the Customers & Receivables reports menu, you see a more comprehensive report that shows individual transactions for each aging period.

Customizing Aging Reports

If you don't need to see all of the columns in the A/R Aging Detail report, or if you'd prefer to see the information displayed in a different manner, you can customize the report. Start by clicking the Customize Report button at the top of the window to open the Modify Report window. Table 5-2 shows you how to make several customizations.

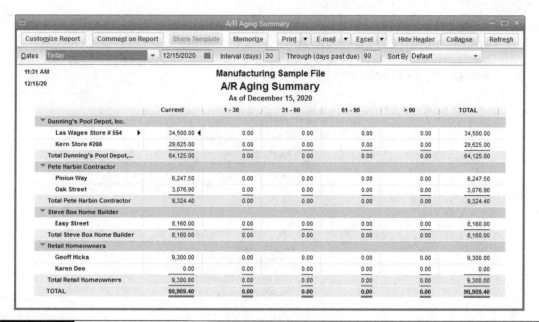

FIGURE 5-4 Use the A/R Aging Summary to find past-due balances.

Customization	Procedure
Customize a column	To remove a column, scroll through the Columns list and click to remove the check mark, and then click OK to accept your changes. The column disappears from the report. To include a column heading, click that column listing to place a check mark next to it and click OK.
Filter information	Click the Filters tab to select a filter and then set the conditions for it. Each filter has its own specific type of criteria.
Configure a header or footer	Customize the header and footer text by making changes in the Header/Footer tab. Eliminate any Header/Footer field by removing the check mark from the field's check box. For fields you want to print, you can change the text. You can also change the layout by choosing a different Alignment option from the drop-down list.
Customize appearance	Click the Fonts & Numbers tab to change the format of the report. You can change the way negative numbers are displayed, and you can change the fonts for any or all of the individual elements in the report.

TABLE 5-2 A/R Aging Detail Report Customization Procedures

Small Business Tip New in QuickBooks Pro, Premier, Accountant, and Enterprise 2016 Desktop editions is the ability to run a report with the dates "This Fiscal Year-to-Last Month" as the date, as seen next. This feature is a direct result of requests by QuickBooks users!

Memorizing Aging Reports

When you close a report window, QuickBooks may ask if you want to memorize the report with the changes you made (if you told QuickBooks to stop asking this, you won't see the message). Click Yes so you don't have to go through all the modifications again.

If you do not see the memorize report prompt, you can still memorize your redesigned report. Click the Memorize button in the report window. When the Memorize Report dialog appears, enter a new name for the report, optionally save it within a report group, and click OK. This report name appears on the list of memorized reports when you choose Reports | Memorized Reports from the menu bar. Only the criteria and formatting are memorized, so each time you open the report, the data QuickBooks generates is from current transaction records, so you get current, accurate information.

No matter what the format of your report, you'll probably want to print it. While you're in a report window, click the Print button at the top of the window and select Report to bring up the Print Reports dialog. If the report is wide, use the Margins tab to set new margins, and use the options on the Settings tab to customize other printing options. You can also use the Fit Report To options to fit all the columns or rows on your report to a page.

Customer and Job Reports

In addition to the accounts receivable reports, QuickBooks has reports designed to give you information about specific customers and jobs. Choose Reports | Customers & Receivables to see the list.

Finance Charges

Imposing finance charges can help offset the time and resources needed to collect past-due balances and can act as an incentive to get your customers to pay on time. You configure finance charges in the Preferences dialog: choose Edit | Preferences. Then click the Finance Charge icon in the left pane and select the Company Preferences tab. Complete the fields, as described next. Click OK to save your settings when you're done.

- **Annual Interest Rate**   Replace the default data (0.00%) with any positive number to enable the finance charges feature. The rate you enter is annual: 18% = 1.5% per month.
- **Minimum Finance Charge**   QuickBooks calculates the finance charge based on the rate you entered in the preceding field. If the charge is less than what you enter, the amount is rolled up to this minimum.
- **Grace Period**   Enter the number of days "grace" you give before finance charges are assessed.
- **Finance Charge Account**   If no account exists, create one here as an Income type.
- **Assess Finance Charge On Overdue Finance Charges**   Not all states allow this, so check with the appropriate agency.
- **Calculate Charges From Due Date/Invoice Date**   Select the appropriate action.
- **Mark Finance Charge Invoices "To Be Printed"**   QuickBooks creates an invoice for each finance charge. You can print those invoices by selecting this option.

Assessing the Charges

Assess finance charges just before you create customer statements, which is commonly a monthly chore. Choose Customers | Assess Finance Charges from the menu bar. The Assess Finance Charges window opens with a list of all the customers with overdue balances. If you have any customers that have made payments that you haven't yet applied to an invoice, or if any customers have credits that you haven't yet applied to an invoice, an asterisk (*) appears to the left of the customer or job name. Close the Assess Finance Charges window, correct the situation, and then return to this window.

Change the Assessment Date field (which displays the current date) to the date on which you actually want to impose the charge. This date appears on customer statements.

When you press TAB to move out of the date field, the finance charges are recalculated to reflect the new date.

If you don't want to include a customer to be assessed a finance charge, click in the Assess column to remove the check mark from the customer name. All customers with overdue balances are included when you assess finance charges. If you reserve this process for only a few customers, choose Unmark All, and then reselect the customers you want to include.

You can quickly change the calculated total if you wish. Click the amount displayed in the Finance Charge column to activate that column for that customer and enter a new amount. If you need to calculate the new figure, press the equal sign (=) on your keyboard to use the QuickBooks built-in calculator.

Once all the calculations and figures are correct, click Assess Charges in the Assess Finance Charges window. When you create your customer statements, the finance charges appear. If you've opted to skip printing the finance charge assessments as invoices, there's nothing more to do. To print the finance charge invoices, be sure to select the Mark Invoices "To Be Printed" check box on the Assess Finance Charges window. Choose File | Print Forms | Invoices. The list of unprinted invoices appears, and unless you have regular invoices you didn't print yet, the list includes only the finance charge invoices. If the list is correct, click OK to continue on to the printing process.

Sending Statements

Monthly statements remind customers of outstanding balances and provide detailed documentation of your records, which your customers can match against their own records.

Before creating statements, you create any transactions that should appear on the statements. Invoices and payments appear automatically, but you may want to add statement charges. A *statement charge* is a charge you want to pass on to a customer for which you don't create an invoice. Some companies use statement charges instead of invoices for invoicing regular payments, such as monthly dues or quarterly retainer charges.

You must add statement charges before you create the statements so the charges appear on the statements. Statement charges use items from your Item List, but you cannot use taxable items, items that have percentage discounts, or items that represent a payment transaction. Statement charges record directly in a customer's register or in the register for a specific job.

To create a statement charge, choose Customers | Enter Statement Charges from the menu bar to open the customer register. By default, QuickBooks opens the register for the first customer in your Customers & Jobs List; use the drop-down list at the top of the window to select a different customer. Using your TAB key, move through the register's fields. When all the fields you want to use are filled in, click Record to save the transaction. Continue to select customers and/or jobs to enter additional statement charges.

Creating Statements

Before you start creating your statements, ensure that all the transactions that should be included on the statements have been entered into the system. When all customer accounts are up to date, choose Customers | Create Statements to open the Create Statements dialog, shown next.

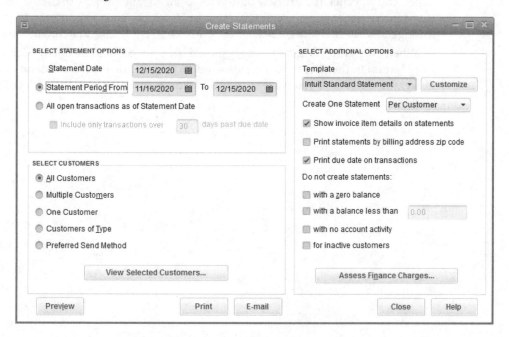

- **Date range**   The Statement Period From and To fields determine which transactions appear on the statement. The printed statement displays the previous balance (the total due before the From date) and includes all transactions that were created within the date range specified for that statement period. The starting date should be the day after the last date of your last statement run.

- **All Open Transactions As Of Statement Date**   The statement shows only unpaid invoices and charges and unapplied credits.

- **Customers**   If you want to send statements only to a select group of customers, click the Multiple Customers option to display a Choose button next to the option. Click the Choose button to bring up a list of customers, and then select each customer you want to include. You can manually select each customer, or select Automatic and then enter text to tell QuickBooks to match that text against all customer names and select the matching customers. If you're sending a statement to one customer only, select One Customer, and then click the arrow next to the text box to scroll through the list of your customers and select the one you want.

- **Filtering for send methods** Choose to send the statement via E-mail, Mail, or None (no statement will be sent).
- **Print** Specify how you want to print the statements.

You may skip statement creation for customers that meet the criteria you set in the Do Not Create Statements section of the dialog. Before you commit the statements to paper, you can click the Preview button to get an advance look. Use the Zoom In button to see the statement and its contents close up. Click the Next Page button to move through all the statements. Click Close to return to the Create Statements window.

When everything is just the way it should be, print the statements by clicking the Print button in the Create Statements window to open the Print Statements window. Designate the printer you want to use and adjust printer settings, then select Print.

Recording and Paying Your Bills

In this chapter:

- Entering vendor bills

- Using the Bill Tracker

- Using purchase orders

- Applying and managing reimbursable items

- Paying your bills and writing the checks

- Managing sales tax

You can pay your vendors in two different ways in QuickBooks: enter the bill into QuickBooks when you receive it and pay it later, or simply write a check without entering it beforehand. This chapter covers both ways and tells you how to link those expenses to customers (if need be) to be reimbursed for the expense.

Entering a bill into QuickBooks and paying it later is called *accrual accounting*. That means an expense is recognized by QuickBooks when you enter the bill, not when you actually pay the bill. Your Accounts Payable account should always equal the total of unpaid bills in your company file. However, if your taxes are filed on a cash basis, where an expense isn't recognized until you actually *pay* the bill, QuickBooks understands how to report your financial picture on a cash basis.

Record Vendor Bills

To enter your bills, choose Vendors | Enter Bills from the menu bar. When the Enter Bills window opens (see Figure 6-1), fill out as much information as you can from the bill.

You see four distinct areas: the ribbon bar at the top, with tabs and buttons for most bill payment tasks; the form section, for information about the vendor and the bill; the details section (at the bottom), where you record the data related to your general ledger accounts; and a History pane on the right side of the form. When you create a new bill for a current vendor, this pane has information about them, including their most recent transactions. To close this pane, simply click the arrow at the top-left corner of the History pane.

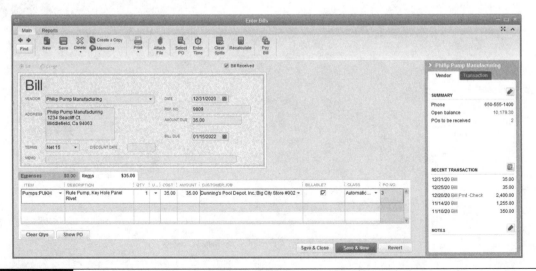

FIGURE 6-1   The Enter Bills window has four distinct areas.

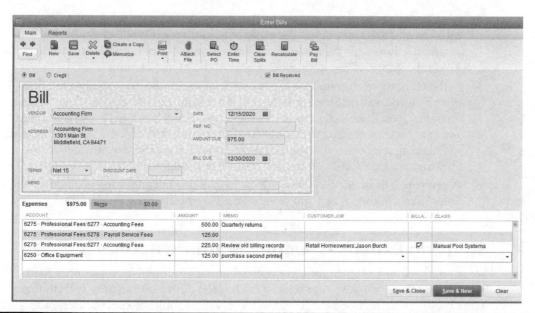

FIGURE 6-2   One or more expense accounts and customers can be assigned to a single bill.

There are two tabs in the details area of the Enter Bills window: Expenses and Items. In this section, we cover bills you post directly to an expense account; handling inventory items is covered a bit later in this chapter in the section "Purchase Inventory Items." Some bills can be assigned to one or more expense accounts or among multiple customer or job accounts, as shown in Figure 6-2.

If you have more than one Accounts Payable account, you may see an A/P Account field drop-down list at the top of the Enter Bills window.

Filling in the Details

In the Vendor field, click the arrow to choose the vendor from the list. If the vendor isn't on the list, choose <Add New> to add this vendor to your QuickBooks Vendors list. Then fill out the rest of the Enter Bills window.

1. In the Date field, enter the bill's date. The due date appears in the Bill Due field, based on your terms with this vendor. If no terms have been set, the due date appears using the QuickBooks default of ten days.

2. Enter the vendor's invoice number in the Ref. No. field and the bill amount in the Amount Due field. If there is no invoice number, consider using the bill's date as the invoice number.

3. In the Terms field, if the terms don't show your terms with this vendor, click the arrow to display a list of terms and select the one you need. If the terms you have with this vendor aren't available, choose <Add New> to create a new Terms entry. The Bill Due date changes to reflect the terms.

4. Click in the Account column on the Expenses tab, and click the arrow to display your chart of accounts. Select the expense account for this bill. QuickBooks automatically assigns the amount you entered in the Amount Due field to the Amount column. If you wish, enter a note in the Memo column.

5. In the Customer:Job column, enter a customer or job if you're paying a bill that will be billed to a customer, or if this bill is a reimbursable expense. If you select a Customer, you'll see a check box that includes a check mark in the Billable column. You can uncheck the box with a mouse click to make the expense nonbillable while still keeping it associated with that customer for job costing purposes. If you're tracking classes, a Class column appears; enter the appropriate class.

6. When you're finished, click Save & New to save this bill and bring up another blank Enter Bills window. When you've entered all your bills, click Save & Close.

Splitting Expenses Among Multiple Accounts

Some bills need to be split among multiple accounts. Common examples are a loan repayment, where you post both interest (to Interest Expense) and principal (to the loan's liability account), or a credit card bill that covers multiple expense categories. Entering this type of bill is the same until you begin assigning the expense accounts and amounts in the details area of the Enter Bills window. Enter the first account in the Account column, and QuickBooks applies the entire bill amount in the Amount column. Replace that amount with the total for this expense category.

Then, on the next row, select the next account. As you add each account to the column, QuickBooks assumes that the unallocated amount is assigned to that account. Repeat the process of changing the amount and adding another account until the total amount assigned to the accounts equals the amount of the vendor bill. To change an amount in the Amount Due field, click the Recalculate button on the ribbon bar to have QuickBooks add up the line items.

Using the Bill Tracker

New in QuickBooks 2016 desktop editions is the Bill Tracker. With this feature, you can, with only a few mouse clicks, see all outstanding purchase orders, bills, credit memos, and bill payments, whether by check or credit card. To access the Bill Tracker:

1. From the menu bar, click Vendors | Bill Tracker.
2. Select Bill Tracker from the Navigation Bar, whether you have chosen to display the Navigation Bar at the left side or the top of your QuickBooks window.
3. Click Vendor Center and then Bill Tracker from Icon Bar under the Vendor Center title bar.

	VENDOR	TYPE	NUMBER	DATE	DUE DATE ▲	STATUS	AMOUNT DUE	ACTION
☐	Prentice Pool Materials	Purchase Order	31	11/5/2020	11/5/2020	Open	15,000.00	
☐	Philip Pump Manufacturing	Purchase Order	32	11/5/2020	11/5/2020	Open	175.00	
☐	Philip Pump Manufacturing	Purchase Order	33	11/10/2020	11/10/2020	Open	1,725.00	
☐	Fran's Fasteners	Purchase Order	34	11/18/2020	11/18/2020	Open	1,065.00	
☐	Lipps Pool Supplies	Purchase Order	36	11/21/2020	11/21/2020	Open	14,750.00	
☐	Anderson's Hardware & Tools Supply	Purchase Order	35	11/26/2020	11/26/2020	Open	1,535.00	
☐	Anderson's Hardware & Tools Supply	Purchase Order	39	12/14/2020	12/14/2020	Open	841.00	
☐	Anderson's Hardware & Tools Supply	Bill		12/15/2020	1/14/2021	Open	905.00	
☐	Philip Pump Manufacturing	Bill	4321	1/18/2020	2/2/2021	Open	770.00	
☐	Philip Pump Manufacturing	Bill		10/10/2020	11/9/2021	Open	1,125.00	
☐	Lipps Pool Supplies	Bill		10/10/2020	11/9/2021	Open	6,720.00	
☐	Anderson's Hardware & Tools Supply	Bill	876589	10/15/2020	11/14/2021	Open	1,865.50	
☐	Perry Cutting Company	Bill	98076	10/25/2020	11/24/2021	Open	1,200.00	
☐	Fran's Fasteners	Bill	98076	11/1/2020	12/1/2021	Open	900.00	
☐	Philip Pump Manufacturing	Bill	PU9098	11/1/2020	12/1/2021	Open	5,484.30	
☐	Fran's Fasteners	Bill	AR90876	11/1/2020	12/1/2021	Open	9,627.70	
☐	Perry Cutting Company	Bill	23451	11/1/2020	12/1/2021	Open	1,177.78	
☐	Caylor's Hardware & Adhesives	Bill	67543	11/1/2020	12/1/2021	Open	4,470.00	
☐	Philip Pump Manufacturing	Bill	89076	11/3/2020	12/3/2021	Open	1,125.00	

Showing 1 - 33 of 33

FIGURE 6-3   Use the Bill Tracker to see the funds your business has committed.

Explore the Bill Tracker

As seen in Figure 6-3, the Bill Tracker presents an overview of all money your business has committed to vendors, whether it is a purchase order, a bill you have not yet paid, a credit card purchase, or a check you have written. You can filter by any of the colored blocks seen at the top of the Bill Tracker:

- **Unbilled**   This section displays your current purchase orders for which you have not yet received a bill.
- **Unpaid/Overdue**   In this area, the total amount currently due is displayed. If a bill is overdue, that amount appears in red in the Unpaid section, as seen next.

- **Paid**   This section shows the total funds you have paid in bills in the last 30 days.

Using the Bill Tracker Filters

Under the main sections of the Bill Tracker, there are six buttons with which you can customize the Bill Tracker to meet your needs:

- From the Vendor button, you can select information about a specific vendor. Click one of the boxes, such as Paid; click the downward arrow by Vendor; and select a name from the drop-down list to see all of the bills you have paid to that vendor over the last 30 days. Note that 30 days is the only option available when looking at Paid items.

- Use the Type button to select from several choices, as shown here.

- The Status button allows you to choose All, Open, Overdue, or Paid items.

- Depending on your other choices, the Date filter allows you to narrow by a variety of dates.

- You can group by vendor to see totals for each vendor. Click the right-pointing arrow to the left of the vendor name to see details, as shown next. Note that you can also choose what to do with an item from the Action column.

- The final filter allows you to clear your choices and show all of the information once again.

Other Bill Tracker Features

At the bottom of the Bill Tracker window are two more useful functions. Using the Batch Actions, you can print selected items, pay bills, or close one or more purchase orders. Use Manage Transactions to create new items or edit a selection.

Use Purchase Orders

Use purchase orders to order inventory items or manufacturing parts from your suppliers, or for services or non-inventory items that are not for resale. Inventory items link to the appropriate income account for that item, and non-inventory purchase orders link to an expense account. No amounts are posted to your books because purchase orders exist only to help you track what you've ordered against what you've received. You create the financial transactions when the items and the vendor's bill are received.

When you enable the inventory and purchase order features, QuickBooks creates a nonposting account named Purchase Orders the first time you open the Create Purchase Order window. You can double-click the account's listing to view the purchase orders you've entered, but the data has no effect on your records and doesn't appear in financial reports.

> **Small Business Tip**   Enable purchase orders and inventory through Preferences. From the menu bar, choose Edit | Preferences | Items & Inventory | Company Preferences | Inventory and Purchase Orders Are Active.

Create a Purchase Order

To create a purchase order, choose Vendors | Create Purchase Orders from the menu bar to open a blank Create Purchase Orders window. Fill in the self-explanatory purchase order fields and click Save & New or Save & Close to save the purchase order. If the item you're ordering has a manufacturer's part number (MPN) in the item record, use that data in your purchase order to avoid any confusion. However, you have to customize the purchase order template to display the MPN data. See Chapter 14 for more about customizing templates. See Figure 6-4 for a completed purchase order.

You can print the purchase orders as you complete them by clicking the Print icon on the ribbon bar in the Create Purchase Orders window, or you can print them all in a batch by placing a check mark next to the Print Later option on the Main tab before saving each purchase order. When you're ready to print the batch, click the arrow below the Print button and select Batch. You can also e-mail the purchase orders as you create them, or e-mail them as a batch by selecting Batch from the drop-down list below the E-mail icon on the transaction window's Main tab.

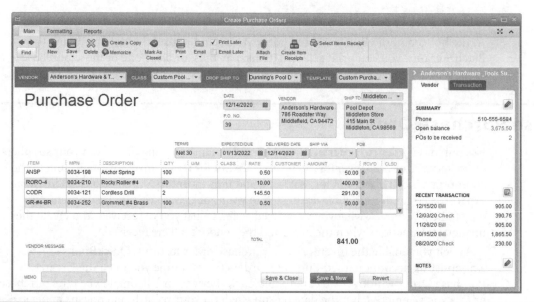

Using purchase orders in QuickBooks can streamline your bookkeeping chores.

When you receive the items and the bill, use the purchase order to automate the receipt of these items and the entry of the vendor's bill.

Purchase Inventory Items

If the vendor bill you're recording is for inventory items, there are some additional factors to consider because the accounting issues (the way you post amounts) are different. Frequently, two transactions are involved when you buy items for inventory:

- You receive the shipment first (with a packing slip).
- You receive the bill for the items that were shipped.

Sometimes the bill comes before the products, often the items arrive first, and sometimes both events occur at the same time (the bill is in an envelope pasted to or included inside the carton). If you created a purchase order for these items, you can use it to automate the receiving and vendor bill entry processes when they and the bill for them arrive.

Receiving Inventory Items Without a Bill

If the inventory items arrive before you receive a bill from the vendor, use the Create Items Receipts window to tell QuickBooks about the new inventory. This form brings the items into inventory so they become available for resale. Use the following steps to receive inventory in this scenario:

1. Choose Vendors | Receive Items from the menu bar to open a blank Create Item Receipts window. Select the vendor name, and if open purchase orders exist for this vendor, an Open POs Exist message appears, as shown next. If you know there isn't a purchase order for this particular shipment, click No, and fill out the Create Item Receipts window manually.

2. If you know a purchase order exists for this shipment, or if you're not sure, click Yes. QuickBooks displays all the open purchase orders for this vendor so you can put a check mark next to the appropriate PO(s). If no PO matching this shipment appears, click Cancel to return to the receipts window to fill in the data manually.
3. If a PO exists, QuickBooks fills out the Create Item Receipts window using the information in the PO. Check the shipment against the PO and change any quantities that don't match.
4. Click Save & New to receive the next shipment into inventory, or click Save & Close if this takes care of all the receipts of goods.

QuickBooks posts the amounts in the purchase order to your Accounts Payable account as an Item Receipt type. When the bill arrives with the actual costs, the Accounts Payable account will be updated accordingly and the transaction type will be changed to Bill.

Technically, an Accounts Payable liability should be connected only to a bill and not an Item Receipt (receipt of goods without a corresponding bill). In most cases, the bill you eventually receive for these goods will have the same unit cost as the Item Receipt. Sometimes, however, the cost per item listed on the Item Receipt may not be the same as the cost per item on the final bill. Whatever the reason, the bill that arrives will presumably have the correct costs, and those costs are the amounts to be posted to the Accounts Payable account.

If this situation occurs, QuickBooks allows you to adjust the initial posting you made to A/P when you received the items so that the new amounts match the bill. This means that on one date your Accounts Payable total and inventory valuation may show one amount, but a few days later, the amount shown is different, even though no additional transactions are displayed in reports. If the interval between those days crosses the month, or even worse, the year, your accountant might have a problem trying to figure out what happened. Now that you understand what happens, you can explain the logic behind the change.

Recording Bills for Items Already Received

When the bill comes *after* you have received items, do *not* use the regular Enter Bills window. This would cause a second posting to Accounts Payable. Instead, do the following:

1. Choose Vendors | Enter Bill For Received Items to open the Select Item Receipt dialog.
2. Select the vendor, and you'll see the current Item Receipt information for that vendor.
3. If you want the date of the bill to be the same as the date you received the item, place a check mark next to the Use Item Receipt Date For The Bill Date option.
4. Select the appropriate listing and click OK to open an Enter Bills window. The information from the Item Receipt is used to fill in the bill information.
5. Change anything in the Items tab that needs to be changed, such as a different cost per unit.
6. Add any shipping or handling charges in the Expenses tab to the appropriate accounts.
7. If you made any changes, you must click the Recalculate button so QuickBooks can match the total in the Amount Due field to the changed line item data.
8. Click Save & Close. Even if you made no changes, QuickBooks displays a message asking if you're sure you want to save the changes. Click Yes. The message appears because you've changed the transaction from a receipt of goods transaction to a vendor bill transaction, and QuickBooks overwrites the original postings that were made when you received the items. If you look at the Accounts Payable register (or the Inventory Assets register) after you receive the items, the transaction type is ITEM RCPT. When you save this transaction, QuickBooks overwrites the entire transaction, changing the transaction type to BILL and uses the new amounts if you made changes.

Receiving Items and Bills Simultaneously

If the items and the bill arrive at the same time, you can enter both at the same time. Choose Vendors | Receive Items And Enter Bill to open the standard Enter Bills window. When you enter the vendor's name, you may see a message telling you that an open PO exists for the vendor. The message dialog asks if you want to receive these goods (and the bill) against an open PO.

Click Yes to see the open POs for this vendor and select the appropriate one. The line items on the bill fill in automatically, and you can correct any quantity or price difference between your original PO and the actual one. When you save the transaction, QuickBooks receives the items into inventory in addition to posting the bill to your Accounts Payable account.

If no PO exists, enter the item quantities and amounts. When you save the transaction, QuickBooks receives the items into inventory in addition to posting the bill to Accounts Payable.

Recording Vendor Credits

When you record a credit from a vendor, you can apply it against an existing open bill or keep it unapplied so you can apply it to a future bill from that vendor. QuickBooks doesn't provide a separate enter credit window; instead, you can change a vendor bill form to a credit form with a click of the mouse by selecting the Credit option near the top of the Enter Bills window, which changes the fields on the form. Choose the vendor from the drop-down list and enter the date of the credit memo.

1. In the Ref. No. field, enter the vendor's credit memo number and the amount.
2. If the credit is not for inventory items, use the Expenses tab to assign an account and amount to this credit. If the credit is for inventory items, use the Items tab to enter the items, along with the quantity and cost, for which you are receiving this credit.
3. Click Save & Close to save the credit (unless you have more credits to enter—in which case, click Save & New).

Small Business Tip   If you receive a return authorization (RA) number, use that as the Ref. No. for your credit. This can help you keep track of when (or if) the actual credit memo is issued by the vendor. When the credit memo arrives, you can replace the QuickBooks Ref. No. with the actual credit memo number. Enter the original RA number in the Memo field for future reference in case there are any disputes.

Use Recurring Bills

Most businesses have at least a few recurring bills that need to be paid every month, such as the rent or mortgage payment, loan payments, or utilities bill. You can make it easy to pay those bills every month without entering a bill each time. QuickBooks provides a *memorized transactions* feature that you can put to work to make sure your recurring bills are covered.

Creating a Memorized Bill

To create a memorized transaction for a recurring bill, first open the Enter Bills window and fill out the information as you normally would. If the amount of a recurring bill isn't always exactly the same, it's okay to leave the Amount Due field blank, as you can fill in the amount each time you use the memorized bill. Before you save the transaction, click the Memorize button on the Enter Bills Main tab. The Memorize Transaction dialog opens.

1. Enter a name for the transaction. Even though QuickBooks enters the vendor name, you can change it to a name that describes the transaction.

2. Select Add To My Reminders List (the default) to tell QuickBooks to issue a reminder that this bill must be put into the system to be paid. Or select Do Not Remind Me if you want to enter the bill yourself. Or select Automate Transaction Entry to have QuickBooks enter this bill as a payable item without reminders. Specify the number of Days In Advance To Enter this bill. At the appropriate time, the bill appears in the Select Bills To Be Paid section of the Pay Bills window.

3. Select the interval for this bill from the drop-down list in the How Often field.

4. Enter the Next Date this bill is due. If this payment is finite, such as a loan that has a specific number of payments, use the Number Remaining field to specify how many times this bill must be paid.

5. Click OK in the Memorize Transaction dialog to save the information, and then click Save & Close in the Enter Bills window to save the bill. If you want to use the bill only to create a memorized version of it, you can cancel the transaction itself before saving it.

Using a Memorized Bill

If you choose to enter the memorized bill manually instead of having it automatically added to the Select Bills To Be Paid section, you must open it to make it a current payable item. To open a memorized bill, press CTRL-T to open the Memorized Transaction List window or, from the Lists menu, select Memorized Transaction List.

1. Double-click the appropriate listing to open the bill in the usual Enter Bills window with the next due date showing. If the Amount Due field is blank, fill it in.

2. Click Save & Close to save this bill so it becomes a current payable item and is listed as a bill that must be paid when you write checks to pay your bills.

Creating Memorized Bill Groups

If you have several memorized bills, all due the first of the month (rent, mortgage, utilities, car payments), you can create a group and QuickBooks will automatically take action on every bill in the group. To use this feature, follow these steps:

1. Press CTRL-T to display the Memorized Transaction List. Right-click any blank spot in the Memorized Transaction window and choose New Group from the shortcut menu.

2. In the New Memorized Transaction Group window, give this group a name (such as 1st Of Month or 15th Of Month).

3. Fill out the fields to specify the way you want to handle the bills in this group, and click OK to save this group.

After you create the group, you can add memorized transactions to it as follows:

1. In the Memorized Transaction List window, select the first memorized transaction you want to add to the group.
2. Right-click and choose Edit Memorized Transaction from the shortcut menu.
3. When the Schedule Memorized Transaction dialog opens with this transaction displayed, select the option Add To Group.
4. Select the group from the list that appears when you click the arrow next to the Group Name field and click OK.

Repeat this process for each bill you want to add to the group. As you create future memorized bills, just select the Add To Group option to add each bill to the appropriate group.

If you have other recurring bills with different criteria (perhaps they're due on a different day of the month, or they're due annually), create groups for them and add the individual transactions to the group.

Reimbursable Expenses

A reimbursable expense is an expense you incurred on behalf of a customer. Even though you pay the vendor's bill, you invoice the customer to recover your costs. There are two common types of reimbursable expenses:

- General expenses, such as long-distance telephone charges, parking and tolls, and other incidental expenses, incurred on behalf of a client. Those portions of the bill that apply to customer agreements for reimbursement are split out when you enter the bill.
- Specific goods or services that you purchase on behalf of the customer.

Options for Managing Reimbursable Expenses

There are two ways to manage reimbursable expenses:

- Enter and pay a bill (or enter a check). When you receive the customer's reimbursement, post it to the same expense account as the bill (or check). This reduces that expense total in your Profit & Loss statements.
- Enter and pay a bill (or enter a check), and then let QuickBooks automatically post the customer's reimbursement to an income account created specifically for this purpose to track totals for both expenses and reimbursements.

Consider discussing these options with your accountant.

To track reimbursed costs from customers, you need to enable reimbursement tracking in QuickBooks and create income accounts that are used for collecting reimbursements. To track reimbursable costs, enable the feature in the Preferences dialog.

1. Open the Preferences dialog and select the Time & Expenses icon in the left pane.
2. Click the Company Preferences tab.
3. In the Invoicing Options section of the dialog, select the Track Reimbursed Expenses As Income check box and click OK.
4. If you prefer to reduce your expense totals by posting reimbursements to the expense account used when you entered a bill, uncheck the Track Reimbursed Expenses As Income check box and click OK.

Applying Automatic Markups

The Time & Expenses Preferences window has an option for setting a default markup percentage. You can use this feature to have QuickBooks automatically mark up expenses you're linking to a customer for reimbursement. Be sure to select (or create) the default account that you want to use to track the income generated by the markup. Most businesses use something like "markup income."

The default markup percentage is unrelated to the option to track reimbursed expenses as income. You can apply this markup whether you're tracking reimbursed expenses as income or posting the reimbursements to the original expense account. You can also override any automatic markup that QuickBooks applies, so filling in a percentage in this field doesn't prevent you from setting up your own pricing formula for any individual item.

The markup percentage that you designate in the Time & Expenses Preferences window can also be applied to the products and services that you sell. Specifically, when you enter an amount in the Cost field when you're creating a new item or editing an existing one, QuickBooks will automatically fill in the item's Price field by marking up the cost with this percentage.

Setting Up Income Accounts for Reimbursement

When you enable the reimbursement tracking option, QuickBooks adds a new field to the dialog you use when you create or edit an expense account. You can configure an expense account so that reimbursements for the expense are posted to an income account. When you post a vendor expense to this account and indicate that the expense is reimbursable, the amount you charge to the customer when you create an invoice for that customer is automatically posted to the income account that's linked to this expense account.

You may want to use numerous expense accounts for reimbursable expenses, since portions of telephone bills, travel expenses, and other costs are often passed on to customers for reimbursement. The easiest way to manage all of this is to enable those expense accounts to track reimbursements and post the income from customers to one account named Reimbursed Expenses. However, QuickBooks requires a one-to-one relationship between a reimbursable expense and the reimbursement income from that expense. As a result, if you have multiple expense accounts for which you may receive reimbursement, you must also create multiple income accounts for accepting reimbursed expenses.

This is a one-time chore, however, so when you've finished setting up the accounts, you can just enter transactions, knowing QuickBooks will automatically post reimbursed expenses to your new income accounts. The best way to set up the income accounts you'll need for reimbursement is to use subaccounts. Then your reports will show the total amount of income due to reimbursed expenses, and you have individual account totals if you have some reason to audit a total.

If you don't already have an income account named Reimbursed Expenses, follow these steps to create the parent account:

1. Open the chart of accounts by pressing CTRL-A or click the Chart of Accounts icon on the Home page. Choose the Add New Account: Choose Account Type dialog, or press CTRL-N.
2. Select Income as the account type and click Continue.
3. In the Add New Account dialog, enter an account number (if you use numbers) and name the account Reimbursed Expenses (or something similar).
4. Click Save & New.

Once you create the parent account, you can create all the subaccounts you need, using the same steps you used to create the parent account. Don't forget to edit any of your existing expense accounts that you'll use to invoice customers for reimbursements. Select the account and press CTRL-E to open the account record in Edit mode. Then select the check box to track reimbursed expenses and enter the appropriate income account.

Recording Reimbursable Expenses

To be reimbursed by customers for expenses you incurred on their behalf, you must enter the appropriate data while you're filling out the vendor's bill (or writing a direct disbursement check to a vendor when you did not enter a bill). After you enter the account and the amount, click the arrow in the Customer: Job column and select the appropriate customer or job from the drop-down list. Charge portions of an expense to one or more customers by splitting the total expense among those customers when you enter the vendor bill.

Entering data in the Customer: Job column automatically places a check box with a check mark inserted in the Billable? column. The expense is charged to the customer, and you can pass the charge along to the customer when you create an invoice. Uncheck the check box if you don't want to bill the customer for the expense but you still want to track what you're spending for the customer or the job. This disables the reimbursement feature, but the expense is still associated with the customer/job so that you can track job costs.

Pay Your Bills

When it's time to pay your bills, you may find that you don't have the cash or credit available to pay every bill that's entered, or even to pay the entire amount due for each bill. There are many opinions about how to decide what to pay when money is tight, and the term "essential vendors" is often used in such cases. "Essential" can be a subjective term, since having electricity can be just as important as buying inventory items. Check with your accountant, but here are some ideas: Pay the government and taxes first and never use payroll withholding money to pay bills. When possible, it's better to send multiple vendors small checks than to send a large payment only to a couple of vendors who have been applying pressure. Vendors dislike being ignored much more than they dislike small payments on an account.

Viewing Your Unpaid Bills

In addition to the new Bill Tracker dashboard, QuickBooks provides reports for you to learn more about your vendor bills. For example, to see a list of each unpaid bill totaled by vendor, choose Reports | Vendors & Payables | Unpaid Bills Detail. By default, the report is sorted by vendor name, but you can re-sort the list using the Sort By field by Date, Due Date, or Open Balance. Often, choosing to sort by Due Date or Aging is helpful as you decide which bills need urgent attention.

Double-click any entry to see the original bill you entered, including all line items and notes you made in the Memo column.

You can filter the report to display only certain bills by clicking Customize Report and selecting the Filters tab in the Modify Report dialog. Use the filters to change what's displayed in the report.

When you're ready to tell QuickBooks which bills you want to pay, choose Vendors | Pay Bills. In the Pay Bills window, make your selections by placing a check mark next to the bills you want to pay, as seen in Figure 6-5. You can also choose which open bills to work with in this window by using the following filters:

- **Due On Or Before** Displays all the bills due on or before the date displayed. The default date is ten days from the current date.
- **Show All Bills** Shows all the bills in your system, regardless of when they're due.
- **A/P Account** When you use multiple Accounts Payable accounts, a drop-down menu appears. If you don't have multiple Accounts Payable accounts, this field doesn't appear in the window.
- **Filter By** Lets you choose to see open bills for a particular vendor or all vendors.
- **Sort By** Enables you to sort by Due Date (the default), Discount Date, Vendor, and Amount Due.

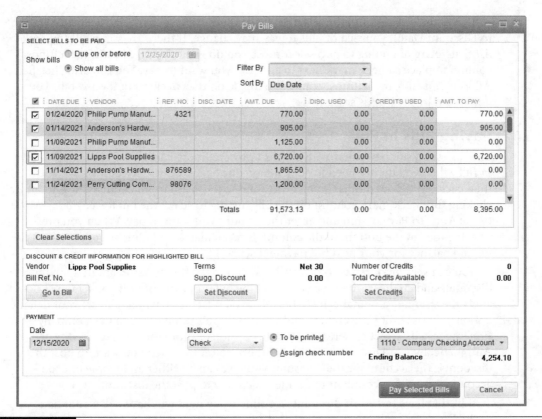

FIGURE 6-5   Quickly choose what bills to pay in the Pay Bills window.

The following fields are in the Payment section of the Pay Bills window:

- **Date**   This date appears on your checks. By default, it is the current date, but you can change it. Tell QuickBooks to date checks on the day of printing by changing the Checking Preferences. If you merely select the bills today and wait until later to print the checks, the payment date set here still appears on the checks.

- **Method**   The drop-down list displays Check and Credit Card by default. If you pay by printing QuickBooks checks, be sure to select the To Be Printed option.

When you finish selecting payments, click the Pay Selected Bills button. The Payment Summary dialog opens, where you can choose when to print the checks. If you prepare checks manually, select Assign Check Number, and when you click the Pay Selected Bills button, QuickBooks opens the Assign Check Numbers dialog so you can specify the starting check number for this bill-paying session. The Account drop-down list displays the checking or credit card account you want to use for these payments.

If you made changes to the selection fields (perhaps you changed the Sort By option to Discount Date), your list of bills to pay may change. If there are some bills on the list that you're not going to pay, select those you do want to pay. Click in the leftmost column to place a check mark next to each bill you want to pay. You can also click Select All Bills and click the leftmost column to toggle off the check mark for any bills you don't want to pay in this session.

Paying Bills in Full

The easiest bills to pay either with checks or by credit card are those you want to pay in full, when you do not need to consider credits or discounts. Select the bills, and then click Pay Selected Bills. If you don't want to pay a bill in full, adjust the amount by clicking the check mark column on the bill's listing to select the bill for payment. Move to the Amt. To Pay column and enter the amount you want to pay. When you press TAB, the total at the bottom of the column is recalculated and QuickBooks reserves the unpaid balance for your next bill payment session.

You can set a preference to determine if you make the decision about applying discounts and credits at the time you select the bill for payment or if you let QuickBooks apply the amounts automatically to bills that you select for payment. To set your default options, choose Edit | Preferences and select Bills on the left pane. In the Company Preferences tab, select either or both of the options Automatically Use Credits or Automatically Use Discounts, and enter the account to which you want to post the discounts. The account for the discounts you take can be either an income or expense account. Ask your accountant to decide which way to post the discount.

Bills that have terms for discounts for timely payment will have a discount date in the Disc. Date column. If you enabled automatic application of discounts and credits, when you select the bill by clicking the check mark column, the discount is automatically applied. You can see the amount in the Disc. Used column; the Amt. To Pay column also adjusts accordingly.

If you're making a partial payment and want to adjust the discount, click the Set Discount button to open the Discount And Credits window and enter the amount of the discount you want to take. Click Done, and when you return to the Pay Bills window, the discount is applied and the Amt. To Pay column has the correct amount.

To take a discount after the discount date, select the bill for payment, and then click the Set Discount button to open the Discount And Credits window. The amount showing for the discount is zero. Enter the discount you would be entitled to if you paid the bill in a timely fashion and click Done.

Applying Credits

If you set the preference for QuickBooks to take credits automatically, when you select a bill for payment for which vendor credits exist, the amount of the credit appears in the Credits Used column, and the Amt. To Pay column is adjusted. If credits are applied automatically and you don't want to take the credit against this bill (perhaps you want to save it for another bill), click Set Credits to open the Discount And Credits window. Deselect the credit and click Done.

If you didn't enable automatic credit application, when you select the bill, the amount of existing credits appears below the list of bills. Click Set Credits to open the Discount And Credits window. Make the appropriate selections of credit amounts, and click Done to change the Amt. To Pay column to reflect your adjustments. If your total credits with the vendor are equal to or exceed the bill you select, QuickBooks does not create a check because the bill is paid in its entirety with credits.

Printing and Sending Bill Payments

When you finish selecting the bills to pay, click Pay Selected Bills. If you chose the option to print checks, QuickBooks displays a Payment Summary dialog. Choose your next step from these choices:

- Choose Pay More Bills to return to the Pay Bills window and select other bills to pay or choose Print Checks to print your checks now.
- Click Done to close the Payment Summary dialog, close the Pay Bills window, and print your checks later.

When you defer check printing, the bill payment checks are posted to the bank account register with the notation "To Print." Choose File | Print Forms | Checks to print your checks. If you selected the Assign Check Number option because you manually write checks, QuickBooks displays the Assign Check Numbers dialog. If you select the option Let QuickBooks Assign Check Numbers, QuickBooks looks at the last check number used in the bank register and begins numbering with the next available number. If you select the option Let Me Assign The Check Numbers Below, enter the check numbers in the dialog.

When you click OK, QuickBooks opens the Payment Summary dialog that displays the payments. Click Pay More Bills if you want to return to the Pay Bills window, or click Done if you're finished paying bills. If you're paying bills online, select the Online Payment option when you select those bills. QuickBooks holds the information until you go online.

Check Writing Without Entering a Bill

You can record and print a check in QuickBooks without first entering a bill. If you use manual checks, you can write your checks and then tell QuickBooks about it later, or you can bring your checkbook to your computer and enter the checks in QuickBooks as you write them. You have two ways to enter these checks in QuickBooks: directly in the bank register or in the Write Checks window.

From the Register

Open the register and enter the check directly in a transaction line. Do the following:

1. Enter the date and press TAB to move to the Number field. QuickBooks automatically fills in the next available check number.
2. Press TAB to fill in the rest of the fields and click the Record button to save the transaction.
3. Repeat the steps until you have recorded all of your manual checks.

From the Write Checks Window

Use the Write Checks window to tell QuickBooks about a check you manually prepared. You can access this window in several ways:

- Click Write Checks on the Home page.
- From the QuickBooks menu bar, select Banking | Write Checks.
- Press CTRL-W.

Whichever method you choose, when the Write Checks transaction window opens, in the Bank Account section, select the bank account you're using to write the checks.

The next available check number appears unless the Print Later option box is checked (uncheck it to have QuickBooks add the number, or leave it checked and type in the number yourself). QuickBooks warns you if you enter a check number that's already been used. Fill out the check, posting amounts to the appropriate accounts. If the check is for inventory items, use the Items tab to make sure the items are placed into inventory. When you finish, click Save & New to open a new blank check. When you're through writing checks, click Save & Close to close the Write Checks transaction window. All the checks you wrote are recorded in the bank account register.

If you pay your bills by printing checks from the Write Checks window and have selected the Print Later box on the toolbar for each check, QuickBooks saves the checks to be printed in a batch instead of one at a time. After all the checks are entered, click Save & Close, and then choose File | Print Forms | Checks from the menu bar. Or, in the last Write Checks window, click the arrow at the bottom of the Print button, located on the toolbar, and choose Batch.

Using QuickBooks to Print Checks

If you want to print your checks from within QuickBooks instead of creating checks manually, you must use checks that are designed specifically for QuickBooks. You can order several check types from Intuit by choosing Banking | Order Checks & Envelopes | Order Checks.

To configure your printer to manage check printing, choose File | Printer Setup from the menu bar. Select Check as the form, and then select the printer you're using for checks.

You have to select a check style that matches your purchased check style. Three styles are available for QuickBooks checks, and a sample of each style appears in the dialog:

- Voucher checks have a detachable section on the check form. QuickBooks prints voucher information on the bottom of the check, including the name of the payee, the date, and the individual amounts of the bills being paid by this check. The check is the width of a regular business envelope.
- Standard checks are just basic checks. They're the width of a regular business envelope (usually called a *#10 envelope*), and if you use a laser or inkjet printer to print the checks, three checks fit on each page. Continuous (dot-matrix) feed printers just keep rolling, since the checks are printed on a continuous sheet with perforations separating the checks.
- Wallet checks are narrower than the other two styles so they fit in your wallet. The paper size is the same as the other checks so you can print, but there's a perforation on the left edge of the check so you can tear the ledger portion off the check.

Adding a Logo and Signature and Changing Fonts

If your checks have no preprinted logo and you have a graphics file of your company logo, select Use Logo or click the Logo button to open the Logo dialog. Click the File button to locate the graphics file. There's also a selection box for printing your company name and address, but when you buy checks, you should have that information preprinted.

Click the Fonts tab in the Printer Setup window to choose different fonts for printed checks. Use the Font button to change the font for all check information, with the exception of your company's name and address. To change the font for this information, click the Address Font button. Click the appropriate button and then choose a font, a font style, and a size from the dialog that opens.

Handling Partial Check Pages on Laser and Inkjet Printers

If you're printing to a laser or inkjet printer, you don't have the advantage that a continuous feed printer provides—printing a check and stopping, leaving the next blank check waiting in the printer for the next time you print checks. See the Partial Page tab to solve this issue. The solution that matches your printer's capabilities is preselected.

Aligning the Printout

Click the Align button to print a sample check and see where the printing lines up on the physical check. You can move the starting points for printing up/down or left/right to make sure everything prints where it's supposed to. When you're finished, click OK in the Printer Setup window to save the configuration data.

Printing Checks in Batches

You can print all your checks batches after you've completed the task of creating them. If you've been working in the Write Checks window, click the Save & New button to continue to create checks. When you're finished, on the last check, click Save, and then click the arrow below the Print icon on the check window and select Batch. You can also click Save & Close when you create the last check, and then choose File | Print Forms | Checks to print the batch.

Either option opens the Select Checks To Print dialog, shown here.

✓	DATE	PAYEE	AMOUNT	
✓	12/01/2019	Wholesale Supply Store	20.00	
✓	02/20/2020	Rand Business Supply Ce...	75.80	
✓	02/20/2020	Express Overnight Shipping	166.00	
✓	02/20/2020	Fran's Fasteners	275.00	
✓	02/20/2020	Lipps Pool Supplies	3,024.90	

Select Checks to Print dialog. Bank Account 1110 · Company Checking... First Check Number 30103. Order Checks. Select Checks to print, then click OK. There are 31 Checks to print for $88,499.69. Buttons: OK, Cancel, Help, Select All, Select None.

By default, all the unprinted checks are selected for printing, but you can deselect checks and they remain in the batch and will be waiting for you the next time you print checks. Click OK to open the Print Checks window.

If your checks were written on different bank accounts, the Select Checks To Print window displays only the checks ready for printing for a specific bank account. Don't forget to put the correct checks in your printer.

If you use the Pay Bills window to create checks for vendors, when you finish selecting the bills and amounts to pay, click Pay Selected Bills. If you selected the To Be Printed option, QuickBooks displays a Payment Summary window with a Print Checks button. If you selected the Assign Check Number option, you're asked to assign a check number in the Assign Check Numbers dialog before you see the summary.

- If these are the only checks you're creating at the moment, click Print Checks.
- If you have additional checks to print, you can click Done and print all your checks at once from the File menu, as described earlier in this section.

In the Print Checks dialog, click Print to begin printing your checks. When all the checks have been sent to the printer, QuickBooks displays the Print Checks – Confirmation window. If all the checks printed correctly, click OK.

Reprinting Checks After a Problem

Sometimes things go awry when you're printing. The paper jams, your printer runs out of toner, or an ink cartridge is empty. If there is a problem, select the check(s) that didn't print properly in the Print Checks – Confirmation window, click OK, and put more checks into the printer. Then click OK and choose File | Print Forms | Checks.

Your unprinted checks are listed in the Select Checks To Print dialog, and the first check number should be the next available check number—if it's not, you can change it.

Track and Pay Sales Tax

You have to turn in all sales tax you have collected to your state's taxing authorities. Instead of using the Pay Bills feature to do this, QuickBooks uses a special system to track and pay sales taxes. Many states have county, city, or parish tax authorities, each with its own rate. Businesses in those states may have to remit the sales tax they collect to all of these authorities, and the sales tax a customer pays is the total of all the taxes from these various tax authorities. As a result, tracking sales tax properly can be a complicated process. The following assumes you've created the sales tax items you need and each item is linked to the appropriate tax authority vendor.

Managing Sales Tax

The Manage Sales Tax feature acts as a "home page" for information and help and offers links to reports and payment forms covered in this section. You can open the Manage Sales Tax window, shown next, by choosing Vendors | Sales Tax | Manage Sales Tax. The menu commands needed to access features and functions are discussed in the following sections, but you can use the links on the Manage Sales Tax window for some of those chores.

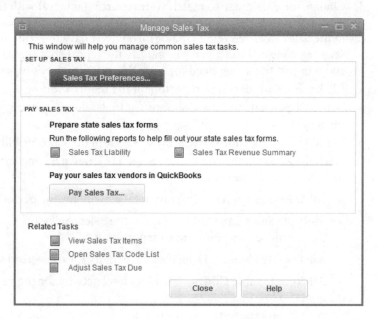

Running Sales Tax Reports

At the intervals determined by your taxing authority, you need to report your total sales, your nontaxable sales, and your taxable sales, along with any other required breakdowns. Of course, you also have to write a sales tax payment check or checks to remit the taxes.

Sales Tax Liability Report

QuickBooks has reports to help you fill out your sales tax forms. Choose Vendors | Sales Tax | Sales Tax Liability. Use the Dates drop-down list to select an interval that matches the way you report to the taxing authorities. QuickBooks chooses the interval you configured in the Preferences dialog, but that interval may apply to your primary sales tax only. If you collect multiple taxes due at different intervals, you must create a separate report with the appropriate interval to display those figures.

Tax Code Reports

If you have to report specific types of taxable or nontaxable sales, you can obtain that information by creating a report on the tax code you created for that purpose.

1. Choose Lists | Sales Tax Code List and select the tax code for which you need a report.
2. Press CTRL-Q to see a report on the sales activity with this tax code.
3. Change the date range to match your reporting interval with the sales tax authority (this isn't a sales tax report, so QuickBooks doesn't automatically match the settings in the Sales Tax Preferences dialog). You don't have to create these reports one sales tax code at a time; you can modify the report so it reports all of your sales tax codes or just those you need for a specific tax authority's report.
4. Click the Customize Report button on the report window.
5. In the Display tab, use the Columns list to deselect any items you don't require for the report.
6. In the Filters tab, choose Sales Tax Code from the Current Filter Choices list.
7. Click the arrow to the right of the Sales Tax Code field and from the drop-down list, choose from these options:
   - **All Sales Tax Codes**   Displays total activity for the period for every code.
   - **Multiple Sales Tax Codes**   Opens the Select Sales Tax Code window; select the specific codes you want to report on.
   - **All Taxable Codes**   Displays total activity for the period for each taxable code.
   - **All Non-Taxable Codes**   Displays total activity for the period for each nontaxable code.
8. Click OK to return to the report window.

Pay the Sales Tax

After you check the figures, it's time to pay the tax, using the following steps:

1. Choose Vendors | Sales Tax | Pay Sales Tax to open the Pay Sales Tax dialog. In the Pay From Account drop-down, select the bank account to use.

2. Check the date that's displayed in the Show Sales Tax Due Through field. It must match the end date of your current reporting period (for instance, monthly or quarterly).

3. Click in the Pay column to insert a check mark next to those items you're paying now. If you have the same reporting interval for all taxing authorities, just click the Pay All Tax button (the label changes to Clear Selections).

4. If you're going to print the check, be sure to select the To Be Printed check box at the bottom of the dialog. If you write the check manually, or if you remit sales tax online using an electronic transfer from your bank, uncheck the To Be Printed check box. Then, insert the check number of your manual check, or remove the check number entirely and enter **EFT** (for Electronic Funds Transfer) in the Starting Check No. field.

5. Click OK when you've finished filling out the information.

Small Business Tip   Don't use the bank account register or Write Checks window to pay sales taxes. Such payments do not correctly apply to your sales tax reports. Instead, use the Pay Sales Tax method described in this section.

Adjusting Sales Tax Amounts

You can adjust the amount of sales tax due at any time. To do this, select the appropriate sales tax item in the Pay Sales Tax window and click the Adjust button to open the Sales Tax Adjustment dialog.

Specify the amount by which to reduce the amount due. You may also need to increase the amount due, if necessary. Specify an Adjustment Account and click OK to return to the Pay Sales Tax dialog, where the amount has changed to reflect your adjustment.

Working with Bank and Credit Card Accounts

In this chapter:

- Working with transfers and other monies

- How to handle petty cash

- Recording and tracking credit card transactions

- Understanding the important reconciliation process

- Finding and correcting balancing issues

You can enter most transactions easily in your bank and credit card accounts. However, in some situations you may need to account for your entries differently. Also, reconciling bank and credit card accounts, although one of the most important tasks connected with financial record keeping, is, sadly, one of the most avoided tasks. When you use QuickBooks, however, the job of reconciling your accounts becomes a very manageable one. This chapter covers how to deal with banking and credit card transactions that are not simply receiving and paying funds, and how to verify that your QuickBooks accounts match your bank and credit card statements. In Chapter 8, you'll learn about downloading your information directly into QuickBooks.

Deposit Money That Isn't from Customers

Even though QuickBooks takes care of recording the deposits into your bank account when you receive money from customers, sometimes you may receive money that's unconnected to a customer payment. This might be rebate checks from manufacturers or stores; infusion of capital from an owner or partner; or a loan from an owner, partner, officer, or bank, for example.

You can use one of two ways to deposit noncustomer payments into your bank account. If the deposit is the only deposit you're making and it will appear on your statement as an individual deposit, you can record the deposit directly in the bank account register. If you're going to deposit the check along with other checks, use the Make Deposits window.

Using the Account Register for Deposits

To work directly in the bank account register, open the register by choosing Banking | Use Register, and select the appropriate bank account from the Use Register dialog, shown here.

When the account register window opens, the Date field in next available transaction line is highlighted and the current date is displayed. To record the deposit directly into the bank account, follow these steps:

1. Change the date if necessary, and then press TAB to move to the Number field.
2. Delete the check number if one automatically appears (or wait until you enter the amount in the Deposit column, at which point QuickBooks deletes the check number).

3. Press TAB to move to the Deposit column, or click in the Deposit column and enter the amount of the deposit.

4. Move to the Account field and assign the deposit to the appropriate account. Use the Memo field to enter an explanation in case your accountant asks you about the deposit.

5. Click the Record button.

Small Business Tip From anywhere in QuickBooks, use the shortcut keys CTRL-R TO open the Use Register dialog and choose your bank account register. From within the Banking menu, use the SHIFT-R keyboard shortcut combination to open the Use Register dialog. And, to open the Banking menu, from anywhere in QuickBooks, use the ALT-B keyboard combination.

Using the Make Deposits Window

Sometimes it's better to use the Make Deposits window for a deposit that's not related to a customer payment (such as a rebate from a vendor) because you're planning to deposit the check along with other checks, and you want your deposit records to match the bank statement. In this case, follow these steps:

1. Choose Banking | Make Deposits to open the Payments To Deposit window.

2. Select the deposits you're taking to the bank by clicking to the left of each check. Note that the check you want to deposit (for a noncustomer payment) is not listed here because the window shows only the money you've received through customer payment transactions.

3. Click OK to move to the Make Deposits window.

4. Click either in the From Account column of the blank line under the last entry or in the Received From column if you need to track the payee (which is optional), as shown in Figure 7-1.

5. Select the account to which you want this deposit to be posted, or enter data in the Memo, Chk No., and Pmt Meth. columns. (Don't forget the Class field if classes apply to this item.)

6. Enter the amount. Your check is added to the total of the deposit you're making. You can, if necessary, enter a payee name in the Received From column, but QuickBooks doesn't require that. Most of the time, a payee isn't needed. For example, if you're depositing a rebate on a purchase you made, there's a good chance the company that wrote the check doesn't exist in your QuickBooks system, and there's no point in adding a name you don't need to produce reports about.

	Make Deposits	— □ X

◆ Previous ◆ Next 🖫 Save 🖨 Print ▼ | 🖳 Payments 🗐 History | 🗐 Attach

Deposit To [Company Chec ▼] Date [12/15/2020 📅] Memo [Deposit]

Click Payments to select customer payments that you have received. List any other amounts to deposit below.

RECEIVED FROM	FROM ACCOUNT	MEMO	CHK...	PMT ...	C...	AMOUNT
Thompson Lighting Stores	Undeposited Funds					800.00
Baker's Professional Lig...	Undeposited Funds					680.48
Norton Discount Wareho...	Printing and Reproduction	refund for annual flyer	87125	Check		150.00

	Deposit Subtotal	1,630.48

To get cash back from this deposit, enter the amount below. Indicate the account where you want this money to go, such as your Petty Cash account.

Cash back goes to [▼]   Cash back memo [ ]   Cash back amount [ ]

	Deposit Total	1,630.48

[Save & Close] [Save & New] [Clear]

FIGURE 7-1 Add any noncustomer item to the Make Deposits window.

Noncustomer Deposits

If the money is from an owner or partner, the name should exist in your system in the Other Names list. If the money is from a corporate officer, that officer probably exists as an employee, but don't use the employee name for this transaction. Instead, create the name in the Other Names list to track this deposit. Because you can't have duplicate names in QuickBooks, many users add an extra letter or symbol to the existing name, such as "O" for officer.

If you're depositing the proceeds of a bank loan, you'll need a vendor, because you'll be writing checks to pay back the principal and interest. If you're depositing your own money into the business and the business is a proprietorship or partnership, that's capital and you should post the deposit from a capital account, which is an equity account. If you're depositing the proceeds of a loan—from either yourself as a corporate officer or from a bank—post the deposit from the liability account for the loan. Keep in mind that you may have to create this liability account. If you're making a deposit that's a refund from a vendor, you can post the amount to the expense account that was used for the original expense.

If you type a payee name that doesn't exist in any of your names lists, QuickBooks displays a Name Not Found message (seen next) offering you the following selections:

- **Quick Add**   Lets you enter the name only after choosing a Name Type (Vendor, Customer, or Employee, for example)
- **Set Up**   Lets you create a new name using the regular New Name window
- **Cancel**   Returns you to the original window you were working in so you can either choose another name or delete the name of the nonexistent payee

If you select Quick Add or Set Up, you're asked which type of name you're adding: Vendor, Customer, Employee, or Other. Unless this payee will become a vendor or customer, choose Other.

Transfer Funds Between Accounts

It is common to move money between bank accounts. If you have a bank account for payroll, you have to move money out of your operating account into your payroll account every payday. Some people deposit all the customer payments into an interest-bearing money market or savings account and then transfer the necessary funds to an operating account when it's time to pay bills. Others do it the other way around, moving money not immediately needed from the business operating account to a money market account. Lawyers, agents, real estate brokers, and other professionals have to maintain trust and escrow accounts and move money between them and the operating account. You can use either of those two methods to transfer funds between accounts.

Using the Transfer Funds Transaction Window

QuickBooks offers a Transfer Funds feature, which is the best solution to record a "noncheck" transfer of funds between bank accounts that are at the same (or even different) banks. (The Transfer Funds feature also works if you write a check.) To transfer money between accounts using the Transfer Funds transaction window, follow these steps:

1. Choose Banking | Transfer Funds from the menu bar to open the Transfer Funds Between Accounts dialog.
2. Enter information in the fields.
3. Click Save & Close (or Save & New if you have another transfer to make).

QuickBooks posts the transaction (it is marked as "TRANSFR" in both bank accounts when you open their registers) without affecting any totals in your financial reports. All the work is done on the Balance Sheet, but the bottom line of your Balance Sheet doesn't change because money was neither added to nor removed from your company.

Handle a Returned Check

When you receive, post, and deposit a check from a customer for payment on an open invoice, QuickBooks performs two tasks for you: it reduces your accounts receivable account, and it increases your bank account in the same amount. A week later, when your bank notifies you that your customer's check has been returned, you also need to record that event in QuickBooks to keep both your accounts receivable and bank balance up to date. You may also need to record a returned check taken on a sales receipt (cash sale) or for a deposit that was recorded directly in your bank account register. QuickBooks handles the recording of these events differently.

Recording a Returned Customer Invoice Payment

When you receive notice of a returned customer payment (a "bounced" payment), your first step is to locate the original Receive Payments transaction in QuickBooks. If it is a fairly recent transaction, you can open the Receive Payments window by selecting Customers | Receive Payments and click the left-pointing blue arrow (located above the Find button in the Main tab of the Receive Payments window) until you see the payment. You can also click the Find button to open the Find dialog and search for the payment by customer name, payment amount, or date. Once you've located the bounced payment, follow these steps:

1. Click the Record Bounced Check button located on the Main tab of the Receive Payments window to open the Manage Bounced Check dialog shown here. If the Record Bounced Check button is disabled (grayed out), see "Record Bounced Check Button Not Available or Disabled" later in this chapter.

2. Enter the date and the fee that your bank has assessed you for the returned check and confirm the expense account for that bank fee. If you're using class tracking, you can assign a class (which should be the same class that was used on the invoice transaction that this payment relates to).

3. Enter the fee that you want to charge your customer. When determining this fee, consider the extra time and effort you or your staff are expending on behalf of this customer. Then click Next.

4. Review the Bounced Check Summary (see here) that confirms the following for you:

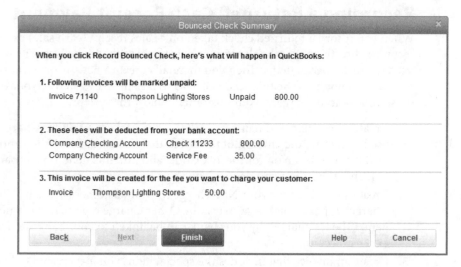

• The original invoice(s) that will now be marked as unpaid

• The amounts that QuickBooks will deduct from your bank account for both the amount of the bounced check and the returned check fee your bank assessed

• That an invoice will be created by QuickBooks for the amount of the returned check fee you want to charge your customer

5. Click Finish to accept the transactions and complete the process. The original customer payment window will now have a "Bounced Check!" watermark.

6. If your customer asks you to redeposit the payment, create a new Receive Payments transaction (with the date of the redeposit) so that you're treating it as if it were a new check. This method will help you keep your records straight and maintain better detail when running customer statements and balance detail reports.

Record Bounced Check Button Not Available or Disabled

If you have followed the previous directions and are not able to access the Record Bounced Check button, ensure the following:

• The payment method/type of your original payment was "Check" and the check number is recorded.

- The check in question is selected in the Payment window.
- The check actually was deposited.
- The check was not bundled with Undeposited Checks and no longer appears in the Payments To Deposit window.

Once you have fixed any of the above issues, the Record Bounced Check button should be available to you.

Recording a Returned Cash Receipt Payment

When you record a returned check taken on a sales receipt (cash sale) or for a deposit recorded directly in your bank account register or in the Make Deposits window, you need to create special items. Then you manually create a new invoice transaction to record the amount of the bounced check as well as the fees you owe your bank and those you want to charge to your customer. Follow these steps:

1. Create a new item and name it "NSF Check." Make it an Other Charge type that's used to capture the amount of the check that bounced. Leave the Amount Or % field blank, select Non for the Tax Code, and link this item to your bank account (whichever account you deposit your checks into).

2. Create a new item for your NSF charge to your customer (name it "NSF Service Charge," for example). Again, use the Other Charge type as this is a nontaxable item. (The fee charged by your bank can be linked to your bank service charge expense account).

3. Create an invoice that includes the special items you just created to handle bounced checks. Be sure the date reflects the date that the payment was returned. When (or if) the new payment arrives, you'll use the Receive Payments window to record the customer's payment.

When you enter the NSF item on the invoice, it credits the bank account, which, in effect, reverses the amount of the original deposit of the check. It also provides both transactions in the Reconcile window when your statement arrives so you can reconcile each entry.

As a final step, don't forget to record the fee that your bank is charging you for your customer's bounced check. The easiest way to record this fee is directly in your bank account register. Simply enter the date and the amount of the fee in the Payment column with a note about the NSF charge in the Memo field.

Void a Check

If a check isn't going to clear your bank, you should void it rather than delete it. Deleting (versus voiding) a check removes all history of the transaction from your register. This is not a good way to keep financial records, especially in the event of an audit. Voiding a check keeps the check number but sets the amount to zero.

The way QuickBooks completes the process of voiding a check differs based on how the check was used. The process starts the same way, however, by opening the bank account register and selecting the disbursement that you want to void. Next, right-click to open the shortcut menu and choose Void Check. If the check to be voided is *not from a closed period*, the check amount is set to zero and the check marked void. As an additional help, put the date you are voiding this check next to the other information, as seen in the next illustration. As you click anywhere in the register window, a message appears warning you that this can affect your financial reports:

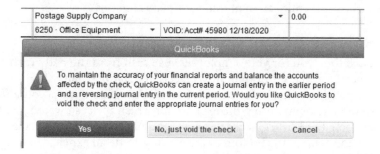

Clicking No keeps the check number along with its current date and then simply sets the amount of the check to zero without making any adjustments to a prior period.

When you're voiding a check that is posted to an asset or liability account, the offer for the automatic journal entries is not made. The check is simply adjusted to zero. Click Record to save the transaction.

Track Cash Disbursements

Most businesses make some purchases with cash. Because the amount is usually small (or "petty"), these minor expenses are often difficult to track. It's not uncommon for receipts to get lost or for cash on hand for the business to disappear. Whether the cash you use in your business is from a petty cash box or from an ATM machine, QuickBooks can help you keep track of every penny.

Keeping a Petty Cash Box

Many businesses keep a petty cash box so they have money on hand to cover such things as a quick trip to the office supply store or the post office. When you decide to keep cash on hand, you must first put money into your petty cash box. Then you need to keep track of how the cash taken *out* of the box is spent, and then you have to put more money into the box to replace what's been spent. When you put money in the cash box, you tell QuickBooks about it by recording a deposit transaction into your petty cash account.

Create a new Bank type account called Petty Cash. If you use account numbers, use a number that fits in with your other bank accounts. Leave the opening balance of the petty cash account at zero, as the beginning balance appears when you make your first deposit into this account.

Putting Money into Petty Cash

Most of the time, you'll write a check (and cash it) to petty cash from your bank account. You can create the name "Petty Cash" in the Vendor or Other Names list. You can use the Write Checks window to do this, or enter the deposit directly in the petty cash account register. Be sure to enter the check number you used in the number field. Cash the check and put the entire amount into your petty cash box.

Recording Petty Cash Expenses

Each time you (or your employees) use cash from the petty cash box, ensure that a receipt for that same amount is placed in the box. Then, when you need to replenish the petty cash box, write a check from your regular bank account for the amount of the reimbursement, noting the expense for which the cash was expended. The advantage of using the Write Checks window (and not the petty cash register) is that you can use the fields at the bottom of the window to tie an expense to a customer or a class for job-costing purposes. Note that you are writing the check for the exact amount of the receipts. That check and the amount of money left in the petty cash box should be the same as the amount shown in your petty cash account on your Balance Sheet.

Tracking Other Cash Withdrawals

Many businesses use ATM and debit cards in their day-to-day transactions. These transactions usually withdraw money from your checking account. However, ATM /debit card transactions can differ from writing checks in that the amount withdrawn often does not have a specific expense attached to it at the time it's withdrawn. To track these amounts, consider creating a special bank account type to post to when recording a debit or ATM withdrawal from your bank account. Then, as the person who made the withdrawal begins handing in receipts, you can debit the appropriate expense account directly from this account's register.

Manage Credit Card Transactions

When you use a credit card to make purchases for your business, you can create a credit card account or treat the credit card as a bill.

Create a Credit Card Account

With this option, you create a credit card account on your Balance Sheet that has its own register and to which you will post individual transactions. The advantage of this method is that, as with your bank account, you can perform a reconciliation of this account and use online banking to download transactions from your credit card company.

To create a credit card account, with the chart of accounts list open, press CTRL-N to open the Add New Account window. Then do the following:

1. Select Credit Card as the account type and click Continue. Enter the name of the credit card (usually the card issuer's name).
2. Enter an account number if you're using account numbers. Optionally, enter a credit card number, which is required if you'll be using online banking, as covered in Chapter 8.
3. Click Save & Close.

You can now enter individual transactions into your account in one of two ways: select Banking | Enter Credit Card Charges to enter your transactions in the Enter Credit Card Charges window, as shown in Figure 7-2 and described next, or enter transactions directly into the credit card account register.

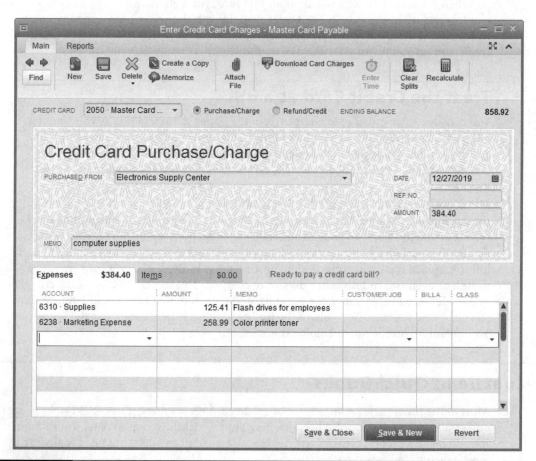

FIGURE 7-2   Use the Enter Credit Card Charges window to record charges on your credit cards.

To use the Enter Credit Card Charges window, select Banking | Enter Credit Card Charges. Then do the following:

1. From the drop-down menu in the Credit Card field, select the credit card to which you want to post transactions.
2. Select either the Purchase/Charge or Refund/Credit option.
3. In the Purchased From field, enter the name where the card was used, if you choose.
4. Enter the date of the transaction or fill in the Ref No. field with the reference number found on the credit card statement.
5. Enter the amount of the charge for each expense category.
6. Use the Expenses tab to add general expenses, or use the Items tab if the transaction was for the purchase of an item for inventory or for a customer. If you track classes, assign the transaction to the appropriate class.

When it's time to make a payment on this card, you will use the Write Checks window and fill in the Pay To The Order Of field with the credit card company name. In the Account column (on the Expenses tab), instead of an expense account, select the *credit card account* from your chart of accounts.

Treat the Credit Card as a Bill

You can also enter credit card charges from the paper statement just as you would a bill from any vendor. Select Vendors | Enter Bills, and then list each transaction that appears on the statement (including any finance charges) in the Expenses tab for general expenses, or use the Items tab if the transaction was for the purchase of an inventory item.

The advantage of this method is that in addition to your charges being posted to the appropriate expense account as you enter the bill, any amount outstanding on the card is included as part of your Accounts Payable account and listed on your reports as such. The drawback of this method, however, is that if you wait for your credit card bill to arrive in the mail, you could be posting these individual credit card charges a month or even two months after they were charged. This can be an issue if the charges you made were in December, for example, and your statement arrives in January, the start of a new tax year. Be aware of the timing of these expenses and consult with your accountant if you choose to employ this method.

Reconcile in QuickBooks

Most of the time, performing a bank or credit card reconciliation in QuickBooks is easy and straightforward. If you've been keeping your QuickBooks up to date, you shouldn't have to make a lot of "catch-up" entries because most of the data you need is already in your bank or credit card register.

The Begin Reconciliation Window

Start with the Begin Reconciliation window, seen next, which opens when you click Banking | Reconcile. If you have several bank or credit card accounts, select the account you want to reconcile from the drop-down list in the Account field.

Enter the statement date from your bank statement, and then check the Beginning Balance field in the window against the beginning balance on the bank statement. (Your bank may call it the *starting balance*.) If the beginning balances match, enter the ending balance from your statement in the Ending Balance field. If this is the *first* time you're reconciling the bank account in QuickBooks, your Beginning Balance field in QuickBooks will automatically be zero. Enter the ending balance from your statement in the Ending Balance field in QuickBooks. If the beginning balances don't match and this is not the first time you're reconciling the bank account in QuickBooks, see "Troubleshooting Differences in the Beginning Balance" later in this chapter, and then return to this section of the chapter to perform the reconciliation.

Entering Interest Income and Service Charges

Enter any service charge or interest shown on the statement in the Begin Reconciliation window and choose the appropriate accounts for posting. If you use the Bank Feeds feature (aka online banking) and the interest payments and bank charges have already been downloaded and entered, do *not* enter them again in the Begin Reconciliation window. They'll be in the register list you see in the next window, and you can clear them as you clear checks and deposits.

Use the Service Charge field to enter a standard monthly charge. If there are other charges, such as NSF fees or charges for ordering new checks, enter the charges into your bank register. Use the Memo field to explain the transaction.

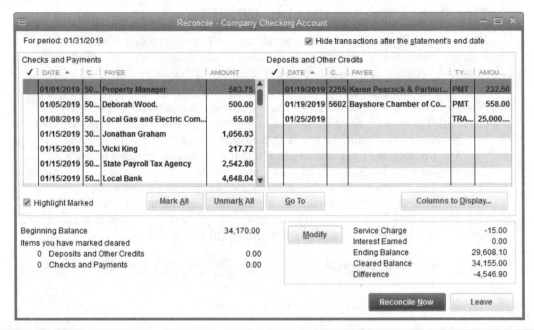

FIGURE 7-3 Uncleared transactions appear in the Reconcile window.

Working in the Reconcile Window

After you've filled out the information in the Begin Reconciliation window, click Continue to open the Reconcile window, shown in Figure 7-3. You can arrange the way transactions are displayed to make it easier to work in the window.

By default, QuickBooks sorts transactions first by date and then by transaction number. For example, in the Checks And Payments pane, if multiple checks have the same date, those checks are sorted in numerical order.

Reconciling is easier if you sort the data to match the way your bank arranges the statement. For instance, if you have several electronic payments in addition to checks, and your bank lists the electronic payments separately from checks, click the CHK # column header to list withdrawals without check numbers separately from checks.

Shorten the list by selecting the option Hide Transactions After The Statement's End Date. Theoretically, transactions created after the statement ending date will not have cleared the bank. Removing them from the window leaves only those transactions likely to have cleared. If you select this option and your reconciliation doesn't balance, deselect the option so you can clear the transactions in case a postdated check was cashed early or you made a mistake on the date of the original transaction. You may have entered a wrong month or even a wrong year, which resulted in moving the transaction date into the future.

Clearing Transactions

Next, mark the cleared transaction. If this is your first bank reconciliation in QuickBooks, in the Deposits And Other Credits pane of the Reconcile window, you'll see a deposit transaction that represents the beginning bank balance entered either via a journal entry or directly in the check register when you set up your QuickBooks data file. You'll need to "clear" this transaction during your first reconciliation. When you clear a transaction in the Reconcile window, a check mark appears in the leftmost (Cleared) column to indicate that the transaction has cleared the bank. If you clear a transaction in error, click again to remove the check mark—it's a toggle.

Here are some shortcuts:

- If all, or almost all, of the transactions have cleared, click Mark All. Then deselect the transactions that didn't clear.
- Mark multiple contiguous transactions by dragging down the Cleared column.
- Click the Highlight Marked check box so that the items you mark as cleared have a shaded background, making them easier to distinguish from those that haven't cleared.
- If the account you're reconciling is enabled for online access (using the QuickBooks Bank Feed feature), click Matched to automatically clear all transactions that were downloaded and matched. QuickBooks asks for the ending date on the statement and clears each previously matched transaction up to that date.

As you check each cleared transaction, the Difference amount in the lower-right corner of the Reconcile window changes. The goal is to get that figure to 0.00.

Adding Transactions During Reconciliation

If you find a transaction on the statement that is not in your register, you don't have to leave the Reconcile window. You can just enter the transaction into your register by right-clicking anywhere in the Reconcile window and choosing Use Register from the shortcut menu. When the account register opens, record the transaction. Then return to the Reconcile window, where that transaction is now waiting for you to clear it.

If the statement shows a deposit that doesn't appear in your Reconcile window, don't add the deposit to your register until you check the Payments To Deposit window (choose Banking | Make Deposits). Often the payments appear there, still awaiting deposit into the QuickBooks register, even though you already may have physically deposited those checks into the bank.

Select the payments that match the total shown on the bank statement and go through the Make Deposits function. When you're finished, the deposit appears in the Reconcile window. If the deposit isn't in the Payments To Deposit window, then you forgot to enter a transaction. Enter the transaction now, using the appropriate transaction window. Make sure you deposit it into the bank account to have it appear in the Reconcile window.

Voiding or Deleting Transactions During Reconciliation

If you find a transaction in the Reconcile window that should not be there, you can either delete or void the transaction. To delete a transaction, double-click its listing in the Reconcile window to open the original transaction. Then right-click and select Delete. QuickBooks asks you to confirm the deletion. The transaction disappears from the Reconcile window and the bank register.

To void a transaction, double-click its listing in the Reconcile window to open the original transaction. Then right-click and select Void, which changes the amount to zero. Voiding a transaction is almost always the preferred method of removing a transaction because QuickBooks retains most all the details of the transaction and allows you to add a note for future reference. Deleting, on the other hand, removes a transaction completely, making it more difficult for your accountant or you to track down a change in an account balance or report that occurred as a result of the deletion.

Editing Transactions During Reconciliation

Sometimes you'll want to change some of the information in a transaction. Whatever the problem, you can correct it by editing the transaction. Double-click the transaction's listing in the Reconcile window to open the original transaction window. Enter the necessary changes and close the window. Answer Yes when QuickBooks asks if you want to record the changes, and you're returned to the Reconcile window where the changes are reflected.

Resolving Missing Check Numbers

Most banks list your checks in order and indicate a missing number with an asterisk on the bank statement. For instance, you may see check number 5003 followed by check number *5007 or 5007*. When a check number is missing, it means one of three things: the check is still outstanding, the check number is unused and is probably literally missing, or the check cleared in a previous reconciliation.

If a missing check number on your bank statement is puzzling, check its status. To see if the check cleared in the last reconciliation, open the Previous Reconciliation report by choosing Reports | Banking | Previous Reconciliation.

To investigate further, right-click anywhere in the Reconcile window and choose Missing Checks Report from the shortcut menu. When the Missing Checks dialog opens, select the appropriate account (if you have multiple bank accounts). You see asterisks indicating missing check numbers. If a check number is listed in your Missing Checks report, it doesn't exist in the register. It may be missing because you deleted the check that was assigned that number, the check is physically missing (usually because somebody grabbed one or more checks to carry around), or checks jammed while printing and you restarted the print run with the number of the first available check. QuickBooks doesn't mark checks as void in that case; it just omits the numbers in the register and they show up in the Missing Checks report.

Finishing the Reconciliation

If this isn't the first reconciliation you're performing, there's a good chance that the Difference figure at the bottom of the Reconcile window displays 0.00. Click Reconcile Now and print either a summary or detail reconciliation report (or both).

Printing the Reconciliation Report

When you have a balanced reconciliation, QuickBooks offers congratulations and offers to print a reconciliation report. You can click the dialog's Close button to skip the report, but it's a good practice to print and keep a copy of it with your bank statement. Whether you print, view, or cancel, QuickBooks saves the report and you can view them in the future by choosing Reports | Banking | Previous Reconciliation.

QuickBooks offers two reconciliation reports: Detail and Summary. The Detail report shows all the transactions that are cleared and all the transactions that haven't yet cleared as of the statement closing date. Any transactions dated after the statement closing date are listed as *New Transactions*. The Summary report breaks down your transactions in the same way, but it doesn't list the individual transactions; it shows only the totals for each category: Cleared, Uncleared, and New. Selecting the Detail report makes it easier to resolve problems in the future, since you have a list of every check and deposit and when it cleared.

When you choose to print one or both reports, the Print Reports dialog opens so you can select the printer. Then you can print the report to the selected printer and file it with that month's bank statement in case you ever need to refer to it. You can also print the report to a file—ASCII text, comma-delimited, or tab-delimited. However, this option is not available if you decide to print both reports.

Viewing the Last Reconciliation Report

Even if you don't display or print a reconciliation report after you reconcile, QuickBooks saves the report and stores it for you as a Previous Reconciliation report. This can be extremely helpful when you're trying to track down a discrepancy in your beginning bank balance the next time you do a reconciliation.

Click Reports | Banking | Previous Reconciliation to open the Select Previous Reconciliation Report dialog. You're given the option of running the Summary, Detail, or both reports in one of two ways:

- Include transactions cleared at the time of the reconciliation—essentially giving you a snapshot of what the reconciliation looked like at the time it was completed. This report prints only as a PDF file.

- Include transactions cleared at the time of the original reconciliation *plus* any changes made to the transactions since the original reconciliation. Once the report is displayed, you can export it to Excel by clicking the Excel button at the top of the report window.

If You Don't Balance

If the account doesn't reconcile (the Difference figure isn't 0.00), you can stop the reconciliation process without losing all the transactions you cleared. Click the Leave button in the Reconcile window. Clear your mind, and when you restart the reconciliation process, all the entries you made will still be there.

Finding and Correcting Problems

To investigate the cause of a difference between the ending balance and the cleared balance, try the following: Count the number of transactions on the bank statement. Then look in the lower-left corner of the Reconcile window, where the number of items you have marked cleared is displayed. Mentally add another item to that number for a service charge you entered or an interest amount you entered in the Begin Reconciliation window. If the numbers differ, the problem is in your QuickBooks records; there's a transaction you should have cleared but didn't or a transaction you cleared that you shouldn't have. Also, check the total deposits and withdrawals shown on the bank statement. They should match the total shown in the QuickBooks reconciliation window.

If you're sure you didn't make any mistakes clearing transactions, do the following:

- Check the amount of each transaction against the amount in the bank statement.
- Check your transactions and make sure a deposit wasn't inadvertently entered as a payment (or vice versa). A clue for this is a transaction that's half the difference. For example, if the difference is $220.00, find a transaction that has an amount of $110.00 and make sure it's a deduction if it's supposed to be a deduction (or the other way around).
- Check for transposed figures. A clue that a transposed number is the problem is that the reconciliation difference can be evenly divided by nine.

Correct the problem when you find it, and when the Difference figure is 0.00, click Reconcile Now.

Making an Adjusting Entry

If you cannot find the reason for the difference in the beginning balances and you've reached the point where it isn't worth your time to keep looking, go ahead and click the Reconcile Now button. QuickBooks presents an option to make an adjusting transaction at the end of the reconciliation process that will post to an expense account that is automatically created, called Reconciliation Discrepancies. If you ever learn the reason for the difference, you can void the adjustment made in this account post and then clear the correct transaction.

Troubleshooting Differences in the Beginning Balance

If this isn't the first time you've reconciled the bank account, the beginning balance that's displayed on the Begin Reconciliation window should match the beginning balance on the bank statement. That beginning balance is simply the ending balance arrived at from the last reconciliation you did. If the beginning balance doesn't match the statement, it means that you or someone else working in your QuickBooks file did one (or more) of the following:

- You changed the amount on a transaction that had previously cleared.
- You voided or deleted a transaction that had previously cleared.
- You removed the cleared check mark from a transaction that had previously cleared.
- You manually entered a cleared check mark on a transaction that had not cleared.

You have to figure out which one of those actions you took after you last reconciled the account, and QuickBooks has a tool to help you. Click the Locate Discrepancies button on the Begin Reconciliation window to open the Locate Discrepancies dialog. Click Discrepancy Report in the Locate Discrepancies dialog to see a report showing the details of any transactions that were cleared during a past reconciliation that were later changed or deleted. If the Reconciled Amount column shows a positive number, the original cleared transaction was a deposit; a negative number indicates a disbursement.

The Type Of Change column provides a clue about the action you must take to correct the unmatched beginning balances:

- **Uncleared**   The check mark was removed in the Cleared column of the register.
- **Deleted**   You deleted the transaction.
- **Amount**   You changed the amount of the transaction. The difference between the amount in the Reconciled Amount column and the amount in the Effect Of Change column is the amount of the change.

This report doesn't offer a Type Of Change named Void, so a voided transaction is merely marked as changed, and the text in the Type Of Change column is Amount. A transaction with a changed amount equal to and opposite of the original amount was almost certainly a transaction you voided after it cleared.

Use the information in the Discrepancy Report to correct the problems you created by changing previously cleared transactions.

Correcting Changed Transactions

If you cleared or uncleared a transaction manually, open the bank register and undo this action by clicking in the Cleared column (designated by a check mark) until a check mark appears next to the transaction. If you changed the amount of a transaction that had cleared and the transaction still exists in the register with an amount, change the amount back to the original amount for that transaction.

Replacing Voided or Deleted Cleared Transactions

If the beginning balance is incorrect because you removed a transaction that had cleared (either by voiding or deleting it), you have to put the transaction back into your register. You can get the information you need from the Discrepancy report.

- If a transaction is there but marked VOID, re-enter it using the data in the reconciliation report. That transaction wasn't void when you performed the last reconciliation; it had cleared. Therefore, it doesn't meet any of the reasons to void a transaction.

- If a transaction appears in the reconciliation report but is not in the register, it was deleted. If it cleared, it can't be deleted. Re-enter it using the data in the reconciliation report.

- Check the amounts on the printed check reconciliation report against the data in the register to see if any amount was changed after the account was reconciled. If so, restore the original amount.

If you re-enter a transaction that was voided or deleted after it cleared and you put a check mark into the Cleared Column, QuickBooks adds it to your Reconcile window with a check mark already in place. This action doesn't adjust your opening balance on the Begin Reconciliation window, but it does readjust the math so the current reconciliation works and next month's opening balance will be correct.

Undoing the Last Reconciliation

QuickBooks lets you undo the last reconciliation, which means that all transactions cleared during the reconciliation are uncleared. This is a good way to start over if you're "stuck" with the current reconciliation and the problems seem to stem from the previous reconciliation (especially if you forced the previous reconciliation by having QuickBooks make an adjusting entry). Click the Undo Last Reconciliation button on the Begin Reconciliation window. QuickBooks suggests you click Cancel and back up your company file before continuing. Backing up is an excellent idea, because you can restore the data back to its reconciled state in case you don't get the results you were expecting. Then, begin reconciling again, click Undo Last Reconciliation, and click Continue. This process removes the cleared status of all transactions cleared during the last reconciliation and leaves the amounts you entered for interest and bank charges so you don't need to re-enter them.

When the process completes, QuickBooks displays a message confirming that fact. Click OK to clear the message and return to the Begin Reconciliation window. If there was an adjustment entry during the last reconciliation, click Cancel to close the Begin Reconciliation window. Delete the adjustment entry; it's the entry posted to the Reconciliation Adjustment account. Hopefully, you won't need another adjusting entry.

Start the reconciliation process again for the same month you just "undid." The data that appears is the same data that appeared when you started the last reconciliation, including the last reconciliation date, the statement date, and the beginning balance. Enter the ending balance from the bank statement.

Using Bank Feeds

In this chapter:

- Setting up bank feeds
- Viewing and adding transactions in the Bank Feeds Center
- Paying your bills online
- Transferring money between accounts online

Chapter 8

With QuickBooks Bank Feeds (known as online banking in earlier QuickBooks versions), you use the Internet to connect to and download your bank and credit card account information into your QuickBooks file. When you see the word "bank" or "financial institution," it can also be referring to your credit card company. Many financial institutions offer one of the following two methods to allow you to connect with and download this information:

- **Direct Connect** With this method, your financial institution exchanges data interactively with QuickBooks. This enables you to take advantage of additional Bank Feeds features, such as transaction data downloads directly into your QuickBooks bank register, transfers between bank accounts, electronic messages between you and the financial institution, and online bill payments (optional at some financial institutions). Some financial institutions charge a fee for some or all of the services available through Direct Connect.
- **Web Connect** Use this manual import method when your financial institution doesn't provide a way to connect your QuickBooks data directly to the data on its own server or you choose not to pay a fee. Using this method, you access a page on the bank's website, where you can view your account data, download your transactions, and import the downloaded file into QuickBooks.

Set Up Bank Feeds

To use Bank Feeds, your bank must support either transaction downloads or online bill paying. If your bank supports only online account access and doesn't support online bill paying, you can still work directly with the QuickBooks Bank Feeds to automate your bill payment process. If you haven't signed up for online services with your bank and you're not sure if your bank has online services, choose Banking | Bank Feeds | Participating Financial Institutions to see the Financial Institutions Directory web page, as shown here.

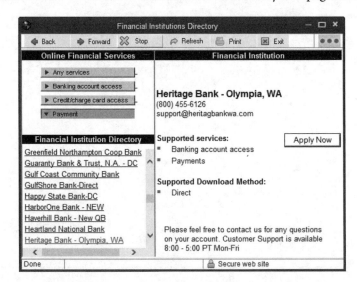

The four choices at the top of the left pane determine the contents of the Financial Institutions Directory list that QuickBooks displays. The window opens with the Any Services choice pre-selected, and all the banks listed provide some type of online service. If you're interested in a particular online service (for example, you want to know about bank account access to download transactions), select that option, and the list of banks changes to those that offer the selected service.

Scroll through the list to find your bank and click its listing. The right pane of the Financial Institutions Directory window displays information about your bank's online services. If your bank isn't listed, you cannot utilize the Bank Feeds feature.

Click the Apply Now button if you want to start the application process. If no Apply Now button appears, follow the instructions for setting up online services at the bank—usually the bank's website displays a phone number. If online applications are available, fill out the form and submit the information. Your bank will send you information about using its online service, a login name, and a PIN or password. You need this information to enable the bank account for Bank Feeds in QuickBooks.

After you receive your login ID and a PIN or password from your bank, return to QuickBooks, which will walk you through the process of enabling Bank Feeds for your bank account. The steps differ depending on whether your bank uses Direct Connect or Web Connect.

Enabling Bank Feeds Using Direct Connect

After you receive your ID and PIN or password, you can enable a bank account for online access with Direct Connect:

1. Choose Banking | Bank Feeds | Set Up Bank Feed For An Account. You see a message from QuickBooks saying that it will temporarily close all open windows. Click Yes to continue. Step 1 of the Bank Feed Setup window opens. Enter the name of your financial institution, or choose from the list at the right side of the window.

2. In the next window, enter the User ID and Password your financial institution provided, and then click Connect.

3. In the next window, link your account with the bank (or credit card) account that you created in QuickBooks. If you have not already created this account in QuickBooks, select Create New Account from the QuickBooks Accounts drop-down list. Then click Connect.

4. The Bank Feed Setup window confirms that you've successfully enabled your account to receive Bank Feeds. Click the link Download Your Transactions From Bank Feeds at the bottom of the window to initiate your first download from the Bank Feeds Center.

Enabling Bank Feeds Using Web Connect (Manual Import)

After you receive your login information from your bank (as described in the previous section), you can enable a bank account to download as a Web Connect file as follows:

1. Choose Banking | Bank Feeds | Setup Bank Feed For An Account. QuickBooks displays an "Updating Branding Files" message. When that process is complete, enter the name of your financial institution. If QuickBooks displays matching names, select one from the list offered.

2. Once you select a financial institution, the Manually Import Transactions window opens, listing the steps required to download and import the transaction file (see Figure 8-1).

3. Click the link provided in Step 1 to be redirected to your bank's login page. If you don't want to download your transactions at this time, click Close.

4. Log in, and then find the transactions that you want to import into QuickBooks. Your bank probably displays criteria selections for a date range and may also offer the option Since Last Download (which you can select after this initial download).

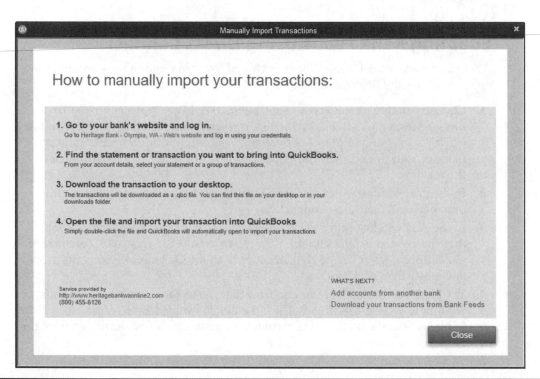

FIGURE 8-1   QuickBooks displays directions to import your transactions manually using Web Connect.

5. After you make your selections, your bank generates a file (it should have the extension .qbo) and displays a File Download dialog asking whether you want to open the file or save it to your computer.

   a. If you click Open, QuickBooks asks if you want to import the file into your bank account now or save it and import later.

   b. If you click Save, save the file to your desktop or your download folder.

6. When you're ready to import the file, choose Banking | Bank Feeds | Import Web Connect Files and select the file you saved. You can also double-click the filename and it will automatically import the transactions into your QuickBooks file. These transactions are now available to you in the Bank Feeds Center.

Work with Bank Feeds Center Transactions

When you have downloaded transactions for the first time, the Bank Feeds Center opens automatically. From now on, however, if you're using the Direct Connect method, you'll both download and view transactions right from the Bank Feeds Center. If you're using the Web Connect (manual) method, you'll start by logging into your bank to download your transactions.

Viewing the Downloaded Transactions

When transactions have been downloaded, the Bank Feeds Center displays your account information, showing the status of all of your accounts. If there are transactions ready to be added, a Transaction List button appears, as shown here.

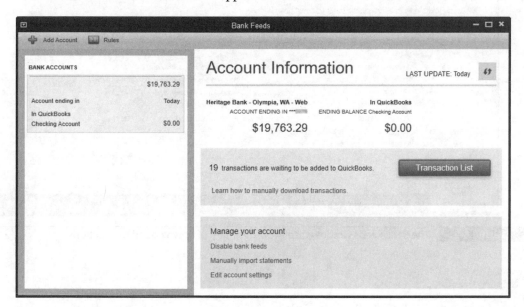

If you are receiving feeds from more than one financial institution (for example, you may have online bank account access at one financial institution and online credit card access at another), select the appropriate account from the list in the Bank Accounts area on the left side of the Bank Feeds window.

If there are no new transactions to review when you select an account from this list, click the Download Transactions button to get the latest transactions from your financial institution. If QuickBooks indicates that downloaded transactions are waiting to be added, click the Transaction List button to begin the process of reviewing and adding these transactions to your account register. The list is a summary of the status of the transactions that need to be reviewed or that require action for each of the accounts listed in the Bank Accounts area, as shown in Figure 8-2.

You can view and enter transactions in two ways: via the default Express mode or via Classic mode. Both modes offer the same functionality, with the exception that the renaming rules created in Express mode are not available in Classic mode. Likewise, aliases created in Classic mode are not available in Express mode. To switch between modes, choose Banking | Bank Feeds | Change Bank Feeds Mode.

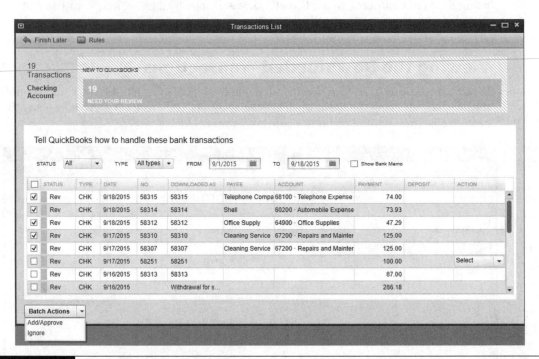

FIGURE 8-2 The Bank Feeds window displays a summary of downloaded transactions.

Adding Transactions to the Account Register in QuickBooks

From the Transaction List window, you tell QuickBooks how to handle each downloaded transaction. You can work directly in this list to assign/change the account, customer, or vendor name for each transaction listed. You can also filter the list of transactions that appear by their status. Each of the drop-down lists makes it possible to customize what you see.

- **Status** This filter allows you to choose to see
  - All downloaded transactions
  - Transactions that need your review
  - Transactions that were changed by existing rules (see "Renaming Rules," later in the chapter)
  - Transactions that have been matched automatically
- **Types** Use the Types filter to tell QuickBooks to show
  - All types of transactions
  - Transfers
  - Checks
  - Deposits
  - General journal
  - Credit card charges
  - Credit card credits
- **Dates** Use the From and To date filters to change the scope of the list
- **Show Bank Memo** Check this option to include any bank memo information included in your download

Start with Matched Transactions

QuickBooks tries to match downloaded transactions to transactions already entered in your register. When you filter your Bank Feeds Transactions list to show auto-matched transactions, the word "Auto" appears in the Status column, indicating that the transaction listed was already entered directly in the bank register. If you have multiple matched transactions and you don't need to review them further, click the check box next to each one, click the Batch Actions drop-down menu (located at the bottom of the Transactions List window), and select Add/Approve to add them to your QuickBooks register.

If you want to work with just one matched transaction at a time, use the Select drop-down menu in the Action column, where you'll see four options, shown here:

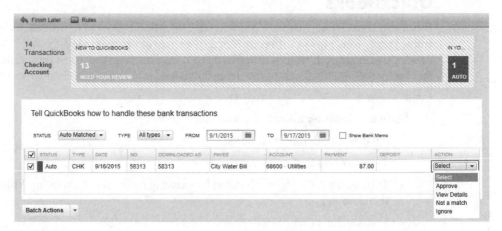

- **Approve**   Select this option to add this transaction to your register.
- **View Details**   Select this option to see more transaction detail to confirm that it's a match.
- **Not A Match**   Select this option to manually match this transaction to another one in your register.
- **Ignore**   Select this option to delete the transaction from the Bank Feeds Transactions list.

Add Renamed Transactions

Renamed transactions have been changed by QuickBooks based on a renaming rule that you created. Filter your Transactions list to show renamed transactions. The letters "Cha" appear in the Status column in the Transactions List window for these transactions.

If you have multiple renamed transactions and you don't need to review them further, click the check box next to each one, click the Batch Actions button (located at the bottom of the Transactions List window), and select Add/Approve to add them to your QuickBooks register. If you want to work with just one renamed transaction at a time, use the Select drop-down menu in the Action column, where you'll see four options:

- **Quick Add**   Selecting this option adds this transaction to your register.
- **Add More Details**   This option allows you to add more transaction detail before adding the transaction to your register. You can also add a new customer, vendor, or account if it doesn't already exist in your QuickBooks file.
- **Match To Existing Transaction**   Select this option to manually match this transaction to one already in your register.
- **Ignore**   Select this option to delete the transaction from the Bank Feeds Transactions list.

Renaming Rules

When the designation "Cha" appears in the Status column in the Transactions List window, it means that a downloaded transaction was changed by a renaming rule. You use a renaming rule to tell QuickBooks that you want to use a particular name for a vendor or payee when a transaction is downloaded into the Bank Feeds Center. QuickBooks automatically creates a renaming rule the first time you assign a payee to a downloaded payment transaction and there is no matching entry in your register. You can also create your own renaming rules by clicking the Rules link at the top-left corner of the Bank Feeds or Transactions List window. This opens the Rules List window, where you'll use the Manage Rules drop-down menu at the bottom of the window to create, edit, or delete a rule.

When you create a new rule, in the Add Rules Details dialog, you can choose to rename the vendor or payee based on whether the name associated with the downloaded transaction contains, starts with, ends with, exactly matches, or does not contain the text or characters that you enter.

Add Unmatched Transactions

Unmatched transactions usually require a review and more detail before they can be added to a register. Filter the Status list in the Transactions List window to show unmatched transactions. The letters "Rev" appear in the Status column in the Transactions List window for these transactions. Use the Select drop-down menu in the Action column, seen here, to take one of these actions:

- **Quick Add**   Select this option to add this transaction to your register.
- **Add More Details**   Select this option to add more transaction detail before adding the transaction to your register. You can also add a new customer, vendor, or account if it doesn't already exist in your QuickBooks file.
- **Select Bills To Mark As Paid**   This option allows you to connect this payment to a bill you have previously entered. This is extremely useful if you have used the Check function rather than the Pay Bills function to pay a bill. This option opens the Transaction Details | Select Bills To Mark As Paid dialog, where you can apply this payment to an outstanding vendor bill. In the Vendor field, select the vendor with an open A/P bill to which this downloaded payment is linked. QuickBooks displays the open bills for the vendor. Select the bill to pay with this transaction, and change the Amount To Pay if the transaction represented a partial payment. You can also select multiple bills for this vendor if you paid more than one bill with this payment.

- **Match To Existing Transaction** Select this option to manually match this transaction to one already in your register. This can happen when the check number in your check register is different than the actual check number that cleared your account.
- **Ignore** Select this option to delete the transaction from the Transactions list.

Adding a Downloaded Deposit to the Register

You may need to apply a downloaded bank deposit to more than one existing QuickBooks transaction (such as open invoices, for example). From the Select drop-down menu in the Actions column for a downloaded deposit transaction, choose Add More Details to do the following:

- Match this deposit to an existing customer payment already received in QuickBooks by finding and selecting it on the Undeposited Funds tab, which contains all the current transactions waiting for deposit. You will then see these transactions in the Payments To Deposit window. (Click the Record Deposits button on the Home page to open this window.)
- Apply that payment now by finding and selecting the open invoice(s) on the Open Invoices tab, which lists all the current open invoices in your company file.

Choose the appropriate tab, and then choose the matching transaction or multiple transactions that total up to the amount of the downloaded transaction.

Ignoring (Deleting) Unmatched Transactions

Sometimes the downloaded file contains transactions that can't be matched. This can occur when you don't download transactions frequently and some of the transactions you download have already been cleared during a reconciliation. You can't match transactions that have already been reconciled within QuickBooks. You should delete these transactions. If you don't, they'll be there waiting for you every time you download new transactions.

- To delete multiple transactions, select the check box next to each one in the Transactions List window, click the Batch Actions button (located at the bottom of the Transactions List window), and select Ignore.
- To delete individual transactions, use the Select drop-down menu in the Action column and select Ignore.

You can apply the Ignore action to matched and renamed transactions, so pay attention to the Status column to avoid deleting transactions you intend to add to QuickBooks.

Use QuickBooks to Pay Your Bills Online

When you pay your bills or write checks, QuickBooks gives you the option of sending these payments electronically to your vendors. You can either use your own bank to transmit these payments to your vendors (if it offers online bill payment services or Direct Connect) or use the QuickBooks Bill Pay Service and have QuickBooks send these payments for you.

Using the QuickBooks Bill Pay Service

From the Banking menu, select Bank Feeds | Learn About Online Bill Payment. You will be taken to the QuickBooks Bill Pay website, as seen in Figure 8-3. This is a monthly fee-based service, although you can enroll for one month for free.

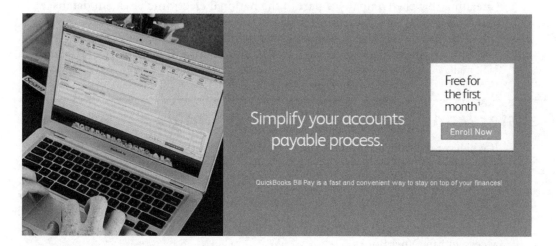

Simplify your accounts payable process.

Free for the first month[1]

Enroll Now

QuickBooks Bill Pay is a fast and convenient way to stay on top of your finances!

Features and Benefits

With electronic payment services for small businesses, you can:

- **Streamline Routine Tasks:** Automating the accounts payable process allows you to concentrate on more critical business issues.
- **Improve Financial Management:** Electronic payment provides small businesses with more accuracy in payables processing and greater control over cash flow.
- **Realize Significant Cost Savings:** Considering labor, supply costs and processing time, a small business can save thousands per year by handling accounts payable online.
- **Gain Convenient Access:** Businesses can pay bills anytime from anywhere they can access the Internet.
- **Be Assured of Complete Security:** All payments are fully backed by the CheckFree Guarantee.

> Additional QuickBooks Bill Pay Features

Pricing

QuickBooks Bill Pay is FREE for the first month. After your free trial, the service is $15.95 per month for up to 20 payments, and $6.95 for each additional set of 10 payments.[1]

Enroll Now

Security

Protecting the security of your financial information is a priority. Your online payment instructions are sent using a secure Internet connection and SSL encryption technology, and protected with a password (PIN) issued only to you.

How It Works

Write checks as you normally would in QuickBooks. Instead of selecting "Print Later", select "Pay Online" and choose the date on which you would like the payment to be delivered.

OR

Pay bills as you normally would in QuickBooks. Select "Online Bank Payment" and choose the date on which you'd like the payment to be delivered.

FIGURE 8-3   QuickBooks Bill Pay can simplify your payables process.

Once you've completed the sign-up process, you can use either the Write Checks or Pay Bills feature in QuickBooks as you normally would. If you are writing a check instead of selecting To Be Printed, select Pay Online. Be sure to fill in the date that you want the payment to be delivered (you can schedule a payment up to one year in advance). If you are using the Pay Bills feature, pay your bills as you normally would and select Online Bank Payment as your payment method. Again, choose the date that you want the payment delivered.

After you've entered your checks or paid your bills, open the Bank Feeds Center and click the Send Items button. If your vendor is set up to receive electronic payments (meaning that the company is part of the national electronic payment database), QuickBooks electronically transfers your payments from your bank to your vendor /payee on the date you've specified. If your vendor is not able to receive electronic payments, a paper check (generated by the QuickBooks Bill Pay service) is sent via U.S. mail.

Transfer Money Between Accounts Online

If you have multiple accounts at your financial institution (for example, you may have a money market account for your business in addition to your checking account) and the financial institution uses Direct Connect, you can transfer money between those accounts within QuickBooks. To transfer money online, you must have applied at your financial institution for online banking for both accounts. You'll probably have a unique PIN for each account. In addition, you must have enabled both accounts for online access within QuickBooks.

You can transfer funds between online accounts using the online transfer funds function or direct manual entry. The simplest way to move money between your online accounts is to use the QuickBooks Transfer Funds Between Accounts window, which you reach by choosing Banking | Transfer Funds from the menu bar.

Specify the sending and receiving accounts (remember that both must be enabled for Direct Connect online access), and enter the amount you want to transfer. Be sure to select the option Online Funds Transfer in the Transfer Funds Between Accounts window. Click Save & Close. Then choose Banking | Bank Feeds Center. Click the Send Items button to send the transfer to your bank.

In the Account Information section of the Bank Feeds window, click the Transfers hyperlink to open the Fund Transfers To Be Sent window. Make sure the transfer transactions you want to send to your bank have check marks next to them. Close this window and click the Send Items button.

Part Three

Payroll

I f you have employees, the chapters in this section are required reading. In Chapter 9, you'll learn how to track the time your employees (and subcontractors) spend on customer jobs using the built-in QuickBooks time-tracking feature and how to use this information to bill your customers and in job-costing reports. You'll learn how to use the time tracked in a timesheet to prepare a paycheck. Then, you will see how to create items specific to payroll and how to set up your employee information to prepare for payroll.

Chapter 10 covers essentially everything else you need to know about running your payroll in QuickBooks, including how to ensure that all payroll taxes due are remitted to the government on time.

Establishing QuickBooks Payroll

In this chapter:

- Tracking time

- Formatting timesheets

- Running, editing, and printing timesheets

- Working with mileage

- Learning about payroll in QuickBooks

- Creating employee templates and setting them up

Chapter 9

This chapter covers the tools QuickBooks provides for you to track time and mileage and use this information to recover reimbursable costs from customers, develop an accurate job-costing system, analyze expenses, and pay employees. The built-in time tracking lets you record the amount of time you and your staff spend completing a project or doing work for either a customer or for your company.

Set Up Time Tracking

QuickBooks may already have turned on the built-in time-tracking features for you, depending on your responses when setting up your company. To see if time tracking is enabled, choose Edit | Preferences from the QuickBooks menu bar. Select Time & Expenses by scrolling to the last category in the left pane, and click the Company Preferences tab. Make sure the Yes option is selected.

By default, QuickBooks assumes your workweek starts on Monday. However, some businesses use a different workweek, such as a Sunday-to-Saturday pattern, for tracking time. If you're tracking time for employees and you plan to use the timesheets for payroll, ensure you have matched the workweek to the days your pay period covers.

QuickBooks has two options for tracking time: a weekly timesheet and a timesheet on which you can enter a single activity. To view them, click Enter Time on the Home page or, from the menu bar, click Employees | Enter Time. The Weekly Timesheet is shown in Figure 9-1.

Adding Time Trackers

You can track time for your employees, outside contractors (vendors), or yourself. Everyone who must keep track of his or her time must first exist in QuickBooks and, of course, fill out a timesheet.

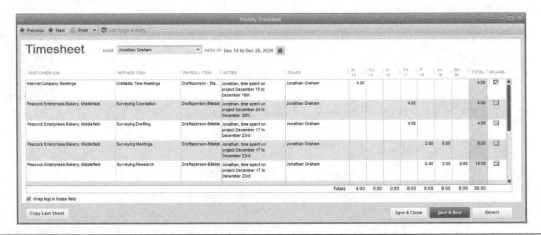

FIGURE 9-1   Use the QuickBooks Weekly Timesheet to enter daily tasks for each employee.

If you established the QuickBooks payroll feature when you first set up your company, you may already have employees in your QuickBooks system, and you can use timesheets to track their time. You can create a paycheck from the data entered on each timesheet. For this to work, however, you must modify the employee record as follows:

1. Choose Employees | Employee Center to open the Employee Center, and click the Employees tab to display the list of employees.
2. Select the employee for whom you want to use time tracking.
3. Click the Edit icon to open the Edit Employee dialog. You can also right-click the employee's name in the Employees list and select Edit Employee.

From the Edit Employee dialog, select the Payroll Info tab. At the bottom of the Earnings area, select the Use Time Data To Create Paychecks check box on the bottom left. Click OK, as seen here.

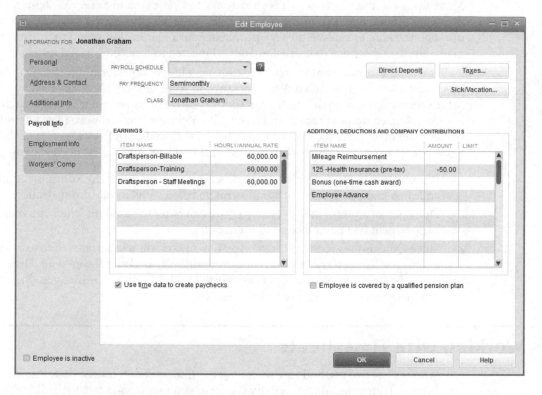

Should you need to track employees' time to create job-costing reports or invoice a customer, you can use QuickBooks timesheets without using time data to create paychecks. In that case, ensure that the Use Time Data to Create Paychecks box is cleared. Even if you do not use QuickBooks for payroll, you can create employees in the Employee Center to track time and use the timesheet data for an outside payroll service.

Tracking Vendor Time

Any vendor in your system that you pay for his or her time can have that time tracked so you can bill your customers. Often, these vendors are outside contractors or subcontractors. To bill the customer, you just record the time in a timesheet and mark the hours as "billable."

Tracking Other Workers' Time

If you need to track the time of people who are neither employees nor vendors, use the Other Names list. For example, if you pay employees using QuickBooks payroll, but you take a draw instead of a paycheck, add your name to the Other Names list to track your own time. If your company is a proprietorship or a partnership and you have no employees, enter the owner or partner names in the Other Names list to track time.

Adding Tasks

Many tasks you track in timesheets already exist in your system as service items and are the items you use when you invoice customers for services. However, because you can use time tracking to analyze the way people in your organization spend their time, you may want to add service items that are not connected to tasks performed for customers.

For example, if you want to track the time people spend performing administrative tasks, add a service item called Administrative to your Item List. You can even be more specific by naming the particular administrative tasks you want to track, such as bookkeeping, equipment repair, and so on. To enter new items, choose Lists | Item List from the menu bar. Press CTRL-N to open the New Item dialog. Select Service as the item type, as only service items are tracked in timesheets, and name the new item.

- If you're specifying administrative tasks, create a service named Administration and then make each specific administrative task a subitem of Administration.
- Don't put an amount in the Rate box. You can enter the amount when you make the payment (via payroll or vendor checks).
- Since QuickBooks requires that you assign an account to a service, choose or create a "dummy" (or placeholder) revenue account, such as Other Revenue or Time Tracking Revenue. No money is ever posted to the account, because you don't ever sell these services directly to customers.

Working with Timesheets

QuickBooks has two methods for recording the time spent on tasks: Single Activity and Weekly Timesheet. Single Activity is a form you use to enter what you did when you performed a single task at a specific time on a specific date. For example, a Single Activity form may record the fact that you made a telephone call on behalf of a customer, you repaired some piece of equipment for a customer, or you performed some administrative task for the company.

As seen earlier in Figure 9-1, the Weekly Timesheet is a form in which you indicate how much time and on which date someone performed work in a given week. Each

Weekly Timesheet entry can also include the name of the customer for whom the work was performed. You can also print a blank timesheet that an employee can fill out and use to enter time into QuickBooks all at once at the end of a week.

Setting the Format for Displaying Time

When you enter time in the timesheet forms, you can use either the minutes (*hh:mm*) format or a decimal format (6.5). To establish a default, choose Edit | Preferences and in the General category select the Company Preferences tab. Use the options in the Time Format section of the dialog to select the format you prefer. If you set the preference to decimal and then enter time as 1:30, when you press TAB to move to the next field, QuickBooks changes the entry to 1.50 (or the other way around when you choose Minutes). The following message appears when you select the Single Activity time option to remind you.

Tracking a Single Activity

To track one event or task with a Single Activity form, choose Employees | Enter Time | Time/Enter Single Activity. You will see a screen similar to the one shown next.

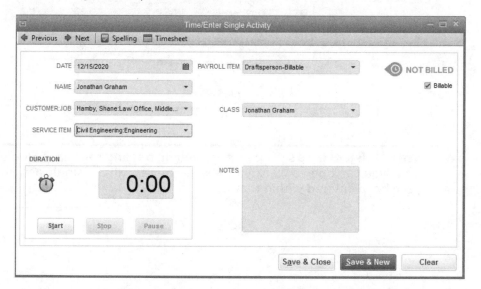

To track the time on any single activity, click the Start button in the Duration box of the Time/Enter Single Activity window as you begin the task. To pause the counting when you're interrupted, click Pause. Then click Start to pick up where you left off. To stop timing, click Stop. The elapsed time displays. The stopwatch always displays time in the *hh:mm:ss* format. If you set your format preference to decimal, QuickBooks converts the time when the stopwatch is stopped.

Fill out the following fields:

- **Date**   Default is the current date. Although you can change the date to an earlier one, you cannot change the date if you're using the stopwatch.
- **Name**   Choose a name from the drop-down list of vendors, employees, and other names.
- **Customer: Job**   Select the customer or job, even if the customer is not to be billed.
- **Service Item**   Choose the item from the drop-down list, and enter the amount of time in the Duration box.
- **Payroll Item**   If available, select the payroll item that applies to this time. This only appears when you have linked the employee to time tracking.
- **Class**   If you have activated Classes, select the class from the drop-down list. If you've linked the employee to the time-tracking system and also enabled class tracking, the class field does not appear unless you turn on the Earnings Item option in Payroll & Employees Preferences.
- **Notes**   Enter any appropriate information. You can transfer these notes to both the invoice and job reports.

When the activity form is complete, click Save & New to fill out another Single Activity form or click Save & Close to finish. The "Stopwatch Is Running" message appears asking if you want to stop the timer, as seen here.

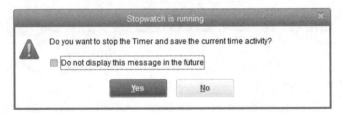

Using Weekly Timesheets

A Weekly Timesheet records the same information as the Single Activity form, except that the information is recorded in week-at-a-time blocks, and you have the option to enter the same timesheet information in batches for both employees and nonemployees. Refer to Figure 9-1 for an example.

To use the Weekly Timesheet form, choose Employees | Enter Time | Use Weekly Timesheet. Use the instructions that follow to fill out the timesheet.

1. In the Name field, select either an individual employee or a vendor name from the drop-down list. Optionally, choose either Multiple Names (Payroll) or Multiple Names (Non-Payroll), located at the top of the Name drop-down list, as seen next, to create multiple timesheets with the same information for the names you've selected in your list. This latter option is useful if you've got a team of employees or contractors working on the same project and performing the same work for the week.

2. By default, the form opens to the current week. Click the calendar icon if you need to select a different week.

3. In the Customer:Job column, select the customer or job connected to the activity.

4. In the Service Item column, select the appropriate service item.

5. For an employee whose paycheck is linked to timesheets, use the Payroll Item column to select the payroll item that fits the activity. (If the name selected in the Name field is not an employee whose paycheck is linked to timesheets, the Payroll Item column disappears.)

6. In the Notes column, enter any necessary notes or comments.

7. Click the column that represents the day in which an activity occurred, and enter the number of hours worked on this task. Repeat across the week for each day that the same activity was performed for the same customer or job. The total hours entered appear in the Total column.

8. Move to the beginning of the next row to enter either a different activity or the same activity for a different customer, repeating this action until the timesheet is filled in for the week.

9. For each row, indicate whether the time is billable in the Billable column. Click the check box to remove the check mark in the Billable column if the time on this row is not billable. QuickBooks marks all time entries linked to a customer as billable.

10. Click Save & New to create a timesheet for a different week. Click Save & Close when you are finished entering time.

You can copy the previous week's timesheet by clicking the Copy Last Sheet button after you enter the current date in the Timesheet window and select a name. This is useful for workers who have similar timesheet data every week. This description frequently applies to your office staff or to outside contractors who are performing large jobs that take multiple weeks. For some employees whose work is usually for the office and not charged to a customer, the timesheet may be identical from week to week.

Reporting Timesheet Information

Before you use the information on the timesheets to invoice customers or pay workers, you should go over the data on the timesheet reports. You can view and customize reports, edit information, and print the original timesheets.

Running Timesheet Reports

To run reports on timesheets, choose Reports | Jobs, Time & Mileage. The following reports provide information on time tracking:

- **Time By Job Summary**   Reports the amount of time spent for each service on your customers and jobs.
- **Time By Job Detail**   Reports the details of the time spent for each customer and job, including dates and whether or not the time was marked as billable. A billing status of Unbilled indicates the time is billable but hasn't yet been used on a customer invoice, as seen in Figure 9-2.
- **Time By Name**   Reports the amount of time each user tracked.
- **Time By Item**   Shows an analysis of the amount of time spent on each service your company provides, including the customers for whom the services were performed.

Editing Entries in a Report

While you're browsing the report, you can double-click an activity listing to navigate to the original entry. You can make changes in the original entry, such as selecting or deselecting the billable option, or change the Notes field by adding a note or editing the content of the existing note. Before you use the timesheets for customer billing or payroll, make sure you examine them and make any needed corrections. In fact, you may want to take this step before you view any of the Jobs, Time & Mileage reports.

The most common revision is the billable status. If outside contractors or employees are filling out timesheets, it's not unusual to have some confusion about which customers receive direct-time billings. In fact, you may have customers to whom you send direct-time bills only for certain activities and provide the remaining activities as part of your basic services.

To check timesheets, open a new weekly timesheet and enter the name of the person connected to the timesheet you want to view. Use the Previous or Next arrows at the top

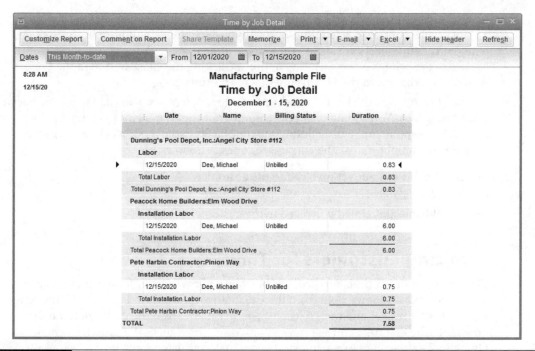

FIGURE 9-2   The Time By Job Detail report can show labor costs that need to be billed.

of the Timesheet window, or use the calendar icon to move to the timesheet you want to inspect. Then edit the information as necessary. If needed, change the number of hours for any activity item, change the billable status, and view (and edit if necessary) any notes. If you've already used the timesheet data to create an invoice for the customer or to pay the employee, the changes you make to the timesheet do not automatically update these documents.

Printing Weekly Timesheets

Employees often print their weekly timesheets and deliver them to the person responsible for monitoring and managing employee hours. Frequently, this is the same person who handles your payroll-related activities. To print timesheets, choose File | Print Forms | Timesheets from the QuickBooks menu bar to open the Select Timesheets To Print window. In this window, you can do the following:

- Change the date range to match the timesheets you want to print.
- By default, all timesheets are selected. To remove a timesheet, select its listing and click the column with the check mark to deselect that listing. You can click Select None to deselect all listings and then select and add check marks to one or more specific users.
- To print any notes in their entirety, select the Print Full Activity Notes option. Otherwise, the default selection to print only the first line of any note.

The Select Timesheets To Print dialog has a Preview button, and clicking it displays a print preview of the selected timesheets. If you click the Print button in the Preview window, the timesheets are sent to the printer immediately, giving you no opportunity to change the printer or any printing options. Clicking the Close button in the Preview window returns you to the Select Timesheets To Print dialog.

Click OK to open the Print Timesheets window, where you can change the printer or printing options. You should change the number of copies to print to match the number of people to whom you're distributing the timesheets. Note the last column, which indicates the billing status. The entries are codes, as follows:

- **B**   Billable but not yet invoiced to the customer
- **N**   Not billable
- **D**   Billable and already invoiced to the customer

Invoicing Customers for Time

Once you've entered time, marked it as billable, and reviewed it for accuracy, it's easy to invoice your customer right from the Create Invoice window. From the Home page, select Create Invoices and then select a customer name from the Customer: Job drop-down list. The first time you select a customer for which there is a timesheet entry, QuickBooks shows a message informing you that the customer or job you've selected has outstanding billable time, as seen next. You are prompted to either select the outstanding billable time (as well as any costs) to add to the invoice or exclude time and costs now and leave them available for invoicing at a later date. You can also have QuickBooks save your choice by checking the Save This As A Preference check box.

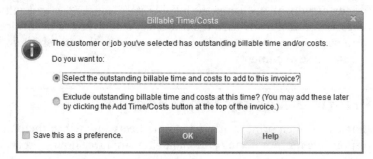

If you choose the option to add the outstanding billable time to your invoice, QuickBooks displays the Choose Billable Time And Costs window. Select the Time tab to view all the unbilled time assigned to that customer or job. Click the Select All button to invoice your customer for all the time that appears in this window, or place a check mark next to only those hours that you're ready to invoice.

By default, each time entry that has a different service item will appear as a separate line item on the invoice. To combine the hours for all items in this window as one line item on the printed copy of the invoice (the detailed view will still appear on your screen), place a check mark in the Print Selected Time And Costs As One Invoice Item check box at the bottom of the window. Clicking the Options button gives you additional ways to customize how information from timesheets is included in invoices.

Tracking Mileage

You can use QuickBooks to track your vehicles' mileage, as shown next. You can use the mileage information to track the expenses connected to vehicle use, to use mileage as part of your job-costing efforts, to bill customers for mileage expenses, or to maintain records for your vehicle-use tax deduction. Your accountant may be able to use the vehicle mileage data on your income tax return. You can deduct either the actual mileage expense or your other vehicle expenses; you can't deduct both. Your accountant, working with the figures you provide as a result of mileage tracking, will make the decision.

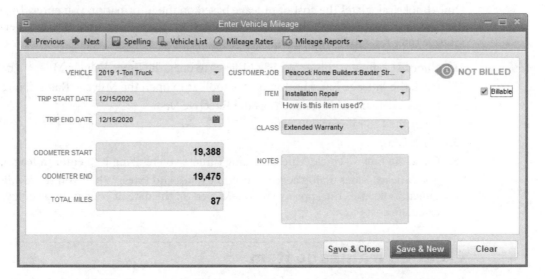

To track a vehicle, you first need to add that vehicle to your Vehicle list. Once the vehicle is in your QuickBooks system, you can begin tracking its mileage. Of course, you also need to make sure that everyone who uses the vehicle is tracking mileage

Trip Start Date	Trip End Date	Starting Odometer	Ending Odometer	Customer: Job

TABLE 9-1   Suggested Mileage Form

properly, so you should create, print, and distribute a form for this purpose, with specific categories to fill in, such as the one shown in Table 9-1.

Small Business Tip   Check with your insurance agent to ensure that your company's insurance policy shows each employee's driver's license information and that your coverage includes each driver.

Entering Mileage Rates

To track the cost of mileage, make sure you have accurate mileage rates in your system. These change frequently, so you'll have to keep up with the latest IRS figures. QuickBooks calculates the cost of mileage based on the information you enter. To get the current rate, check with the IRS (www.irs.gov) or ask your accountant. To enter mileage rates for your own use, use the following steps:

1. Choose Company | Enter Vehicle Mileage to open the Enter Vehicle Mileage dialog.
2. Click the Mileage Rates button on the toolbar to open the Mileage Rates dialog.
3. Select a date from the calendar as the Effective Date.
4. Enter the IRS rate for that date.
5. Click Close.
6. Close the Enter Vehicle Mileage dialog (unless you're using it to enter mileage).
7. The Mileage Rates dialog accepts multiple dates and rates. When you track mileage, QuickBooks uses the appropriate rate, based on the date of your mileage entry, to calculate costs.

Creating a Mileage Item

If you plan to invoice customers for mileage expenses, you must create an item (call it Mileage, Travel, or something similar). The item you create can be either a Service or Other Charge type.

- If you want to charge your customers for mileage as a reimbursable expense and post your reimbursements as income, use an Other Charge item type and select the option This Item Is Used In Assemblies Or Is A Reimbursable Charge. Then enter the appropriate expense and income accounts.

- If you want to charge your customers for mileage and reduce your mileage expenses with reimbursed amounts, select the expense account to which you post your mileage expenses.

It's important to understand that the mileage rate you entered in the Mileage Rates dialog is *not* automatically transferred to the item you create for mileage. Therefore, you must manually fill in the rate for the item and update it when the IRS rate changes. You can use the same rate you used in the Mileage Rates dialog or enter a different rate to create a markup—or even a markdown, if you wish.

Entering Mileage

After you've configured your company file for mileage charges, you can track the mileage in the Enter Vehicle Mileage dialog as follows:

1. Choose Company | Enter Vehicle Mileage.
2. Select the appropriate vehicle from the drop-down list in the Vehicle field and enter the following data:

   - The dates of the trip.

   - The odometer readings (QuickBooks calculates the total miles for you). You can skip the odometer readings and enter the total mileage manually, but entering the odometer numbers creates a report entry that's closer to what an IRS auditor wants to see (the IRS likes "logs" that include odometer readings).

   - If you want to bill the customer for mileage, place a check mark in the Billable check box and select the Customer: Job, the item you created for mileage, and the class (if you're tracking classes).

   - If you don't want to bill a customer but you want to track job costs, select the Customer: Job, but don't place a check mark in the Billable check box.

You can add mileage charges to customer invoices in the same fashion as time charges.

Creating Mileage Reports

QuickBooks includes four vehicle mileage reports, found in Reports | Jobs, Time & Mileage. Select the report from the submenu. If you're working in the Enter Vehicle Mileage dialog, the reports are available in the drop-down list when you click the arrow next to the Mileage Reports button at the top of the dialog. See Table 9-2 for more information.

Report	Explanation
Mileage By Vehicle Summary	Run this report for any date range to see the total miles and the mileage expense for each vehicle you track.
Mileage By Vehicle Detail	View details about each mileage entry you created. For each vehicle, the report displays trip end date, total miles, mileage rate, and mileage expense. No customer information appears in the report, but you can double-click any listing to open the original mileage entry to see if it's billable or linked to a job.
Mileage By Job Summary	View the total number of miles linked to customers or jobs. The report displays total miles for all customers or jobs for which you entered an item and displays billable amounts for any mileage entries you marked billable.
Mileage By Job Detail	View information about each trip for each customer or job. The report contains the trip end date, billing status, item, total miles, sales price, and amount.

TABLE 9-2   Vehicle Mileage Reports

Payroll Setup

Now that you understand how QuickBooks tracks hours, you can process your payroll through QuickBooks, as this section explains. If you have not yet set up payroll, consult with your accountant for advice on choosing the payroll option that fits your business needs and to ensure that your setup is fully compliant with your local and state taxing authorities.

QuickBooks Desktop Payroll Services

QuickBooks offers a variety of payroll services designed to work with your company data. Each service requires a separate fee paid to Intuit. Here's a brief recap of what's currently available:

- **Basic Payroll**   Provides tax tables and automatic calculations of paycheck deductions and employer expenses for up to three employees. No tax forms are included, so you either need to work with your accountant on tax filings or prepare your tax forms manually. QuickBooks makes it easy to prepare tax forms manually by providing detailed reports in Excel.
- **Enhanced Payroll**   Adds tax forms and e-filing for both federal and state reporting.
- **Full Payroll**   Turns the job of running your payroll, depositing withholdings, paying employer contributions, and printing and filing government forms over to QuickBooks. All you have to do is enter your employees' hours.

Additional plans are available, such as Intuit's Online Payroll service, which does not require that you use QuickBooks for your accounting, and Enhanced Payroll for Accountants, which lets you prepare payroll for up to 50 companies (including preparing federal and state forms) and includes After The Fact payroll data entry capability. If you're looking for a complete solution, consider the Intuit Full Service option—you enter your employees' time, and Intuit handles the rest.

Enabling a QuickBooks Payroll Service

As you begin, be sure the Full Payroll feature preference is enabled in your QuickBooks company file by choosing Edit | Preferences | Payroll & Employees | Company Preferences | Full Payroll. Selecting this option enables payroll-related information fields for employees and adds a Turn On Payroll button in the Employee section of the QuickBooks Home page. Click the Turn On Payroll button to learn about and sign up for one of the QuickBooks payroll offerings.

When the sign-up process is completed, download the files you need to run payroll. The new files are automatically added to your QuickBooks system; you don't have to do anything to install them. In addition to the payroll software, the current tax table is added to your system. After payroll is installed, your Employees menu has all the commands you need to run payroll.

Processing Your Payroll Manually in QuickBooks

If you have only one or two employees, you may choose to run a manual payroll in QuickBooks. Remember that when you process your payroll manually, no withholding or tax will automatically be calculated for any paycheck you create; you have to subscribe to the QuickBooks payroll service for that. You can use the Employer's Circular E from the IRS, calculate the deductions, and enter them manually when you create paychecks.

However, you need to set up your file to allow you to enter these amounts manually, and the only way to tell QuickBooks you want to exercise this option is via the Help menu.

1. Select QuickBooks Help from the main Help menu to open the Have A Question? window.
2. In the Search field, type **manual payroll**, and then click the magnifying glass (search) icon. QuickBooks displays several Help articles. Click the article titled "Process Payroll Manually (Without A Subscription To QuickBooks Payroll)."
3. Follow the instructions as shown in the link "If You Prefer To Process Your Payroll Manually." If you do elect to process your payroll manually, you'll still need to set up Employees and Payroll items and track Payroll Liabilities.

The decision to run a manual payroll should be made only after careful consideration and consultation with your accountant and when you have only one or two employees. It is up to you to ensure that the calculations are correct and that you have a workable system to remit withholdings to the appropriate agency in a timely manner.

Setting Up Your Payroll

To produce accurate paychecks, you need to add accounts to your chart of accounts; create payroll items (salary, wages, and so on); and identify the payroll taxes you have to withhold, the payroll taxes you have to pay as an employer, and company contributions or deductions. You also need to set up tax information for each employee, such as dependents and deductions.

You can set up these payroll elements either using the Payroll Setup Wizard or manually. The following sections cover the steps in setting up payroll manually, and later you'll learn to use the Payroll Setup Wizard. Review both to decide which way you want to do the setup.

Add Payroll Accounts to the Chart of Accounts

You may need to create new accounts in your chart of accounts for payroll. QuickBooks automatically adds the Payroll Liabilities and Payroll Expenses accounts when you enable payroll. Use subaccounts for payroll liabilities and payroll expenses, because it makes it easier to keep track of individual liabilities and expenses. Be sure to link your payroll items to these subaccounts and not to the parent account. Then, when you create reports, any balances in the subaccounts are totaled in the parent account.

Add Vendors

Running payroll creates liabilities for payroll taxes and employee benefits withheld or deducted. In QuickBooks, the government agency or employee benefit provider to which you remit these withheld amounts needs to be a vendor. Then, when you set up the payroll item that tracks the withholding or deduction, you assign that item to the appropriate vendor.

For withholding of federal income taxes, Medicare, Federal Insurance Contributions Act (FICA), and the matching employer Medicare and FICA payments, you can assign the United States Treasury Department as the vendor. Since January 1, 2011, the IRS requires that all payroll tax deposits be made electronically using the Employer Federal Tax Payment System (EFTPS). EFTPS deposits can be made online or by telephone, from the convenience of your home or office. If you haven't already done so, you'll need to go to the EFTPS website (www.eftps.gov) to learn more and enroll.

For local and state income tax, unemployment, disability, workers comp, and deductions for benefits such as health insurance, set up a vendor for each agency you need to pay. Most states now offer electronic payments for payroll remittances on their websites, but if you use checks, you probably have forms or coupons that should accompany your payments.

Adding Payroll Items

QuickBooks uses *payroll items* to list compensation or deduction amounts on a payroll check. The number of individual payroll items that make up a paycheck may

Item	Description
Employee Earnings	These can be salaries; hourly, overtime, or double-time wages; bonuses; and/or commissions.
Sick and/or Vacation Pay	These vary by industry and company policy.
Federal Tax Withholdings	Federal Income Tax (FIT), Social Security (FICA), and Medicare.
Advanced Earned Income Credit	Check with your accountant regarding this item.
State and Local Tax Withholdings	These vary by state and locality. Some areas have both state income and local income taxes.
State Unemployment and Disability	These taxes vary by state, but nearly each state has unemployment and disability taxes.
Retirement or Pension Plan	These deductions vary by industry.
Insurance	Medical and life insurance deductions.
Union Dues	These vary by industry and locale.
Garnishments	Such as child support, collection agencies, and the like.

TABLE 9-3 **Payroll Items**

be more than you thought. Consider the items in Table 9-3, which are typical of many businesses.

You can view your payroll items and create new ones by choosing Lists | Payroll Item List to open the Payroll Item List, as seen in Figure 9-3. Although QuickBooks adds

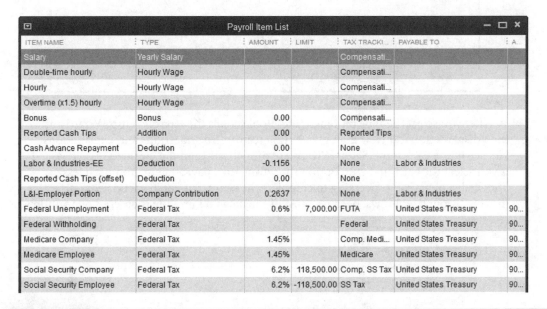

ITEM NAME	TYPE	AMOUNT	LIMIT	TAX TRACKI...	PAYABLE TO	A...
Salary	Yearly Salary			Compensati...		
Double-time hourly	Hourly Wage			Compensati...		
Hourly	Hourly Wage			Compensati...		
Overtime (x1.5) hourly	Hourly Wage			Compensati...		
Bonus	Bonus	0.00		Compensati...		
Reported Cash Tips	Addition	0.00		Reported Tips		
Cash Advance Repayment	Deduction	0.00		None		
Labor & Industries-EE	Deduction	-0.1156		None	Labor & Industries	
Reported Cash Tips (offset)	Deduction	0.00		None		
L&I-Employer Portion	Company Contribution	0.2637		None	Labor & Industries	
Federal Unemployment	Federal Tax	0.6%	7,000.00	FUTA	United States Treasury	90...
Federal Withholding	Federal Tax			Federal	United States Treasury	90...
Medicare Company	Federal Tax	1.45%		Comp. Medi...	United States Treasury	90...
Medicare Employee	Federal Tax	1.45%		Medicare	United States Treasury	90...
Social Security Company	Federal Tax	6.2%	118,500.00	Comp. SS Tax	United States Treasury	90...
Social Security Employee	Federal Tax	6.2%	-118,500.00	SS Tax	United States Treasury	90...

FIGURE 9-3 The Payroll Item list includes both tax and wage items.

some items to the list when you enable payroll services, you are usually missing local taxes, medical benefits deductions, and other payroll items. Also, the items that *do* exist may be missing information about the vendor, so you'll have to edit them accordingly.

To add a new payroll item, from the Payroll Item List window, select Payroll Item | New or press CTRL-N to open the Add New Payroll Item window. Select one of two methods for setting up payroll items: EZ Setup or Custom Setup.

EZ Setup of Payroll Items

With the EZ Setup option, when you click Next, you see a list of payroll item types, as shown next. The descriptions are brief, but you can create any type of pay, deduction, or company benefit, paid by the company, the employee, or both. The only types of payroll items you cannot create in EZ Setup are state and local payroll taxes, including state unemployment and/or disability taxes.

After you select the type of item, QuickBooks loads the Payroll Setup Wizard and then displays the Add New dialog from that feature. The questions and explanations you see in the EZ Payroll Setup Wizard are more basic than the questions you're asked if you select the Custom Setup option for setting up a payroll item. You need less knowledge of payroll processing to complete the setup, but you'll spend more time moving through windows, because most of the data you provide is entered one window at a time.

If you know nothing about payroll about deductions, benefits, or the accounting and legal issues involved with payroll benefits and deductions, consult with an accounting professional when payroll is involved. However, QuickBooks does give good, easy to understand explanations of the requested information.

For example, if you're setting up a benefit such as health insurance, pension benefit, or a benefit in a cafeteria plan, QuickBooks asks you if the benefit cost is borne entirely by the company, entirely by the employee, or shared between both. Depending on your answer, you move through the subsequent windows to set up the necessary payroll item(s). In addition, if the employee contributes some or all of the cost, you have to know whether it's a pre-tax or after-tax deduction, and you have to know how the deduction affects the employee's W-2 form. This is yet another reason to discuss your payroll setup with your accountant first!

Custom Setup of Payroll Items

If you select the Custom Setup option, the list you see when you click Next is all inclusive. You can set up all the payroll item types offered in the EZ Setup list of payroll types, plus you can set up state and local payroll items. You'll find that, unlike the EZ Setup, each window in the Custom Setup Wizard contains most of the fields for the required information, resulting in fewer steps needed to complete the setup of a payroll item.

Keep in mind, however, that if you have a health benefit with costs shared between the company and the employee, the Custom Setup Wizard isn't going to remind you that you have to set up two items: first one for the employee deduction and another for the company payment. In this instance, you have to start the wizard again to select Company Contribution in the second wizard window to set up the company side of the Health Benefits item.

Setting Up Employees

You have a great deal of information to fill out for each employee, and some of it is probably the same for all or most of your employees. The information about your employees *must* be accurate; otherwise, you may have to adjust payroll information inside QuickBooks and then report the changes to the IRS, both of which mean more work for you and potential confusion with the IRS about your payroll data.

To save yourself a lot of time, you can create a new employee default template. The information you put into the template is added automatically to the Payroll Info tab for each new employee you create, as shown here.

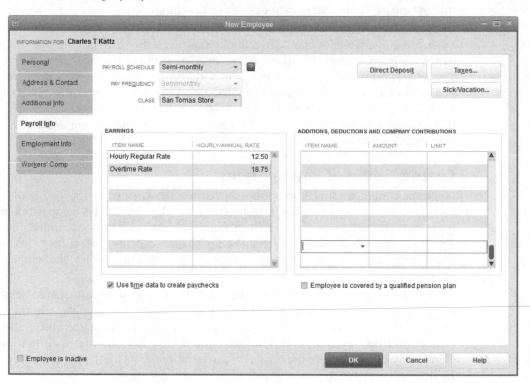

Creating an Employee Template

To access the template, open the Employee Center by choosing Employees | Employee Center from the menu bar. In the Employee Center window, click the Manage Employee Information button at the top of the window and choose Change New Employee Default Settings from the submenu that appears. This opens the Employee Defaults window, where you can enter the data that applies to most or all of your employees.

1. Click in the Item Name column of the Earnings box, and then click the arrow to see a list of earnings types that you've defined as payroll items. Select the one that is common enough to be suitable for a template.

2. In the Hourly/Annual Rate column, enter a wage or salary figure if one applies to most of your employees. Otherwise, skip it and enter each rate in the employee record.

3. Click the arrow in the field to the right of the Payroll Schedule field and select a schedule. See Chapter 10 for more information.

4. Select a pay frequency (if you created schedules and selected one, QuickBooks automatically uses that schedule to fill in the Pay Frequency field).

5. Use the Class field if you've enabled classes to track data.

6. If you use QuickBooks, time-tracking features to pay employees, you see a Use Time Data To Create Paychecks check box. Select the check box to enable that feature.

7. If all or most of your employees have the same adjustments, click in the Item Name column in the Additions, Deductions, And Company Contributions box, and then click the arrow to select the appropriate adjustments.

8. Click the Taxes button to open the Taxes Defaults dialog, and select those taxes that are common and therefore suited for the template. The State tab and the Other tab (usually local payroll taxes) contain tax data that often applies to all or most of your employees.

9. Click the Sick/Vacation button to set the terms for accruing sick time and vacation time if your policy is similar enough among employees to include it in the template.

10. When you are finished filling out the template, click OK to save it.

Creating Employees

You're ready to add your employees. Choose Employees | Employee Center. Click the New Employee button at the top of the window to add your first employee. The New Employee form opens on the Personal tab. Enter the new employee's data, as described here:

- **Personal**   Enter basic data about your new hire.
- **Address & Contact**   Enter address, phone numbers, e-mail, and emergency contacts information. You must have at least the address to file W-2 forms.
- **Additional Info**   Use this tab to enter an (optional) employee number or create custom fields using the Define Fields button to track additional information.
- **Payroll Info**   Enter earnings, taxes, and deductions. (If you've chosen to enter payroll manually, this tab is named "Compensation" and does not include tax or deduction information.)

  1. Click the Taxes button to open the Taxes dialog.
  2. Enter the federal and state tax information. QuickBooks builds in a great deal of state information.
  3. On the Other tab, apply any local payroll tax that applies to this employee.
  4. Click the Sick/Vacation button and enter the hours and dates for this employee.
  5. When you are finished, click OK to return to the Payroll Info tab.

- **Employment Info** Enter hiring date and other employment and job details here. See "Understanding Employment Types" next to determine the employee type.
- **Workers Comp** If you use either the Enhanced or Assisted Payroll service, the workers comp tracking feature appears. You can disable it in the Payroll & Employees Preferences. Assign the applicable workers comp code, or select Exempt if this employee is exempt from workers comp.

Understanding Employment Types

There are four options in the Type field on the Employment Info tab of the New Employee form. What you select may have an impact on your tax returns, so check with your accountant if you have any questions. Table 9-4 explains the four types.

Type	Explanation
Regular Employee	Someone you hire from whom you deduct taxes and issue a W-2.
Officer Employee	An officer of a corporation. If your business isn't incorporated, you have no officers. Selecting Officer as the type has no impact on running your payroll (calculations, check printing, and so on); it only affects reports.
Statutory Employee	Someone working for you deemed by the IRS as an employee instead of an independent contractor. Check with your accountant before assigning this type.
Owner Employee	No payroll tasks are performed for this type of employee. This employee type is appropriate if you own a company that is a proprietorship because the money you pay yourself is posted to an equity account called Owner's Draw. If the business is a partnership, the amounts paid to the owners are distributions.

TABLE 9-4 Employee Types in QuickBooks

Paying Employees and Payroll Taxes and Creating Forms

Chapter 10

n this chapter:

- Entering year-to-date payroll information
- How payroll is set up in QuickBooks
- Scheduling payroll
- Running and reviewing the payroll
- Understanding the Payroll Center
- Determining, remitting, and tracking payroll liabilities
- Preparing W-2 forms
- Using Excel for taxes

Handle Year-to-Date Payroll Data

To make historical data entry easier, consider going live with payroll at the beginning of a calendar year. However, if you start using QuickBooks mid-year, you must enter the historical information about paychecks you have entered so far for this year. This way, QuickBooks can perform all of the required year-end tasks. For example, you cannot give your employees two W-2 forms: one from your "pre-QuickBooks" system and another from QuickBooks.

No matter what your fiscal year may be, your payroll year is the calendar year. Even though you can start using QuickBooks payroll for the current period before you enter historical data, remember that the absence of historical data may affect some tax calculations. Also, year-to-date payroll information on pay stubs for the employees will be incorrect until you enter historical payroll data. If there are withholding amounts that cease after a certain amount, you have to adjust the deductions on the current paychecks manually so that QuickBooks can calculate the maximum deduction properly and stop deducting these amounts.

Entering Year-to-Date Totals

If you start using QuickBooks payroll in the middle of the year, you need to enter the year-to-date payroll totals to date into your QuickBooks company file. Consider the following:

- You need the total of all payroll amounts entered by quarter because 941 reports are due quarterly.
- You can't enter summarized data for the current quarter (the quarter your start date falls in). Instead, for the current quarter, you must enter data for each individual pay period (weekly, biweekly, semimonthly, or monthly). For previous quarters, you can enter quarterly totals.

Manually Entering Payroll History in Batches

Once you have entered all of your employees, you can use a shortcut that launches a process for entering year-to-date payroll information. This process replicates the historical balance-entry windows that QuickBooks Payroll Setup offers, but some people find this method easier to use, especially if they've chosen to set up their payroll manually.

1. Choose Help | About QuickBooks (*version 2016*) Desktop to display the product information window. Then press CTRL-SHIFT-Y. The Set Up YTD Amounts Wizard, shown next, opens to walk you through the steps of entering year-to-date summary information for each employee. Click Next to begin.

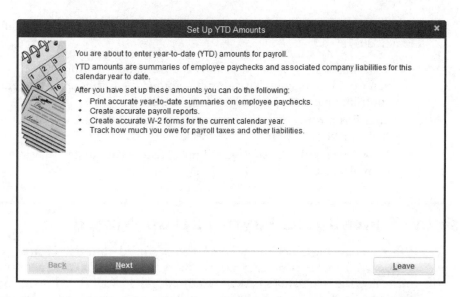

2. In the next two windows, the wizard asks you to specify three dates. It's important to note that the dates you enter might not be the same for all three categories.

   - The date your Payroll Liability and Payroll Expenses accounts are affected. When should the data you're entering be posted to payroll item liability and expense accounts?

   - The date your payroll bank accounts are affected. When should the net paycheck amounts be posted to your payroll bank account?

   - The check date of the first paycheck you'll create using QuickBooks payroll. This paycheck posts to all relevant accounts; there are no historical balances. Click Next when you've entered this third date.

3. On the Employee summary information page, you'll see your list of employees. Highlight a name and then click the Enter Summary button to open the YTD Adjustment window for that employee.

4. Enter the YTD amounts for wages and withholdings for each payroll period. Click OK after you've completed the entries for each employee. You'll be brought back to the Employee summary information page in the Set Up YTD Amounts Wizard. Click the Leave button to close the Set Up YTD Amounts Wizard.

Choosing the Correct Dates When Entering Year-to-Date Payroll

This example should help you understand how to enter the dates in these categories. For the purpose of these examples, let's assume you're entering historical information as of the end of April 2017, and your first QuickBooks-produced paychecks will be Friday, May 1, 2017.

- Your first posting of liabilities and expenses should be April 1, 2017, because you would (hopefully) have already remitted the withholdings and employer contributions for the quarter ending March 31, 2017.
- Your first posting of bank account amounts should be May 1, 2017, the date of the first QuickBooks-produced paycheck.
- Your "first paycheck using QuickBooks" date is your first payday in May. In this example, that day is May 1, 2017.

Use the QuickBooks Payroll Setup Wizard

When you use the QuickBooks Payroll Setup Wizard, shown in Figure 10-1, to set up your payroll, the setup process can take more time than it takes to perform those tasks manually. The wizard does have some advantages: it's user friendly with explanations throughout, and you can use it to set up all the components required for payroll, including entering your historical data. It also has a Finish Later button so that when you open the wizard again, you can pick up where you left off.

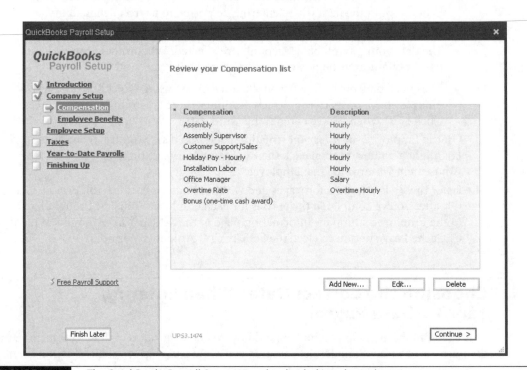

FIGURE 10-1 The QuickBooks Payroll Setup Wizard is divided into logical sections.

Regardless of whether you use the Payroll Setup Wizard to set up all your components or to enter historical data only, be sure to set up all the vendors and accounts you need to remit payroll withholding and employer payroll expenses first.

Start by choosing Employees | Payroll Setup from the QuickBooks menu bar. The wizard window opens with all the tasks listed in the left pane. The first few screens are informational, indicating the data you need to complete the wizard (the same information about employees, payroll items, deductions, and so on that were discussed in Chapter 9). The real work starts with the Company Setup pages, where the wizard begins to guide you through the necessary details of your payroll setup.

Company Setup Section

In the Company Setup section, the wizard starts with compensation, which means payroll items for salary, hourly wages, bonuses, and so on. If you've already created your payroll items, they appear in the wizard window, and you can click Edit to view or change the settings. If you haven't yet set up payroll items, click Add New to open a mini-wizard that walks you through the process.

The types of payroll items the Company Setup section of the wizard helps to set up include types of compensation, benefits, paid time off, and other additions and deductions, such as workers comp, auto expense reimbursement, garnishments, union dues, and so on.

Setting Up Employees in the Wizard

After the Company Setup section, the wizard moves on to the Employee Setup section. You can add each employee in the wizard, moving through a series of windows in which you enter information about the employee's personal information, pay structure, and tax status. For each employee, you designate the taxes and benefits that affect the employee.

When you finish entering employee information, the wizard displays the list of employees. If any employee is missing information, the wizard indicates the problem. If you entered your employees manually, the wizard automatically finds the employee records and displays the same list if problems exist.

Some missing information isn't critical to issuing paychecks, but QuickBooks requires the information in the employee record. If any employee in the list has the notation Fix This Error Now, it means critical information is missing and the system either won't be able to issue a paycheck or won't be able to issue a W-2 form at the end of the year. Select the employee and click Edit to move through the wizard and fix the problem.

Setting Up Payroll Taxes in the Wizard

In the Taxes section, you tell the wizard about the federal, state, and local taxes you're responsible for. These are payroll items, so if you haven't set up all these items beforehand, you can use the wizard to do so now. As you finish each section, the wizard displays a list of all the taxes for that section. If you set up your taxes as payroll items manually, the wizard finds those entries and uses them to populate the list. If the wizard finds anything amiss in your setup of any tax, the problem is displayed in the Description column. Choose Edit to make the needed changes.

Entering Payroll History in the Wizard

You enter historical payroll data in the Year-to-Date Payroll section. The wizard presents a set of windows, starting with a window that asks if you've issued paychecks this year outside of QuickBooks. If you answer Yes, the next window displayed is the Payroll Summary window, where you have access to three preformatted tables. Click the Edit button next to each of these payroll categories to open the associated worksheet and enter the information.

Running Data Review

Next is the Data Review section, which is optional. QuickBooks asks if you'd like to go over your payroll settings. If you select Yes, the wizard runs a payroll checkup routine. At this point, your setup is complete, and from here you can click Finish or go straight to the Payroll Center, where you'll have access to essentially everything that relates to managing your payroll.

Running a Payroll Checkup

You can run a Payroll Checkup whenever you make changes to your payroll components (employees, taxes, and so on) by choosing Employees | My Payroll Service | Run Payroll Checkup. The QuickBooks Payroll Setup Wizard walks you through a task list of payroll items, and each section of the wizard's task list is checked for errors. The errors the checkup may find include missing information, invalid information, or any other data that doesn't match QuickBooks' built-in payroll standards.

Payroll Schedules

If your company pays salaried employees and officers on a weekly basis and pays hourly workers on a biweekly basis, for example, using a payroll schedule makes it easy to ensure you're paying the proper employees at the proper time. When you create a payroll schedule, you define how often you pay your employees and define the pay period (the workdays covered by the paycheck), the date on the paycheck, and the date you prepare the payroll. (However, the date you prepare the payroll differs from the paycheck date if you're using direct deposit, which requires you to transfer payroll information two days before the paycheck date.)

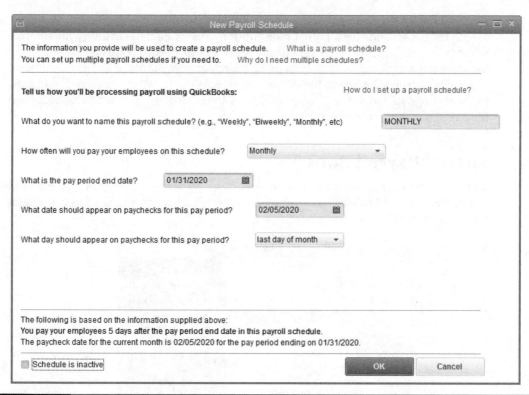

Establish payroll schedules using the New Payroll Schedule dialog.

Creating a Payroll Schedule

To create a payroll schedule, choose Employees | Add Or Edit Payroll Schedules. When the Payroll Schedule List window opens, select Payroll Schedule | New (or press CTRL-N) to open the New Payroll Schedule dialog. Use the dialog seen in Figure 10-2 to complete the following:

- A name for this schedule. Use descriptive text if you're setting up multiple schedules, such as "Weekly-Hourly," "Commissions Only," and so on.
- The pay period frequency for this schedule.
- The next pay period end date. This is the time period covered by the paycheck, which often is not the same as the paycheck date, such as paychecks issued on Thursday for the period ending the previous Friday.
- The next paycheck date.

The dialog includes additional fields for monthly or semimonthly payrolls. For example, if you issue paychecks semimonthly, you can select specific dates, such as the

10th and the 25th, or you can select one midmonth date and then select Last Day Of Month for the second check in that month. After you create the schedule, QuickBooks offers to assign the schedule automatically to any employees who are configured for the same pay frequency as the new schedule. Each employee record has a field for the applicable payroll schedule in the Payroll Info tab. When you link the payroll schedule to the appropriate employees, those employees appear when you select the schedule on the day you're preparing paychecks.

Special Payroll Runs

You can create payroll checks at other times as well. When you choose Employees | Pay Employees, in addition to the subcommand Scheduled Payroll, you see two commands for special payroll runs (shown here):

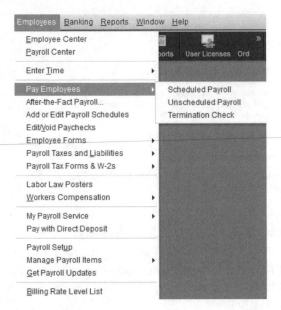

- **Unscheduled Payroll**   Select this special payroll category if you need to create bonus checks, commission checks, or any other type of paycheck that differs from a regularly scheduled payroll run.
- **Termination Check**   To use this option, you must first enter a release date in the Employment Info tab of the employee's record. Be sure this release date is after the check date because QuickBooks removes the name from the Enter Payroll Information window as of that date, which means that you can't create a final paycheck for this person.

When you're ready to create the check, select the terminated employee by placing a check mark in the column to the left of the employee name. Next, fill in the pay period ending date, the check date, the termination date, and the hours (or amount the employee is salaried). Click Continue; approve or change the paycheck details; and then print the check, assign a check number for a manual check, or issue a direct-deposit check.

> **Small Business Tip** If you rehire a terminated employee, you have to delete the release date in the Employment Info tab of the Edit Employee screen.

Run Payroll

When you are ready to run your first payroll, begin creating payroll checks as follows:

- If you don't use payroll schedules, choose Employees | Pay Employees | Unscheduled Payroll to open the Enter Payroll Information dialog.
- If you have payroll schedules, choose Employees | Pay Employees | Scheduled Payroll to open the Employee Center with the Payroll tab selected (the Pay Employees function appears in the right pane). Select the appropriate schedule and click Start Scheduled Payroll to open the Enter Payroll Information dialog.

Select the employees to pay. If all the employees are receiving paychecks (the usual scenario), click Check All. For hourly employees configured for automatic payroll amounts using timesheets, the number of hours is prefilled. For hourly employees not paid from timesheets, you must fill in the number of hours for this paycheck.

Changing Paycheck Data

If you want to make changes to a paycheck, click the employee's name to open the Preview Paycheck dialog. You can add a payroll item such as a bonus, assign the paycheck to a customer or job, or add a deduction such as a repayment of a loan or garnishment. Click Save & Next to move to the next employee, click Save & Previous to go back to a previous check, or click Save & Close to return to the Enter Payroll Information dialog. If you want to make a change to a paycheck after you have printed it, you will need to "unlock" the information to make this change. Contact your payroll professional before doing this for the first time.

Reviewing the Payroll Run

Click Continue in the Enter Payroll Information dialog to display the Review And Create Paychecks window, which displays all the financial information for this payroll run. If anything looks incorrect, click Back to reconfigure the paychecks or make other needed corrections.

Fill out the options for producing the paychecks (print the checks or automatically assign check numbers in the bank account register for manual checks), and then click Create Paychecks. QuickBooks creates the checks and displays the Confirmation And Next Steps dialog.

If you're printing paychecks, you can click Print Paychecks, or you can wait and print them by choosing File | Print Forms | Print Paychecks, as seen next. If you have direct-deposit employees, click Print Pay Stubs. When the pay stubs are printed, click the Send Payroll Data button on the Confirmation And Next Steps dialog. This opens the Send Center window, and you can upload the direct-deposit data to Intuit for processing. You can e-mail the pay stubs using the security standards built into the process (see the Help files for details).

If you have another payroll schedule to run today (perhaps both weekly and biweekly employees are paid today), repeat all the processes as outlined here.

➼ Net-to-Gross Calculations for Enhanced Payroll Subscribers

If you subscribe to the Enhanced Payroll service, you can enter the net amount of a check and let QuickBooks calculate the gross amount. This is useful for bonus checks or another special payroll check for which you need to make sure the employee receives a net check of a certain amount.

During the payroll run (either a regular payroll or a special payroll for this individual paycheck), select the relevant employee. In the Preview Paycheck window, select the option Enter Net/Calculate Gross, located in the lower-right corner, and then enter the net amount for this paycheck. QuickBooks automatically calculates the gross amount and the deductions to arrive at the net amount you entered.

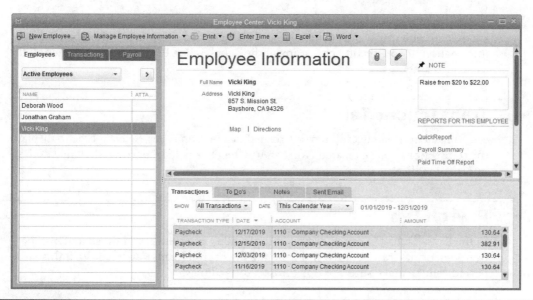

FIGURE 10-3   Your employees' information is stored in the Employee Center.

The Employee Center

All the employee information you've entered and the payroll schedules and paychecks you've created are easily accessed via the Employee Center, shown in Figure 10-3. The Employee Center contains reporting information about your payroll and provides links to all the functions in the payroll system. It's a central location for everything you need to do or need to know.

To open this window, choose Employees | Employee Center from the menu bar. If you subscribe to a QuickBooks payroll service, the left pane of the Employee Center contains three tabs: Employees, Transactions, and Payroll. If you don't have a payroll plan subscription, the pane lacks a Payroll tab.

Employees Tab

When you select an employee on the Employees tab, QuickBooks displays information from the employee's record on the top part of the right pane and displays transaction information for that employee on the bottom part of the right pane. You can change the choices in the Show and Date fields to filter the transaction information. Notice the three additional tabs located just above the employee transaction information. They allow you to add and manage To Do's, Notes, and e-mails sent to an employee.

You can open any listed transaction by double-clicking it. For example, if you open a paycheck, you can see the original check along with a summary of the financial information. If you need to check any of the details, click Paycheck Detail to see all the calculated amounts.

Transactions Tab

The Transactions tab lists all payroll-related transaction types. Select a type to display the transactions you've created. You can use the Date field to narrow the range of the information displayed.

Payroll Tab

In the Payroll tab, you can view upcoming liability payments (and those that may be overdue), create transactions, and generate the payroll forms you need. Visit this tab periodically to make sure you don't miss any deadlines.

Customizing the Employee Center

You can tailor the way the Employee Center displays information. Resize the panes by moving your mouse pointer over the edge of any pane; when the pointer changes to a vertical bar with right and left arrows, drag the pane in either direction. In addition, you can expand the pane to show the full List view by clicking the arrow button located at the top of the Employees tab. Use the same button to collapse the pane to show both the list and the detail panes.

You can customize the columns that QuickBooks displays in the left pane of the Employees tab by right-clicking anywhere on the list and choosing Customize Columns. You can also customize the information displayed in the right pane when you select an employee's name in the Employees tab or when you select a transaction type on the Transactions tab. Right-click anywhere in the right (Transaction) pane and select Customize Columns.

Tracking and Remitting Payroll Liabilities

All of the tasks involved in reporting on and paying your payroll liabilities using QuickBooks have a logical order, although the steps may differ depending on the state and municipality you're in.

Confirm Payroll Payment Schedules

When you run payroll, QuickBooks maintains a payment schedule behind the scenes that keeps track of the amounts and due dates for all the payroll liabilities and employer expenses that accumulate. Use this payment schedule to make sure you remit your payroll obligations on time. Most of the information required for scheduling payments is probably already in your system from when you set up payroll items. To view the schedule and correct any problems, choose Employees | Payroll Taxes And Liabilities | Edit Payment Due Dates/Methods.

This opens the Payroll Setup Wizard's Tax Payments window. As you move through each page, if any data is missing or does not match the content or format the payroll system expects, the wizard highlights the listing with a problem icon. Double-click the problem listing so you can edit it and fix the problem. QuickBooks usually provides a hint about the problem in the window that opens.

Report and Remit Payroll Tax Liabilities

When you create payroll checks, QuickBooks tracks the taxes that are due as liabilities. To see your scheduled liabilities, choose Employees | Payroll Taxes And Liabilities | Pay Scheduled Liabilities. The Pay Liabilities tab shows the list of taxes and other liabilities currently owed, as shown here.

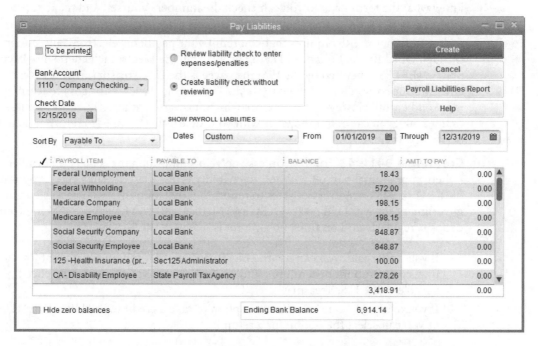

Select the liability you want to pay and click the View/Pay button. The first time you pay liabilities, QuickBooks asks you to select the appropriate bank account (if you have more than one). The Liability Payment transaction window opens. Continue to view and pay until all the current liabilities are set for payment.

Federal Tax Liabilities

Payments to the federal government involve two payroll taxes:

- 941/944/943 taxes, which cover withholding, Social Security, and Medicare
- 940 taxes, which are the federal unemployment taxes

941/943 Payments   The federal government requires you to report and remit the withheld amounts, along with the matching employer contributions, at a specified time. That time period is dependent upon the size of the total withholding amount you've accumulated. You may be required to remit monthly, semimonthly, weekly, or within three days of the payroll. Check the current limits with the IRS or your accountant.

There's a formula for determining the size of the 941/943 payment. It is the sum of these amounts for the period: federal withholding, plus FICA (Social Security) withholding, plus Medicare withholding, plus the matching employer contributions for FICA and Medicare.

You don't have to do the math—QuickBooks does it for you. But it's a good idea to know what the formula is so you can check the numbers yourself and make sure you have sufficient funds in your bank account to cover the next payment.

In addition, the IRS requires that you remit your payments electronically, either through QuickBooks Enhanced Payroll or by using the Electronic Federal Tax Payment System (EFTPS) operated by the IRS; the payee is the U.S. Treasury. If you haven't already done so, you'll need to go to the EFTPS website (www.eftps.gov) to learn more and enroll. However, if your employment taxes for a quarterly period are less than $2,500, you can remit the taxes with your quarterly (Form 941) return in lieu of depositing them.

Creating a 941/943 Form   Unless you've been notified that you're a Form 944 filer (where your annual payroll withholding liability is less than $1,000 a year), you must file a 941 or 943 form every quarter to report the total amount you owe the federal government for withheld taxes, FICA, and Medicare. If you have been making your deposits regularly and on time, no amount is due with the 941/943.

- If you underpaid, you can use the EFTPS system to remit your payment for the underpaid amount or remit the underpayment with your form with a check payable to the U.S. Treasury.
- If you overpaid, you can select the option to take a credit toward the next 941/ 943, or you can select the option for a refund.

QuickBooks will prepare your 941/943 report using the information in your QuickBooks payroll registers. If QuickBooks isn't preparing your federal forms (either because you're doing payroll manually or you subscribed to the QuickBooks Basic Payroll service), you can prepare your forms manually with the use of Excel worksheets that QuickBooks provides. See the section "Tax Form Worksheets in Excel" at the end of this chapter. Creating the form is quite easy.

1. Choose Employees | Payroll Tax Forms & W-2s | Process Payroll Forms. The Payroll tab in the Employee Center opens to show the list of tax forms available for filing.
2. Select Federal Quarterly Form 941/Sch B – Employer's Quarterly Federal Tax Return (or Federal Quarterly Form 943A – Employer's Annual Federal Tax Return for Agricultural Employees) and click the File Form button. The File Form window opens.
3. Select the filing period. You can also click the Auto-Fill Contact Info button to have QuickBooks automatically copy the contact information you provide in this window to future tax forms you need to complete. Click OK.
4. The Payroll Tax Form window opens to the selected form. The first window is an interview; enter the appropriate data, and click Next to continue.
5. Use the guidelines presented in the following sections to move through the wizard.

To enter information in a blank field, click your cursor in the field to activate it, and then type the data. The typed text appears in blue, but that's just a signal to you that the data was entered manually; QuickBooks doesn't print the form in color.

Editing Prefilled Data

Follow these steps to edit data:

1. Right-click the field and choose Override from the menu that appears.
2. Enter the replacement data in the override box and press the TAB key.
3. The new data replaces the original data in the field, and the text is green to remind you that you manually replaced the data that was exported from QuickBooks.

If you change your mind and decide that the data automatically supplied by QuickBooks should remain in the form, right-click in the field and choose Cancel Override.

Data You Cannot Change

Do *not* edit the following types of data on the Form 941 or on any payroll tax form:

- Federal Employer Identification Number (EIN)
- Filing period (if you're trying to change the filing period, start the process again and select the appropriate date range)
- Totals (these are calculated by QuickBooks; if a total is wrong, edit the erroneous number, and QuickBooks will recalculate the total)

Checking for Errors

Before you finalize the contents of Form 941/943, click the Check For Errors button. QuickBooks examines the content and displays any errors in the Errors box that opens at the top of the form. If there aren't any problems, the Errors box reports this too.

Click any error to move automatically to the field that's causing the problem, and then correct the information:

- If the problem is in a field you filled out, correct the data and press the TAB key.
- If the problem is in a field that was prefilled but you changed the content by overriding the data, right-click the field and select Cancel Override.

When you press TAB to replace the data in the field, the error listing should disappear from the Errors box. If it doesn't, you have to figure out what's wrong with the data and correct it. When the error is fixed, you can close the Errors box by clicking the Close Errors button.

Saving and Reopening an Unfinished Form

If you get interrupted while you're preparing your 941, 943, or 940 form, you can save it with the data you already filled in so you don't have to start from scratch when you resume your work. Click Save And Close to save the form with its current contents. To return to work on the saved form, you'll need to open the form again, following the steps from the previous section, again selecting the form and a date range. QuickBooks asks if you want to use the saved draft. If you made changes, you'll have to start a new form instead of opening a saved draft. Changes could include an additional paycheck being issued within the date range for some reason or a payment you made to the IRS as a remittance for this report period.

Printing or Submitting Form 941/943

You can print the form from QuickBooks, save it as a PDF, or submit the form electronically. If you choose to print, be sure to use these printing criteria:

- The form must be printed with black ink on white or cream-colored paper.
- The paper size must be 8.5 by 11 inches.
- The paper must be 20-pound weight or heavier.

The printed report doesn't look exactly like the blank form you received, but it's perfectly acceptable to the government. Print two copies: one to mail and one for your files.

If you've set up for e-filing with your QuickBooks Payroll subscription, click the Submit Form button to file your 941/943 electronically. If you have not set up this form for e-filing, open the Employee Center and click the Payroll tab to open the Payroll Center. Then click the File Forms tab and click Start Filing Electronically in the Other Activities area. (If you've already chosen e-file for any form filing, click Manage Filing Methods instead.)

940 Payments

The Federal Unemployment Tax Act (FUTA) provides unemployment compensation to workers who have lost their jobs, usually after the workers' state benefits have been exhausted. The FUTA tax is paid by employers; no deductions are taken from employee wages. Companies must make FUTA payments if either of the following scenarios exists:

- During this year or last year, you paid wages of at least $1,500 in any calendar quarter.
- During this year or last year, you had one or more employees for at least part of a day for a period of 20 weeks (the weeks do not have to be contiguous).

You don't have to make the deposit until you owe the entire amount, but you can make deposits until you reach that amount if you wish.

Currently, the FUTA tax is 6 percent of gross wages up to $7,000 per employee, but the federal government gives employers up to a 5.4 percent credit for paying their state unemployment taxes. So if you're entitled to the maximum 5.4 percent credit, the FUTA tax rate after the credit is 0.6 percent. QuickBooks assumes you're paying your state unemployment taxes and calculates your FUTA liability accordingly.

Preparing the 940 Form   The 940 form (FUTA) is filed annually. To create your Form 940:

1. Choose Employees | Payroll Tax Forms & W-2s | Process Payroll Forms. The Payroll tab in the Employee Center opens to show the list of tax forms available for filing.

2. Select Annual Form 940/Sch A – Employer's Annual Federal Unemployment (FUTA) Tax Return. Click the File Form button to open the File Form window.

3. Select the filing period. You can also click the Auto-Fill Contact Info button to have QuickBooks automatically copy the contact information you provide in this window to future tax forms you need to complete. Click OK.

4. The Payroll Tax Form window (it's the first window of a wizard) opens with the Form 940 Interview displayed. The top section of the interview window asks about your state and federal unemployment payments. Below that section is a series of questions aimed at determining whether any of your payroll expenses covered exempt payment types. Exempt payments are wages you paid that are exempt from FUTA taxes. QuickBooks checks your payroll items to track several categories of exempt payments, and if you've used these payroll items, QuickBooks fills in the amounts. If you had any exempt payments that are not in the payroll items that QuickBooks automatically checks, fill in the amount directly on the appropriate field. Check the IRS rules for preparing Form 940, or check with your accountant. You can also get more information about this form by clicking the link View Details About This Form located at the bottom of the Payroll Tax Form window.

5. Click Next to see the form itself. Fill out any fields that aren't automatically prefilled by QuickBooks from your payroll records. Continue to click Next and follow the instructions that appear on the screen.

State and Local Income Taxes

Your state and local payroll liabilities vary depending upon where your business is located and where your employees live (and pay taxes). Besides income taxes, you may be liable for unemployment insurance and disability insurance. Most states have some form of an income tax, which might be calculated as a flat or sliding percentage of gross income or a percentage based on the federal tax for the employee.

Local (municipal or county) taxes also vary widely in their approach:

- Some cities have different rates for employees of companies that operate in the city. There may be one rate for employees who live in the same city and a different rate for nonresidents.
- Your business might operate in a city or town that has a *payroll head tax* (a once-a-year payment that is a flat amount per employee).

QuickBooks Enhanced Payroll supports most state forms. State and local taxing authorities also provide coupons, forms, or an online service for remitting income tax withholding. The frequency with which you must pay might depend on the size of your payroll, or it might be quarterly, semiannual, or annual, regardless of the amount. Some municipal authorities have e-pay available.

It's a good idea to create different vendor names for state unemployment insurance (SUI), state disability insurance (SDI), and state income tax withholding to make sure you don't accidentally send checks for the wrong component and to prevent QuickBooks from issuing a single check for the grand total. The vendor record for each vendor name may have the same payee (State Department of Revenue), but the vendor names are different.

Other State Liabilities

If your state has SUI or SDI or both, you have to pay those liabilities when they're due. Commonly, these are quarterly payments. Not all states have SUI or SDI, and some have one but not the other. Some states collect SUI and SDI from the employee and the company; some collect only from the company. Check the rules for your state, or talk to your accounting professional.

Nontax Payroll Liabilities

The rules for remitting the paycheck deductions and employer contributions for other reasons, such as health benefits, pension, and workers compensation, are specific to your arrangements with those vendors.

There are many ways to handle how these payments are posted, and you have to decide what makes sense to you and to your accountant. For example, if you pay a monthly amount to a medical insurer, you may want to post the employee deductions back to the same expense account you use to pay the bill. That way, only the net amount is reported as an expense on your taxes.

To remit liabilities that are not a scheduled liability in QuickBooks, you can use the Unscheduled Liabilities window. Choose Employees | Payroll Taxes And Liabilities | Create Custom Liability Payments. Select the paycheck date range you need, and then select the liability you want to remit.

Workers Comp

QuickBooks Enhanced and Assisted Payroll offerings include workers comp, and the setup options are available in the Payroll & Employees category of the Preferences dialog. Click the Workers Compensation button on the Company Preferences tab to open the Workers Comp Preferences dialog. Select Track Workers Comp to enable the feature.

When Workers Comp is enabled, you can also opt to see reminder messages to assign workers comp codes when you create paychecks or timesheets. In addition, you can select the option to exclude an overtime premium from your workers comp calculations (check your workers comp insurance policy to see if you can calculate overtime amounts as regular pay).

Prepare W-2 Forms

On or before January 31 of each year, you must print and send W-2 forms to your employees for the previous calendar year. By February 28, you need to send or e-file copies to the appropriate government agencies as well. When you run your payroll in QuickBooks, this process is very straightforward. You start by selecting the form and the employees, and then move to the process of creating and printing or electronically sending the forms. To do so:

1. Choose Employees | Payroll Tax Forms & W-2s | Process Payroll Forms. The Payroll tab in the Employee Center opens to show the list of tax forms available for filing.
2. Select Annual Form W-2/W-3 –Wage And Tax Statement/Transmittal. Click the File Form button. The File Form dialog opens.
3. Select the filing period and the employees for which you want to process W-2 forms. You can also click the Auto-Fill Contact Info button to have QuickBooks automatically copy the contact information you provide in this window to future tax forms you need to complete. Click OK.

4. The Select Employees For Form W-2/W-3 window opens, listing all your employees that have received a paycheck during the year, as shown here. By default, all employees are selected and the current status of the W-2 printing process is noted.

5. Click Review/Edit to display the first page of the Payroll Tax Form window, which explains the steps you'll go through as you step through the wizard. Click Next to move through the wizard.

6. In the screens that follow, each employee's W-2 form is presented. If any nonfinancial data is missing (such as an address or ZIP code), you must fill it in. If prefilled information is incorrect, right-click the appropriate field and select Override. Enter the correct information, and press TAB to add that information into the field. Changes you make to nonfinancial information are not written back to the employee record. You must make the same changes there.

7. Click the Check For Errors button to see if anything is amiss on any employee's form. If errors appear in the Errors box at the top of the form, click the error's listing. QuickBooks automatically takes you to the appropriate field to correct the information.

8. When everything is correct, load your W-2 forms in the printer (even if you're e-filing, you'll likely be printing the copy that goes to the employee) and click Submit Form to open the Print/E-file Form dialog.

9. If you enrolled in an agency's e-filing program, have an active Enhanced Payroll subscription, and there are no errors on the form, the option to e-file these forms will be available to you. Otherwise, only the Print button will be active. Select the option to open the Print W-2 And W-3 Forms window.

10. Click Print when all of these settings are just the way you want them. You must also print or e-file the W-3 form, which is a summary of your W-2 forms.

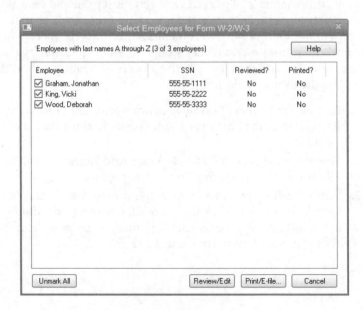

You can make your employees' W-2 forms available online at no extra charge if you have a QuickBooks payroll subscription. Using this service eliminates the need to print and mail W-2 forms to your employees since they can view and print their own W-2 information directly from an Intuit website called ViewMyPaycheck.com. Also, if your employees use TurboTax to prepare their own personal tax returns, they can view and download their W-2 forms directly into TurboTax. To learn more about this service, click the Tell Me More link at the bottom of the Print W-2 And W-3 Forms window.

Tax Form Worksheets in Excel

If QuickBooks isn't preparing your payroll forms (either because you're doing payroll manually or you subscribed to the QuickBooks Basic Payroll service), you can prepare your forms manually with the use of Excel worksheets that are available from QuickBooks.

To access the worksheets, choose Reports | Employees & Payroll | More Payroll Reports In Excel | Tax Form Worksheets as seen here. Because this Excel file has macros, depending on how you've configured Excel's security options, you might have to tell Excel to let the macros run.

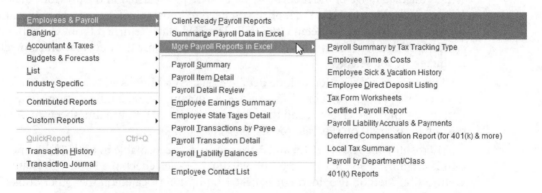

When the QuickBooks Tax Worksheets dialog appears, seen next, select the form and filing period you need. Next, click the Options/Settings button to open the

QuickBooks Tax Forms Workbook Options/Settings dialog, where you'll configure the report.

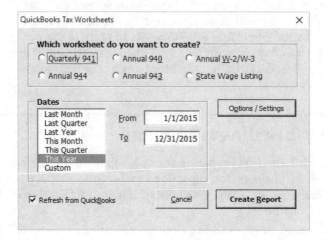

By default, the option to update worksheet headers is checked. This means the header of a printout of the worksheet contains the company name and address information, as well as the date range of the report (the date range you selected in the previous dialog). If you are planning to print the report, you need to know the date range, so make sure this option is selected. By default, the Hide Detailed Data Returned From QuickBooks option is selected, which means the workbook displays only the information connected to the report you selected.

If you deselect the option to hide detailed data, QuickBooks adds a second worksheet named Data to the workbook. This worksheet contains detailed information about the employees, the payroll items, and the job-costing links (if you use timesheets to do job costing for payroll) on separate rows.

Microsoft Office 2010, 2013, and 2016 products are available in both 32-bit and 64-bit versions. If you're using a 64-bit version of Excel, check the Force Alternate Connection Method Provided For Excel 64-bit option (located on the QuickBooks Tax Forms Workbook – Options/Settings dialog) to complete the export.

Use QuickBooks E-file

If you have chosen a subscription to the QuickBooks Enhanced Payroll service, you can file your 941, 940, W-2, and W-3 forms using QuickBooks e-file. To do so:

1. Change the filing method of the form you want to e-file by clicking Employees | Payroll Center.
2. Click QuickBooks Payroll Setup | Tax Forms | Related Form Activities | Edit Payment Due Dates/Methods | Schedule Payments.

3. Click the form you wish to e-file and select Edit. Change the payment method to e-file.

After you have made your changes in QuickBooks, in about 10 to 14 days, you'll receive a 10-digit personal identification number to use when filing these forms.

When the form is due, submit the form in QuickBooks.

1. Click Process Payroll Forms.
2. Review the form to ensure it is correct.
3. Click Submit Form | E-file.
4. Enter your contact information and the 10-digit PIN you received.

Small Business Tip Check with your state agencies to see if they will allow you to e-file as well.

Using QuickBooks Reports, Planning Tools, and Budgets

Part Four of this book covers how to gain insight into your company's finances by using the information that you've entered into your QuickBooks file. In Chapter 11, you learn how to run the reports you need to analyze your business and pay your taxes. Also covered in this chapter is the External Accountant, a special user login identity that lets your accountant examine, troubleshoot, and fix data entry problems. You will also find step-by-step instructions for customizing reports so they display exactly the data you and your accountant want to see. In Chapter 12, you learn how to create a budget and become familiar with the other planning and forecasting tools that come with QuickBooks.

Useful QuickBooks Reports and Analysis Tools

In this chapter:

- Exploring the Report Center
- Using standard QuickBooks reports
- Using the Company Snapshot and the Insight tab
- What the "External Accountant" means
- Making reports meet your needs
- Using comments on reports
- Sharing and memorizing reports

Chapter 11

As you have seen, QuickBooks makes it easy to enter and keep track of your business's transactions. This chapter explains how to run, analyze, and customize the reports that help you better manage your day-to-day operations and give you insight into how your business is doing. This chapter introduces you to the most common reports that QuickBooks users rely on and explains the information contained in them. Then you learn how to customize and memorize *any* QuickBooks report with your own settings.

Start with the Report Center

In the Report Center, you can get a dynamic preview of the built-in reports that are available in QuickBooks. It's also where you can access reports that have been contributed by other QuickBooks users and keep track of reports that you especially like by adding them to your list of favorites. Choose Reports | Report Center or click the Reports icon on the Icon Bar to get there (see Figure 11-1).

To view samples of the reports in a particular category, start by selecting a report category from the Standard tab on the left. QuickBooks displays a sample and a short description of the reports available for that category in the main window, depending on the view you've chosen. Next, select the view to display the category. The Report Center has three view types: Carousel, List, and Grid (the default view). See the options for setting each view at the right side of the Report Center screen, as seen next. All views

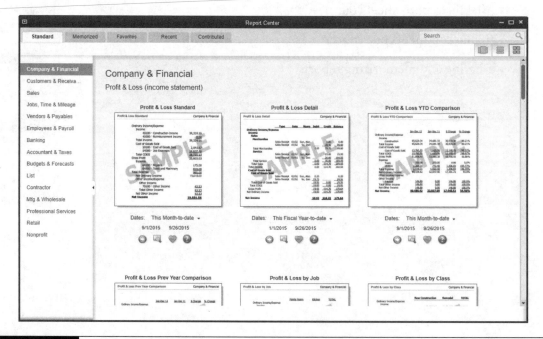

FIGURE 11-1 Profit & Loss reports shown in the Report Center's Grid view

provide the same options and quick access to multiple reports, but they're arranged in different ways. Experiment with the different views to find the one that works best for you. If you double-click the report display or description itself, the report opens; it's not a sample—it's an actual report based on your company's information.

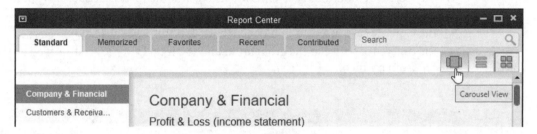

In addition to the Standard tab that is displayed by default when the Report Center opens, four other tabs give you quick access to reports that you've memorized, chosen as favorites, and most recently viewed. You can see reports that have been contributed by others or shared by you, or you can search for a specific report.

When you create and view a report, you can investigate the information that's shown by drilling down to the details behind the displayed totals. Position your mouse over a total, and your mouse pointer turns into a magnifying glass with the letter "Z" (for zoom). Double-click to see the details behind the number. If the report is a summary report, the detail report that opens is a list of transactions that made up the total on the original report. You can drill down into each listing to see the original transaction. If the report is a detail report, the list of individual transactions displays. You can drill down into each listing to see the original transaction.

Standard Financial Reports

Accountants, bookkeepers, and business owners can keep an eye on the company's health and financial status with a group of reports that are referred to as the *standard financial reports*. Your banker may ask to see these reports for loans and lines of credit, and if you sell your business, these are the initial reports the potential buyer wants to see.

Profit & Loss Report

Your Profit & Loss report is probably the one you'll run most often, as it shows if your company is making money. A Profit & Loss report is also called an *income statement*. It shows the total of all your income accounts and all your expense accounts, and then puts the difference between the two totals on the last line. If you have more income than expenses, the last line is a profit; if not, that last line is a loss. Several variations of the Profit & Loss report are available in QuickBooks. These can be accessed by choosing Reports | Company & Financial from the QuickBooks menu bar, the Icon bar, or the Report Center.

Perhaps the most widely used, the Profit & Loss Standard report, shown in Figure 11-2, is a basic report that follows a conventional format:

- The income is listed and totaled by both account and subaccount.
- The Cost Of Goods Sold accounts are listed, and the total is deducted from the income total to show the gross profit.
- The expenses are listed and totaled by both account and subaccount.
- The difference between the gross profit and the total expenses is displayed as your net ordinary income (or loss).

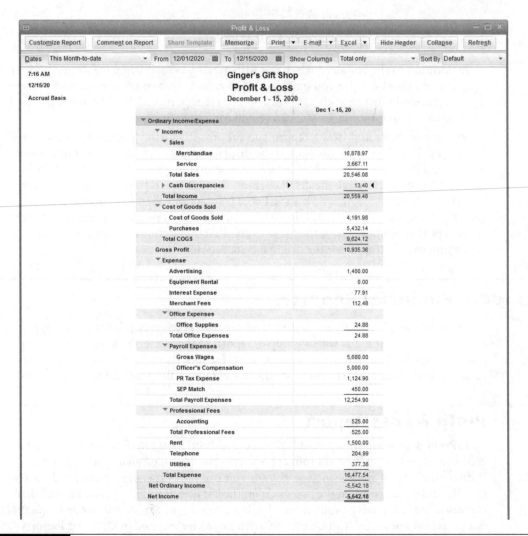

FIGURE 11-2 Most businesses rely on the information in the Profit & Loss Standard report.

When you run a Profit & Loss report, the default date range that QuickBooks sets is the current month to date. The default date setting shows information for the current month through the date you run the report, so you need to change the date range to see any other time period. New in QuickBooks 2016 is the ability to run any report with the dates "This Fiscal Year-to-Last Month," as seen next. Many QuickBooks users asked for this enhancement.

Click the Collapse button on the report menu bar to show income and expense totals by parent account only. To return the report to its default format, click the Expand button to view report totals by account and subaccount. Table 11-1 details other Profit & Loss reports.

Small Business Tip   By default, QuickBooks shows negative amounts with a leading minus sign. It is often easier to read financial reports with negative amounts encased in parentheses. To change a single report to show parentheses, select Customize Report | Fonts & Numbers | In Parentheses and click OK. To change all future reports to this format, select Edit | Preferences | Reports & Graphs | Company Preferences | Format | Fonts & Numbers | In Parentheses and click OK.

Report	What It Contains
Profit & Loss Detail Report	This report lists every transaction for every account in the Profit & Loss format.
Profit & Loss YTD Comparison Report	The YTD (year-to-date) Comparison report compares the current month's income and expense totals with the year-to-date totals for each income and expense account.
Profit & Loss Prev Year Comparison Report	This report is for the current year to date, with an additional column that shows last year's figures for the same period. There are two useful additional columns that show you the difference between the years in either dollars or percentage.

TABLE 11-1   Additional Profit & Loss Reports in QuickBooks

Balance Sheet

A Balance Sheet report shows only the totals of the Balance Sheet accounts (assets, liabilities, and equity) from your chart of accounts. This information is critical to understanding your business's financial health. The Balance Sheet balances because it's based on the age-old accounting formula:

Total Assets = Total Liabilities + Total Equity

QuickBooks offers several Balance Sheet reports, and each of them is explained in Table 11-2.

Trial Balance

A *trial balance* is a list of all the accounts in your chart of accounts and their current balances. It's a quick way to see what's what on an account-by-account basis. Most accountants ask to see a trial balance when they're preparing your taxes or analyzing the health of your business. To see a trial balance, choose Reports | Accountant & Taxes | Trial Balance. Your company's trial balance displays on your screen, and you can scroll through it to see all the account balances. The bottom of the report shows a total for debits and a total for credits, and they're equal.

By default, the trial balance displays every account (including inactive accounts), even if an account has a zero balance. That's because most accountants want to see the entire list of accounts, and sometimes the fact that an account has a zero balance is meaningful.

Report	What It Contains
Balance Sheet Standard Report	This report lists the balance in every Balance Sheet account (unless the account has a zero balance) and subtotals each type of asset, liability, and equity in addition to reporting the totals of those three categories. By default, the report displays totals for the year to date at the date you run the report, but you can change the time period.
Balance Sheet Detail Report	This report displays every transaction in every Balance Sheet account. By default, the report covers a date range of the current month to date. Even if it's early in the month, this report is lengthy.
Balance Sheet Summary Report	This report is a quick way to see totals, and it's also the easiest way to answer the question, "How am I doing?" All the Balance Sheet accounts are subtotaled by type.
Balance Sheet Prev Year Comparison Report	This report shows what your financial situation is compared with a year ago, and it displays these four columns: • The year-to-date balance for each Balance Sheet account • The year-to-date balance for each Balance Sheet account for last year • The amount of change in dollars between last year and this year • The percentage of change between last year and this year

TABLE 11-2   Balance Sheet Reports in QuickBooks

Cash Flow Reports

The list of reports in the Company & Financial submenu includes two cash flow reports: Statement Of Cash Flows and Cash Flow Forecast. The difference between them is that the Statement Of Cash Flows displays historical information, and the Cash Flow Forecast looks ahead and forecasts cash flow based on the history in your company file.

Statement Of Cash Flows

The Statement Of Cash Flows report displays the history of your cash position over a given period (by default, the Dates field is set to This Fiscal Year-To-Date, but you can change the date). This is one of the reports you'll probably be asked for by a banker or a potential buyer. This is an accrual report that self-modifies to report on a cash basis, and the lines on the report show you the adjustments made behind the scenes to provide cash-based totals. If you have no asset accounts that involve money owed to you—such as accounts receivable (A/R) or loans you made to others—and no liability accounts that involve money you owe—such as accounts payable or loans—then no adjustments have to be made because you're essentially operating your business on a cash basis.

A cash flow report has several categories and, depending on the general ledger postings, QuickBooks provides category totals for operating activities, which are those transactions from general business activities; investing activities, which are transactions involved with the acquisition and sale of fixed assets; and financing activities, which are transactions concerned with long-term liabilities, and, if the business is not a C-Corp, postings of owner/partner investments in the business and draws from the business.

QuickBooks uses specific accounts for this report, and you can view and modify those accounts as follows:

1. Click Reports | Company & Financial | Statement Of Cash Flows Report, and click the Classify Cash button at the top right of the report window to open the Reports & Graphs Preferences window.
2. In the Company Preferences tab, click the Classify Cash button found in the Statement Of Cash Flows section at the right of the window, as seen in Figure 11-3.
3. In the Classify Cash dialog also seen in Figure 11-3, add or remove accounts or move an account to a different category.

Cash Flow Forecast

The Cash Flow Forecast report predicts your cash flow as of a specific date range (by default, the next four weeks, but you can change this). The forecast predicts cash in and cash out and then displays the cash balances that result from those cash flows. This report is based on income predicted from current receivables and outgo predicted by current payables. If your business operates mostly on a cash basis (you collect payment from customers at the time of the sale and you write direct disbursement checks instead of entering vendor bills), there's not much future cash flow for QuickBooks to predict.

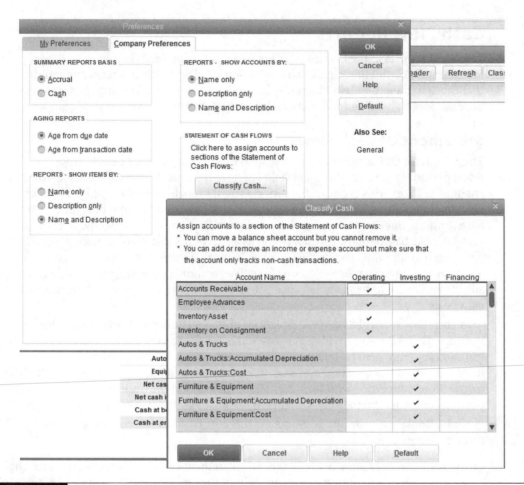

FIGURE 11-3 You can modify your Statement Of Cash Flows report.

This report assumes that both you and your customers pay bills based on their terms. If your customers pay late, you can tell QuickBooks to "re-predict" the flow of cash and the dates you can expect that cash by using the Delay Receipts field at the top of the report window. In the Delay Receipts field, enter the number of days after the due date that you expect to receive money from your customers. QuickBooks has no field on the report window for you to enter the number of days you take beyond the terms your vendors offer; this report assumes you always pay on time.

Other Useful Reports

QuickBooks offers many other financial reports on your transactions categorized by the type of activity for those transactions. Here's a brief overview of those reports.

Sales Reports

If you choose Reports | Sales, you see a list of built-in reports you can use to see your sales reported in a summarized or detailed fashion. Table 11-3 explains the contents of each report.

Vendor Reports

Choose Reports | Vendors & Payables to track vendor payment data. The list of reports in the submenu includes A/P aging, Form 1099 data, and other useful data such as the Unpaid Bills Detail report, which lists every outstanding bill and vendor credit as of the report date. Of course, the Bill Tracker is another tool that is useful in this regard.

Inventory and Purchasing Reports

If you enable inventory tracking, choose Reports | Purchases *or* Inventory. QuickBooks contains Purchase reports, which give detail on purchases you've made and can be sorted and totaled by vendor or item. Open Purchase Order reports can also be found on the Purchases submenu and can be listed by item or customer.

Several inventory reports are available to get your inventory value and stock status as of the report date. The Inventory Valuation Detail report is one report you can use to quickly determine your current on-hand quantities and inventory asset value.

Employees & Payroll Reports

The Employees & Payroll submenu, shown next, provides a number of reports, depending on how you and your accountant want to analyze your financials.

Report	Contents
Sales By Customer Summary	Total sales for each customer and job; does not include reimbursed expenses or sales tax
Sales By Customer Detail	Each transaction that's included in the Sales By Customer Summary report
Sales By Item Summary	Summary of sales, subtotaled by item type
Sales By Item Detail	Each transaction that's included in the Sales By Item Summary report
Sales By Rep Summary	Summary of sales totaled by sales rep; does not include reimbursed expenses or sales tax
Sales By Rep Detail	Each transaction that's included in the Sales By Rep summary report
Sales By Ship To Address	Totals for each unique address you ship to
Sales Graph	Bar and pie graphs of sales totals (you can display data by customers, items, and reps)
Pending Sales	All sales transactions currently marked "Pending"

TABLE 11-3 Sales Reports Built into QuickBooks

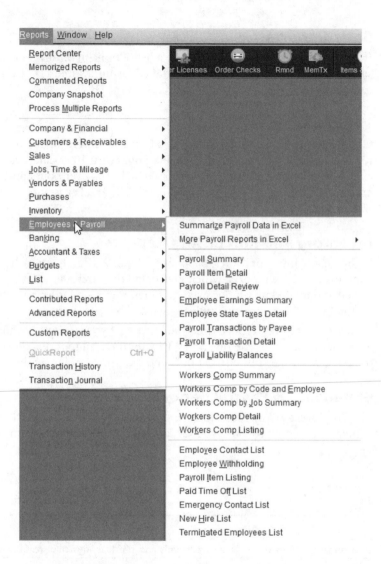

Banking Reports

To track your bank balance activities, you can display reports on them, including check and deposit detail data, missing check numbers, and reconciliations. See Chapter 7 to learn about troubleshooting problems with the reconciliation reports in this Reports submenu.

Reporting by Class

If you use class tracking and have assigned classes to all of your income and expense transactions, you can run both individual class reports and reports on all classes. To report on a single class, open the Class list and select the class on which you want to report. Then press CTRL-Q to open a QuickReport on the class. This report gives you a list of all the transactions that have been assigned to that class. When the Class QuickReport appears, you can change the date range or customize the report as needed. Using the Sort By drop-down list, you can also sort the report by type to group together transactions of the same type (such as invoice, bill, and so on).

If you want to see one report on all the classes, open the Class list and click the Reports button at the bottom of the list window. Choose Reports On All Classes, and then select Profit & Loss By Class, Profit & Loss Unclassified, or Graphs. The Graphs menu item offers a choice of an Income & Expenses graph or a Budget Vs. Actual graph.

- **Profit & Loss By Class Report**   The Profit & Loss By Class report is the same as a standard Profit & Loss report, except that each class uses a separate column. This report is also available on the submenu by choosing Reports | Company & Financial.

- **Profit & Loss Unclassified Report**   This report displays P&L totals for transactions in which items were not assigned to a class. You can drill down to the transactions and add the appropriate class to each transaction.

- **Graphs That Use Class Data**   You can also display graphs for income and expenses sorted by class or a graph that compares budget versus actual figures sorted by class.

Accountant & Taxes Reports

The reports that you or your accountant will need at the end of the year or to identify entries that may need adjusting are found in the Reports | Accountant & Taxes submenu.

Audit Trail Reports

The Audit Trails are active behind the scenes, keeping track of all the accounting and credit card transactions that you (and all your QuickBooks users) add, modify, or delete in your company file. The Audit Trail reports list these transactions along with the date; the time; and the user who entered, modified, or deleted the transaction. The Audit Trail reports should be your go-to report if you are concerned about entries in your QuickBooks file (like missing or changed transactions). Consider running this report on a regular basis to verify that all transactions are appropriate. Choose Reports | Accountant & Taxes | Audit Trail *or* Customer Credit Card Audit Trail.

Voided and Deleted Transactions Detail and Summary Reports

QuickBooks offers two reports you can use to track voided and deleted transactions. Both reports are available by choosing Reports | Accountant & Taxes and then selecting either of these reports: Voided/Deleted Transactions Summary or Voided/Deleted

Transactions Detail. The summary report displays a summary of all voided and deleted transactions in the selected period. Use the detail report to see detailed information about both the original transaction and the change. The detail report displays the credit and debit postings and the posting accounts. If items (including payroll items) were involved in the transaction, they're also displayed.

Company Snapshot and the Insights Tab

To get a quick answer to the question "How's business?" use the Company Snapshot window (see Figure 11-4). Click Snapshots from the Icon Bar to open this window. This customizable window displays an easy-to-understand summary of the money that's moved in and out, provides information on tasks you should perform, account balances, and A/R and A/P data by customer/vendor.

Click the Add Content link at the top of the window to add graphs and tables to your "dashboard." Double-click an area in a graph or table to display a more detailed report or to see an account's register. You can modify the report content (such as date ranges), rearrange the positions, or completely remove a graph or table from the Snapshot window. To view more detail on any of the information presented in the snapshot view, just double-click any element. The data displayed in the Company Snapshot window is

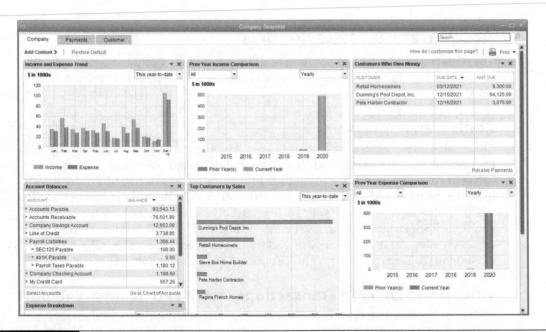

FIGURE 11-4   View a summary of your financial status using the Company Snapshot.

always appropriate for the permissions granted to the current user. Various elements of the window are displayed or hidden, depending on the current user's permissions.

When you click Home from the Icon Bar, two tabs appear: the Home Page tab, which helps you navigate in QuickBooks, and the new Insights Dashboard tab. This tab contains several analytic tools in graph form that you can customize and drill down through for more information. Like the Company Snapshot, this tool provides useful information about your business.

External Accountant

An External Accountant is a specific type of user who has the same rights as the QuickBooks Admin but with the following exceptions: the External Accountant cannot create, edit, or remove users, nor can the External Accountant view customer credit card numbers when you have enabled the QuickBooks Credit Card Protection feature. Create an External Accountant user so that when your accountant (or a bookkeeper from your accountant's office) comes to your office, certain Accountant tools are available, as discussed in the next section.

To create an External Accountant user, you must be logged into QuickBooks as the Admin (only the QuickBooks Admin can create users).

1. Choose Company | Set Up Users And Passwords | Set Up Users, and in the User List dialog, select Add User.
2. Enter the user name and password and click Next.
3. Select External Accountant and click Next. QuickBooks asks you to confirm this action—click Yes.
4. Click Finish to create the External Accountant.

Many companies have already set up a user name for the accountant. Even if the accountant's login provides full permissions, the Client Data Review tool isn't available on the Company menu unless an External Accountant is logged in. You can edit the accountant's user account to convert it to an External Accountant by selecting the accountant's user account and clicking Edit User. Don't change the user name and password data. Click Next, select External Accountant, and follow the prompts to save this user name as *External Accountant*.

Accountant Toolbox and the Accountant Center

The Accountant Center is available via the Company menu when an External Accountant user logs into your QuickBooks file. Your accountant uses these tools to examine your QuickBooks data and troubleshoot any data entry mistakes or other potential problems in your company file. He or she will see an option on the Company File called Accountant ToolBox, as seen next.

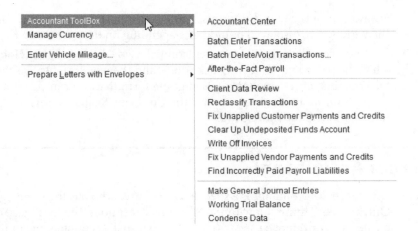

Once this person signs in with his or her Intuit ProAdvisor password, he or she can review your data and make any necessary corrections. (These tools are also available on a limited trial basis for non-ProAdvisors.) The toolbox allows your outside accountant to perform many batch tasks, enter after-the-fact payroll, review the current year's data, and perform several other functions. Changes made by the External Accountant during a review are separate from the changes made by any regular QuickBooks user, including the Admin user, in the Audit Trail reports.

Small Business Tip   In QuickBooks 2016 Premier Accountant Desktop, these tools are available on the QuickBooks menu bar. Select Accountant | Accountant Center.

Customizing Reports

The report customization tools in QuickBooks allow you to work with your financial information in the way that makes the most sense for you. Use these tools to select and sort almost any piece of information stored in your QuickBooks company file, from the smallest detail to the broadest overview.

All report customization efforts start with opening one of the standard QuickBooks reports. Click the Customize Report button to open the Modify Report dialog, shown next. This is where you begin the process of customizing the format and content of the report.

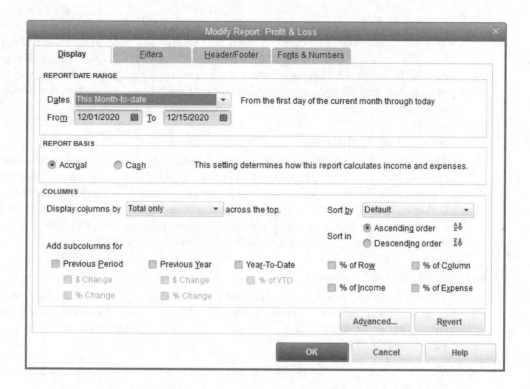

The Display Tab

The Display tab is filled with customization options. Some of these options are also on the report window itself, such as the Dates, Report Basis, and Sort By fields.

You can select accrual or cash basis for most QuickBooks reports. When you run a cash basis report, the report only shows actual cash transactions. This means that, for example, an invoice (revenue) won't show on a report if a customer has not yet paid you, and a bill (expense) won't appear on the report if you have not yet paid the vendor for that bill.

Small Business Tip Remember that accrual-based accounting recognizes income when it is earned and expenses when they are incurred. Cash-based accounting recognizes income when it is received and expenses when they are paid.

When you run an accrual basis report, it shows all the transactions you've entered. This means revenue is reflected in the report when you create an invoice, and expenses are reflected when you enter a bill. By default, QuickBooks displays financial reports as accrual-based reports because these are more useful for getting an overview of the state of your business. However, if you file taxes on a cash basis, a cash-based report is easier to use for tax preparation.

Selecting Columns

The real power in the Display tab is in the Columns list (which exists only in detail reports, not in summary reports). You can select and deselect columns so the report displays only the information you need. Any custom fields you created appear in the Columns list, which adds even more power to your ability to customize reports in a meaningful way. For example, if you want to show the percentage of total income each line item represents, check the % Of Income box to add that subcolumn.

Advanced Options

To further specify how QuickBooks selects data, some reports have an Advanced button. It is on the Display tab of the Modify Report dialog. Click the button to open the Advanced Options dialog. The options you see vary, depending on the report, as shown in Table 11-4.

The Filters Tab

The Filters tab, shown next, has a robust set of tools that you can use to customize a report to display the exact information that you want it to. Explore all the options

Option	Explanation
Display Rows/Columns	These options specify the rows or columns to include or exclude. Choose *Active* in which some financial activity, including $0.00, has occurred; *All*, regardless of activity or balance; and *Non-zero* in which amounts are other than zero.
Reporting Calendar Options	*Fiscal Year* uses the Company Info financial year, *Calendar Year* starts in January, and *Tax Year* uses a year that starts in the tax year specified in the Company Info window.
Include	*All* includes all accounts whether there was activity or not, and *In Use* includes only accounts that had postings in the selected date range.
Open Balance/Aging Options	*Current (Faster)* displays the open balance as of today and is faster to run, and *Report Date* displays the open balance as of the ending date of the report. Payments received after the ending date of the report are not included in the calculation.
Show Only Rows And Columns With Budgets	Some budget reports have this option, which displays only accounts used in your budgets.

TABLE 11-4 Advanced Options Available in QuickBooks Reports

in this tab to get a feel for its capabilities and power. Each filter option is shown in alphabetical order. .Scroll through the list to see your options.

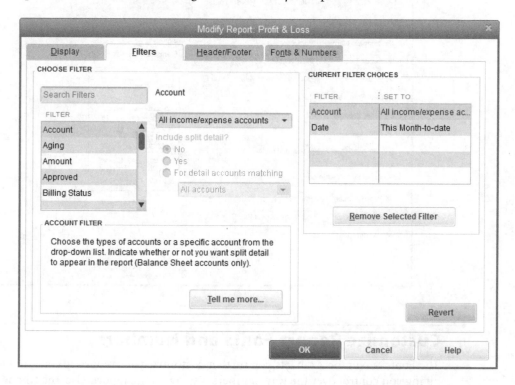

If you want to see only certain types of transactions on the report, use the Transaction Type filter to select the type you want to see; for example, in a report on sales and customers, you might want to see only credit memos. Once you've selected that filter, you've created a "Credit Memos By Customer Detail" report. Consider memorizing a filtered report so you can use it frequently. Memorizing customized reports is covered later in this chapter. Keep in mind that each filter has its own options. As you add and configure filters and notice the effect on your reports, you'll learn to use filters effectively.

Customize Report Headers and Footers

You can customize what appears on the header and footer of your report by changing the options on the Header/Footer tab, shown next. The options you set here have no bearing on the figures in the report; they are simply a descriptive label on the report that appears in either the header or footer. Note that there are options for both.

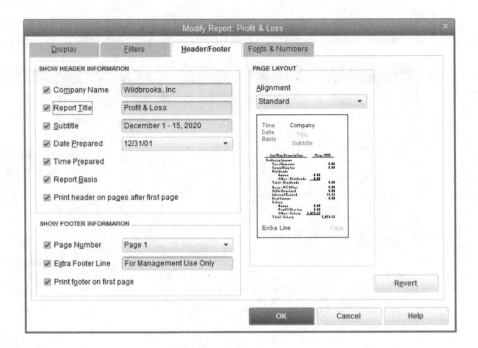

Customize Report Fonts and Numbers

The Fonts & Numbers tab lets you further customize your report by changing fonts and giving you control over the way numbers display on the report. Use The Change Font For list to select an element of the report for which you want to change the font size or style, for example, a column label or report totals.

On the right side of the Fonts & Numbers tab, you can control the way numbers display and print on your report. Select a method for showing negative numbers. If you wish, you can also select a method for displaying all the numbers on the report. *Divided By 1000* reduces the size of the numbers by showing them as multiples of 1,000. This is useful for companies that report seven- and eight-digit numbers, whereas *Without Cents* eliminates the decimal point and the two digits to the right of the decimal point from every amount. Only the dollars show, not the cents. QuickBooks rounds the cents to the nearest dollar. (Accountants frequently enter numbers in this manner for tax preparation purposes.)

Comment on Reports

A useful tool is the ability to add comments to nearly every part of a transaction, as shown in Figure 11-5. Click the Comment On Report button on any report to open the Comment On Report dialog box.

1. Check the small comment box by the item you question to open the Comments section.

2. Create as many comments as you need and click Save. A dialog box appears asking you to name the report. Give it a new name and click Save.

3. You will see a Saved Successfully message telling you that you can find this report again in Reports | Commented Reports.

Memorize Customized Reports

Once you've customized a report to display the information you want in the manner in which you want it, you can avoid the need to go through all this work again by memorizing the report. However, before you memorize a report, change its name in the Header/Footer tab so when you use it in the future, you know exactly what you're looking at.

Click the Memorize button on the report's button bar to open the Memorize Report window, where you can give this customized report a name. QuickBooks gives you the option to save the report in a report group and to share the report you've just customized with others (both of these options are discussed in this chapter).

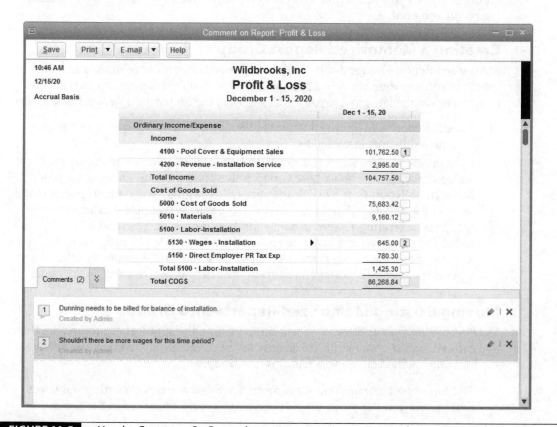

| FIGURE 11-5 | Use the Comment On Report button to customize a report with your own comments. |

By default, QuickBooks uses the report name in the Header/Footer tab. If you didn't change that title, be sure to use a reference to the report type in the memorized name. If you use a name such as My Report, you'll have no idea what the report displays.

Using a Memorized Report

Open a memorized report by choosing Reports | Memorized Reports from the QuickBooks menu bar and selecting the report from the submenu. When you open the report, all your customized settings are the way you configured them, but the data changes to reflect up-to-date information.

Using Memorized Report Groups

After you discover the power available in creating and memorizing customized reports, you may find yourself creating quite a number of special reports. At some point, it becomes difficult to select the report you need in the list of memorized reports. To save time and confusion, QuickBooks has a feature called Memorized Report Groups. These report groups let you store reports by category, which makes it easier to locate exactly the report you need.

Creating a Memorized Report Group

Memorized Report Groups display in the Memorized Report List window and on the submenu you see when you select Memorized Reports on the Reports menu. However, to create or manipulate groups, you have to work in the Memorized Report List window.

1. Choose Reports | Memorized Reports | Memorized Report List to open the Memorized Report List window.

2. Click the Memorized Report button at the bottom of the window to display the window's menu, and choose New Group. Enter a name for this group in the New Memorized Report Group dialog and click OK. The group you created appears in the window list, and its listing is boldfaced. Choose a name that fits the category for the group you're creating. Common names for these groups are Year-End, Monthly, and so on. The more straightforward the name, the easier it is to place reports in the group and find those reports when you need them. Continue to add groups to reflect the types of memorized reports you've already created or expect to create in the future.

Moving Existing Memorized Reports into Groups

Start by moving your existing memorized reports into the appropriate groups, and then you can save reports you memorize directly in the correct group. You can use either of the following methods to move a report into a group:

- *Edit each report to add the name of the group.* Select the report's listing and select Edit Memorized Report or simply press CTRL-E. Select the Save In Memorized

Report Group option, and then select the appropriate group from the drop-down list.

- *Drag each report to a group by indenting the report name under the group name.* First, drag each report listing (using the small diamond icon to the left of the report name) so it's under the group listing, and then drag to the right, indenting the report name under the group name. Note that any report listing indented under a group listing is automatically a member of that group.

You can drag listings to groups only if the Report Name column heading bar at the top of the window is the only column heading. If you see a column to the left that has a diamond as the heading, click the diamond to hide that column. (To reverse the process, click the Report Name heading to reveal the diamond.)

If the report you want to include in a group is a standard, built-in report available on the Reports menu, add the report to a group. Open the standard report and click the Memorize button. In the Memorize Report dialog, put the report into the appropriate group.

Saving a Memorized Report in a Group

After you've created groups, you can save memorized reports directly to a group. When you've perfected the customizations you need, click Memorize on the report window. In the Memorize Report dialog, enter the report name, select the Save In Memorized Report Group option, and then select the appropriate group from the drop-down list.

Processing Report Groups

One of the best things about creating groups for your memorized reports is that you can process all the reports in a group at once, such as printing all the reports in one fell swoop or e-mailing them to your accountant all at once.

To process a group of reports, double-click the group's listing in the Memorized Report List window to open the Process Multiple Reports dialog. You can deselect any report you don't need at the moment.

Sharing Reports You've Customized

When you modify a report, you can share its template (meaning only the customized report structure you've created and not your company's actual financial data) with other QuickBooks users. Simply click the Share Template button at the top of the report window and give your report a title and description. You can decide if you want to share the report with the rest of the QuickBooks world.

Your shared report will then be listed on the Memorized tab in the Report Center. What's more, you can access reports that others have decided to share. In the Report Center, select the Contributed tab. Check to see what reports other QuickBooks users in your industry have shared.

Exporting Your Report Data to Excel

If you need to perform some additional analysis of your QuickBooks data, or even change the appearance of a report in ways that QuickBooks doesn't allow, you can easily send the contents of a QuickBooks report to Excel. At the top of every report window is an Excel drop-down menu that has two options: Create New Worksheet and Update Existing Worksheet. If you choose the first option, QuickBooks either creates a new file (workbook) that contains a new worksheet or creates a new worksheet in an existing workbook. If you choose the second option, QuickBooks opens a window that allows you to browse to an existing Excel workbook. QuickBooks can send the report information and update the existing Excel report data accordingly, using much of the existing formats and formulas in the workbook.

Using the QuickBooks Budget and Planning Tools

In this chapter:

- Budgeting in QuickBooks

- Creating your budget

- Making reports with your budgeted information

- Projecting cash flow

Chapter 12

A budget is a tool for tracking your business's progress against your plans. A well-prepared budget can also help you decide when it's best to make a major purchase, hire additional staff, or draw money out of your business account. The ability to project profitability and cash flow by using actual data and then applying "what if " scenarios helps you decide whether you can increase or decrease expenses and prices. This chapter shows you how to make the budgeting and planning tools built into QuickBooks work for you.

How QuickBooks Handles Budgets

Before you begin creating a budget, you need to know how QuickBooks manages budgets and the processes connected to them. This section presents an overview of the QuickBooks budget features so you can understand them and keep them in mind when you create your budgets. Profit & Loss budgets can be created from scratch or by using the actual figures from the previous year.

Types of Budgets

QuickBooks offers several types of budgets:

- Budgets based on your Balance Sheet accounts
- Profit & Loss budgets based on your income and expense accounts
- Profit & Loss budgets based on income and expense accounts and a customer or job
- Profit & Loss budgets based on income and expense accounts and a class

Budget Data Is Saved Automatically

In QuickBooks, once you begin creating a budget, the data you record is stored in the budget window and reappears whenever you open that window. You create a budget by choosing Company | Planning & Budgeting | Set Up Budgets.

You can create only one of each type of budget for the same year. For example, if you create a Profit & Loss budget, enter and record some figures, and then decide to start all over by launching the Create New Budget Wizard, you can't create a new Profit & Loss budget for the same year. Instead of creating a new budget, the wizard displays the data you already configured. You have no way of telling QuickBooks, "Okay, save that one; I'm going to do another one with different figures." You can change the figures, but the changes replace the original figures. You're editing a budget; you're not creating a new budget document.

Creating Multiple Budgets

Once you've created your first budget, regardless of type, the next time you select Company | Planning & Budgeting | Set Up Budgets, the budget window opens with the last budget you created. If the budget is a Profit & Loss or Balance Sheet budget, you cannot create a second budget of the same type for the same year. However, you can create a budget of a different type, such as Profit & Loss with Customer: Job or Profit & Loss with Class. To do so, click the Create New Budget button in the budget window and go through the wizard to select different criteria (Customer: Job or Class).

After you've created a Customer: Job budget or a Class budget, you can create another budget using a different customer or job or a different class (or using different accounts for the same customer, job, or class). See the sections "Customer: Job Budgets" and "Class Budgets" for instructions on creating multiple budgets of those types.

Deleting a Budget

QuickBooks does let you delete a budget. This means if you want to create multiple budgets of the same type (perhaps you feel better if you have a "Plan B" budget), you have a workaround to the "no two budgets of the same type" rule. Export the original budget to Microsoft Excel, and then delete the original budget and start the process again. To delete a budget, choose Edit | Delete Budget from the QuickBooks menu bar while the budget window is open.

Understanding the Budget Window

Before you start entering figures, you need to learn how to manage your work using the buttons on the budget window shown in Figure 12-1:

- **Copy Across**   When you have entered a figure in one month's row, click this button to copy the same number across the rest of the months.

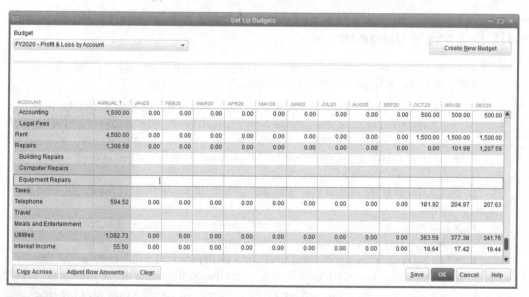

FIGURE 12-1   Use the Budget window to create a new budget in QuickBooks.

- **Adjust Row Amounts** With this button, the Adjust Row Amounts dialog appears. See "Enter Budget Amounts" later in this chapter for more information.
- **Clear** Deletes all figures in the budget window. You can't use this button to clear a row or column.
- **Save** Records the current figures and leaves the window open so you can continue to work.
- **OK** Records the current figures and closes the window.
- **Cancel** Closes the window without offering to record the figures.
- **Create New Budget** Starts the budget process anew, opening the Create New Budget Wizard. If you've entered any data, QuickBooks asks if you want to record your budget before closing the window. If you record your data (or have previously recorded your data with the Save button), when you start anew, the budget window opens with the same recorded data, and you can change the figures.

Tasks to Perform Before You Start Your Budget

Before you create a budget, check the following details:

- Add any new accounts before you start your budget. The first month of the budget must be the same as the first month of your fiscal year.
- Ensure all the accounts you want to include in your budget are active. Inactive accounts aren't available in the budget window.

Profit & Loss Budgets

The most common and useful budget you can create is a Profit & Loss budget, which helps you plan for future income and expenses.

1. Choose Company | Planning & Budgeting | Set Up Budgets. If this is the first budget you're creating, the Create New Budget Wizard opens to walk you through the process. If you've already created a budget, the Set Up Budgets window appears with your existing budget loaded. Click Create New Budget to launch the Create New Budget Wizard.
2. Enter the year for which you're creating the budget and select the Profit And Loss option.
3. Click Next and select No Additional Criteria for this budget. Customer: Job and Class budgets are covered later in this chapter.
4. Click Next. You'll see an option to create a budget from scratch or from the figures from last year's activities. In this case, select the option to create a budget from scratch.
5. Click Finish to open the budget window, where all your income and expense accounts are displayed.

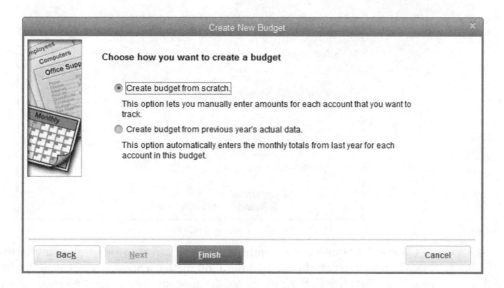

Enter Budget Amounts

To create budget figures for an account, select the account and then click in the column of the first month for which you want to budget. Enter the budget figure, press TAB to move to the next month, and enter the appropriate amount. Repeat until all the months for this account have your budget figures. As you enter each monthly amount and press TAB, QuickBooks automatically calculates and displays the annual total for the account.

QuickBooks provides the following shortcuts to save you from some of the more repetitive tasks when entering budget figures.

Copy Numbers Across

To copy a monthly figure from the current month (the month where your cursor is) to all the following months, enter the figure and then click the Copy Across button. The numbers are copied to all the rest of the months of the year. The Copy Across button is also the only way to clear a row. Delete the figure in the first month (or enter a zero) and click Copy Across. The entire row is now blank (or filled with zeros).

Automatically Increase or Decrease Monthly Figures

After you've entered figures into all the months on an account's row, you can raise or lower monthly figures automatically. For example, you may want to raise an income account by an amount or a percentage starting in a certain month because you expect to sign a new customer or a new contract. Select the first month that needs the adjustment, and click the Adjust Row Amounts button to open the Adjust Row Amounts dialog, as seen here.

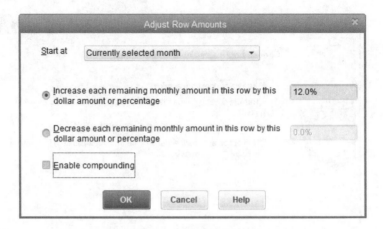

Choose 1st Month or Currently Selected Month as the starting point for the calculations. You can choose 1st Month no matter where your cursor is on the account's row. You must click in the column for the appropriate month if you want to choose Currently Selected Month; however, you can click the first month to make that the currently selected month.

To increase or decrease the amount in the selected month and all the following months by a specific amount, enter the amount. To increase or decrease the amount in the selected month and all columns to the right by a percentage, enter the percentage rate and the percentage sign.

If you select Currently Selected Month, the Adjust Row Amounts dialog adds an option named Enable Compounding. When you enable compounding, the calculations for each month are increased or decreased based on a formula starting with the currently selected month and taking into consideration the resulting change in the previous month. QuickBooks calculates a compounded increase (or decrease) using a dollar amount or percentage.

Creating a Budget from Last Year's Data

If you used QuickBooks last year, you can create a budget based on last year's figures. To use last year's real data as the basis of your budget:

1. Open the Create New Budget Wizard by choosing Company | Planning & Budgeting | Set Up Budgets. When the Create New Budget Wizard opens, enter the year for which you're creating the budget and select the Profit And Loss budget option. Click Next.
2. Select any additional criteria, such as a customer, job, or class. Click Next.
3. Select the option to create the budget from the previous year's actual data, and click Finish.

The budget window opens with last year's actual data used for the budget figures. For each account that had activity, the ending monthly balances appear in the appropriate month. You can change any figures you wish using the procedures and shortcuts described earlier.

Customer: Job Budgets

If you have a customer or a job that warrants it, you can create a Profit & Loss budget to track the financials for that customer or job against a budget. Customer: Job budget reports aren't accurate unless you're faithful about assigning every appropriate revenue or expense transaction to the customer or job.

To create your first budget for a customer or a job:

1. Choose Company | Planning & Budgeting | Set Up Budgets. If you already created another budget of a different type (Profit & Loss or Class), the budget window opens with the last budget you created. Click the Create New Budget button in the budget window to launch the Create New Budget Wizard. If this is your first-ever budget, the Create New Budget Wizard appears automatically.
2. Select the year for your budget, and choose Profit And Loss as the type. Click Next.
3. Select the option Customer: Job. Click Next.
4. In the next window, specify whether you want to create the budget from scratch or from last year's data. Click Finish.

In the Set Up Budgets window, select the Customer: Job for this budget from the drop-down list. Enter budget figures using the following guidelines:

- The expenses you track depend on the scope of the job. For example, you may only want to budget the cost of outside contractors or supplies so if prices rise, you can have a conversation with the customer about overruns.
- Enter a monthly budget figure for each account or for each month the project exists, or enter a total budget figure in the first month. The last option lets you compare accumulated data for expenses against the total budgeted figure by creating modified reports, where you change the report date to reflect the elapsed time for the project and filter the report for this job only.
- If the project is lengthy, you may budget some accounts for some months and other accounts for other months. For example, if you have a project that involves purchases of goods followed by installation of those goods or training for the customer's employees, you might choose to budget the purchases for the first few months and then the cost of the installation or training (either by tracking payroll or outside contractors) for the months in which those activities occur.
- If you want to track payroll costs against a job, use the QuickBooks Time and Billing features.

Class Budgets

If you use class tracking to track branch offices, company divisions, or company departments, you can link your budget to any class to create very useful class budgets. If you look at your class-based reports and find yourself asking, "Aren't those expenses higher than they should be?" or "Why is one class less profitable than the other classes?" you might want to budget each month to get a handle on where and when expenses got out of hand. If you ask, "Is this department contributing the income I expected?" include income accounts in your budget. You can use income accounts in class budgets to provide incentives to your employees, perhaps a bonus to a manager if the reality is better than the budget.

To create a class-based budget, use the steps described earlier to create a budget and choose Class in the Additional Profit And Loss Budget Criteria window. When the budget window opens, a Current Class field appears. Select the class for which you're creating a budget from the drop-down list. Then begin entering data.

Balance Sheet Budgets

A Balance Sheet budget can be challenging to build because it's difficult to predict the amounts for most Balance Sheet accounts—with the exception of fixed assets and loans. In fact, the transactions that affect fixed assets and loans are usually planned and therefore don't need budget-to-reality comparisons to allow you to keep an eye on them.

If you still feel the need to create a Balance Sheet budget, choose Company | Planning & Budgeting | Set Up Budgets. If this is your first budget, the Create New Budget Wizard opens. Otherwise, when an existing budget appears, click the Create New Budget button. When the Create New Budget Wizard opens, select the year for which you want to create the budget and select the Balance Sheet option. Then click Next, and because the next window has no options, there's nothing for you to do except click Finish. The budget window opens, listing all of your Balance Sheet accounts, and you can enter the budget figures.

Budget Reports

QuickBooks provides a number of budget reports to see how you're doing. To get to the reports, choose Reports | Budgets from the menu bar, and then select one of the following reports:

- Budget Overview
- Budget vs. Actual
- Profit & Loss Budget Performance
- Budget vs. Actual Graph

Budget Overview

This report shows the accounts you budgeted and the amounts you budgeted for each month. Accounts not included in the budget do not display. If you created multiple budgets, select the one you want to view from the drop-down list and click Next. In the next window, select a report layout (the options differ, depending on the type of budget). Click Next, and then click Finish. The Overview report type produces the display you'd see if the window you use to create a budget had a button labeled Print The Budget.

This report includes inactive accounts if you input figures for that account when you prepared the budget and later made the account inactive. This can be confusing if you print this report as the "official" budget for your company.

If you use subaccounts in your budget but only want to see parent account budget totals, click the Collapse button at the top of the report window. The button name changes to Expand, and clicking it puts the subaccount lines back into the display.

To condense the numbers, use the Columns drop-down list to select a different interval. The default is Month, but you can choose another interval and QuickBooks will calculate the figures to fit. For example, you might want to select Quarter to see four columns of three-month subtotals and a Total column.

If you want to tweak the budget or play "what if" games by experimenting with different numbers, click the Excel button to send the report to Microsoft Excel.

Customer: Job Budget Overview

If you created budgets for customers or jobs, select <FYxxxx> Profit & Loss By Account And Customer: Job in the first window and click Next. Select a report layout from the drop-down list (as you select each option from the list, QuickBooks displays a diagram of the layout). The name of each layout is a hint about the way it displays in the report. The first word represents the rows, and the word after "by" represents the columns. So, for Customer: Job By Month, Customers: Jobs are shown in rows and months are displayed as columns.

The following choices are available:

- **Account By Month**   Lists each account you used in the budget and displays the total budget amounts for all customer budgets you created for each month that has data. No budget information for individual customers appears.
- **Account By Customer: Job**   Lists each account you used in the budget and displays the fiscal year total for that account for each customer (each customer has its own column).
- **Customer: Job By Month**   Displays a row for each customer that has a budget and a column for each month. The budget totals for all accounts—individual accounts are not displayed—appear under each month. Under each customer's row is a row for each job that has a budget.

Class Budget Overview

If you created a Class budget, select Profit & Loss By Account And Class in the first window and click Next. Select a report layout from the drop-down list. You have the following choices:

- **Account By Month**   Lists each account you used in the budget and displays the total budget amounts for all Class budgets you created for each month that has data. No budget information for individual classes appears.
- **Account By Class**   Lists each account you used in the budget and displays the yearly total for that account for each class (each class has its own column).
- **Class By Month**   Displays a row for each class that has a budget and a column for each month. The total budget (not broken down by account) appears for each month.

Balance Sheet Budget Overview

If you created a Balance Sheet budget, select <FYxxxx> Balance Sheet By Account for the budget in the first window, and then click Next. QuickBooks displays a graphical representation of the report's layout (it's a monthly layout similar to the layout for the Profit & Loss budget). Click Finish to see the report.

Budget vs. Actual

This report's name says it all—it shows you how your real numbers compare to your budget figures. For a standard Profit & Loss budget, the report displays the following data for each month of your budget for each account:

- Amount posted
- Amount budgeted
- Difference in dollars
- Difference in percentage

The choices for the budget type are the same as the Budget Overview report, so you can see account totals, customer totals, or class totals to match the budgets you've created. When the report opens, only the accounts you used in your budget show budget figures.

You can also use the options in the Modify Report window to make the following changes:

- Change the report dates.
- Change the calculations from accrual to cash to remove any unpaid invoices and bills so that only actual income and expenses are reported.

Memorize the report so you don't have to make the same modifications next time you want to view a comparison report. Click the Memorize button at the top of the report window and then give the report a meaningful name. Only the formatting changes you make are memorized, not the data. Every time you open the report, it displays current data. To view the report after you memorize it, choose Reports | Memorized Reports from the QuickBooks menu bar.

Profit & Loss Budget Performance

This report is similar to the Budget vs. Actual report, but it's based on the current month and the year to date. For that time period, the report displays your actual income and expenses compared to what you budgeted. By default, the date range is the current month, but you can change that to see last month's figures or the figures for any previous month. This report is available for all types and can be modified to customize the display.

Budget vs. Actual Graph

This report just opens; you have no choices to select first. All the choices are in the graph that displays in the form of buttons across the top of the report window. Click the type of report you want to see.

Work with Budget Data Outside of QuickBooks

If you need to manipulate your budget data or have report formatting needs beyond what QuickBooks offers, you can export this data to Excel or to a delimited text file. Exporting to Excel can be useful for creating customized budget reports using your QuickBooks data, whereas exporting to a text file gives you the option to make changes to your budget data that can be imported back into QuickBooks.

Exporting a Budget Report to Excel

Although you can export any budget report to Excel, many use the Profit & Loss Budget Overview report for this purpose. Choose Reports | Budgets | Budget Overview. Select the desired Profit & Loss report and click Next. Select a report layout, click Next, and then click Finish.

With the report open, click the Excel button at the top of the report window. From here, you can choose to create a new worksheet or update an existing worksheet. Select Create New Worksheet if this is the first budget you're exporting. If you're exporting multiple budgets in this manner, you can select an existing workbook and create separate worksheets for each budget.

Exporting Budgets to Delimited Text Files

When you export budgets to a delimited text file (QuickBooks adds the file extension .iif to the exported file), you can't select specific budgets to export—it's all or nothing. To export your budget data:

1. Choose File | Utilities | Export | Lists To IIF Files from the QuickBooks menu bar.
2. When the Export dialog opens, it displays all the QuickBooks lists. Select the item named Budgets, shown next, and click OK.

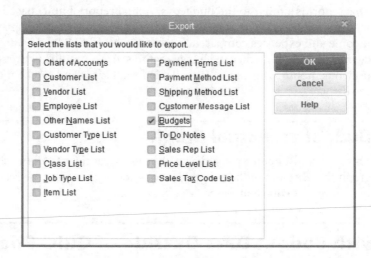

3. Another Export dialog opens. Select a folder in which to save this exported file, or leave it in your QuickBooks folder (the default location).
4. Give the exported list a filename (for example, QBBudgets). QuickBooks will automatically add the extension .iif to the filename.
5. Click Save. QuickBooks displays a message telling you that your data has been exported successfully.
6. Click OK.

Open the file using Excel (or any spreadsheet program). Note that the file shows a row of budget data for every year that you've created one in QuickBooks. If you only want to work on the figures for one year, you have to delete the unwanted rows. The budget year is indicated by the date found in the STARTDATE column. Updating the date in the STARTDATE column will create a budget for the year you've entered when the file is imported back into QuickBooks. Be sure that any changes you make to the file while it is open in Excel are saved in the original text (.iif) format if you plan on importing your changes back into your QuickBooks file.

Importing Budgets Back into QuickBooks

The only practical reason you'd import budgets back into QuickBooks is to copy a budget to another year to use as the basis for another year's budget. Although you can also edit the actual budget figures you've exported to an .iif file, it's easier to work directly in the QuickBooks budget window. To play "what if" games or to sort the budget differently, it's easier to work in Excel or some other spreadsheet program.

Before you can import the file, you must save it as a delimited text file, choosing Tab as the delimiter. You must also change the filename extension to .iif. Then follow these steps to bring the budget into QuickBooks:

1. Choose File | Utilities | Import | IIF Files from the menu bar to open the Import dialog.
2. Locate and double-click the file you saved.
3. When QuickBooks displays a message telling you the import was successful, click OK.

You can view the imported budgets in any budget report or in the budget window. QuickBooks checks the dates and changes the budget's name to reflect the dates. When you select a budget report or choose a budget to edit in the budget window, the available budgets include both the budgets you created in QuickBooks (FY2021, for example) and the budgets you imported after changing the date (FY2022).

Project Cash Flow

The Cash Flow Projector is a tool you can use to build a report that projects your cash flows using your own criteria. This tool uses data in your company file and then lets you remove and add accounts and even adjust figures. These features make it easier to achieve the projection parameters and results you need.

> **Small Business Tip**   You may see a message that QuickBooks 2016 has updated this feature to work with your current browser version.

The Cash Flow Projector is rather powerful if you understand the accounting terminology and principles of determining cash flows. You can design specific cash flow scenarios, which might be useful in planning for an expansion or other major business event. This section gives you an overview.

To ensure accuracy, make sure you've entered all transactions, including memorized transactions, into your QuickBooks company file. Then launch the Cash Flow Projector by choosing Company | Planning & Budgeting | Cash Flow Projector. The program operates like a wizard, and the opening window (as seen in the illustration) welcomes you and offers links to information you should read before you begin. Each ensuing wizard window has a button labeled Preview Projection.

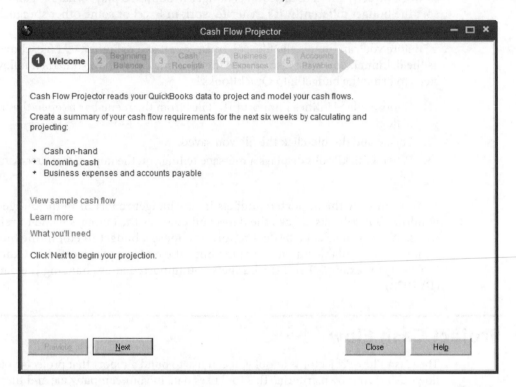

Click Next to display the Beginning Balance window, as seen in Figure 12-2. Select the cash accounts you want to include in your projection. The software calculates a beginning balance by adding together the balances of all the accounts you select. You can adjust that calculated balance to change the beginning balance of the cash flow projection. This is useful if you know that the current balance of any account contains an amount that you don't want included in the projection, such as an income item that is earmarked for spending today or tomorrow and therefore shouldn't be counted.

Click Next to move to the Cash Receipts window. You must select a projection method from the drop-down list, shown next. If you don't understand the terminology in the list, discuss it with your accountant. One of the choices is I Want To Project Cash Receipts Manually, which is useful if your accountant has some particular method in mind or if you don't have A/R totals to guide you because you run a retail business.

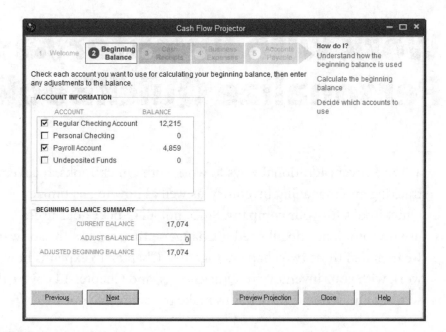

FIGURE 12-2   The Cash Flow Projector helps you understand and control your company's cash flow.

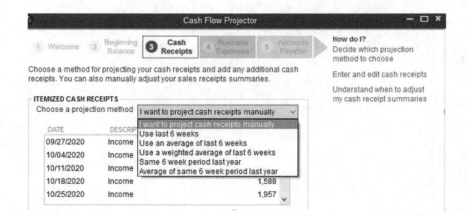

The next two wizard windows look similar, but they deal with expenses, starting with expenses that are not accounts-payable expenses (expenses for which you write direct checks instead of entering bills and any unique expenses that qualify as "one- time-only"), and moving on to accounts-payable expenses, including recurring bills you've entered into your system. In both windows, you can enter specific expenses or adjusted total expenses.

This brief discussion gives you a basic understanding of the ways you can use this tool for your business. If you think you'd benefit from generating a variety of cash flow scenarios, introduce this tool to your accountant so together you can see all the ways it can be applied to suit your business needs.

Work with Inventory and Personalize QuickBooks

Part Five covers additional ways to work with QuickBooks. It covers tracking and managing inventory, as well as how to customize QuickBooks for your company. Since not all QuickBooks users use inventory, nor do all need to change settings within the software, we included these two chapters together. Chapter 13 explains how to work with your inventory in QuickBooks, and Chapter 14 covers the settings QuickBooks provides to make the software your own.

Manage Inventory in QuickBooks

In this chapter:

- Understanding an inventory item
- Learning to track inventory
- Using subitems
- Doing an inventory count

Accurately keeping track of inventory items is no easy task. In fact, for many businesses, the warehouse can be a source of frustration and erroneous information. (The term "warehouse" is used generically here to indicate the place where you store inventory, but it may be your basement or garage instead of a physical warehouse.) This chapter covers how to set up and make adjustments to your inventory. You learned how to purchase, receive, and manage your inventory in Chapter 6.

What Is an Inventory Item?

An inventory item is a product you manufacture, assemble, or purchase for the purpose of selling to a customer. Inventory also includes items you store to use in the normal course of business that are resold to customers as part of other services. However, if you're a plumber and you store valves, pipes, and other plumbing parts to use when you perform a job, you may choose to track these items as non-inventory, especially if they are low-value items. If you're a consultant who uses consumables or supplies in the course of your consulting work and you keep them on hand to sell to customers, you can also choose not to track them as inventory.

QuickBooks provides the item type "non-inventory part" that you can use to indicate products you used on a job when you invoice customers. You can create reports on those items to track quantity and revenue amounts. These item types don't require the kinds of details and tax reports that inventory items do. In general, the types of businesses that typically track inventory are manufacturers (who may use inventory parts to create other inventory parts), wholesale distributors, and retailers.

Set Up QuickBooks for Inventory Tracking

To track inventory, first enable the inventory feature. Choose Edit | Preferences and select the Items & Inventory category in the left pane. Move to the Company Preferences tab to see the inventory options. When you turn on the inventory feature, you also turn on the purchase order feature (although you don't have to use purchase orders to use the inventory feature). The dialog offers two more options to keep your inventory records accurate as seen next:

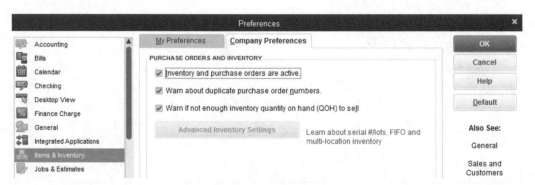

- **Warn About Duplicate Purchase Order Numbers** When enabled, if you use a PO number that's already in use, QuickBooks will display a message warning you of that fact. (The system doesn't prevent you from using the duplicate number, but it's a good idea to heed the warning to avoid problems.)
- **Warn If Not Enough Inventory Quantity On Hand (QOH) To Sell** When enabled, QuickBooks flashes a warning if you fill out a sales transaction that has a quantity greater than the currently available units of that product. You can continue the sale if you wish and track the unfilled quantity as a backorder (covered later in this chapter).

Click OK when you have made your choices. QuickBooks closes all the open windows to update your choices.

Depending on your version of QuickBooks, the Company Preferences tab of the Items & Inventory Preferences dialog may show an Advanced Inventory Settings button and an Enable button for Unit of Measure. The Advanced Inventory feature, available only in QuickBooks Enterprise Solutions, allows you to track inventory across multiple locations. Click the Learn About Serial #/Lots, FIFO And Multi-Location Inventory link to see if it's a fit for your business and learn how to upgrade to QuickBooks Enterprise Solutions. The Unit of Measure feature is available in most Premier editions and all Enterprise editions of QuickBooks.

Accounts Required for Inventory Are Automatically Created

After you've enabled inventory tracking and are ready to create your first inventory item, QuickBooks adds the following accounts to your chart of accounts:

- An Other Current Asset account named Inventory Asset
- A Cost Of Goods Sold account

Create Inventory Items

Now you're ready to create your first inventory item. Open the Item List (choose Lists | Item List from the menu bar) to open the Item List window. Select Item | New (or press CTRL-N) to open the New Item dialog, and select Inventory Part from the drop-down list as the item type. Fill in the information using these guidelines, as shown in Figure 13-1:

- The Item Name/Number is what you will use to reference the item in the software—which is not necessarily the same way you'd describe this item to your customers in sales transactions. This field must be unique in your Item List.

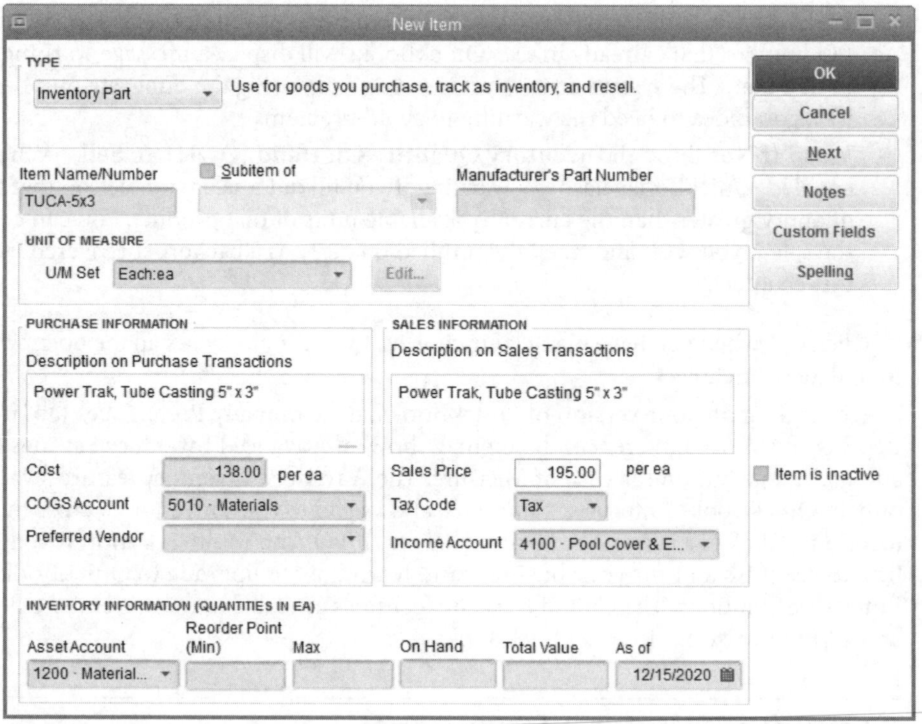

FIGURE 13-1 Use the New Item dialog to enter your inventory parts.

- The Manufacturer's Part Number (useful if you're a distributor or retailer) lets you include the manufacturer's part number on your purchase orders. If you purchase from a distributor instead of a manufacturer, enter the distributor's part number. This makes creating an accurate purchase order much easier. This number can be added as a column in all sales transaction forms, except credit memos.

- The text you enter in the Description On Purchase Transactions field appears when you create a purchase order. The text you enter in the Description On Sales Transactions field appears in sales transaction forms, such as invoices, estimates, and sales receipts.

- Enter a cost, as this appears automatically in a purchase order. QuickBooks does *not* use this figure for posting cost of goods sold; instead, it uses the *average* cost of this item based on your item receipt and inventory adjustment transactions as covered later in this chapter.

- If you enter a Sales Price, that amount is entered when you create sales transactions. Many leave this blank and change it on individual sales transactions.

- Choose the Tax Code for this item, which indicates whether the item is taxable to customers.

- Select the appropriate posting accounts for Cost Of Goods Sold (COGS) and Income accounts.
- If you prefer to purchase this item from a specific vendor, enter it in the Preferred Vendor field.
- Enter a number in the Reorder Point field that reflects the minimum quantity you want to have in stock. If you've enabled the Reminders feature, QuickBooks will issue a reminder about reordering when this quantity is reached. To turn on the Reminders feature, choose Edit | Preferences and click the Reminders category. On the My Preferences tab, select the Show Reminders List When Opening A Company File check box. On the Company Preferences tab, choose either Show Summary or Show List for the Inventory To Reorder option.

Do not enter anything in the On Hand or Total Value fields. Instead, let QuickBooks track these values as you receive items into inventory and/or use the inventory adjustment feature, covered later in this chapter. See Chapter 3 for more information about the Notes and Custom Fields buttons.

Use Subitems

Subitems are useful when items include choices and you want all the choices to be part of a larger hierarchy so you can sell them easily and track them efficiently. Perhaps you sell shoes and want to separate them by type, such as sandals, sneakers, boots, and so on.

Creating the Parent Item for a Subitem

To have a subitem, you must first create a parent item. Here are some guidelines for creating an inventory item that's designed to be a parent item:

- Use a generic name for the item; the details are in the subitem names.
- Use uppercase to make the item easier to see (especially in a long list of items).
- Do not enter a description—save that for the subitems—the cost or the price, or a reorder point or the quantity on hand.
- Enter the Inventory Asset, COG, and Income accounts because they are required fields for all inventory items.

Creating Subitems

Having created the parent item, subitems are easy to create. Open a blank New Item window either by selecting Item | New or pressing CTRL-N and follow these steps:

1. Select the Type (in most cases, this will be Inventory Part as you are creating a subitem to an Inventory Part).

2. In the Item Name/Number field, enter the code for this item. It can be a color, a size, a manufacturer name, or any other code that makes this subitem unique when compared with other subitems under the same parent item.

3. Check the Subitem Of box, and then select the parent item from the drop-down list that appears when you click the arrow to the right of the field.

4. Enter the Manufacturer's Part Number (for creating purchase orders).

5. Optionally, enter any descriptions you want to appear on purchase orders and sales transactions, the cost you expect to pay for this item and a preferred vendor, and the sales price.

6. Enter the general ledger account information (Inventory Asset, Cost Of Goods, and Income accounts).

7. Enter the reorder point if you use that feature.

8. *Do not* enter anything in the On Hand or Total Value fields. Instead, let QuickBooks track these values as you receive items into inventory and/or use the inventory adjustment feature.

9. Click Next to enter another inventory item, or click OK if you're finished.

Small Business Tip QuickBooks 2016 issues a warning if you try to deactivate items that still have quantities on hand.

Count Inventory

Some business owners dread doing a physical inventory. However, no matter how careful you are with QuickBooks transactions, no matter how strict your internal controls are for making sure everything that comes in and goes out is accounted for, you may find, like most businesses, that your physical inventory does not match your QuickBooks figures and you will have to make adjustments.

Printing the Physical Inventory Worksheet

When it's time to count your inventory, start by printing a Physical Inventory Worksheet, shown next. To open the worksheet, select Reports | Inventory | Physical Inventory Worksheet. This report lists your inventory items and subitems in alphabetical order, along with the current quantity on hand, which is calculated from your QuickBooks transactions. In addition, a column is set up to record the actual count as you walk around your warehouse with this printout (and a pen) in hand. Click the Print button in the worksheet window to bring up the Print Reports window. In the Number Of Copies box, enter as many copies as you need.

Customize the Physical Inventory Worksheet

When first opened, the Physical Inventory Worksheet displays only basic information about the inventory that you carry. Depending on the way you plan on carrying out your physical inventory, you may find that you need more information. By default, only the inventory items that have an active status are displayed. So if you made any inventory items inactive and you think (or know) there are still units in stock of that item, consider filtering the report to show the inactive items so you can identify any on-hand quantities for these items. Also, if any items are obsolete or discontinued, be sure to adjust their quantities or value to zero. If you think they may have a resale value, consider making them active again.

You might want to print separate worksheets by vendor because you want to divide up and assign the counting process to your staff accordingly. In that case, filter the report by Preferred Vendor. If you want to start your physical inventory by targeting your highest-value items first, you could add a column for either Cost or Price and re-sort your report by that column, with the highest value items at the top. You could also filter the report to display items with a cost above a certain dollar amount.

You can find all customization options by clicking the Customize Report button at the top of the Physical Inventory Worksheet window. This action opens the Modify Report window that contains four tabs. Use the Display tab to add or remove columns and the Filters tab to set one of the multiple filters available that allow you to control the items' display. Use the Header/Footer tab to customize the name of the report and the appearance of other titles that appear on the report. The Fonts & Numbers tab lets you change the font size and color.

Planning the Physical Count

Although QuickBooks doesn't have a built-in automatic "freeze" feature, consider following these steps during your physical count to perform this process manually:

1. Print the Physical Inventory Worksheet *only* when you're ready to start counting.
2. Enter and print invoices as usual, but mark them as pending (by clicking the Mark As Pending button on the Create Invoice ribbon bar) until your physical inventory is complete. Don't pick and pack the inventory for these invoices until after the count! Once you're finished with your counting, and readied the items for shipment, mark these pending invoices as final by clicking the Mark As Final button on the Create Invoice ribbon bar.
3. Don't receive inventory into QuickBooks until after the count.
4. If inventory arrives during the count, don't unpack the boxes until after the count.

It is a good idea to have one person in charge who knows who is counting what. When each counter is finished, their sheet should be handed to the person in charge, who ideally will be the person who enters the counts into QuickBooks. After the count, bring in any inventory that's arrived during the count. Then start picking and packing the orders that were placed during your physical inventory.

Making Inventory Adjustments

After you've finished counting the inventory, you may find that the numbers on the worksheet don't match the physical count. In fact, it's almost a sure bet that the numbers won't match. In many cases, the physical count is lower than the QuickBooks figures. This is called *shrinkage*. Shrinkage is a way of describing unexplained missing inventory.

Adjusting the Count

Use the Adjust Quantity/Value On Hand window to tell QuickBooks about the results of your physical count. Choose Vendors | Inventory Activities | Adjust Quantity/Value On Hand to open the Adjust Quantity/Value On Hand window shown in Figure 13-2. Follow these steps to complete this form:

1. From the Adjustment Type drop-down menu, select Quantity.
2. Enter the date. Inventory adjustments are usually dated at the end of the month, quarter, or year.
3. In the Adjustment Account field, enter the inventory adjustment account in your chart of accounts. The section "About the Inventory Adjustment Account" tells which account you should use.

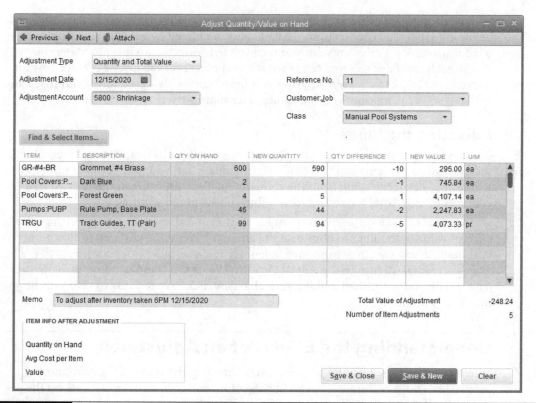

Adjust Quantity/Value on Hand

Previous · Next · Attach

Adjustment Type	Quantity and Total Value ▼		
Adjustment Date	12/15/2020 📅	Reference No.	11
Adjustment Account	5800 · Shrinkage ▼	Customer:Job	
		Class	Manual Pool Systems ▼

Find & Select Items...

ITEM	DESCRIPTION	QTY ON HAND	NEW QUANTITY	QTY DIFFERENCE	NEW VALUE	U/M
GR-#4-BR	Grommet, #4 Brass	600	590	-10	295.00	ea
Pool Covers:P...	Dark Blue	2	1	-1	745.84	ea
Pool Covers:P...	Forest Green	4	5	1	4,107.14	ea
Pumps:PUBP	Rule Pump, Base Plate	46	44	-2	2,247.83	ea
TRGU	Track Guides, TT (Pair)	99	94	-5	4,073.33	pr

Memo   To adjust after inventory taken 6PM 12/15/2020

Total Value of Adjustment   -248.24
Number of Item Adjustments   5

ITEM INFO AFTER ADJUSTMENT

Quantity on Hand
Avg Cost per Item
Value

Save & Close   Save & New   Clear

FIGURE 13-2   Adjust for shrinkage in the Adjust Quantity/Value On Hand window.

4. Use an optional reference number to track the adjustment.

5. Click the Find & Select Items button to open the Find & Select Items window. Here you tell QuickBooks which items you want to adjust.

6. Click the Add Selected Items button to add the items selected to the adjustment window. Notice the Include Inactive check box at the bottom of the Find & Select Items window.

7. In the Adjust Quantity/Value On Hand window, the Customer: Job field appears in case you're sending items to a customer but didn't include the items on any invoices for that customer or job. This is a way to create a transfer of the inventory where the inventory count is changed and the cost posted to the customer or job.

8. If you use the class tracking feature, a Class field appears if the adjustment can be assigned to a class.

9. Use either the New Quantity column or the Qty Difference column to enter the count. Whichever column you use, QuickBooks fills in the other column automatically.

10. Anything you enter in the Memo field appears on your Profit & Loss Detail report, which prevents the question "What's this figure?" from your accountant.

When you complete the entries, the total value of the adjustment you made is displayed below the Qty Difference column. That value is calculated by using the average cost of your inventory. For example, if you received ten widgets into inventory at a cost of $10.00 each and later received ten more at a cost of $12.00 each, your average cost for widgets is $11.00 each. If your adjustment is for minus one widget and you didn't sell any of that item in the interim, your inventory asset value is decreased by $11.00.

Adjusting the Value

You can be more precise about your inventory valuation; in fact, you can override the average cost calculation and enter a true value when you fill out this transaction window. Select Total Value from the Adjustment Type drop-down menu. Two new columns named Total Value and New Value appear in the window.

The value of the total adjusted count for each item is displayed. You can change the current value of the item to eliminate the effects of averaging costs up to this point (although as you continue to receive inventory items, QuickBooks continues to use average costing). Return to the Adjust Quantity/Value On Hand window and enter the data. When you've finished making your changes, click Save & Close to save your new inventory numbers.

Understanding the Effects of an Adjustment

When you adjust the inventory count, you're changing the value of your inventory asset. After you save the adjustment, the inventory asset account register reflects the differences for each item. Because QuickBooks is a double-entry bookkeeping system, there has to be an equal and opposite entry made to another account.

For example, when you sell items via customer invoices, your inventory asset decreases while at the same time your cost of goods sold increases. When you're adjusting inventory, however, there is no sale or purchase involved. In most cases, the offsetting entry is to an Inventory Adjustment account created specifically for this purpose.

About the Inventory Adjustment Account

Before you can make adjustments to your inventory, you should first create an account to receive that adjustment. Most users name it the Inventory Adjustment account, and it can either be a Cost Of Goods Sold (COGS) or an expense type of account. Check with your accountant on what account type works best for your situation.

If you use a COGS account when you use the Adjust Quantity/Value On Hand window, QuickBooks issues a warning message when you enter your adjustment account in the Adjustment Account field. If your accountant wants you to use a cost of goods account, be sure to select the option to stop showing this message before you click OK to continue working in this window.

Making Other Adjustments to Inventory

You can use the Adjust Quantity/Value On Hand window to make adjustments to inventory at any time and for a variety of reasons unconnected to the periodic physical count:

- Breakage or other damage
- Customer demo/sample units
- Gifts or bonuses for customers or employees
- Removal of inventory parts to create built or preassembled inventory items

The important thing to remember is that tracking and periodically adjusting inventory isn't done just to make sure that you have sufficient items on hand to sell to customers. Equally important is the fact that your inventory is an asset, just like your cash, equipment, and other assets. As such, it affects your company's worth in a substantial way.

Run Inventory Reports

You'll probably find that you run reports on your inventory status since, for many inventory-based businesses, inventory status reports are the second most important set of reports, next to current accounts receivable balance reports. QuickBooks provides several useful inventory reports, shown next, which you can access by choosing Reports | Inventory.

Inventory Valuation Summary
Inventory Valuation Detail

Inventory Stock Status by Item
Inventory Stock Status by Vendor

Physical Inventory Worksheet
Pending Builds

Inventory Valuation Summary Report

This report gives you a quick assessment of the value of your inventory. By default, the date range is the current month to date, but you can change that to suit your needs. Each item is listed with the following information displayed in columns:

- **Item Description**   The description of the item, if you entered a description for purchase transactions.
- **On Hand**   The current quantity on hand, which is the net number of received items and sold items. Because QuickBooks permits you to sell items you don't have in stock (a very bad idea, which can wreak havoc with your financials), it's possible to have a negative number in this column.

- **Avg Cost** QuickBooks calculates the average cost of an item each time you record the purchase of more units of the item. It adds the cost of the new items to the cost of the remaining old stock, then divides by the total number of both new and old items.
- **Asset Value** The value posted to your Inventory account in the general ledger. The value is calculated by multiplying the number on hand by the average cost.
- **% Of Tot Asset** The percentage of your total inventory assets that this item represents.
- **Sales Price** The price you've set for this item. This figure is obtained by looking at the item's configuration window. If you entered a price when you set up the item, that price is displayed. If you didn't enter a price (because you chose to determine the price at the time of sale), $0.00 displays. QuickBooks does not check the sales records for this item to determine this number, so if you routinely change the price when you're filling out a customer invoice, those changes aren't reflected in this report.
- **Retail Value** The current retail value of the item, which is calculated by multiplying the number on hand by the sales price (if the sales price is set).
- **% Of Tot Retail** The percentage of the total retail value of your inventory that this item represents.

Inventory Valuation Detail Report

This report lists all the transactions that affect the on-hand value of each item in your inventory—including sales and purchases. The report shows no financial information about the price charged to customers because your inventory value is based on cost. You can double-click any transaction line to see the details of that transaction.

Inventory Stock Status Report

There are two Stock Status reports: Inventory Stock Status By Item and Inventory Stock Status By Vendor. The information is the same in both reports, but the order in which information is arranged and subtotaled is different. You can use these Stock Status reports to get quick numbers about inventory items, including the following information:

- The preferred vendor
- The reorder point
- The number currently on hand
- A reminder (a check mark) for ordering items that are below the reorder point
- The number currently on order (a purchase order exists but the order has not yet been received)
- The next delivery date (according to the data in the purchase orders)
- The average number of units sold per week

Pending Builds Report

If you're using the Premier or Enterprise edition of QuickBooks and you build and track *assembly items,* this report details the current state of items you assemble from existing inventory items (called *builds*). If you find that you need this feature, consider upgrading to either of these editions by going to www.quickbooks.intuit.com.

Inventory QuickReports

QuickBooks provides a reporting feature called QuickReports that provides detailed sales and purchase information about an individual item. QuickReports are available from the Item List window and are the fastest way to take a look at all the transactions for an item.

In the Item List window, select an item and click the Reports button (at the bottom of the list) to open a drop-down menu from which you can select the QuickReport for that item. You can change the date range for the report, and you can double-click any transaction line to drill down to the transaction details.

Filtering Using Custom Fields in the Item Report

New in all desktop versions of QuickBooks 2016 is the ability to filter by your custom fields when creating item-based reports. You can add up to five custom fields in items. QuickBooks Pro, Premier, and Accountant desktop versions allow you to add up to seven custom fields in the Customer, Employee, and Vendor lists to provide your company with great detailed reports. (The total combined custom fields for these lists can be 15. In QuickBooks Enterprise, you can add up to 12 fields to each list for a combined total of 30 custom fields.)

In our example, we are creating a Physical Inventory Worksheet showing all inventory parts that are located in the warehouse. One of our custom fields is entitled Location, as shown here.

1. To use a custom field, Select Reports | Inventory | *name of your report* (we are using Physical Inventory Worksheet).
2. Click the name of the report you want to create.
3. Enter any dates that pertain to this report.

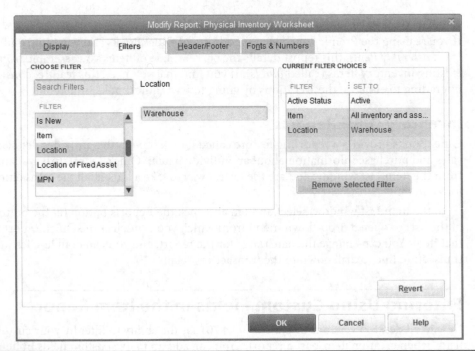

FIGURE 13-3 QuickBooks 2016 desktop versions allow you to use custom fields as filters.

4. Click Customize Report and select the Filters tab. Scroll down to the custom field name you want to use.
5. Enter the name in the box that appears. In our example, we have chosen the Custom field Location and chosen Warehouse as the term by which to filter, as seen in Figure 13-3.
6. Click OK to run your report.

Customizing QuickBooks for Your Company

In this chapter:

- Setting your options in Preferences
- Attaching documents and working with the Doc Center
- Using e-mail in QuickBooks

The Preferences settings in QuickBooks allow you to control the way you complete tasks, how data is entered, and how it is reported. Many QuickBooks users change or tweak these preferences periodically. You can also customize the templates included with QuickBooks. The ability to customize templates means that you can modify the way information displays in a transaction window, which makes it easier to fill in a form with just the information that you need. You can capture additional information about your transactions, and, once captured, this information is available in reports.

QuickBooks offers several ways to connect with your customers, potential customers, and vendors. With QuickBooks, you can attach documents to invoices or vendor bills and utilize the numerous e-mail features to make your business grow.

Customize Settings and Options

Your settings and options for the available QuickBooks features are maintained in the Preferences dialog, which you open by choosing Edit | Preferences from the QuickBooks menu bar. Access each category in the Preferences dialog by clicking the appropriate icon in the left pane. Although every category has the two tabs, My Preferences and Company Preferences, not every category has options available on each tab.

- The My Preferences tab is where you configure your preferences as a QuickBooks user. Each user you create in QuickBooks can set his or her own My Preferences. QuickBooks will apply the correct preferences as each user logs into the company file.
- The Company Preferences tab is the place to configure the way the QuickBooks features work for the current company, regardless of the logged-in user. Only the Admin or an External Accountant user can change settings in the Company Preferences tab.

As you configure options and move from one category of the Preferences window to another, you're asked whether you want to save the changes in the section you just left.

This chapter covers all of the Preferences categories. However, you may also find some additional details about a specific preference category in a relevant chapter. Access all Preferences from the QuickBooks menu bar by choosing Edit | Preferences.

Accounting Preferences

Click the Accounting icon on the left pane of the Preferences dialog to open these preferences. No options display in the My Preferences tab, as there are only Company Preferences available for this section.

You can choose to use account numbers, and, if so, you should also select the option Show Lowest Subaccount Only. This is a useful option because when you see an account number in a drop-down list in a transaction window, you see only the subaccount. If the option is not selected, you see the parent account followed by the subaccount, and if the field display doesn't show the entire text, it's hard to determine which account has been selected. Although you sometimes can extend the width of the field, it is easier to simply display the subaccount.

> **Small Business Tip** If you have accounts without account numbers in your chart of accounts, you cannot choose the Show Lowest Subaccount Only option. This is true even if the account is not active.

The option to require accounts means that every item and transaction you create in QuickBooks has an assigned account. If you disable this option, transaction amounts not assigned to an account post to Uncategorized Income or Uncategorized Expense and show as such on reports. This information is not useful when you want to analyze your business.

You can also enable the Class feature, which lets you create Profit & Loss reports for divisions, departments, or other categories by which you've decided to analyze your business. The other options on this dialog are self-explanatory, except for the Closing Date section, which is discussed in detail in Chapter 17.

Bills Preferences

In the Bills category, you have the opportunity on the Company Preferences tab to set options for the way you enter and pay vendor bills:

- *You can set default terms.* Although QuickBooks defaults to ten days, you can change this setting. When you create terms and link those terms to vendors, QuickBooks ignores the default for any vendor that has terms configured.
- *You can tell QuickBooks to take discounts and credits automatically when you're paying vendor bills.* If you choose the discounts option, you'll be asked to select a Default Discount Account to which QuickBooks will post your discounts.

Calendar Preferences

The My Preferences tab has all the settings available in this preference area. This means that the choices you make here apply when you log into QuickBooks. Other users will see the default settings unless they also make changes.

The Calendar Settings area on this tab gives you several alternatives on the view (daily, weekly, monthly) that should be set as your default. If you can't decide, you can tell QuickBooks to open the view that you were using the last time you had your calendar window open. Other options in the Calendar Settings area include the number of days you want to appear for each week and the type of transactions your calendar should display. The Upcoming & Past Due Settings give you control over which future and past-due transactions show in your calendar.

Checking Preferences

This category has options in both the My Preferences and Company Preferences tabs. On the My Preferences tab, you can select default bank accounts for different types of transactions. You can skip these options if you only have one bank account. The Company Preferences tab offers several options concerned with check printing, as shown in Table 14-1.

Desktop View Preferences

This is where you can modify the way the QuickBooks window looks and acts. The My Preferences tab, shown next, contains basic configuration options. In the View section, you can specify whether you always want to see one QuickBooks window at a time or view multiple windows. These are your personal settings; other users may establish their own settings in the My Preferences section on their computers.

Option	How It's Used
Print Account Names On Voucher	If you print voucher checks, this option means that the text on the stub displays posting accounts. Only use this option if you keep and file check vouchers.
Change Check Date When Non-cleared Check Is Printed	When you print checks, the current date becomes the check date. If this option is not chosen, the check date you specified when you filled out the check window is used, even if that date has already passed.
Start With Payee Field On Check	Enable this option to force your cursor to the Payee field when you first bring up the Write Checks window. Otherwise, the Bank Account field is the first active field.
Warn About Duplicate Check Numbers	This option means that QuickBooks warns you if you attempt to save a check with a number that already exists.
Autofill Payee Account Number In Check Memo	If you fill in your account number in the Account No field on the Payment Settings tab in the vendor record, the number appears in the Memo section on the lower-left section of the check.
Select Default Accounts To Use	When you write checks, you won't have to select the bank account from a drop-down list in the transaction window.
Bank Feeds (Online Banking)	Choose how to download transactions. Express Mode uses a Transaction List window. If you select Classic (Register) mode, the work of processing and categorizing your transactions happens while in a register view.

TABLE 14-1 Checking Preference Options

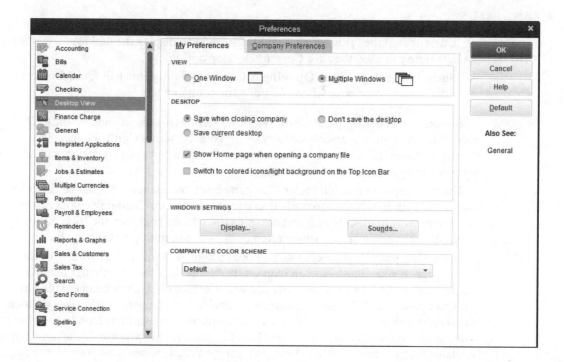

- **One Window**   Limits the QuickBooks screen to show one window at a time, even if you have multiple windows open. The windows are maximized and stacked atop each other, with only the top window visible.
- **Multiple Windows**   Choose to make it possible to view multiple windows on your screen. Selecting this option activates the arrangement commands on the Window menu item, which allows you to stack or arrange windows so that more than one window is visible at a time.

In the Desktop section, you can also specify what QuickBooks should do when you open and exit the software; choose among the following options:

- **Save When Closing Company**   This means that QuickBooks remembers the state of the desktop when you close the company file or exit QuickBooks. Whichever QuickBooks windows were open when you left will reappear when you return.
- **Save Current Desktop**   When you choose this option, the next time you open QuickBooks, it displays the desktop as it was the last time you worked in your company file.
- **Don't Save The Desktop**   This tells QuickBooks to display an empty QuickBooks desktop (unless you enable the Show Home Page When Opening A Company File option) when you open this company file or when you start QuickBooks again after using this company file.

- **Keep Previously Saved Desktop**   This is available only when you select Save Current Desktop. This option tells QuickBooks to display the desktop as it was the last time you used the Save Current Desktop option.
- **Show Home Page When Opening A Company File**   This tells QuickBooks to display the Home page when you open the company file.

Buttons are available to configure Windows settings for display and sounds. Clicking either button opens the associated window in your Windows Control Panel. The display and sounds configuration options you change affect your computer and all your software, not just QuickBooks.

Use the drop-down menu under Company File Color Scheme to change the color associated with the QuickBooks file that you're working in. Changing colors can be an effective way to quickly differentiate one QuickBooks company file from another—especially helpful if you find you're often doing work in multiple company files.

In the Company Preferences tab, you can customize some of the contents of the Home page. If you want to add an icon on the Home page for a particular feature (such as Estimates), this tab also tells you whether that feature has been enabled in your company file. If the feature hasn't been enabled, click the feature's name to open its category in the Preferences dialog. Turn the feature on to add its icon to the Home page, and then click the Desktop View icon to return to this window. If the item is not available (such as Invoices), it means that feature already appears on your Home page.

Finance Charge Preferences

In the Company Preferences tab, you configure finance charges. Read the complete discussion about this topic in Chapter 5.

General Preferences

This dialog contains options for the way you work in QuickBooks. There are settings on both the My Preferences and Company Preferences tabs.

The My Preferences Tab

The My Preferences tab options, explained in Table 14-2, offer a number of ways to control the way QuickBooks behaves while you're working in transaction windows.

The Company Preferences Tab in General Preferences

The Company Preferences tab in the General section has the following options:

- **Time Format**   Select a format for entering time, choosing between decimal (for example, 11.5 hours) or minutes (11:30).

Option	How It's Used
Pressing Enter Moves Between Fields	This option tells QuickBooks to use the ENTER key to move between fields instead of the TAB key.
Automatically Open Drop-Down Lists When Typing	As you type the first few letters of a listing, the drop-down list appears and you move to the first listing that matches what you typed.
Beep When Recording A Transaction	Deselect if you don't want to hear sound effects. With this default option, you can control sounds by clicking the Sounds button and then the Sounds tab.
Automatically Place Decimal Point	When you enter numbers in a currency field, a decimal point is placed automatically to the left of the last two digits when you enable this feature. Therefore, if you type 5421, when you move to the next field, the number changes to 54.21.
Warn When Editing A Transaction	This option, selected by default, tells QuickBooks to flash a warning message when you change any transaction and try to close the transaction window without explicitly saving the changed transaction.
Bring Back All One Time Messages	One-time messages are those dialogs that include a Don't Show This Message Again option. If you clicked that Don't Show option on any message dialogs, select this check box to see those messages again.
Turn Off Pop-Up Messages For Products And Services	Selecting this option stops pop-up messages connected to products and services available from Intuit.
Show ToolTips For Clipped Text	If text in any field is cut off, hovering your mouse over the text displays the entire text.
Warn When Deleting A Transaction Or Unused List Item	This option produces a warning when you delete a transaction or a list item that has not been used in a transaction.
Keep QuickBooks Running For Quick Startups	With this option, QuickBooks starts automatically and runs in the background whenever you start your computer.
Automatically Remember Account Or Transaction Information	This option tells QuickBooks to prefill information in a bill, check, or credit card transaction window, based on previous transactions for the same vendor. When enabled, you can choose either of these suboptions: • Automatically Recall Last Transaction For This Name • Pre-fill Accounts For Vendor Based On Past Entries
Default Date To Use For New Transactions	This option tells QuickBooks whether you want the Date field to show the current date or the date of the last transaction you entered.
Keep Custom Item Information When Changing Item In Transactions	This option determines what QuickBooks does when you change the description text or the price for an item in a sales transaction form. If you select *Always*, QuickBooks will keep the descriptive text you wrote. If you select *Never*, QuickBooks fills in the description that goes with the new item you selected. If you select *Ask*, as soon as you change the item, QuickBooks asks if you want to change only the item and keep your customized description on the invoice.

TABLE 14-2   My Preferences Options in the General Preferences Tab

- **Always Show Years As 4 Digits**   If you prefer to display the year with four digits (01/01/2014 instead of 01/01/14), select this option.
- **Never Update Name Information When Saving Transactions**   By default, QuickBooks asks if you want to update the original information for a name when you change it during a transaction entry. If you don't want this opportunity and always want the record to remain as is, select this option.
- **Save Transactions Before Printing**   The rule that a transaction must be saved before it's printed is a security precaution. Keeping this option enabled will prevent anyone who has access to your QuickBooks file from printing an invoice or check without the transaction being recorded. It's recommended that you keep this default setting.

Integrated Applications Preferences

You can let third-party software access and share the data in your QuickBooks files. Click the Integrated Applications icon and move to the Company Preferences tab to specify the way QuickBooks works with other software programs. The first time that other applications attempt to make a connection to the QuickBooks file you're working in, you're asked to approve the link. If you click Yes, basic information for that program is recorded and appears in this dialog so that you do not have to reapprove future connections.

Items & Inventory Preferences

Use this dialog to enable the inventory function and set options for processing inventory transactions. Only the Company Preferences tab has options, as shown here:

- **Inventory And Purchase Orders Are Active**   Select this option to tell QuickBooks that you want to enable the inventory feature; the ability to create and track purchase orders is automatically enabled with that option.
- **Warn About Duplicate Purchase Order Numbers**   When this option is enabled, any attempt to issue a purchase order with a PO number that already exists will generate a warning.
- **Warn If Not Enough Inventory Quantity On Hand (QOH) To Sell**   This option turns on the warning feature that is useful during customer invoicing. If you sell ten widgets but your stock of widgets is fewer than ten, QuickBooks displays a message telling you there's insufficient stock to fill the order. You can still complete the invoice; it's just a message, not a limitation, but you should order more widgets immediately.

The Company Preferences tab of the Items & Inventory Preferences dialog also contains an Advanced Inventory Settings and a Unit Of Measure button. If you find that both of these buttons are not "live," it's because these features are only available in the QuickBooks Premier and Enterprise editions (Advanced Inventory is only available at the Enterprise level). Click the Learn More links to see if either of these features is a fit for your business and learn how to upgrade to either one of these versions of QuickBooks.

Jobs & Estimates Preferences

Use the Company Preferences tab of this dialog to configure the way your estimates work. The options are self-explanatory. If you use estimates, see Chapter 4 for more information about creating estimates and how to save time and increase accuracy by creating invoices from estimates.

Multiple Currencies Preferences

The Company Preferences tab has options enabling the ability to do business in multiple currencies. The available options are Yes and No, but if you select Yes, QuickBooks prompts you to make a backup of your company file before finalizing your decision because this feature cannot be turned off once it's been turned on. From this window, you'll also tell QuickBooks what your home currency is.

Even if you're sure you want to work in multiple currencies in QuickBooks, make a backup, and use a name for the backup file that indicates what you're doing (such as <Company Name>PreMulticurrency.qbb). Then, if you decide you don't want to use this feature immediately after turning it on, you can restore your backup file and proceed as before.

Payments Preferences

In the Payments Company Preferences tab, in the Receive Payments section, there are three options:

- **Automatically Apply Payments** This option tells QuickBooks to apply payments automatically to open invoices. If the payment amount is an exact match for an open invoice, it is applied to that invoice. If the payment amount is smaller than any open invoice, QuickBooks applies the payment to the oldest invoice. If the payment amount is larger than any open invoice, QuickBooks applies payments, starting with the oldest invoice, until the payment amount is used up.
- **Automatically Calculate Payments** When this option is enabled, you can begin selecting invoices to pay in the Receive Payments window before entering

the amount of the customer's payment check. When you've finished selecting invoices, either paying them entirely or applying a partial payment, the amounts you've applied should equal the amount of the check you received. This is efficient if a customer has many invoices (some of which may have credits or may have an amount in dispute) and has attached instructions about the way to apply the checks.

- **Use Undeposited Funds As A Default Deposit To Account**   Selecting this option automates the process of depositing all cash received into the Undeposited Funds account. Otherwise, each customer payment and sales receipt offer the choice of depositing the cash into either a bank account or the Undeposited Funds account.

You will also see Online Payments as an option. Click Credit Card and/or Bank Transfer to activate these payment methods. If you have not yet set up your QuickBooks Payments feature, select either option and follow the links to sign up for this fee-based service.

Payroll & Employees Preferences

Use the Company Preferences tab of this category to set all the configuration options for payroll. Refer to Chapter 10 for an explanation of the selections in this window.

Reminders Preferences

The Reminders category of the Preferences dialog has options on both tabs. The My Preferences tab has one option, which enables the display of the Reminders List when you open the company file.

The Company Preferences tab lists all the available reminders, and you can select the ones you want to use. Keep in mind that these selections won't take effect unless you select the Show Reminders List When Opening A Company File check box on the My Preferences tab.

For each item, decide whether you want to see a summary (just a listing and the total amount of money involved), a complete detailed list, or nothing at all. You can also determine the amount of lead time you want for your reminders. If you notice that some of the options are grayed out, it's because they're only available in QuickBooks Premier or Enterprise edition.

Reports & Graphs Preferences

This section of the Preferences window also has choices on both tabs, so you can set your own user preferences and then set those options that affect the current company. Using the My Preferences tab, you can customize your experience when working with reports and graphs.

Prompt Me To Modify Report Options Before Opening A Report

If you find that almost every time you select a report you want to customize it, you can tell QuickBooks to open the Modify Report window whenever a report is brought to the screen by selecting this option.

Reports And Graphs Settings

While you're viewing a report or a graph, you can make changes to the format, the filters, or the data behind it. Most of the time, QuickBooks automatically changes the report or graph to match the changes. Sometimes, however, if there is anything else going on (perhaps you're also online, or you're in a network environment and other users are manipulating data that's in your report or graph), QuickBooks may not make changes automatically. The reason for the shutdown of automatic refreshing is to keep your computer running as quickly and efficiently as possible. At that point, QuickBooks has to make a decision about when and how to refresh the report or graph. You must give QuickBooks the parameters for making the decision to refresh:

- **Prompt Me To Refresh** Choose this option to see a message asking you whether you want to refresh the report or the graph after you've made changes to the data behind it. When the reminder appears, you can click Yes to refresh the data in the report.
- **Refresh Automatically** Choose this option if you want up-to-the-second data and don't want to bother to click the Refresh button. If you work with QuickBooks across a network, this could slow down your work a bit because whenever any user makes a change to data that's used in the report/graph, it will refresh itself.
- **Don't Refresh** Choose this option if you want to decide for yourself when to click the Refresh button on the report window, without any reminder from QuickBooks.

Graphs Only

Give QuickBooks instructions about creating your graphs, as follows:

- **Draw Graphs In 2D (Faster)** Choose this to display graphs in two dimensions instead of three. This doesn't limit your ability to see trends at a glance; it's just not as high-tech. The main reason to consider this option is that the 2-D graph takes less time to draw on your screen.
- **Use Patterns** Choose this to draw the various elements in your graphs with black-and-white patterns instead of colors. For example, one pie wedge may be striped, another speckled. This option is handy if you print your graphs to a black-and-white printer.

Move to the Company Preferences tab of the Reports & Graphs category to set company preferences for reports, as shown next.

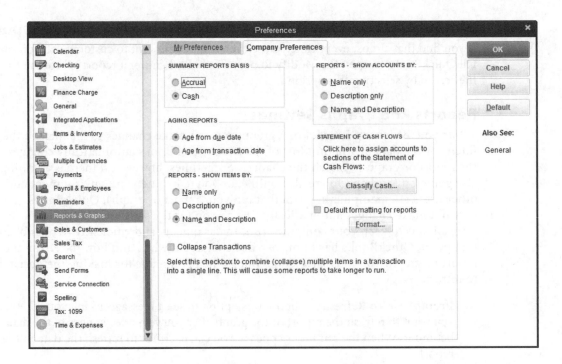

Summary Reports Basis

Specify whether you want to see summary reports as accrual based or cash based. You can always change the basis in the Modify Report dialog when you actually display the report.

Aging Reports

Specify whether you want to generate A/R and A/P aging reports using the due date or the transaction date.

Reports—Show Accounts By

Specify whether you want reports to display account names, account descriptions, or both. If you enabled account numbers, those numbers are part of the account names.

Reports—Show Items By

Specify whether you want reports that include items to display just the item name, the item description, or both.

Setting Report Format Defaults

Set the default formatting for reports by clicking the Format button and making changes to the default configuration options for parts of reports that aren't data related but instead control the look of the reports.

Configuring the Statement Cash Flows Report

A cash flow report is really a complicated document, and before the days of accounting software, accountants spent many hours creating such a report (and charged a lot of money for doing so). QuickBooks has configured a cash flow report format that is used to produce the Statement Of Cash Flows, which is available in the list of Company & Financial reports.

You can view the format by clicking the Classify Cash button, but if you plan on using this report on a regular basis, it's a good idea to check with your accountant before you reassign accounts. You can learn about cash flow reports in Chapter 12.

Collapse Transactions

Selecting this option will collapse (combine) a transaction that includes multiple items into one line on a report. When you run a report with this option, you can then use the Expand button at the top of the report window to display the details.

Sales & Customers Preferences

You can set options in the Sales & Customers category on both the My Preferences and Company Preferences tabs. On the My Preferences tab, set the options for invoicing customers for reimbursable expenses and billable time.

- **Prompt For Time/Costs To Add**   Choose this option to tell QuickBooks to open a dialog that displays the current outstanding reimbursable expenses and time associated with a customer whenever you create an invoice or sales receipt for a customer. This is the option to select if you typically need to rebill your customers for out-of-pocket expenses or for time spent on a project.
- **Don't Add Any**   Selecting this option prevents the automatic display of any dialogs about reimbursable expenses when you create a sales transaction. Choose this option if you rarely (or never) seek reimbursement from your customers. If you decide that you *do* want to collect reimbursable expenses during invoice creation, you can click the Add Time/Costs button on the sales transaction form.
- **Ask What To Do**   Select this option to tell QuickBooks to ask you what you want to do whenever you create a sales transaction for a customer with outstanding reimbursable costs. Depending on your selection in that dialog, you can either add the costs to the sales transaction or omit them.

On the Company Preferences tab, set the default options for sales transactions.

Usual Shipping Method

Use this to set the default shipping method if you use the same shipping method most of the time.

Usual FOB

Set the FOB language for invoices. FOB (Free On Board) is the location from which shipping is determined to be the customer's responsibility. This means more than just paying for freight; it's a statement that says, "At this point, you have become the owner of this product." The side effects include assigning responsibility if goods are lost, damaged, or stolen. FOB settings have no impact on your financial records.

Warn About Duplicate Invoice Numbers

This option tells QuickBooks to warn you if you're creating an invoice with an invoice number that's already in use.

Choose Template For Invoice Packing Slip

Select a default packing slip to use when you print packing slips. If you've created customized packing slips, you can make one of them the default.

Enable Collections Center

Selecting the Enable Collections Center check box makes the Collections Center feature available. Once enabled, an icon with the same name is added to the Customer Center for easy access. Its purpose is to help you keep track of past due and almost past due customer balances while also giving you an easy way to send e-mail reminders to the customers that are listed there.

Custom Pricing

Choose one of two options: No Custom Pricing and Enable Price Levels. Price levels are a way for you to customize your prices by customer.

Sales Tax Preferences

If you collect sales tax, you must set your sales tax options. Although there are no options in the personal preferences section, most of the selections in the Company Preferences are defined by state tax laws and state tax reporting rules, as shown next. Check with your accountant and read the information that came with your state sales tax license. For more information about managing sales taxes in QuickBooks, see Chapter 6.

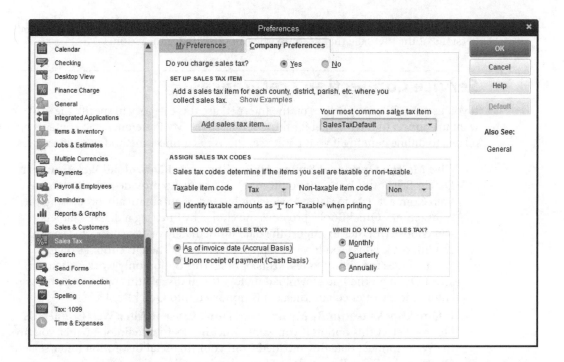

Search Preferences

The Search feature allows you to quickly search in all areas of your company file for things like transactions, names, amounts, dates, QuickBooks features, and so on. By default, the Search field is included on the QuickBooks Icon Bar, whether you use the Top or Left Icon Bar. If you use the Top Icon Bar, you can remove the Search field on it by unchecking that option at the top of the My Preferences tab. You can also tell QuickBooks whether to search the Help files or your QuickBooks file when a search term is entered in this field.

The preferences listed on the Company Preferences tab give you the option of updating your search information either automatically (as often as every five minutes) or manually.

Send Forms Preferences

If you send transactions to customers via e-mail, the My Preferences tab offers the opportunity to automatically select the Email Later option on a sales transaction if the current customer is configured for e-mail as the preferred send method. You can choose whether to send this information via Outlook or a compatible web e-mail service like Yahoo! or Gmail. You can also use QuickBooks E-mail, which is a subscription-based offering. Click the Check For Valid Subscriptions button to learn more or to confirm your own subscription.

On the Company Preferences tab, you can use Email Templates to design multiple versions of the message that accompanies an e-mailed transaction.

Service Connection Preferences

If you use QuickBooks services on the Internet, use this category to specify the way you want to connect to the Internet for those services. The My Preferences tab contains options related to online banking if your bank uses the Web Connect method of online access:

- **Give Me The Option Of Saving A File Whenever I Download Web Connect Data**   Select this option if you want QuickBooks to provide a choice to save Web Connect data for later processing instead of automatically processing the transactions. QuickBooks provides the choice by opening a dialog that lets you choose whether to import the data immediately or save it to a file so you can import it later (you have to supply a filename). The QuickBooks dialog also includes the ability to reset this option. This option only works when you select Open on the File Download dialog. If you disable this option, the file is automatically opened and the data is imported into QuickBooks.
- **If QuickBooks Is Run By My Browser, Don't Close It After Web Connect Is Done**   Select this option if you want QuickBooks to remain open after you process the Web Connect data downloaded from your financial institution (after selecting Open on the Download dialog). If you deselect this option, QuickBooks closes automatically as soon as your data is processed.

The following connection options are available on the Company Preferences tab (these options don't apply to payroll services or online banking):

- **Automatically Connect Without Asking For A Password**   Lets all users log in to the QuickBooks network automatically.
- **Always Ask For A Password Before Connecting**   Forces users to enter a login name and password in order to access QuickBooks Services.
- **Allow Background Downloading Of Service Messages**   Lets QuickBooks check the Intuit website for updates and information periodically when you're connected to the Internet.

Spelling Preferences

The Spelling section presents options only on the My Preferences tab. This is where you control the way the spell checker in QuickBooks works. You can instruct QuickBooks to check spelling automatically before saving, sending, or printing any form. In addition, you can specify those words you want the spell checker to skip, such as Internet addresses, numbers, and all capital letters that probably indicate an abbreviation, as shown next.

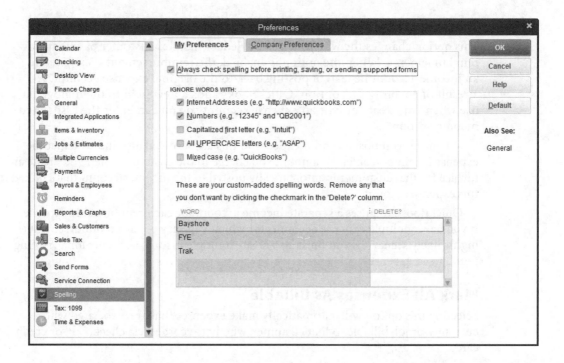

Tax:1099 Preferences

If you need to file 1099-Misc forms, select the Company Preferences tab of this window to access a wizard that will help you establish the 1099 form options you need. For each type of 1099 payment, you must assign an account from your chart of accounts. To make these assignments, use the Click Here link under If You Want To Map Your Accounts To Boxes On Form 1099-MISC. If you're ready to prepare your 1099s, including mapping accounts, use the Click Here link to launch the 1099 Wizard. For complete information about 1099s, see Chapter 17.

Time & Expenses Preferences

Use this section in the Company Preferences tab to turn on time tracking and to tell QuickBooks the first day of your work week (which becomes the first day listed on your timesheets). Configure invoicing options as explained in the following sections.

Mark All Time Entries As Billable

Selecting this option makes hours entered in a timesheet that are associated with a customer or job billable to that customer.

Track Reimbursed Expenses As Income

This option changes the way your general ledger handles customer payments for reimbursements. When the option is enabled, the reimbursement is assigned to an income account instead of posting back to the original expense account. As a result of enabling this option, QuickBooks adds a new field to the dialog you use when you create or edit an expense account so you can enter the associated income account.

Whenever you post a vendor expense to this account and also indicate that the expense is reimbursable, the amount you charge to the customer when you create an invoice for that customer is automatically posted to the income account that's linked to this expense account.

QuickBooks requires a separate income account for each reimbursable expense. If you have multiple expense accounts for which you may receive reimbursement (a highly likely scenario), you must also create multiple income accounts for accepting reimbursed expenses.

Mark All Expenses As Billable

Selecting this option will automatically make expenses that are associated with a customer or job billable to that customer, whether recorded via check, bill, or credit card.

Default Markup Percentage

You can preset a markup for reimbursed expenses and for items that have both a cost and price. QuickBooks uses the percentage you enter here to automate the pricing of inventory items. When you're creating an inventory item, as soon as you enter the cost, QuickBooks automatically adds this percentage and displays the result as the price. If you enter a default markup percentage, use the Default Markup Account field to select an account to which you want to post the resulting markup amounts.

Customize Transaction Templates

QuickBooks makes it easy to customize the forms you use to create transactions. Forms such as invoices, purchase orders, statements, and so on are called *templates* in QuickBooks, and there are two options available when customizing templates.

The first allows you to create brand-new template designs from an online template gallery. You can then save these templates to your template list. The second option gives you the ability to work with and modify the appearance of an *existing* template or to create a new template based on an existing one from within the program. This section focuses on the second option. You can use an existing template as the basis of a new template, copying what you like, changing what you don't like, and eliminating what you don't need. Existing templates can be customized in two ways:

- **Basic customization**   Change the appearance by customizing the fonts, colors, and other output settings only. These are minor changes that can be made to your templates, including the built-in Intuit templates.
- **Additional customization**   Customize the fields and columns that appear on the template. These are major changes and require you to create a new template with a new template name.

Basic Customization of Templates

To make minor changes to an existing template, locate and open the desired template in the Templates list by choosing Lists | Templates. Double-click the desired template to open the Basic Customization window. You can also open a template in the Basic Customization window while you're creating a new transaction (like an invoice, for example). In this case, on the Formatting tab located on the ribbon bar at the top of the form window, select Manage Templates. Choose the template you want to modify and click OK to open the Basic Customization window (see Figure 14-1).

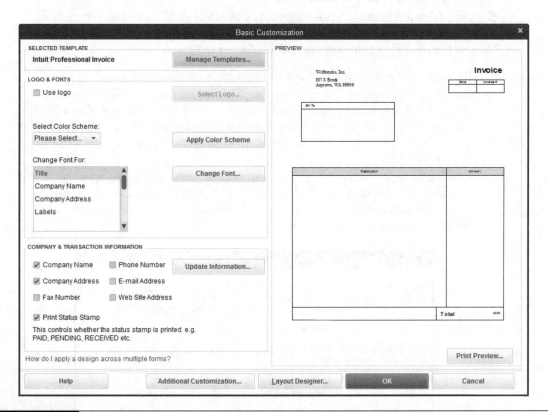

FIGURE 14-1   Use the Basic Customization dialog to make small changes to Intuit templates.

Small Business Tip Templates that have the word "Intuit" in their name are designed to work with preprinted forms you purchase from Intuit (although you can use them with blank paper or letterhead). Except for the Intuit Packing Slip, you can only perform basic customization on these templates. To use Intuit templates as the basis for additional customization, you must make a copy of the template and create a new template.

Managing Templates

Click Manage Templates to view, copy, or rename a template. The Preview pane (located on the bottom-right) displays a layout of the template as it currently looks and displays the template name at the top. In the Template Name field at the top of the Preview pane, you can delete the current name (unless it's an original Intuit template) and replace it with the name you want for the new template. Clicking OK returns you to the Basic Customization dialog.

Adding a Logo to a Template

You can add your company logo to a template by selecting the Use Logo check box. Navigate to the folder in which you have stored your logo graphic file, and select the file. Use the following guidelines to add a logo to a template:

- The logo should be a square shape to fit properly on the template.
- QuickBooks accepts all the common graphic formats for your logo. However, the graphic loads when you print the template, and graphic files saved in a BMP, TIFF, or PSD format tend to be larger than other formats and may take quite some time to load each time you print. The most efficient format in terms of size and resolution is JPG.
- Your logo appears in the upper-left corner of the form, unless you open the Layout Designer (covered later in this chapter) to reposition it. (If you are customizing a template with Intuit in its name, you will be warned to create a copy to make additional changes, as shown next.)

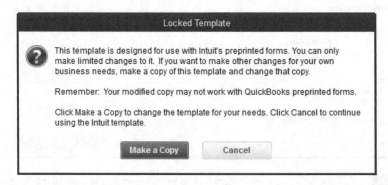

- You won't see the logo on the screen version of the template.
- If you can't place the logo in the size and position you prefer, consider having stationery printed and using it as the paper source for the template.

Customizing Colors on a Template

You can change the color of the lines that appear on the template by selecting a color scheme from the drop-down list in the Select Color Scheme field. Click Apply Color Scheme to save the change and see its effect in the Preview pane on the right side of the dialog.

You can also change the color of any text that's printed on the form by using the features for changing fonts (covered next) and selecting a color for the font.

Customizing Fonts on a Template

To change the fonts for any elements on the template, select the element in the Change Font For list and click Change Font. Select a font, size, style (such as bold or italic), effects, or color.

Customizing the Company Information on a Template

You can select and deselect the text that appears in the name and address block of your templates. The data comes from the Company Information dialog, which you can open by clicking Update Information to make sure that the data exists.

Printing Status Stamps on Templates

You can select or deselect the option to print the status stamp on a transaction template (PAID, RECEIVED, and so on). The status stamp prints at an angle across the center of the header section of the template. If you deselect the status stamp, you are only removing it from the printed copy of the form; the screen copy always shows the status.

The List of Templates

If you've just started using QuickBooks, you may be confused by the template names you see in the Templates list (Lists | Templates). The templates that appear in the list depend on the preferences you set and the transactions you've created.

By default, QuickBooks installs Invoice templates, a Statement template, and a Packing Slip template. You won't see a Purchase Order template unless you enable Inventory & Purchase Orders and open the built-in Purchase Order template by choosing Vendors | Create Purchase Orders. As soon as the Create Purchase Orders transaction window opens, the Purchase Order template appears on the list (close the transaction window without creating a purchase order if your only purpose was to add the template to the list). The same convention applies to Sales Receipts, Estimates, and other QuickBooks templates.

Additional Customization of Templates

You can make major changes to templates to suit your needs as well as your taste. QuickBooks calls this the Additional Customization feature. Start your customization by selecting an existing template on which to base your new template. Select the Customize Data Layout button located on the Formatting tab, which is located on the ribbon bar at the top of the form's window. If you are attempting to modify an Intuit template, the Locked Template dialog appears, instructing you to make a copy of the template; otherwise, the Additional Customization window opens (see Figure 14-2).

Custom fields you create in a Names list appear in the Header section of transaction windows, whereas custom fields you create in the Item List appear in the Columns section of transaction windows.

Customizing the Template Header

The header section of the Additional Customization dialog includes all the fields that appear above the line items in a transaction form. You can add or remove fields on the

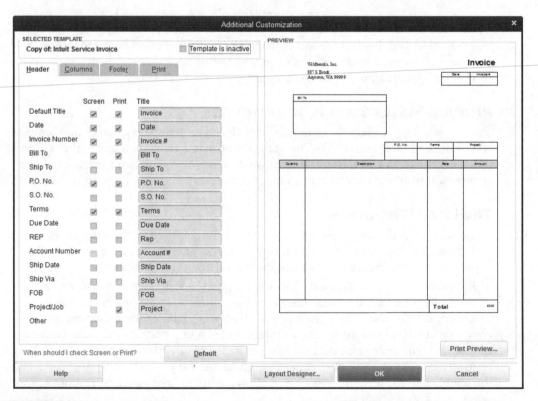

FIGURE 14-2 The Additional Customization dialog lets you point and click to redesign a template.

screen form, the printed form, or both. The Preview pane on the right is a preview of the printed form, and as you add or remove fields from the printed form, you see the changes reflected there.

There are some changes to the header section that you may want to make based on the way you've set up your QuickBooks company file. For example:

- If you assign account numbers to your customers, you may want to display the Account Number field (only available on the printed version).
- If you use reps, either as commissioned salespersons or as customer support contacts, you can add the Rep field to both the screen and printed versions.
- If you're tracking jobs for the majority of your customers, add the job name to the form (only available in the printed version). QuickBooks uses the term "project" because that's the commonly used term in most businesses (the exception is the construction trade, where "job" is a common term). If you refer to jobs as "jobs" with your customers, you can change the text.

Customizing the Template Columns

On the Columns tab of the Additional Customization dialog, you can add or remove columns that appear in the line item section of the transaction form. If you created custom fields for items, they're available for any template you design.

If progress invoicing is turned on, another columns tab, called Prog Cols, is available for customizing the transaction form you use when you create a progress invoice against an estimate.

Customizing the Template Footer

The Footer tab contains the elements that appear at the bottom of the transaction form. If you want to add fields to this section of the printed transaction form, you'll have to use the Layout Designer to maneuver the positioning because you don't have a lot of space to work with.

Setting the Print Option

On the Print tab, you can configure the printer settings for just this template by selecting the option Use Specified Printer Settings Below For This Invoice. If you want to use the same invoice printer settings that you used in your printer setup (File | Printer Setup | Invoices), you can select that option as your default.

Using the Layout Designer

As you customize the printed forms, you can see the effects in the Preview pane. If you notice some overlapping fields, or if you think the layout looks too crowded, you can use the Layout Designer to reposition the elements on the form. Click Layout Designer to open your template in the Layout Designer window, as shown in Figure 14-3.

The Layout Designer is a powerful and complicated feature, and it's beyond the scope of this book to go into deep detail about it. The more you work with it, however, the better you'll get at making it work for you. It's a good idea to make a copy of an existing invoice template and experiment on that copy before you make changes to your "live" template.

If you use window envelopes to mail your invoices, be sure the Show Envelope Window option at the bottom of the Layout Designer is selected before you start. The

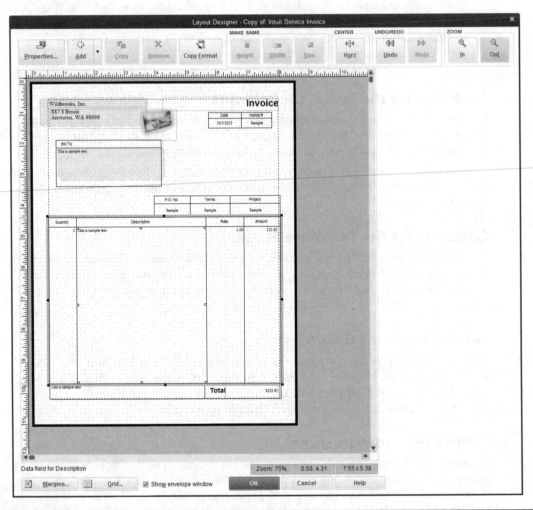

areas of the form that appear in envelope windows are highlighted in green. This helps you avoid moving any fields into that area.

Select any element to put a frame around it. Now you can perform an action on the frame, as follows:

- To change the size of the element, position your pointer on one of the sizing handles on the frame and then drag the handle to resize the element.
- To move an element, position your pointer inside the frame and, when your pointer turns into a four-headed arrow, drag the frame to a different location on the form.
- Double-click an element's frame to see a Properties dialog that permits a variety of changes for the selected element.
- To change the margin measurements, click the Margins button at the bottom of the Layout Designer.
- Click the Grid button to open the Grid And Snap Settings dialog, where you can eliminate the dotted line grid, change the spacing between grid lines, or turn off the Snap To Grid option (which automatically aligns objects to the nearest point on the grid).
- Use the toolbar buttons to align, resize, and zoom into the selected elements. There are also Undo and Redo buttons, just in case.

When you finish with the Layout Designer, click OK to move back to the Additional Customization window. If everything is just the way you want it, save your new template by clicking OK. This new template name appears on the drop-down list when you create transaction forms.

Document Management

QuickBooks lets you store other documents with your QuickBooks transactions.

The Doc Center

The Doc Center holds documents and files on your computer that you can then "attach" to or associate with a specific transaction or record in QuickBooks. For example, a purchase order a customer sends to you via e-mail or snail mail can be saved or scanned into the Doc Center. Later, with the customer's invoice open, click the Attach (paper clip) icon at the top of the Create Invoices window and browse to the document that you've saved on your computer through the Doc Center. A copy of the PO will then be easily retrievable right from the invoice. To open the Doc Center, click the Docs button on the Icon Bar, or from the QuickBooks menu bar, select Company | Documents | Doc Center, as seen here.

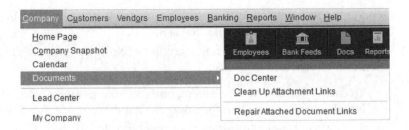

Using the Attach File Feature

The Attach File feature allows you to attach files of any type to a QuickBooks list record or transaction. You'll see an Attach File icon at the top of all transaction windows, as well as in all QuickBooks centers.

Once you've attached a file or scanned image, it is easily accessible via the Doc Center, as shown here (which you can open by clicking the Docs button on the Icon Bar). For example, you might want to attach a scanned copy of a customer's purchase order to the invoice that you generate for them in QuickBooks, or maybe you'll need to attach an e-mailed copy of a vendor's bill when you enter it into QuickBooks. Or you might want to attach a file or image to a vendor record.

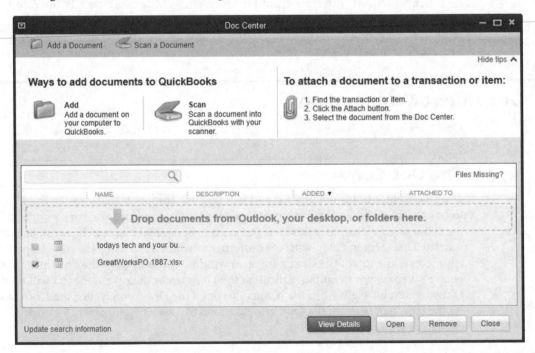

To attach a file or image to a transaction (such as an invoice or estimate), open the transaction and click the Attach File button, shown next. To attach a document to a customer or vendor record, highlight the record's name in the appropriate center, and then click the Attach (paper clip) icon. The Attachments window opens, giving you the option of attaching a document directly from your computer, your scanner, or the Doc Center.

A QuickBooks transaction or record that has an attachment will display a blue icon (a paper clip attached to a piece of paper), indicating that an attached file or image exists. Click this icon to open the Doc Center to view this and other files and documents stored there.

E-mail Forms and Reports

You can e-mail documents and reports directly from QuickBooks as PDF attachments to e-mail messages. E-mailing works exactly the same as printing forms and reports. That is, you can e-mail each individual transaction as you create it or save the transactions and e-mail them in a batch.

If you're using Outlook or a compatible web-based e-mail service, QuickBooks can send e-mail to your customers either directly through your e-mail software or your e-mail service. If you use e-mail software other than the supported software, you can use QuickBooks E-mail, which provides a server-based e-mail service. You have to sign up for this, and additional fees may apply.

You can e-mail any report (either as a PDF file or as an Excel file), and you can also e-mail all of the following QuickBooks transaction forms:

- Invoices
- Estimates
- Sales receipts
- Credit memos
- Statements
- Purchase orders
- Pay stubs (if you use QuickBooks payroll and have signed up for direct deposit)

Setting Up E-mail

Your e-mail setup options can be found by selecting Edit | Preferences | Send Forms. If QuickBooks finds a copy of one of the supported e-mail software applications (such as Outlook) on your computer with an active profile installed (an *active profile* is an e-mail account established in the software, and the software is the default e-mail software on your computer), the Send Forms category on the My Preferences tab shows this as the default e-mail method. If these options aren't displayed, you must use the QuickBooks E-mail service to send transaction forms and reports.

The My Preferences tab also shows an option, Auto-check The "Email Later" Checkbox If Customer's Preferred Delivery Method Is E-mail, to instruct QuickBooks to select Email Later automatically on every transaction linked to a customer that has e-mail set as their preferred delivery method (set on the Payment Settings tab of the customer record). If you configure a customer's delivery method as e-mail, make sure you enter the customer's e-mail address as well.

When creating purchase orders, you'll also have the option to e-mail later if you want to send those transactions in a batch. This option works only if you've entered an e-mail address for the vendor on their Address Info tab in their record.

On the Company Preferences tab, you can use e-mail templates to design multiple versions of the message that accompanies an e-mailed form (such as invoices, purchase orders, and estimates, to name a few). Click the Add, Edit, or Delete buttons to create, modify, or delete an e-mail template.

Sending E-mail

To send a single transaction form by e-mail, click the Email button at the top of the transaction form. Or select Email Later (located next to the Email button) before saving the transaction to send the e-mail in a batch.

Using Your E-mail Software

If QuickBooks uses Outlook to send transaction forms or reports, the standard Create Message window appears:

- If the customer's or vendor's e-mail address is stored in QuickBooks, it's automatically inserted into the To: field.
- If the customer's or vendor's e-mail address is not available, QuickBooks searches your e-mail software address book. If the name/e-mail address is found, the entry in the To: field is underlined to indicate the name has been matched to an existing address book entry.
- If the customer's or vendor's e-mail address is not available in either place, you'll need to add it to your QuickBooks file.

The Subject field is prefilled with *<Transaction Number>* from *<YourCompanyName>*. The Attachment field is prefilled with the name of the PDF file of the transaction form. The text of the message is prefilled by QuickBooks, using the text in the Send Forms Preferences dialog, discussed in the previous section.

Using QuickBooks E-mail

If you're not using one of the supported e-mail applications and you've activated the QuickBooks E-mail service, QuickBooks fills out the message and attaches the document in the same way it does when you're using your own e-mail software.

When you click Send Now, QuickBooks opens a browser window and takes you to the QuickBooks Billing Solutions website. If this is the first time you're e-mailing invoices, follow the prompts to complete the sign-up process, and then QuickBooks will send the e-mail. Thereafter, your e-mail is sent automatically. An additional feature of this Billing Solutions service is the ability to accept online payments from your customers that receive an invoice from you via this service (additional fees may apply).

Small Business Tip If you use the QuickBooks Billing Solutions, enter your own e-mail address in the CC: or BCC: field of the message window so you have a record of the e-mail. (If you use your own software, you have a copy in the Sent Messages folder.)

Additional Tasks in QuickBooks

Part Six covers features and tasks in QuickBooks that are more general in nature. These chapters cover information such as explaining how to keep your data secure and how to protect it from disasters. In Chapter 15, you'll also see step-by-step instructions on how to maintain the integrity of the important financial information you track in QuickBooks.

In Chapter 16, you learn about using journal entries, special transactions that are used to make changes directly to an account without using a regular transaction (such as an invoice or check). Chapter 17 shows you how to share your company information with others, including your accountant. You'll learn how to make an Accountant's Copy, a special copy of your file that allows your accountant to examine your books and make the necessary adjustments to your QuickBooks data and what you can do to prepare your QuickBooks data for year end. This part ends with Chapter 18, which is a blend of tips and solutions that may prevent some errors before they happen or help you fix errors that have occurred.

Keeping Your QuickBooks Data Secure and Healthy

n this chapter:

- Deleting and eliminating company files

- Backing up your files and restoring from a backup

- Creating a portable company file

- Using the Verify and Rebuild utilities

- Making your file smaller

- Working with QuickBooks updates

The bookkeeping chores you complete in QuickBooks ensure that you're tracking important information about your business and how it's performing. Just as important as these tasks is the need to take care of the "health" of your QuickBooks company data file. In particular, it's important to keep your software up to date and make sure your data is not cluttered with very old or irrelevant transactions and list items. Finally, it's critical that you decide on and adopt a backup routine that you can rely on.

Delete Company Files

Sometimes, you have a valid reason to get rid of a company file. Perhaps you created a company to experiment with and you no longer use it, or you've been promoted and someone is taking over your job and you no longer need to keep a QuickBooks company file on your local computer.

QuickBooks doesn't have a Delete File command from within the program itself, but you can delete the file from your hard drive through Windows Explorer or My Computer. Before you delete the file, however, read the following sections carefully so you don't encounter a problem the next time you open QuickBooks.

How QuickBooks Loads Company Files

When it opens, QuickBooks automatically opens the company file that was loaded when you last exited the software. It's best to make sure that you don't have the about-to-be-deleted company file loaded when you close QuickBooks. Otherwise, the next time you open the program, it will try to "find" the deleted file, which can be confusing to both you and the software. To prevent this, take one of the following actions:

- Choose File | Open Or Restore Company to select another company file other than the one you're about to delete, and then exit the program. If you have no other companies, use one of the sample companies that came with your program.
- Choose File | Close Company/Logoff to close the current file and have no company file loaded if you shut down QuickBooks and reopen it.

Deleting the File

To delete a company file, open Windows Explorer in Windows 7 or File Explorer in Windows 8.1 or Windows 10. Navigate to the folder that holds your company files. Then delete the file *companyname*.qbw and the associated *companyname*.dsn and *companyname*.nd files. To complete the task, you'll also need to delete the *companyname*.tlg file separately (you may also see an LGB file that can be removed as well).

> **Small Business Tip**   Consider creating a separate folder on your hard drive for your QuickBooks company files. Having a separate folder allows you to find your files quickly, and you can back up everything simply by backing up the folder.

Eliminating Deleted Files from the Company File List

QuickBooks tracks the company files you've opened and lists the most recently opened files on the Open Previous Company submenu (under the File menu) to make it easier to move among files. You don't have to open a new dialog to select one of those files; you just click the appropriate listing. The submenu lists the company files you've opened, starting with the most recent.

After you delete a company file, its "ghost" listing may still appear on the Open Previous Company submenu or in the No Company Open window. You or another user could inadvertently select it, which produces a delay followed by an error message. You can clear the list of company files that you see in the Open Previous Company menu or in the No Company Open window by clicking the Edit List link on the No Company Open window.

In the QuickBooks Edit Company List window, select a company file that you want to hide from the list and click OK.

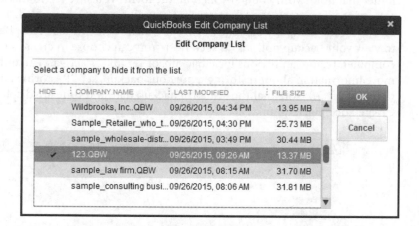

This changes the company files that are listed in the Open Previous Company menu, as well as the No Company Open Window, to the current company file only. QuickBooks again begins to track the files that you're working on, so as you open different company files, it rebuilds the list.

Back Up and Restore Files

Backing up your QuickBooks data is an incredibly important task and should be done on a daily basis. In addition, once a week, it's a good idea to use removable media to make an extra backup and then take that backup off-site.

If you need to use a backup file, you can't open it the way you open a regular company file; instead, it has to be restored using the QuickBooks Restore command, as discussed in the following section.

Backing Up

Do this every day! You don't have to create a manual backup every day as described here if you set up scheduled backups (covered later in this section); you'll still be making a daily backup—you just won't have to remember to initiate it.

Intuit says that backing up a file across the network results in a backup that isn't a full backup. Unfortunately, backing up a company file that is located on your computer can also result in a backup file that's missing some information, although the problem isn't as severe.

If you do payroll in-house, any payroll forms you saved (940, 941, W-2, etc.) are not backed up. Luckily, you can back up those forms separately by copying them to your backup media. Look for a folder named *<YourCompanyFile>* Tax Forms History in the folder that holds your company files; all the forms you save are in that folder. You might also print a hard copy of each important payroll form you have filed. To create a local backup of the company currently open in QuickBooks, choose File | Back Up Company to view your backup options, as seen next. You can choose to create a backup on a local computer, restore a previous local backup, or set up (or activate) an online backup. (For more information about restoring a previous backup, see "Restoring a Backup" later in this chapter.) Note that the last local backup date and time are displayed above the Create Local Backup link.

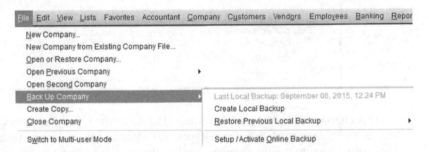

Select Create Local Backup to open the Create Backup Wizard as seen in Figure 15-1.

If you choose Setup/Activate Online Backup from this dialog, QuickBooks opens a browser and takes you to a website with information about the QuickBooks online backup service (a fee-based service). From there, you can learn more about the service

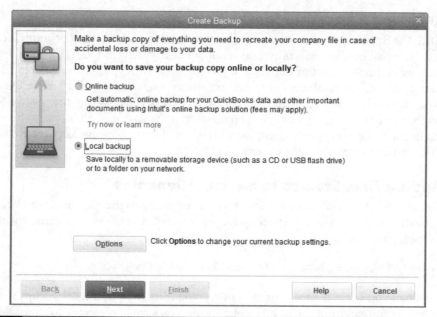

FIGURE 15-1   The Create Backup Wizard helps you protect your valuable information.

(which allows you to back up not only your QuickBooks data, but also other critical business files) or sign up for the service. Intuit offers a free trial so you can learn how this service works.

With the Local Backup option selected, click the Options button to set the location of the backup in the Backup Options dialog, shown here. Use the guidelines in the following sections to select options in this dialog.

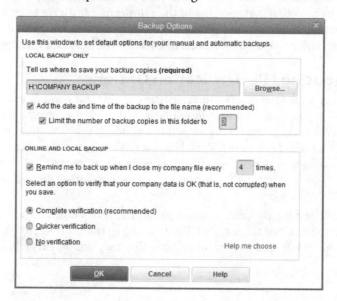

Selecting a Location for the Backup

Click the Browse button to select the location for this backup. The optimum location is an external hard drive, a universal serial bus (USB) drive, a CD/DVD, or a drive on another computer on your network (if you have a network). If you select a local drive, such as the "C" drive on the computer on which your company file is kept, QuickBooks issues a warning message when you click OK. Unless you're saving the file to a folder on the drive that is going to be backed up later in the day or at night, heed the warning. Putting a backup on your current hard drive could make your backup irretrievable if this hard drive experiences a catastrophic failure.

Adding Time Stamps to Backup Filenames

You can select the option to append a date/time stamp to the filename, which lets you tell at a glance when the backup file was created. The backup filename has the following format:

```
CompanyFilename(Backup Sept 09,2015 04 36 PM).QBB
```

When you select the time-stamp option, you can create multiple backups in the same location. You can limit the number of backups you save in a specific location. Multiple backups over continuous days provide an option to restore a backup from two days ago (or longer) if you think the backup you made yesterday may have some corrupted data. During backup, QuickBooks notes the number of backups you opted to keep; when a backup is made that exceeds that number, QuickBooks asks if you want to delete the extra backup, always choosing the oldest backup as the one to delete.

Setting Backup Reminders

You can ask QuickBooks to remind you about backing up when you close a company file by selecting that option and then indicating the frequency. Hopefully, this prompt won't be necessary because you are already backing up every day. However, if you think you'll still need to be reminded to back up your file, use this option.

Choosing File Verification Options

You can ask QuickBooks to verify the data in your company file before backing up by selecting either verification option. Although this can increase the amount of time it takes to complete the backup, it is a good idea to take the time when backing up at the end of a day or work shift. However, if you're performing a quick backup because you want to make changes in your file, or you're about to perform some other action that makes you think you want a quick backup for safety, you can select the option No Verification.

When time permits, it is best to run the verify utility. To do so, select File | Utilities | Verify Data. See the section "Verify and Rebuild a Company File," later in this chapter, for more information on completing this very important task.

Choosing When to Save the Backup

After you have chosen the location for your backup and set the other options in the Backup Options dialog, click OK to return to the Create Backup dialog. Click Next to choose when to create this backup. You have three choices:

- Save It Now
- Save It Now And Schedule Future Backups
- Only Schedule Future Backups

The second and third choices are concerned with scheduling automatic and unattended backups, a subject that's covered later in this chapter in the section, "Scheduling Backups."

Assuming you're creating a backup now (the option chosen by default), click Next. QuickBooks opens the Save Backup Copy dialog with your location selected and the backup filename in the File Name field. Click Save.

Back Up to a CD

If you're using QuickBooks on a computer running Windows Vista, Windows 7, Windows 8.1, or Windows 10, you can select your CD drive as the backup target. QuickBooks saves the backup to the default folder on the hard drive that holds files waiting to be written to a CD, and the software displays a message telling you your data has been backed up successfully to that location. When you click OK, QuickBooks may display a dialog offering online backup (you can choose to learn more about this service or close the dialog to proceed). From here, you can choose to burn the CD using the Windows CD Writing Wizard (Burn Now) or using your own CD-burning software (Burn Later), as seen next.

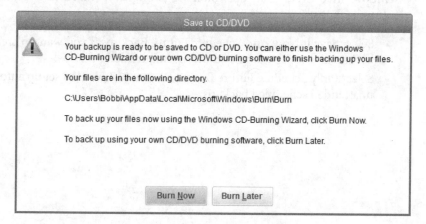

You may see a balloon over the notification area of your taskbar, telling you that files are waiting to be written to the CD (the standard notification when you burn CDs in Windows). You don't have to click the balloon to open the folder that holds the file because the QuickBooks backup feature automatically opens the Windows CD Writing Wizard and copies the file to the CD.

If you choose Burn Later, when you're ready to burn your CD, Windows looks in the folders under your name in C:\Users\<*username*>\AppData\Local\Microsoft \Windows\ Burn in Windows 7 and uses the backup files that QuickBooks created to burn to the CD. In Windows 8.1 and 10, the file is in C:\Users\<*username*>\AppData \Local\Microsoft\Windows\Burn\Burn. You can open your CD-burning software and direct it to that location, or you can use the Windows CD Writing Wizard by following these steps:

1. Select the CD drive in My Computer, where Windows displays the file(s) waiting to be written to the CD.
2. Choose File | Burn To Disc in Windows 7, 8.1, and 10.
3. When the Windows CD Writing Wizard appears, follow the prompts to move your backup file to the CD.

Scheduling Backups

QuickBooks offers both automatic backups and unattended backups (which are also automatic). You can schedule either or both of these types of backups from the same wizard that walks you through the backup process described in the previous sections. Click through the wizard windows until you get to the second window titled Create Backup. You'll see two options that allow you to schedule future backups:

- Select Save It Now And Schedule Future Backups if you want to create a manual backup and set up automatic and/or unattended backups.
- Select Only Schedule Future Backups if you just want to set up automatic and/or unattended scheduled backups.

Clicking Next after either selection brings you to the wizard window shown here.

Configuring Automatic Backups

An automatic backup is one that takes place whenever you close the company file. Closing a file is an action that can take place under any of the following circumstances:

- You open another company file.
- You choose File | Close Company (or File | Close Company/Logoff if you've set up users for the company).
- You close QuickBooks with this company file loaded.

Set the frequency of automatic backups to match the way you use QuickBooks and the way you work in this company file. For example, if you open QuickBooks with this company file loaded in the morning and keep QuickBooks open all day without changing companies, set a frequency of 1 to make sure you have at least one backup each day (you can also set up another scheduled backup for that evening). The automatic backup is created using the settings, including the location, you configured in the Options dialog.

Configuring Scheduled Backups

You can configure QuickBooks to perform a backup of your company files at any time, even if you're not working at your computer. This is a cool feature, but it doesn't work unless you remember to leave your computer running when you leave the office. Before you leave, make sure QuickBooks is closed so all the files are available for backing up (open files are skipped during a scheduled backup). Also, keep in mind that scheduled backups cannot be made to a CD/DVD.

To create the configuration for an unattended backup, click New to open the Schedule Backup dialog, shown here.

You can give the backup a descriptive name (it's optional), but if you're going to create multiple unattended backup configurations, it's a good idea to identify each by name. For example, if you're backing up to an external hard drive on Monday, Wednesday, and Friday, name the backup "QB Backup M-W-F."

Be sure the target drive is available at the time you designate. Ensure the USB or other removable drive is attached before leaving the computer, or be sure the remote network computer you're using for backup storage isn't shut down at night.

If you don't want to overwrite the last backup file every time a new backup file is created, select the option Number Of Backup Copies To Keep and specify the number. QuickBooks saves as many backup files as you specify (up to 99), each time replacing the first file with the most recent backup and copying older files to the next highest number in the filename. These backup files are saved with the file extension .qbb and include a date and time stamp. Create a schedule for this unattended backup by selecting a time and a frequency.

If you're on a network, QuickBooks displays the Enter Windows Password dialog. The password in question is not to your QuickBooks user and password configuration; it's your Windows logon name and password. You can create multiple unattended backups and configure them for special circumstances. For instance, in addition to a nightly backup, you may want to configure a backup every four weeks on a Saturday or Sunday (or during your lunch hour on a weekday) to create a backup on a removable drive that is stored off-site. Be sure to bring your backup media to the office on that day and take it back to the off-site location when the backup is finished.

Mapped drives are unique to your Windows login name. If you log off of Windows before you leave the office (not the same as shutting down the computer, which would prevent the backup from running), you cannot use a mapped drive to create your backup. Although it's not common to take the trouble to log off of Windows, if you do normally log off, use the full path to the remote folder you're using as the target backup location instead of the mapped drive letter. The format of the full path (called *Universal Naming Convention* or UNC) is

```
\\ComputerName\ShareName
```

Restoring a Backup

You just turned on your computer and it sounds different, a lot noisier. In fact, it seems to be a grinding noise. You wait and wait, but the usual startup of the operating system fails to appear. Eventually, an error message about a missing boot sector appears (or some other equally troubling message). Nonetheless, you have invoices to send out, checks to write, and tons of things to do, and if you can't accomplish those tasks, your business suffers. It may be time to replace your hard drive or get a new computer.

If your computer is fine (none of the grinding noises), perhaps it's your QuickBooks program that won't open, or it opens but reports a data error when it tries to open your file. In either case, follow these steps to restore your latest backup file:

1. Start QuickBooks. If the opening window tells you there's no company file open and suggests you create one (if this is a fresh installation of the software), ignore that message.
2. If you backed up to removable media, access the external hard drive, or put the disc or USB flash drive that contains your last backup into its slot. If you backed up to a network share, be sure the remote computer is running. If you purchased the QuickBooks online backup service, be sure you've configured your Internet connection in QuickBooks.

3. Choose File | Open Or Restore Company. Choose Restore A Backup Copy and click Next.

4. Select Local Backup if your backup files are on removable media or on a remote computer on the network. Select Online Backup if you subscribe to that QuickBooks service. Then click Next. (If you use the QuickBooks online backup service, at this point, follow the prompts to restore your backup.)

5. If you selected Local Backup, the Open Backup Copy dialog appears. Navigate to the folder or drive where your backup is stored.

6. Select the backup file—if you store multiple backups with time stamps embedded in the filename, select the most recent backup.

7. Click Open, and then click Next to continue with the Restore Wizard.

8. In the Save Company File As dialog, select the folder to which you're restoring the file and click Save.

9. If you're restoring to an existing company because the problem was a corrupt data file, QuickBooks asks if you want to replace the existing file. Click Yes. Then, just to make sure, QuickBooks displays a warning that you're about to overwrite/delete the existing file. That's fine; it's what you want to do, so type **Yes** in the dialog and click OK.

QuickBooks displays a message that your data files have been restored successfully and opens the file (if you have to log in, the login dialog displays first, and the success dialog appears after you log in).

The Portable Company File

A portable company file is a copy of your QuickBooks company file that has been condensed to save disk space to make it "portable," that is, smaller than a backup (QBB) copy. Portable files are designed to move data between computers, such as your home computer and your office, so you can work at home and then bring the updated file back to the office. However, ensure that no one at the office is working with the QuickBooks file while you are gone, as the entries they make will not appear in your file once you have restored it in the morning.

Creating a Portable Company File

To create a portable company file, choose File | Create Copy, select Portable Company File, and click Next. In the Save Portable Company File dialog, select a location for the file (by default, QuickBooks selects Desktop as the location).

If you're taking the file to another computer (perhaps you're taking it home), choose removable media such as an external drive or other USB drive, and take the media with you. Or, save the file on your hard drive and then send it to the person who will be working with the file (such as your accountant), by e-mail; through a cloud storage service; or by burning it to removable media such as a flash drive, DVD, or CD and sending that media to the recipient.

Small Business Tip Do not substitute making a full backup as part of your regular backup routine with creating a portable company file. Why? Because a portable company file does not contain an important transaction log file that a full backup (QBB) file has. This file is located in the same folder as your company file (the QBW file), and its filename is *<YourCompanyFilename>*.tlg. In many cases, Intuit Technical Support can use the log file and your most recent backup to recover data up to the point of the transactions saved at the time of the backup file you supply.

Click Save. QuickBooks displays a message telling you it has to close the company file to create the portable file. Click OK. It takes a while to create the file, and when it's done, QuickBooks issues a success message.

Overwriting Your Data File by Restoring a Backup or Portable File

Restoring a portable or backup file to a computer that has an existing QuickBooks company file may cause you to lose any work you've performed in the existing file. The process of overwriting the existing file with the portable or backup copy deletes the existing file and replaces it with the data in the portable or backup copy.

If you're the only person who works in the company file and you take a portable or backup file to another computer (such as your home computer), then work on the file and bring it back to the office, it's safe to overwrite the office copy with the changes that are made when you restore. Nobody has created any transactions since you created the portable or backup file, so deleting the original file doesn't delete any new transactions.

However, if you send a portable or backup file to someone else and then continue to work in the original file, you can't restore the file when it's returned unless you're prepared to lose all the work you did in the meantime. You have four ways to avoid this situation:

- Stop working on the file until the portable or backup file is returned. Then, when you restore to the company file, you don't lose any data.
- Have the person who's performing work in the portable or backup file send you a list of the transactions that were entered, instead of returning the file, and enter those transactions in the existing company file.
- Restore the file to a different location or use a different filename (or both). You can open the restored company file and see what's new and then add that data to your real company file.

- Send an Accountant's Copy to the person doing the off-site work (this person needs to be using QuickBooks Accountant's edition). Creating and working with an Accountant's Copy is covered in Chapter 17.

To restore a portable company file, either on your home computer or on the office computer after you've worked on the file at home and saved it as a portable file, follow these steps to use the wizard that guides you through the process:

1. Choose File | Open Or Restore Company.
2. In the Open Or Restore Company window, select Restore A Portable File and click Next.
3. In the Open Portable Company File dialog, navigate to the folder or removable media drive that holds the file, select the file, and click Open.
4. The next window that appears is the informational window about where to restore the file. Click Next.
5. The Save Company File As window opens, which allows you to choose where you want to save the restored file. Use one of the guidelines described next to select a location and filename:

   - **Replacing the Existing Company File with the Portable File**   If you're deliberately replacing a company file, select the folder that holds the original company file and use the same filename as your company file. QuickBooks displays a warning that you're about to overwrite the existing file and asks if you want to replace it; click Yes. To make sure you really understand what you're about to do, QuickBooks displays the Delete Entire File dialog and asks you to confirm your action. Type **Yes** and click OK to continue.
   - **Creating a Different Company File from the Portable File**   If you want to create a separate company file to avoid overwriting the work you did in your real company file, change the location or the filename (or both) before you click Save.

After the portable company file is uncompressed, it's loaded in the QuickBooks window so you can work in it.

Verify and Rebuild a Company File

QuickBooks 2016 has improved their utilities that verify and rebuild the data in your company file. Verifying a company file checks the integrity of your QuickBooks data. To verify your data, select File | Utilities | Verify Data. You are told that QuickBooks needs to close all open windows. If you want to continue, click OK. The Verify utility runs. If your file is large, this may take a few minutes.

If QuickBooks finds any issues with your data, you see a message that you can view the errors or rebuild the file, as shown next.

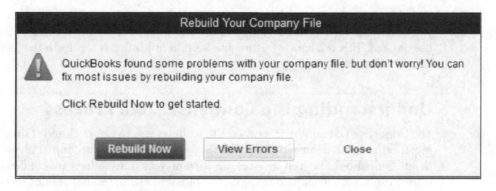

If you want to see the errors, clicking the View Errors button opens a window describing the problems. The report shows both errors that QuickBooks can fix and those the program cannot fix. Each error has a link in the form of an arrow that expands to show the details of the error.

You can choose to print the report and close the window or select Rebuild Data to start rebuilding your file right away. Before you start the rebuild, QuickBooks asks you to make a backup and reminds you *not* to use your existing backup disk (or location). *Be sure to follow this advice!*

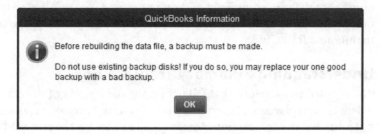

The Rebuild routine will attempt to resolve the issue with the data. When the process is complete, you will see a report showing the errors that have been fixed. If QuickBooks found errors it cannot fix, those errors are listed first. However, if you can't easily decipher the report's contents or the Rebuild routine continues to indicate a problem with the data, select the link to QuickBooks Technical Support for help.

Condense Your Data

To help reduce the size of your data file, QuickBooks provides a feature that enables you to remove certain transaction and list data in your company file that you no longer use or need. This is a handy feature, but keep in mind that it results in the loss of details about transactions.

Understanding the Condense Data Process

The Condense Data utility is a process that allows you to delete closed transactions and replace them with a journal entry that shows totals posted to accounts. If you subscribe to any QuickBooks payroll services, no current-year transactions are condensed. Open transactions, such as unpaid invoices and bills and estimates that are not marked "Closed," are not removed. Before removing the data, QuickBooks creates an archive copy of your company file, which you can open to see the original transactions that were removed.

Choosing a Date

QuickBooks asks you for the date you want to use as the cutoff date. Everything you no longer need before that date is removed, if it can be safely removed without interfering with the transactions that remain. No open transactions are removed; only those that are completed and safe to remove are affected. Also, any transactions before the cutoff date that affect current transactions are kept so the details are maintained in the file.

Understanding Summary Transactions

The detailed transactions that fall within the parameters of the condensing date are deleted and replaced with summary transactions. Summary transactions are nothing but journal entry transactions that show the totals for the removed transactions, one for each month. The account balances are not changed by removing data because the summary transactions maintain those totals.

What to Expect After the Condense Process Is Complete

After you clean up the file, you won't be able to run detail reports for those periods before the cutoff date. However, summary reports will be perfectly accurate in their financial totals. You will be able to recognize the summary transactions in the account registers because they will be marked with a transaction type GENJRNL. You can open the archived file if you need to see the original transaction details.

Run the Condense Data Utility

To select this feature, click File | Utilities | Condense data to open the Condense Data dialog, shown next.

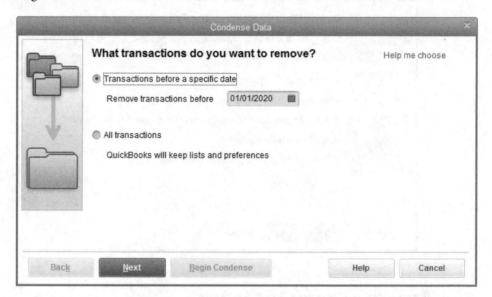

You see two cleanup methods. You may see a warning about losing your budget data when your file is condensed because some budgets are based on detailed postings. Click Yes. (Chapter 12 explains how to export your budgets to Excel and import them back into QuickBooks.)

For this discussion, select the Transactions Before A Specific Date option. Read "Removing All Transactions" later in this section to learn about the other option. By default, QuickBooks inserts the first day of the previous fiscal year as the date. Usually, it's a good idea to go back a bit more if you've been using QuickBooks for several years without performing a cleanup. Click Next when you've entered the cutoff date.

Condensing Inventory Transactions

If you track inventory in your QuickBooks file, the next window asks you how you want QuickBooks to handle the removal of transactions that involve inventory. If your file is not set up to track inventory, you're asked to tell QuickBooks about the transactions you want to remove from your file.

Selecting Additional Transactions to Remove

In the next wizard window, you can select one or more types of existing transactions to remove, as shown next, even though they wouldn't be removed automatically during a file cleanup process. For example, if you have a transaction marked "To Be Printed" that's more than a year old, you probably aren't planning to print it and you probably forgot you ever created it. When you've made your selections, click Next.

Removing Unused List Entries

In the next window, you can select the lists that may have entries that won't be used after old transactions are removed. Click the list(s) you want QuickBooks to examine to determine whether there are unused listings and, if so, remove them.

Click Next to see an informational window in which the condense process is explained. Click Begin Condense to start the process. QuickBooks automatically makes a full copy of your file for you and at the end of the condense process displays a message giving you the location on your computer that this copy was saved to.

This is not an everyday backup; it's a full copy of your data file—just the way your file was before you ran the cleanup feature. This means you can open it if you need to see transaction details the next time a customer or vendor calls to discuss a very old transaction.

Removing All Transactions

The Condense Data feature offers an option to strip the file of all transactions, leaving behind only the lists and the configuration settings you created for printers and Edit | Preferences categories. Often, this function is used shortly after you start using

QuickBooks as a way to "start all over." The other reasons you may use this option include the following:

- To start a new file at the beginning of a new year when the current company file has become so large that working in it is slower than you'd like.
- When a company changes its legal structure (from a proprietorship to a corporation or to an LLC), payroll, equity accounts, and other elements of the file must be changed to reflect the new organization type.
- The Remove All Transactions choice won't be available if you have payroll transactions for the current year or if your file contains bank or credit card accounts that are still enabled for online access.

QuickBooks creates a backup of the file before beginning the process and creates an archive of the file before clearing the transactions, so you don't really wipe out the company's history permanently.

Update QuickBooks

QuickBooks provides an automatic update service you can use to make sure your software is up to date and trouble free. This service provides you with any maintenance releases of QuickBooks created since you purchased and installed your copy of the software. A maintenance release is distributed when a problem is discovered and fixed, or when a new feature is added to the software. Note that this service does not provide upgrades to a new version; it just provides updates to your current version.

You can enable automatic updates, which means QuickBooks periodically checks the Intuit update site for updates to your version of QuickBooks. If new files exist, they're downloaded to your hard drive. If you turn off automatic updates, you should periodically check for new software files manually. Use the Update Now tab to select and download updated files.

Configuring the QuickBooks Update Service

Choose Help | Update QuickBooks and move to the Options tab, shown next, to configure the Update feature. You can enable or disable the automatic check for updates. If you're using QuickBooks on a network, you can configure the update service to share downloaded files with other users. When this option is enabled, QuickBooks creates a subfolder on the computer that holds the shared QuickBooks data files, and the other computers on the network use that subfolder as the source of updated files instead of going online and downloading files.

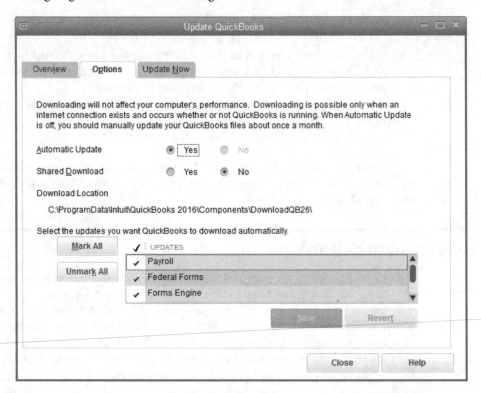

For this to work, every user on the network must open her or his copy of QuickBooks and configure the Update options for Shared Download to reflect the folder location on the host computer. The folder location is displayed on the Options tab when you select the Shared Download option.

Understanding General Journal Entries and Other Special Tasks

Chapter 16

In this chapter, you'll learn about QuickBooks transactions that are neither done every day, nor by every company. You'll learn about using *general journal entries* as explained in the first section of this chapter. Moreover, in our ever-narrowing world, your company may possibly deal in currencies other than the U.S. dollar. If so, you can learn about using more than one currency. In addition, if your company has a computer network and more than one user, you might choose to install QuickBooks on several computers. If so, those instructions are included in this chapter.

The QuickBooks Journal Entries Window

As you work in QuickBooks, the amounts entered in your financial transactions, such as invoices and bills, post automatically to the appropriate accounts in your chart of accounts. However, if necessary, you (or your accountant) can make an adjustment to an account directly. QuickBooks refers to this type of transaction as a general journal entry (aka journal entry).

Use journal entries to enter only financial data that cannot be added to an account via a standard transaction. For example, your accountant may use a journal entry at year end to record annual depreciation of an asset and the associated depreciation expense.

The Make General Journal Entries window, shown in Figure 16-1, is accessed from the Company menu. The format of the transaction window is standardized and cannot be customized in the same way as an invoice template. There are columns for account names and debit and credit amounts. In addition, QuickBooks provides columns you can use to link the data you enter to customers and classes or enter a memo.

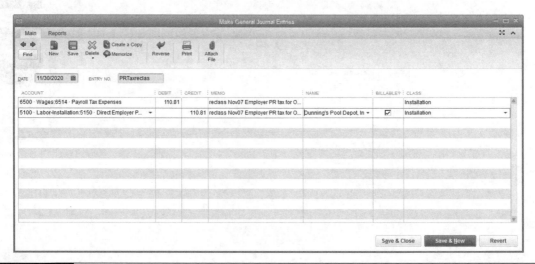

FIGURE 16-1 The Make General Journal Entries window has extra columns so you can track additional information about your entry.

To create a journal entry, follow these steps:

1. Choose Company | Make General Journal Entries. QuickBooks displays a message telling you that automatic numbers are now assigned to journal entries. (You can select the option Do Not Display This Message In The Future before you click OK.) Enable or disable the automatic numbering feature in the Accounting category of the Preferences dialog.
2. In the Account column, select the account you need.
3. Move to either the Debit or Credit column and enter an amount.
4. Optionally, make an entry in the Memo, Name, or Billable? columns.
5. Repeat Steps 2–4 for all the amounts in the journal entry.

As you enter each amount, QuickBooks presents the offsetting total in the next line. For example, if the line items you've entered so far have a higher total for the credit side than the debit side, the next entry presents the balancing offset.

Here are some guidelines to using the columns available in the Make General Journal Entries window:

- Use the Memo column to write a comment about the reason for the journal entry. The memo text appears in the entry of the account's register and on reports, so enter the text on every line of the entry in order to see the explanation, no matter which account register you're viewing.
- Use the Name column to assign a customer, vendor, employee, or other name to the amount on this line of the entry, if you're linking the entry to a name. If the account you're posting to is an A/R (accounts receivable) or A/P (accounts payable) account, an entry in the Name column is required. Note, however, that you cannot use more than one A/R or A/P account in the same journal entry. When you have created such an entry, this message appears. When you need to enter several items that affect either A/R or A/P, you will need to make several journal entries, one for each A/R or A/P item.

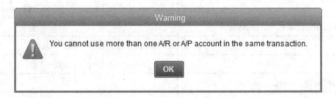

- The Billable? column indicates whether the amount is billable to the name in the Name column.
- If you are using the Class Tracking feature, you'll see a Class column, and you can link the entry to a class. This can be useful if, for example, you'd like to allocate certain overhead costs or assets to different classes.

Create Journal Entries for Depreciation

Depreciation is a way to track the current value of a fixed asset that loses value as it ages. The basis of an asset's depreciation from an accounting point of view is determined by a complicated set of rules, including IRS rules, which can change frequently. Most small businesses enter the depreciation of their assets at the end of the year, but some companies perform depreciation tasks monthly or quarterly.

Depreciation is a special journal entry because the accounts involved are very specific. The account that is being depreciated must be a fixed asset, and the offset entry is to a Depreciation Expense account found in the expense section of your chart of accounts.

Creating Accounts for Tracking Depreciation

Having multiple fixed-asset accounts is not uncommon if you want to track different types of fixed assets separately. For instance, a chart of accounts could have three fixed-asset account categories: Equipment, Furniture & Fixtures, and Vehicles.

It's useful to create a separate subaccount to capture the depreciation entries for each of your fixed assets as well as the purchase of an asset for that asset category. For example, the fixed-asset section of the chart of accounts for the three categories just described could look like the example in Table 16-1.

If you use numbers for your chart of accounts, create a numbering system that makes sense for this setup. For example, if Equipment is 16000, the subaccounts start with 16010; Furniture & Fixtures starts with 16100 and the subaccounts start with 16110; and Vehicle starts with 16200; and so on.

Parent Accounts	Subaccounts
Equipment Assets	
	Equipment Purchases
	Accumulated Depreciation-Equipment
Furniture & Fixtures Assets	
	Furniture & Fixtures Purchases
	Accumulated Depreciation-Furniture & Fixtures
Vehicle Assets	
	Vehicle Purchases
	Accumulated Depreciation-Vehicles

TABLE 16-1   Fixed-Asset Parent Accounts and Subaccounts

Post asset purchases to the subaccount created for purchases, and make the journal entry for depreciation in the Accumulated Depreciation subaccount. Avoid using the "parent" accounts when tracking fixed assets. There are several reasons for this:

- The transactions posted to both the asset subaccount and the Accumulated Depreciation subaccount should be consistent so that you (or your accountant) can look at either one to see a running total instead of a calculated net total.
- Tracing the year-to-year depreciation is easier. If depreciation entries are made annually, open the Accumulated Depreciation subaccount register, and each line represents a year. If you and your accountant choose to enter depreciation entries monthly or quarterly, you can create reports that show annual depreciation for one or more years, using the QuickReports for each depreciation account and setting the dates for the period you wish to see.
- The net value of the fixed assets is correct. A Balance Sheet report shows you the details in the subaccounts and automatically displays the total of the subaccounts in the parent account.

You can refine this example by creating subaccounts and classes for specific fixed assets. For instance, you may want to create a subaccount for each vehicle asset (or one that covers all cars and another that manages all trucks) and its accompanying accumulated depreciation. If your equipment falls under a variety of depreciation rules (for example, manufacturing equipment versus computer equipment), you may want to have a set of subaccounts for each type. You can then use classes to categorize these assets by location or division.

For further precision, you can create a different subaccount for each year of depreciation; for instance, under your Accumulated Depreciation-Vehicle subaccount, you could have Vehicle-Depreciation 2017, Vehicle-Depreciation 2018, Vehicle-Depreciation 2019, and so on. Then your balance sheet shows a complete year-by-year depreciation schedule instead of accumulated depreciation, and the math works.

Creating a Depreciation Entry

To depreciate fixed assets, you need a Depreciation Expense account in the expense section of your chart of accounts. Once that account exists, open the Make General Journal Entries window and choose the first asset depreciation subaccount. In the following example shown in Table 16-2, it's the Accumulated Depreciation account

Account	Debit	Credit
Equipment:Accumulated Depreciation-Equip		5,000.00
Furniture & Fix:Accumulated Depreciation-Furniture & Fix		700.00
LeaseholdImprov:Accumulated Depreciation-LeasImprov		1,000.00
Depreciation Expense	6,700.00	

TABLE 16-2   Depreciation Journal Entry

under the fixed asset Equipment. Enter the depreciation amount in the Credit column. Notice the colon in the account names for the asset accounts. That's how QuickBooks indicates a subaccount.

To help ensure that important transactions such as this depreciation journal entry are posted to the correct subaccount, turn on a company preference that tells QuickBooks to display only the lowest subaccounts, not the parent accounts, when entering transactions. Select Edit | Preferences | Accounting | Company Preferences | Show Lowest Subaccount Only. Keep in mind that this option is available to you only if you use account numbers in your chart of accounts.

Choose the next asset depreciation subaccount and enter its depreciation amount in the Credit column as well. QuickBooks automatically puts the offsetting amount in the Debit column, but just keep moving to the Credit column as you work. Continue until all your depreciation figures are entered in the Credit column.

Now choose the Depreciation Expense account. The total amount of the credits you've entered is automatically placed in the Debit column. Click Save & Close.

Use Journal Entries to Post to Outside Payroll Services

If you use an outside payroll service, to include that information on your company financial statements, you have to tell QuickBooks about the payroll transactions. Your payroll service provider should be able to provide you with a report that gives the details of gross wages and any withholding or deductions so you can enter this information into QuickBooks.

Many businesses make this entry with a journal entry. Like all journal entries, this one is just a matter of entering debits and credits. There are three parts to recording payroll:

- Transferring money to the payroll account (if you use a separate bank account for your payroll)
- Entering the various payroll totals
- Entering the employer expense totals

Transferring Money to the Payroll Account

It's a good idea to have a separate bank account for payroll if you have an outside payroll service. This second account makes it easier to record, track, and reconcile payroll-related transactions. A separate payroll account can be useful even when you do your own payroll.

To transfer the money you need for payroll, choose Banking | Transfer Funds. Select the account that you want to take the funds *from* and complete the transfer *to* your payroll account. Be sure to transfer enough money for the gross payroll, plus the employer payroll expenses, which include the following:

> **Small Business Tip** Remember, entering information into your QuickBooks accounts does not actually transfer the funds. You have to physically transfer the money, either using online banking or writing a check from your main account and depositing it into the Payroll account.

- Employer-matching contributions to FICA and Medicare
- Employer-matching contributions to pension plans
- Employer-matching contributions to benefits
- Employer state unemployment assessments
- Employer FUTA (Federal Unemployment Taxing Authority)
- Any other government or benefit payments paid by the employer

Even though some of these aren't transmitted every payday, consider transferring the amounts at this time anyway. Then, when it's time to pay them, the correct amount of money will be in the payroll account.

Recording the Payroll

Running your payroll produces a detailed set of debits and credits. If your payroll service takes care of remitting your payroll liabilities for you, you can record a single journal entry for the payment side of a payroll run and another separate journal entry for the payment of the employer expenses when they're transmitted. An example of the journal entries you'll make to record this payroll processing scenario is shown in Table 16-3.

If your payroll service doesn't pay your liabilities, leaving you with that task, your check-writing activity will record the payments when you create those checks. So, in this instance, you don't need a second journal entry if you are operating your company on a cash basis. On an accrual basis, enter the liability amounts as a Bill, payable to the appropriate taxing entity and remit the funds using the Pay Bills function.

Table 16-3 shows a typical template for recording the payment side of a payroll run as a journal entry. It's possible that you don't have all the expenses shown in this table. You may have additional withholding categories such as union dues, garnishments against wages, and so on. Be sure you've created a liability account in your chart of accounts for each withholding category you need and a vendor for each transmittal check.

Account	Debit	Credit
Salaries and Wages (expense)	Gross Payroll	
Federal Withholding Tax (liability)		Total Federal Tax Withheld
Federal Insurance Contributions Act (FICA) (Social Security) (liability)		Total Federal Insurance Contributions Act (FICA) Withheld
Medicare (liability)		Total Medicare
Withheld State Income Tax (liability)		Total State Tax
Withheld Local Income Tax (liability)		Total Local Tax
Withheld State Disability Insurance (liability)		Total State Disability Insurance
Withheld State Unemployment Insurance (liability)		Total State Unemployment Insurance
Withheld Benefits Contrib. (liability)		Total Benefits
Withheld 401(k) Contrib. (liability)		Total 401(k)
Withheld Other Deductions (liability)		Total Other Deductions
Withheld Payroll Bank Account (asset)		Total of Net Payroll

TABLE 16-3 Typical Journal Entry to Record Payroll from an Outside Service

Recording Liabilities

If your payroll service takes care of paying your payroll liabilities, you need to make a journal entry for that payment. If you do it yourself, just write the checks from the payroll account, and each item will post to the general ledger. Table 16-4 is a sample journal entry for recording payroll remittances.

The entry involving the transmittal of withholdings is posted to the same account you used when you withheld the amounts. In effect, you "wash" the liability accounts; you're not really spending money—you're remitting money you've withheld from employees.

Account	Debit	Credit
Federal Payroll Expenses (expense)	Employer FICA and Medicare	
Federal Withholdings (liability)	All federal withholdings	
State and Local Withholdings (liability)	All local withholdings	
State Unemployment Taxing Authority (SUTA) (expense)	Employer SUTA	
Federal Unemployment Taxing Authority (FUTA) (expense)	Employer FUTA	
Employer Contributions (expense)	All employer benefits, pensions, etc.	
Payroll Bank Account (asset)		Total of checks written

TABLE 16-4 Typical Journal Entry for Employer-Side Transactions

You can have as many individual employer expense accounts as you need, or you can post all the employer expenses to one account named "Payroll Expenses." However, when you choose to use individual liability and expense accounts, it is easier to determine the total company costs for each item.

Creating Your Own Payroll Entry Template

You can save a lot of time and effort by creating a template for the payroll journal entries. Open a Make General Journal Entries window and fill out the Account column only. Enter the first account, and then press the DOWN ARROW key and enter the next account; keep going until all accounts are listed (see Tables 16-3 and 16-4).

Select the Memorize icon on the Icon Bar of the Make General Journal Entries window, or press CTRL-M. The Memorize Transaction dialog opens as seen next. Name the memorized transaction "Payroll Expense" (or something similar). From here you can

- Select Add To My Reminders List to receive a reminder each payroll. If you choose this option, you have the chance to tell QuickBooks how often to be reminded,
- Select the Do Not Remind Me option because the reports from the payroll company are your reminder.
- Select Automate The Transaction Entry. When choosing this option, you can tell QuickBooks how many more entries to enter automatically and how far in advance to do so.
- Select Add To A Group if you have created a group of journal entries. See "Creating a Memorized Transaction Group" later in this chapter.

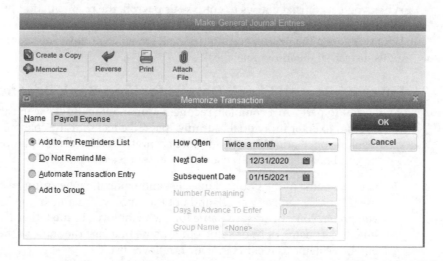

Close the Make General Journal Entries window. QuickBooks displays a message asking if you want to save the transaction you just created. Click No, as you don't have to save a journal entry in order to memorize it. Do the same thing for the boilerplate journal entry you create to record employer remittances.

When you're ready to record a payroll entry, open the memorized transaction. To do so, on the QuickBooks menu bar, choose Lists | Memorized Transaction List. (You can use the keyboard shortcut of CTRL-T as well.) Double-click your payroll boilerplate journal entry, enter the appropriate date, and then enter the data.

Click Save & New if you have to create another journal entry for the employer expenses; otherwise, click Save & Close.

➡ Creating a Memorized Transaction Group

If you have several memorized transactions that are repeated on a regular basis, you can tell QuickBooks to enter them all together by creating a group. To group memorized transactions:

1. From the QuickBooks menu bar, choose Lists | Memorized Transaction List.
2. At the bottom left of the list, select Memorized Transaction | New Group.
3. Enter a name for your new group, and enter how to be reminded.
4. After you have made all your selections, click OK to finish creating the group.

Reconciling the Payroll Account When Using Outside Payroll Services

When you use journal entries to enter your payroll, the reconciliation process is a bit different. You may not have a record of the individual check numbers and payees. When you open the payroll account in the Reconcile window, you see the journal entry totals instead of the individual checks.

Entering Payroll Check Details for Your Bank Reconciliation

If you want to perform a complete reconciliation in QuickBooks, you can use a workaround to enter individual "dummy" payroll checks for the sole purpose of making your bank reconciliation easier and more accurate. You have a little bit of setup to do, but the good news is you can reuse what you set up every payday.

1. Create a name in the Other Names list and name the new entity Payroll. You can use this name for every check and put the employee's name in the Memo field. If you prefer, you can create a name for each employee in the Other Names list using initials, last name only, or some other name that isn't the same as the original employee name as it exists in your Employee list.

2. Open the Write Checks window. Using the bank account that you use for your payroll, enter the individual dummy payroll checks using these guidelines:

   a. The Date is the date of the payroll check.

   b. The No. field is the check number referenced in the report from the payroll service.

   c. You can use "Payroll" as the Pay To The Order Of name (unless you've entered all of your employee names as Other Names, in which case enter the appropriate name, which you can match to the right check number too).

   d. The amount that you enter in the $ field is for the net paycheck (not the gross payroll) amount.

   e. The account is the *same* bank, meaning that the net effect on your bank account is zero and you're not double-counting your payroll expenses.

QuickBooks flashes a message warning you that you're posting the payment to the source account. Click OK, because that's exactly what you want to do. You can select the Do Not Display This Message In The Future check box if you don't want to be reminded each time. You can also enter the checks the payroll service wrote to transmit your withholdings or pay your taxes.

You'll still have to enter your regular payroll journal entry, described earlier, because the total of the checks written and posted to the bank account via the journal entry will need to be cleared as part of the reconciliation, as well as the individual dummy checks you've entered that have cleared the bank.

Creating Journal Entries for Changed Accounts

If, after using QuickBooks for a time, you decide you want to track income or expenses differently, you can use a journal entry to split out these amounts to separate income or expense accounts. For example, instead of using only one income account to keep track of all the products and services sold, you determine that having separate income accounts for on-site service fees and another for in-house services might give more meaningful information.

To create an income journal entry, create the new account(s) and then take the appropriate amount of funds out of the original account and put it into the new account. Income, for example, is a credit-side item, which means you would do the following:

- Debit the original account to reduce the balance for the amount that belongs in the new account.
- Credit the new account to increase the balance for that amount.

Then go to the Item List and change the affected items by linking them to the new income accounts so you don't have to keep making journal entries.

On the expense side, you may decide your insurance accounts should be separated into car insurance, equipment insurance, building insurance, malpractice insurance, and so on. Since expense accounts are debit-side items, the journal entry in this case is created as follows:

- Credit the original expense account to reduce the balance for the amount you're taking out of it and putting into the new account(s).
- Debit the new account(s) to increase the balance for the appropriate amount(s).

You could also consider simply using subaccounts for each item, with Insurance being the parent account.

Set Up and Configure Multiple Currencies

If you do business with customers or vendors in other countries, the multicurrency feature allows you to create transactions in their currencies and track the exchange rates so you always know what the transactions mean to you in U.S. dollars. Before you can begin creating transactions in different currencies, however, you have to complete some configuration and setup tasks.

It's important to be aware that, unlike most of the configuration preferences available in QuickBooks, once you enable multiple currencies, you *cannot* disable it. If you're already using QuickBooks, either because you updated your company files from a previous version or because you began creating transactions before deciding to use multiple currencies, be sure to back up your company file before enabling this feature.

Creating a Special Backup

When you create your backup before turning on multiple currencies, don't use your normal backup routine. Instead, name the backup file differently so you can identify it easily and avoid having the multicurrency backup file overwritten with "regular" backups. For example, when you save your backup file, you might change the name of the file from the usual <*CompanyFileName*>.qbb to <*CompanyFileName*>-BeforeMulticurrency.qbb.

If you decide not to use multiple currencies and don't want to restore the backup (because you'd have to re-enter all the transactions you created while multiple currencies was enabled), it's okay to keep using the company file with multiple currencies enabled as long as you use customers, vendors, and accounts that are not linked to another currency. Some windows and dialogs will continue to have an extra field for currency, but no financial information will be compromised.

Enabling Multiple Currencies

To enable the multicurrency feature, choose Edit | Preferences and click the Multiple Currencies category icon in the left pane. In the Company Preferences tab, select Yes,

I Use More Than One Currency. When you select Yes, QuickBooks displays a warning message, as shown here.

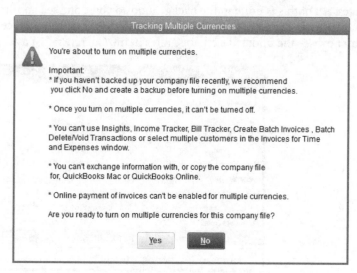

If you've already made a backup, as discussed in the previous section, you can continue. If not, stop the process and create your backup. Then enable multiple currencies.

The Preferences window offers the opportunity to change your home currency from U.S. dollars to another currency. Because QuickBooks tracks payroll, sales tax, online banking, and other basic data in U.S. dollars only, it is best to leave the home currency as the U.S. dollar if your company is based in the United States.

When you have enabled multiple currencies, choose Company | Manage Currency to view the various tools provided by QuickBooks as shown here.

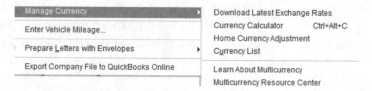

Tracking Exchange Rates

Because QuickBooks tracks both the customer/vendor currency and its worth in your home currency, you need to make sure the exchange rate is accurate. If the exchange rate isn't accurate, your financial reports, which use U.S. dollars, won't be accurate. If you are creating any documents, such as invoices or bill payments, it is a good idea to download today's rate before you begin preparing your documents.

To update the exchange rate for all your active currencies, choose Company | Manage Currency | Download Latest Exchange Rates. QuickBooks goes online to get the current rates. All of this is done in the background so you don't see an Internet page. When your active currencies have been updated, QuickBooks displays a success message, and you can now see the updated exchange rates in the Currency List as seen here.

CURRENCY (1 UNIT)	CODE	EXCHANGE RATE	AS OF DATE
Canadian Dollar	CAD	.747954	09/28/2015
Euro	EUR	1.1235	09/28/2015
Hong Kong Dollar	HKD	.129026	09/28/2015
Japanese Yen	JPY	.008346	09/28/2015
New Zealand Dollar	NZD	.63355	09/28/2015
Philippine peso	PHP	.021369	09/28/2015
Singapore Dollar	SGD	.699766	09/28/2015
US Dollar	USD		

Currency List — Exchange rate: 1 unit foreign currency = x units home currency. Example: 1 USD (foreign) = x units USD (home). Currency | Activities | Reports | Include inactive

Selecting Currencies

QuickBooks provides a long list of currencies you can use, but only the commonly used currencies are active. You can change the list of active currencies to suit your own needs. Remember that only active currencies are updated when you update the exchange rate. Also, only active currencies appear in the drop-down list when you assign a currency to a customer or vendor.

From the Manage Currency options menu, select Currency List. If the list includes only active currencies, select the Include Inactive check box to see the entire list. To activate an inactive currency, click the X in the leftmost column to remove it; to make an active currency inactive, click the leftmost column to place an X in it.

Notice that each currency has a three-letter abbreviation; for example, U.S. dollar is USD. You can, if necessary, create a currency if the one you need doesn't appear on the list, but QuickBooks can't download exchange rates for currencies you add manually. With the Currency List window open, select Currency | New to open the New Currency dialog and configure the currency. (You can also use the keyboard shortcut of CTRL-N.)

Using the Currency Calculator

Once you have activated the currencies you use, you can use the Currency Calculator to calculate what a foreign amount will be in your home currency, or what your home currency will be in the foreign amount, along with the current exchange rate based on the most current rates you have downloaded.

To use the Calculator, select Currency Calculator from the Company | Manage Currency option menu and choose the type of calculation you want. In our example, we've used Exchange Rate, although you can also choose Home Amount or Foreign Amount.

- Home Amount requires you enter the exchange rate as shown on the Currency List you just updated.
- Foreign Amount asks you to enter the exchange rate and the home amount you wish to see in foreign currency terms.
- Exchange Rate requires that you enter the amount of foreign currency and the amount in your home currency, and the exchange rate will appear.

Once you have entered the information in the two appropriate boxes, click Calculate to find your answer.

Small Business Tip   You can learn more about multiple currencies by selecting Learn About Multicurrency from the Manage Currency drop-down menu. However, at this writing, the Multicurrency Resource Center is not active.

Manage Customers and Vendors with Foreign Currencies

You need to identify the currency of every customer and vendor in your company file. QuickBooks automatically assigns your home currency (in most cases, USD) to all customers and vendors, so you need to change only those that do business in a different currency.

When you create customers and vendors who do business in another currency, the basic steps are the same as creating any new customer or vendor in QuickBooks. The only differences are the existence of a Currency field in the New Customer or New Vendor dialog and the lack of an Opening Balance field when you select a currency other than USD. As you create a new customer or vendor and assign them a new currency, QuickBooks automatically adds an Accounts Receivable account and an Accounts Payable account for each currency.

By default, QuickBooks inserts US Dollar in the Currency field, but you can choose another currency from the drop-down list, which displays each currency you have marked as Active.

Changing the Currency for Existing Customers and Vendors

You can change the currency assignment for existing customers and vendors only if they have *no transactions* associated with their names. It doesn't matter whether the current opening balance is $0.00; the existence of any transaction prevents you from changing the currency. For those customers and vendors, you must create a new entity with the new currency.

In addition, you cannot merge customers or vendors that use different currencies. To edit the currency of an existing customer or vendor that has no existing transactions, open either the Customer or Vendor Center, select the name that you want to edit, and click the Edit icon in the upper-right of the Information pane. Select the currency from the drop-down list in the Currency field and click OK.

If you need to change the currency assignment for customers or vendors that have transactions associated with their name, or if you need to do business with them in more than one currency, see the next section.

Creating New Customers and Vendors for Multiple Currencies

To create a new customer or vendor for existing accounts with a foreign currency specification, create the new entity using the following guidelines:

- In the Name field, use the same name as the existing entity, but add text to make the name unique, as QuickBooks does not allow duplicates in the Name field.
- Add text *after* the name so the customer/vendor appears in the right place in drop-down lists in transaction windows. For example, a new customer is created to assign a new currency to an existing customer by adding a three-digit abbreviation for the customer's currency to create a unique name. Remember, you still see the existing customer name in the Customers & Jobs List.

Remember, the data in the Name field doesn't appear on transaction documents; instead, QuickBooks uses the data in the Company Name and Address fields (and, for vendors, there is the field labeled Print Name On Check As).

Managing Existing Open Transactions

When you create new customers and vendors, you have to manage existing open transactions using the original customer or vendor since you cannot accept or make a payment linked to the original entity using the new entity. When the opening balance for the original entity becomes zero, you can make the original customer or vendor inactive so the listing doesn't appear in drop-down lists in transaction windows. Be sure to use the new entity you created for all new transactions.

Viewing Currency Data in Customer and Vendor Centers

After you've enabled multiple currencies, the Customer Center and Vendor Center display currency information in both panes.

In addition, QuickBooks makes the following changes automatically:

- In the List pane, the currency is noted for each customer/vendor and the current balance total displays using the customer/vendor currency, shown here.
- In the Transactions tab of the Details pane, the Amount and Open Balance columns display amounts in the currency of the customer or vendor.

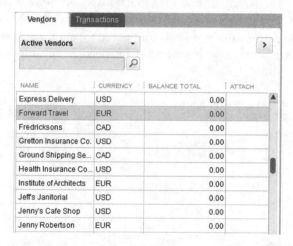

You can change these default settings to make it easier to understand the data you see in the centers. In the List pane, you can add the current balance total in USD to save yourself the need to calculate the "real money," as shown here.

NAME	CURRENCY	BALANCE TOTAL	BALANCE (USD)
Express Delivery	USD	0.00	0.00
Forward Travel	EUR	800.00	-899.06
Fredricksons	CAD	525.00	-392.73
Gretton Insurance Co.	USD	0.00	0.00
Ground Shipping Service	CAD	125.36	-93.78
Health Insurance Comp...	USD	0.00	0.00
Institute of Architects	EUR	2,200.00	-2,472.43
Jeff's Janitorial	USD	0.00	0.00
Jenny's Cafe Shop	USD	0.00	0.00
Jenny Robertson	EUR	300.00	-337.15

You can either remove the Balance Total column for the foreign currency or display both Balance Total columns. If you frequently talk to vendors or customers about current balances, it's handy to have the foreign currency balance in front of you, so having both amounts display makes sense. You can add (or remove) columns to the list by right-clicking anywhere in the list and choosing Customize Columns.

Create Transactions in Other Currencies

When you open a sales or payment transaction window, QuickBooks automatically takes care of the currency issues by adding fields to the transaction window. If the customer or vendor currency is USD, you won't see much difference between the transaction window for multiple currencies and the same transaction window before you enabled multiple currencies. The only real difference is that the text "USD" appears for "Total" amounts.

If the customer or vendor is configured for another currency, the transaction window changes to provide the information you need. For example, Figure 16-2 shows an invoice for a customer in Italy.

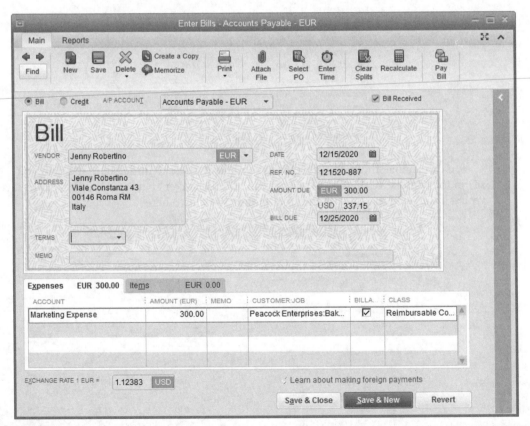

FIGURE 16-2 This invoice displays all the data needed to see the sales total for this invoice in both U.S. dollars and euros for a vendor in Italy.

Notice the following about these transaction windows:

- The A/P account is specific to the currency. The same is true for customer invoices that show A/R accounts for the appropriate currency.
- The amounts in the line items display in the customer/vendor currency.
- There are two totals: one for the transaction currency and one for USD.
- The Exchange Rate field displays the exchange rate used when this transaction was created.

The printed versions of transactions that are sent to customers (invoices, credits, and so on) and vendors (checks) do not display any fields or data related to USD; those fields appear on the screen only for your convenience.

Decide on an exchange rate update schedule that makes sense to you. Keep in mind that if the exchange rate changes between the day you enter an invoice or bill and the day you receive a payment or make a payment, QuickBooks automatically adds an Other Expense account named Exchange Gain or Exchange Loss to track the net amounts that accrue from adjustments in exchange rates for current open balances.

Create Reports on Multiple Currency Transactions

By default, all reports on customer and vendor transactions (such as Aging, Sales, Purchases, and so on) are displayed in your home currency (USD). You can modify the reports so they display the appropriate currencies:

- For Summary reports, click Customize Report, and in the Display Amounts In section, select The Transaction Currency.
- For Detail reports, click Customize Report and select Foreign Amount in the Columns list. You may also want to add the Currency column.

Memorize these reports, using a name that reflects the contents (such as Transaction Currency), so you don't have to customize them each time you create them.

Installing QuickBooks on a Network

If your company has a computer network, there are several differences when you install QuickBooks. Soon after you launch the QuickBooks installer, you need to make some choices about how to install the program on your computer and other computers on your network. Although the choices are straightforward, during the installation, it may not be obvious which choice is right for you when more than one user needs simultaneous access to your QuickBooks file. This section provides you with the background information you need to know, along with some tips to help ensure your multi-user installation goes as smoothly as possible.

License Requirements for a Multi-user Installation

You'll need to purchase a separate QuickBooks license for *each* computer that will have simultaneous access to your QuickBooks data file. In addition, all computers must use the same version, in this case, QuickBooks Pro 2016. QuickBooks Pro comes in one-, two-, or three-user license packs, allowing for up to three simultaneous users (with three unique user login names) to access a company file on a network. You can also purchase a two-user and a three-user pack that allows up to five simultaneous users accessing the company file. Again, each user is required to have a unique user login name.

Multi-user Installation Options

Multi-user installation options depend on the type of network configuration you plan to use. Specifically, the options you choose depend on whether you plan to use a peer-to-peer network, where one of the computers on the network runs QuickBooks and also stores the file, or a dedicated server to host your QuickBooks company file.

It's beyond the scope of this section to provide instruction on which configuration is best in your situation and the steps required for setup. Contact your system administrator or a local IT expert for more information.

Installing QuickBooks on a Peer-to-Peer Network

First, ensure that all the computers that need access to the QuickBooks file are on a network running Windows 7, 8.1 (all editions except Starter and Basic), or Windows 10. Ensure your operating system is up to date with the latest release. Other important tasks to add to your preinstall checklist include these:

- Decide which computer on your network will hold the QuickBooks company file. It should be the fastest computer on your network, and it will be the first computer on which you install QuickBooks.
- Ensure that the other QuickBooks computers on the network have full read/write access to the folder in which you plan on storing your QuickBooks data file.

Insert the QuickBooks CD in your CD drive, or, if you downloaded the program, run the Download Manager to launch the Intuit QuickBooks Installer. A Welcome screen confirms the launch. Click Next and follow these steps:

1. Review and accept the terms of the Intuit Software End User License Agreement. Click Next.
2. In the Choose Your Installation Type window, select Custom And Network Options. Click Next.
3. The Custom And Network Options window opens, giving you three choices. Select the middle option, I'll Be Using QuickBooks On This Computer, AND

I'll Be Storing Our Company File Here So It Can Be Shared Over Our Network. Click Next.

4. Enter your license and product information, found either on your CD or in the e-mail received from Intuit that included your product download link. Click Next.

5. Enter your Intuit ID (which is likely the e-mail address you used when you purchased the software) and click the Validate button. If you don't know your Intuit user name or password, or you don't want to enter it at this time, click the Skip This link to advance to the next window.

6. If this is your first version of QuickBooks, you can accept the suggested folder that the installer recommends. If you're upgrading from a previous version of QuickBooks, you'll have the option of replacing your previous version with QuickBooks 2016 or changing the install location (which keeps the existing version of QuickBooks on your computer). Click Next, and then click the Install button.

For the next several minutes, you'll see a series of informational windows about various QuickBooks features and additional services. Each window contains a status bar to keep you apprised of the progress of your installation.

When the installation is complete, you'll receive a congratulations message and the option to open QuickBooks directly, get help getting started, or both. For the discussion that follows, select Open QuickBooks and click Finish.

Small Business Tip   Most installations are trouble free. But there are times when a setting on your computer that you are not aware of, or even an emergency situation in your office, interrupts your installation. Whatever the reason, choosing not to overwrite and replace your existing QuickBooks installation lets you continue working in your QuickBooks file until any issues with the installation have been resolved. Later, after you're up and running with the new version, you can confidently uninstall the previous version using the appropriate utility in Windows Control Panel.

File Hosting and the Database Server Manager

With your QuickBooks company file open, select File | Switch To Multi-User Mode. Click OK. When you turn on multi-user mode on the first computer on which you've installed QuickBooks, you automatically designate this computer as the *host* of your QuickBooks data file.

In addition, behind the scenes, QuickBooks installs a Database Server Manager program. Running this program along with QuickBooks ensures that other QuickBooks users will be able to access the company file even if the QuickBooks program is not open on this computer. However, the computer itself has to be turned on.

To open and run the QuickBooks Database Server Manager in Windows 7:

1. On the Windows Start menu, select All Programs | QuickBooks | QuickBooks Database Server Manager.
2. On the Scan Folders tab, click the Add Folder button to browse to the QuickBooks file you want to make available to other users. The default location that QuickBooks uses to save company files (which will have a .qbw extension) is C:\Users\Public\Documents\Intuit\QuickBooks\Company Files.
3. When the folder where your QuickBooks file resides is listed in the Folders That Contain QuickBooks Company Files box, click the Scan button. Your file will be configured to ensure that others on the network can open your QuickBooks file.

To open and run the Database Server Manager in Windows 8.1:

1. Find QuickBooks in the Apps menu and select the QuickBooks Database Server Manager.
2. On the Scan Folders tab, click the Add Folder button to browse to the QuickBooks file you want to make available to other users. The default location that QuickBooks uses to save company files (which will have a .qbw extension) is C:\Users\Public\Documents\Intuit\QuickBooks\Company Files.
3. When the folder where your QuickBooks file resides is listed in the Folders That Contain QuickBooks Company Files box, click the Scan button. Your file will be configured to ensure that others on the network can open your QuickBooks file.

Installing QuickBooks on the Client Computers

With your QuickBooks host computer up and running, you're ready to install the program on the other networked computers. Follow these steps:

1. Complete Steps 1 and 2 from the previous section.
2. In the Custom And Network Options window, select the first option, I'll Be Using QuickBooks On This Computer. Click Next.
3. Enter your license and product information, found either on your CD or in the e-mail received from Intuit that included your product download link.
4. Enter your Intuit ID (which is likely the e-mail address you used when you purchased the software) and click the Validate button. If you don't know your Intuit user name or password—or you don't want to enter it at this time—click the Skip This link to advance to the next window.
5. If this is your first version of QuickBooks, you can accept the suggested folder that the installer recommends. If you're upgrading from a previous version of QuickBooks, you'll have the option of replacing your previous version with QuickBooks 2016 or changing the install location (which keeps the existing version of QuickBooks on your computer). I recommend you select the option Change The Install Location. Click Next, and then click the Install button.

For the next several minutes, you'll see a series of informational windows about various QuickBooks features and additional services. Each of these windows contains a status bar to keep you apprised of the progress of your installation.

6. When the installation is complete, you'll receive a congratulations message and the option to open QuickBooks directly, get help getting started, or both.

7. In the No Company Open window, click the Open Or Restore An Existing Company button.

8. In the Open Or Restore Company window, select the Open A Company File option. Click Next.

9. Browse to and open your QuickBooks company file located on the QuickBooks host computer.

After you click Finish, and before proceeding to the No Company Open window, QuickBooks may ask if you want to use this computer to host multi-user access. Answer No to ensure that the first computer that you installed QuickBooks on remains the host computer. If you answer Yes to this question, this computer will become the host, which means that not only will QuickBooks need to be open on this computer, but a user will need to be logged into the company file before any of the other users on the network can work in the file.

Installing QuickBooks on a Client-Server Network

To use QuickBooks on a network with a dedicated server, you must be running one of the following: Microsoft Windows Vista (with User Account Control [UAC] on), Windows 7 or 8.1 (with UAC on), Windows 10, or Windows Server 2008/2011 or 2012 editions. Once you've confirmed that your server operating system meets one of these requirements, follow these installation instructions:

1. On the server computer, insert the QuickBooks CD into the CD drive; if you downloaded the program, run the Download Manager to launch the Intuit QuickBooks Installer. A Welcome screen confirms the launch. Click Next.

2. Review and accept the terms of the Intuit Software End User License Agreement. Click Next.

3. In the Choose Installation Type window, select the Custom And Network option. Click Next.

4. The Custom And Network Options window opens, giving you three choices. Select the last option, I Will NOT Be Using QuickBooks On This Computer. I Will Be Storing Our Company File Here So It Can Be Shared Over Our Network. Click Next.

5. QuickBooks suggests an installation location for the Database Server Manager. You can change the location if you wish by clicking Change The Install Location. Click Next, and then click the Install button.

6. For the next several minutes, you'll see a series of informational windows about various QuickBooks features and additional services. Each of these windows contains a status bar to keep you apprised of the progress of your installation. When the installation of the Database Server Manager is complete, you'll receive a congratulations message and the option to get help getting started.

Installing Both QuickBooks and the Database Server Manager on Your Server

Selecting the I Will NOT Be Using QuickBooks On This Computer option installs the QuickBooks Database Server Manager program and not the full version of QuickBooks. Although this is a perfectly acceptable installation option when installing in a client-server environment, it's also acceptable to install both QuickBooks and the Database Server Manager on the server computer. This can be a good idea because two very important utilities are built into the full QuickBooks program: the Verify and Rebuild utilities. These utilities should only be run locally, meaning that the QuickBooks file being verified and rebuilt should reside on the same computer as the full QuickBooks program.

When both QuickBooks and the Database Server Manager are installed, the QuickBooks program will be "silent" and used only occasionally for maintenance purposes. As a result, it will not affect your licensing requirements, but it will give you peace of mind knowing that you can easily perform routine maintenance on your QuickBooks file when needed.

Posting at Year's End and Sending the Year-End Accountant's Copy

n *this chapter:*

- Making your year-end To Do list

- Running financial reports

- Printing 1099 forms

- Making year-end journal entries

- Getting ready for taxes

- Closing the books

- Creating a year-end backup

- Creating an Accountant's Copy

- Merging the accountant's changes into your file

Whether your company is a large corporation or a small business, the end of the year brings with it several inevitable tasks. There is so much to do—reports to run, corrections to make, entries to create, and adjustments to apply. However, you can relax. Not everything has to be accomplished on January 1. QuickBooks is date sensitive, so you can continue to work in the new year without affecting the totals of the previous year. As long as the dates of new transactions are after the last day of your fiscal year, new transactions do *not* affect your year-end calculations.

Many accountants specialize in supporting QuickBooks, which means they understand the software and know how to use it. At year end, your accountant will want to examine your QuickBooks file to help you close your books and prepare your tax returns. This chapter explains how to prepare year-end forms and reports, close your year, and send an Accountant's Copy to your accountant.

The Year-End To Do List

Some of the tasks covered in this chapter, such as reconciling your bank account and running reports, may already be a part of your monthly routine. Others, however, can be done only at the end of the year. Consider creating a year-end To Do list based on the tasks covered in this chapter. You'll not only be ready for your accountant at tax time, but you can feel confident that your books will be in good shape for the new year.

Reconciling All Bank, Cash, and Credit Card Accounts

In January, when your December statements arrive from your bank and credit card company, be sure to either set those aside or download and print extra copies. Your cash position at year end is important when applying for credit and preparing your tax returns and for general business planning purposes. Reconciling all your bank and credit card accounts will ensure that you can rely on the accuracy of these essential balances. It's also a good time to gather and enter all those petty cash receipts so you can reconcile that account, too. Review Chapter 7 if you don't reconcile regularly.

Inventory Stock Status

Perform a physical inventory. Whereas some businesses reserve the last day of the year to complete their physical inventory, others complete it in the days immediately following the end of the year. With the latter method, you need to adjust the physical count to account for changes (sales and receipt of goods) that occurred after the last day of the year, and then create an inventory adjustment dated the last day of the previous year. Refer to Chapter 13 to learn how to use inventory reports and the Adjust Quantity/Value On Hand window to ensure that QuickBooks accurately reflects your year-end inventory value.

Fixed Assets

Create a report on your fixed asset accounts to see purchases for the year. Your accountant will also need this report as the basis for calculating accumulated depreciation totals for fixed assets you purchased in prior years.

The easy way to create this report is to select any fixed asset account in your chart of accounts. Select Lists | Chart Of Accounts and choose any fixed asset account. Click the Reports button and select QuickReport. (Once you have selected your fixed asset account, you can also press CTRL-Q to run the report.) Click Customize Report, move to the Filters tab, and select Account in the Choose Filter list. Then select All Fixed Assets from the drop-down list in the Account field, and click OK. The resulting report, shown in Figure 17-1, displays detailed information about all your fixed assets, including purchases and accumulated depreciation. Give this report to your tax professional.

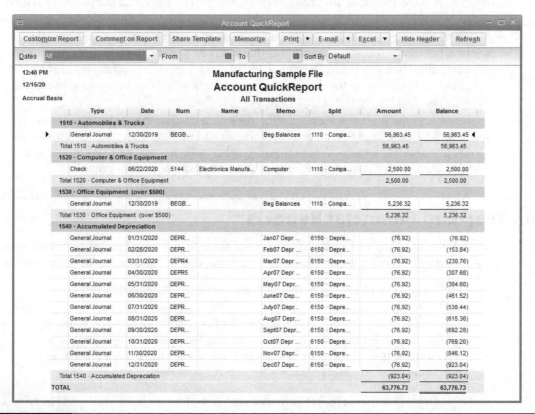

| FIGURE 17-1 | Create a report that shows all the details about your fixed assets to help your tax professional prepare your tax returns. |

Payroll

Payroll reports are always relevant as of the end of the calendar year, regardless of your company's fiscal year setup. See Chapter 10 to learn more about year-end payroll processes, including preparing W-2 forms.

If you use QuickBooks to run your payroll, QuickBooks uses the paycheck date as the basis for calculating payroll totals. For example, if you pay employees on Tuesday for the pay period ending the previous Saturday, all payroll reports are based on the Tuesday paycheck date. That means for 2016, the last payroll figures are reported as of the last Tuesday in December. Paychecks issued in January 2017 for the period including the end of December 2016 are not part of your payroll totals.

Some businesses prefer to track gross salaries and wages as a liability based on the work period and pay off that liability with the paycheck, so they create journal entries to track accrued salaries and wages. Using the same example, in 2016, that accrued entry covers December 27 through January 2 and will be paid with the paycheck issued January 5, 2017.

If you accrue payroll entries and you file taxes on a cash basis, you need to make a journal entry for the accrued amounts that won't be paid by the end of the year. A reversing journal entry dated December 31, 2016, and reversed on January 1, 2017, takes care of maintaining the figures you need. Check with your accountant to see if a year-end accrual for payroll is applicable to your situation.

This is also the time to review any employee benefits that should be reported on W-2 forms and to make sure that all employee names and mailing addresses are up-to-date. This is important information to verify and gather, whether you print your own year-end payroll forms or pass on that information to an outside payroll processor.

Run Year-End Financial Reports

In addition to giving you and your accountant the information required to prepare your tax returns, the standard financial reports you run at year end provide some other benefits:

- They help you and your accountant assess the overall financial health of your business.
- They can provide you with the details behind every transaction you've made in QuickBooks for the year. This gives you one last opportunity to make sure everything is posted correctly *before* you finalize your financial information to determine what you owe in taxes.

Don't forget that these reports have date ranges such as "current year" and "last fiscal year." So if you're working in QuickBooks *after* the last date of your fiscal year, which is quite common, be sure you adjust the report dates to reflect the activities of your *last* fiscal year.

> **Small Business Tip** In QuickBooks 2016, a new report allows you to print reports for the period "Fiscal Year To Last Month," very useful for both you and your accountant.

Profit & Loss Reports

Start with a Profit & Loss Standard report by choosing Reports | Company & Financial | Profit & Loss Standard. By default, when the report opens, the standard date range is the current month to date. Be sure to change it to the fiscal year end that you're preparing.

The report displays the totals for all the income and expense accounts in your general ledger that had any activity for the year. Examine the report, and if anything seems out of the ordinary, double-click the line to see a list of the postings to that account. If the data you see doesn't reassure you, double-click any of the individual posting lines to see the original transaction.

If a transaction seems to be in error, you can take corrective action. You should not delete or void a bill you paid or a customer invoice for which you received payment without consulting your accountant.

You may also find that you posted an expense or income transaction to the wrong general ledger account. If so, you can either change the posting account in the transaction or create a journal entry to correct it. (See Chapter 16 for information on creating journal entries.) Then run the year-end P&L report again and print it.

Year-End Balance Sheet

In many ways, your balance sheet best represents your financial position. It is a good idea to run this report at regular intervals throughout the year and not just at the end of your fiscal year. To run a year-end balance sheet, choose Reports | Company & Financial | Balance Sheet Standard. An analysis of your year-end balance sheet figures can lead to some important follow-up action items. Here are some examples:

- Perform a "reality check" with the balances that QuickBooks shows for your bank accounts with your bank's records: Are they in sync? Make sure your accounts are reconciled to the latest bank statement.
- If you track inventory, is the number that QuickBooks shows an accurate reflection of what's actually on your shelves?
- Consider paying your payroll withholding liabilities in the current year (the year in which they were accumulated) to clear them from the balance sheet. Do the same with any employer contributions you may owe.

- Check to see if your accounts payable and accounts receivable need some housekeeping: Is QuickBooks still showing some open customer invoices or vendor bills that you believe have been paid? New in QuickBooks 2016, if you have designated an External Accountant user, that person can delete or void these old items in a batch, rather than having to change them all at once, as in previous editions.

Small Business Tip An External Accountant user is a special user type in QuickBooks. To create such a user, Set Up Users and Passwords from the manu bar. Select Add User and click Next. Then choose External Accountant, click Next and confirm by clicking Yes on the warning message. While this user type can access nearly all areas of QuickBooks, they cannot create or edit users nor access customer credit card numbers. If you designate your accountant as such a user, they can access your records throughout the year and make changes or review your data. This can eliminate the necessity of creating an Accountant's Copy to send to your accountant at year end. See "Understanding the Accountant's Copy" later in this chapter.

- If you have an Accounts Payable balance, pay as many bills as you can afford in the current year, even if this means you pay vendor bills earlier than their due dates. If you report your taxes on a cash basis, you can gain the expense deduction for this year.

Issue 1099 Forms

If any vendors are eligible for 1099 forms (QuickBooks supports only the 1099-MISC form), you need to print and mail the forms to them by January 31. Some of the work involved in issuing 1099 forms is done during company setup, where you set up the conditions for 1099 tracking. Then, during the year, you need to make sure the transactions you enter are posted to the accounts you identified when you configured these settings. It's also a very good idea to check the latest IRS rules and guidelines about which vendors should receive a 1099 from you. Ensure you have a current tax ID number, either an FEIN (Federal Employer Identification Number) or social security number for each 1099 vendor.

Checking the 1099 Setup

First, make sure your file is set up to track and process 1099 forms: choose Edit | Preferences, click the Tax: 1099 icon, and move to the Company Preferences tab to ensure you've clicked Yes next to the Do You File 1099-MISC Forms? question. Optionally, you can click the first Click Here link (located near the top of the 1099 preference window), which opens the Map Vendor Payment Accounts window in the QuickBooks 1099 Wizard (see Figure 17-2).

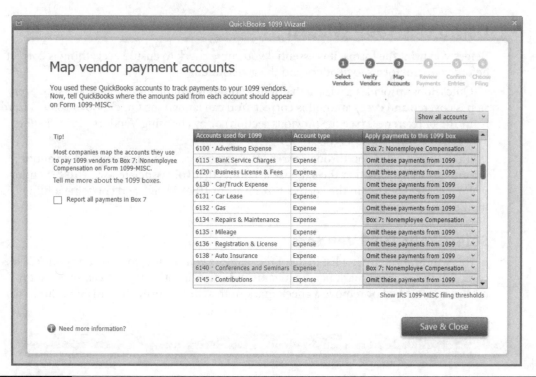

FIGURE 17-2   Use the Map Vendor Payments dialog to select expenses paid to 1099 vendors.

QuickBooks lists the accounts that have payment transactions to 1099 vendors for the previous calendar year. From here, you tell QuickBooks in which box (or category) on the 1099-MISC form you want the totals from each account to appear, or you can simply have all amounts appear in Box 7 (Nonemployee Compensation). To assign an account to a 1099 category, select the category from the drop-down menu.

You also have the option of displaying your entire chart of accounts by selecting Show All Accounts in the drop-down menu at the top-right area of the window. This will give you the opportunity to map additional accounts for 1099 reporting. Click Save & Close to assign all the accounts you've mapped.

You can assign multiple accounts to a 1099 category, but you cannot assign any account to more than one 1099 category. For example, if you have an expense account Sales Commissions and an expense account Outside Services, both of the accounts can be linked to the same 1099 category (Box 7–Nonemployee Compensation). However, once you link those accounts to that category, you cannot use those same accounts in any other 1099 category. Note that you can also access this window via the 1099 Wizard, which is covered in the following section.

Using the 1099 Wizard

Before you print the forms, it is essential you run a check to ensure everything is correct before you send forms to vendors and the government.

QuickBooks provides a wizard that walks you through the process to make sure every step is covered and every amount is correct. You can launch the QuickBooks 1099 Wizard from 1099 Preferences (see the previous section) or by choosing Vendors | Print/E-File 1099s | 1099 Wizard (see Figure 17-3).

This wizard walks you through three important steps: verifying your 1099 vendor information, ensuring that the expense accounts that you associated with 1099 vendor payments are reported in the correct box on form 1099-MISC, and choosing a filing method.

Select Your 1099 Vendors

In this window, you'll see a list of all of the vendors you've entered into your QuickBooks company file. A check mark next to a name indicates that it's already been selected to receive a 1099. Add or remove a check mark in the Create Form 1099-MISC column to

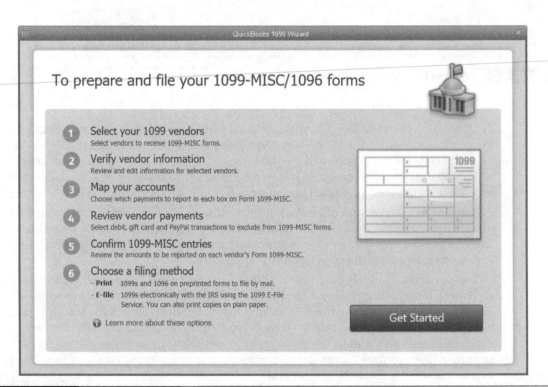

FIGURE 17-3 Use the QuickBooks 1099 Wizard to prepare and file your annual 1099 forms.

change the 1099 status of a vendor. Click Continue when you're ready to advance to the Verify Your 1099 Vendors' Information window.

Verify Your 1099 Vendors' Information

If any of the selected 1099-MISC vendors are missing the required address and tax ID information (or have an invalid tax ID format), those missing fields are outlined in red, as seen here. Enter the missing information directly in the appropriate field(s). Click Continue when you're ready to advance to the Map Vendor Payment Accounts window.

Map Vendor Payment Accounts

This is the same window discussed in the previous section, "Checking the 1099 Setup," but the steps are worth repeating here. QuickBooks lists the accounts that have payment transactions to 1099 vendors for the previous calendar year. From here, you tell QuickBooks which box(es) on the 1099-MISC form you want the totals from each account to appear in, or you can simply have all amounts appear in Box 7 (Nonemployee Compensation). To assign an account to a 1099 category, select the category from the drop-down menu.

You also have the option of displaying your entire chart of accounts by selecting Show All Accounts in the drop-down menu at the top-right area of the window. This will give you the opportunity to map additional accounts for 1099 reporting. Click Continue to assign all the accounts you've mapped and to move on to the Review Payments For Exclusions window.

Review Payments for Exclusions

The IRS requires that you exclude from reporting on Form 1099-MISC any vendor payments you made by credit card, debit card, gift card, or third-party payment providers such as PayPal, because these payments are already being reported to the IRS by these networks directly.

QuickBooks will automatically exclude any payments you made to a vendor using a credit card account that's listed in your chart of accounts, but you'll need to "code" the other payment types so that you can exclude them from your 1099-MISC reporting. Use the View Included Payments report to identify and code these vendor payments that fall into this category, if you didn't do so when you originally entered the payment.

If you see a payment that needs to be coded for exclusion on this report, double-click that payment transaction, and in the check number field, enter one of the following codes that QuickBooks will recognize (be sure to save the updated transaction):

- Debit
- Debitcar
- DBT
- DBT card
- DCard
- Debit cd
- Visa
- Masterc
- MC
- MCard
- Chase
- Discover
- Diners
- PayPal

Once you've updated the information in the check number field for all of the necessary payment transactions, click the View Excluded Payments button to confirm that the transactions that you've modified will now be excluded from your 1099-MISC totals. Click Continue when you complete all of your updates.

Confirm Your 1099 Entries

The Confirm Your 1099 Entries page of the 1099 wizard shows all the vendors for which a form 1099-MISC will be created (see Figure 17-4). To the right of each vendor name, the following information appears:

- The tax ID number associated with that vendor
- The total of all payments included on the 1099
- The total payments to be included in Box 7 (Nonemployee Compensation)

FIGURE 17-4   The QuickBooks 1099 Wizard helps confirm all of your 1099 information.

- The total of all payments to that vendor posted to accounts not mapped to a 1099 category (box)
- The total of all payments made to the vendor

To see the details behind the amounts being displayed for each vendor, double-click anywhere on the row that contains the vendor's information. The 1099 Detail report for that vendor opens, listing all payment transactions that make up the 1099 reporting balance. If you want to investigate—or modify—an individual payment, double-click the transaction in question on the report. When you're satisfied that the amounts you'll be reporting are accurate, click Continue.

Choose a Filing Method

You have two options when choosing how to file your 1099-MISC information to your vendors, your state, and the IRS: e-file your federal and state forms, with a printed copy to send to your vendor, or print all copies.

Click the Go To Intuit 1099 E-File Service button to e-file or to learn more about it (additional fees may apply). Click the Print 1099s button if you prefer to file using this method.

Printing 1099s

The 1099 Print dialog asks you to confirm the year for which you're printing. You'll likely be performing this task in January of the next year. In this case, you'll choose Last Calendar Year as the date range, as shown here. Click OK to move to the Select 1099s To Print dialog. QuickBooks displays the vendors for whom you should be printing 1099s.

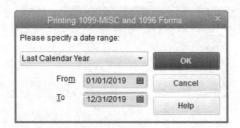

Click Preview 1099 to see what the form will look like when it prints. Zoom in to make sure your company name, address, and employer ID number (EIN) are correct, and check the vendor's information to make sure it's up to date.

Click Close on the Print Preview window to return to the Select 1099s To Print dialog. Then load the 1099 forms into your printer and click Print 1099. If you're using a laser or inkjet printer, set the number of copies at 3. Dot-matrix printers use three-part forms.

When the forms are printed, click Print 1096 in the Select 1099s To Print dialog. Enter the name of the contact person in your company who can answer questions about these forms (the name is printed on the 1096 form).

Print two copies of the 1096 so you have one for your files. Send each vendor a copy of the 1099 form by January 31. Send the government a copy of each 1099, along with a 1096 Transmittal Form. Repeat these procedures for each box number of the 1099-MISC form you are required to print (most small businesses need only Box 7).

Make Year-End Journal Entries

Your accountant may want you to make some journal entries before you close your books for the year, such as the following:

- Enter depreciation.
- Move retained earnings to an account created to hold prior retained earnings, or move retained earnings to owner or partner equity retained earnings accounts.

- Create adjustments needed for cash versus accrual reporting (these are usually reversed on the first day of the next fiscal year).
- Adjust prepaid expenses from asset accounts to expense accounts.

You can send the P&L and Balance Sheet reports to your accountant by exporting the reports to Excel.

You can also send your accountant the Accountant's Copy of your company data and let him or her make the journal entries. You import the changes when the file is returned. (See Chapter 16 for detailed instructions on creating journal entries.) You will learn about using the Accountant's Copy feature later in this chapter.

Getting Ready for Taxes

Most small businesses turn over the job of tax preparation to their accountants, but some business owners prepare their own taxes manually or use a tax software program such as TurboTax.

No matter which method you choose, you should run the reports that tell you whether your QuickBooks data files are ready for tax preparation. Is all the necessary data entered? Do the bottom-line numbers call for some special tax planning or special tax considerations? Even if your taxes are prepared by your accountant, the more organized your records are, the less time the accountant spends on your return, which, hopefully, makes your bill from the accountant smaller.

Checking Tax-Line Information

If you're going to do your own taxes, every account in your chart of accounts that is tax related should have the correct tax form in the account's tax-line assignment. To see if any tax-line assignments are missing, choose Reports | Accountant & Taxes | Income Tax Preparation. When the report appears, all your accounts are listed, along with the tax form assigned to each account. If you created your own chart of accounts instead of accepting a chart of accounts during company setup, the number of accounts that lack a tax form assignment is likely to be quite large.

Before you can prepare your own taxes, you should edit each account to add the tax information. To do so, in QuickBooks 2016 Desktop Pro and Premier, double-click each account listed as <Unassigned> on the Income Tax Preparation report to open the Edit Account dialog. In other versions, you may have to open the chart of accounts, select an account, and select Edit Account. From the Edit Account dialog, select a tax form from the Tax-Line Mapping drop-down list as shown here.

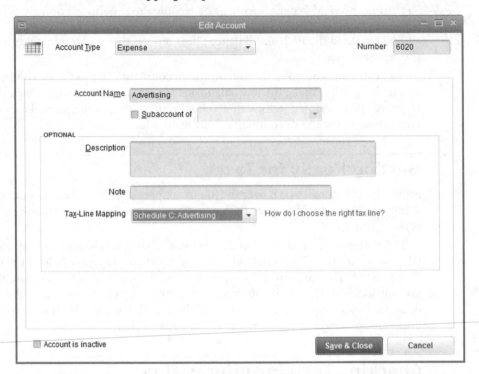

Your selections vary depending upon the organizational type of your company (proprietorship, partnership, S-Corp, C-Corp, and so on). Be sure the Income Tax Form Used field is filled out properly on the Company Information dialog in the Company menu. If it's blank, you won't see the tax information fields on any accounts.

Calculating Other Important Tax Information

Some taxable numbers aren't available through the normal QuickBooks reports. One of the most common is the report on company officer compensation if your business is incorporated. If your business is a C-Corporation, you file Tax Form 1120, whereas a Subchapter S-corporation files Tax Form 1120S. Both of these forms require that you separate compensation for corporate officers from the other employee compensation. You will have to add those totals from payroll reports (either QuickBooks payroll or an outside payroll service).

You can avoid the need to calculate this by creating a separate Payroll item called Officer Compensation and assigning it to its own account (named something like Salaries & Wages—Officers), which you'll also have to create. Then open the Employee record for each officer and change the Earnings item to the new item. Although you can go back to every payroll for the year, it is usually easier to set this up for the following year.

Using TurboTax

If you use TurboTax to do your taxes, you don't have to do anything special in QuickBooks to transfer the information. Open TurboTax and tell it to import the data it needs from your QuickBooks company file.

Almost everything you need is transferred to TurboTax. You'll have to enter some details directly (for example, home-office expenses for a Schedule C form). You can learn more about TurboTax at www.turbotax.com.

Close Your Books

After all the year-end reports have been run, any necessary journal entries have been entered, and your taxes have been filed, it's customary to "close the books" so no user can add, remove, or change any transactions for that year. After taxes have been filed based on the information in your QuickBooks file, nothing should ever be changed. Typically, closing the books occurs some time after the end of the fiscal year, usually within the first couple of months of the current fiscal year, as soon as your business tax forms have been filed.

QuickBooks does not require you to close the books in order to keep working in the software. You can work forever, year after year, without performing a closing process. However, many QuickBooks users prefer to lock the transactions for the previous year as a way to prevent any changes to the data except by users with the appropriate permissions who know the password you created when you closed the books.

Closing the Year by Setting a Closing Date

In QuickBooks, you close the year by entering a closing date. This very important action essentially locks users out of that year's transactions. At the same time, you can configure user rights to enable or disable a user's ability to see, or even manipulate, closed transactions. If you've set up users and passwords for access to your QuickBooks data file, only the QuickBooks users named Admin or a user set up as an External Accountant can set the closing date and password.

1. Choose Company | Set Closing Date. The Preferences window appears with the Accounting | Company Preferences tab selected.
2. At the bottom of this tab, click the Set Date/Password button in the Closing Date section.

3. In the Set Closing Date And Password dialog, enter the closing date (the last date of your fiscal year) and a password.

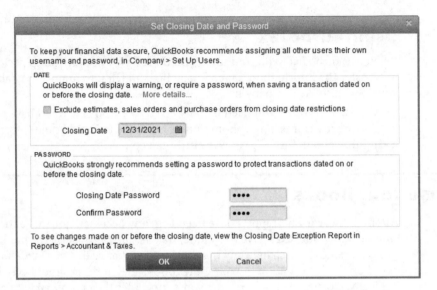

Create a Year-End Backup

After all the numbers are checked, all the journal entries are made, and the books have been closed by entering a closing date, do a separate backup in addition to your normal daily backup. Don't put this backup on the same media you use for your normal backups—the best option is an external hard drive, a CD, flash drive, or cloud-based backup service, which you can label "Year-End Backup 2019" and store off-site. See Chapter 15 to learn more about how to back up your QuickBooks files.

Understanding the Accountant's Copy

Some accountants may ask for a copy of the company file, a backup of your company file (which they restore onto their computer), or a portable company file in order to review and make changes to your QuickBooks file.

If they use any of these methods, you shouldn't work in your QuickBooks file at the same time. If you do continue to work on your local copy on your computer, the transactions you enter will be lost once you restore the copy your accountant returns to you. Why? Because restoring a regular backup overwrites the company file you continued to use. Not a good solution.

QuickBooks has a better solution. Give your accountant a specially designed copy of your company file called the *Accountant's Copy*. Let your accountant do the work at her or his office while you continue to work in your copy. When the file comes back to you with the accountant's changes, QuickBooks can merge the changes from the Accountant's Copy into your copy of the company file. This means the work you do while the accountant is working isn't replaced by the work your accountant does.

When you create an Accountant's Copy, QuickBooks imposes restrictions on the type and extent of transactions you and your accountant can do to make sure you don't work at cross purposes. Only the Admin or External Accountant user can create an Accountant's Copy, and the company file must be operating in Single-User mode to accomplish this task.

Creating an Accountant's Copy

QuickBooks has three methods for delivering your created Accountant's Copy to your accountant:

- **Save a file**   You can save an Accountant's Copy on removable media (external hard drive, CD, DVD, or flash drive) and send or deliver it that way. You can also send it via e-mail, although sometimes people can't e-mail the file because of the size limits set by their ISP (Internet service provider) and/or their accountant's ISP.
- **Send a file using a "cloud" secure storage system**   There are several free online storage systems into which you can upload your Accountant's Copy at no charge. Your accountant can then download it to her or his computer. Do an Internet search for the most highly rated services, and let your accountant know when the file is available at that site.
- **Send a file to your accountant using a QuickBooks secure server**   If your accountant has subscribed to this service, you can upload for free an Accountant's Copy to a secure server provided by QuickBooks and have your accountant download the file. QuickBooks notifies the accountant of the existence of the file by e-mail and provides a link to the file in the e-mail message.

Saving the Accountant's Copy

To create an Accountant's Copy and save it to a location on your computer or on removable media, choose File | Send Company File | Accountant's Copy | Save File. In the Save Accountant's Copy dialog, be sure the Accountant's Copy option is selected.

Click Next to move to the window to set the dividing date for this Accountant's Copy, as shown here. Your accountant will be able to work on transactions dated on or before that date in his or her copy while you can continue to work and create transactions that are dated after the dividing date in your company file. To learn more about this important date, be sure to read the section "Choosing the Dividing Date." Click Next to save the file.

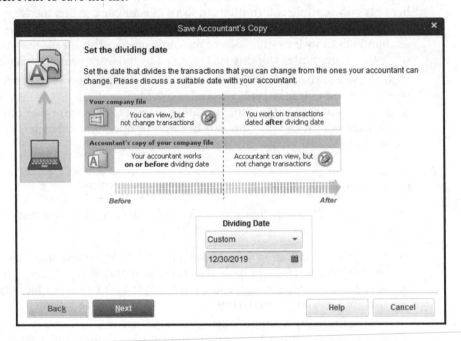

QuickBooks opens the Save Accountant's Copy dialog and creates a filename that incorporates your company filename as well as the date and time of the file's creation. That's an excellent filename, and there's no reason to change it. By default, QuickBooks saves the Accountant's Copy to your desktop, but you can change the location if you wish.

If you're sending the file on a flash drive, change the location by choosing the flash drive in the Save In field at the top of the dialog. If you're planning to send the file on a CD or DVD, save the file to your hard drive and then transfer the file to the CD/DVD. After you save the file, QuickBooks displays a message reminding you of the dividing date and to send the file to your accountant.

If you've password-protected your QuickBooks data file, you must give your accountant the Admin password so he or she can open it.

Sending an Accountant's Copy to an Online Server

To create an Accountant's Copy that is uploaded to a secure server maintained by QuickBooks (or any other service) from which your accountant can download the file, choose File | Accountant's Copy | Send To Accountant, which opens the Send Accountant's Copy dialog that explains the process.

Click Next to establish a dividing date. Your accountant will be able to work on transactions dated on or before that date in his or her copy while you can continue to work and create transactions that are dated after the dividing date in your company file. To learn more about this important date, be sure to read the next section, "Choosing the Dividing Date."

In the next window, enter your accountant's e-mail address twice to confirm the data, your name, and your e-mail address. If an e-mail address exists in the e-mail field of the Company Info dialog (in the Company menu), that address is automatically entered as your e-mail address, but you can change it.

In the next window, enter a password your accountant needs to open the company file in the accountant's version of QuickBooks. It must be a *strong password,* which means it contains at least seven characters, a mixture of letters and numbers, and at least one letter in a different case from the other letters (usually, this means one letter is uppercase).

If your Admin password is a strong password because you enabled credit card security, you can use the Admin password for the upload/download server access. You can also enter a message for your accountant that will appear in the body of the e-mail message, notifying your accountant that you've uploaded the file. E-mail text is not encrypted as it travels around the Internet, so don't use this message to give your accountant the password.

Click Send to upload the file to the server. QuickBooks displays a message telling you it must close all windows to create an Accountant's Copy; click OK to continue. When the Accountant's Copy has been created and uploaded to the QuickBooks server, QuickBooks displays a success message.

QuickBooks then sends an e-mail to both you and your accountant.

Choosing the Dividing Date

The text in the Set The Dividing Date window, seen earlier, explains that your accountant works on transactions dated on or before the dividing date, and you work on transactions dated after the dividing date. You and your accountant should discuss the dividing date you select.

While your accountant is working with the Accountant's Copy, you can continue to work in your QuickBooks file, adding transactions dated *after* the dividing date. There are some limitations, however, in what you can change in your file while an Accountant's Copy is outstanding:

- You can add a new account but not subaccounts. You can also make existing accounts inactive. You cannot add a subaccount to an account that existed before creating the Accountant's Copy.
- If you perform bank or credit card account reconciliation and clear transactions dated on or before the Accountant's Copy dividing date, be sure to advise your accountant that you're performing a reconciliation. Otherwise, if the accountant performs a reconciliation for the same month and/or clears the same transactions, the reconciliation will be undone in your QuickBooks file when you import the accountant's changes.

The dividing date you select should be the period for which you need your accountant to examine your books and make needed changes, which may not be a year-end date.

Some people send an Accountant's Copy with a dividing date matching the date of a report they need for a special reason—such as an income statement and/or balance sheet the bank wants to see because of an existing or potential line of credit. Other users may need an "accountant-approved" detailed report of transactions for the company's partners or a nonprofit association's board (usually a month-, quarter-, or year-end date).

To give your accountant a period in which to insert changes, such as adjusting journal entries or reversing journal entries, set the dividing date about two weeks after the end date you need. For example, if the report you need is as of the end of the last quarter, set the dividing date for two or three weeks after the last quarter-end date.

Merge the Accountant's Changes into Your File

The file your accountant sends back is not a complete QuickBooks company file; it contains only the changes made by your accountant. In addition, the file is encrypted so it can be imported only into the company file you used to create it.

Follow these steps to open the file and import it into the original company file:

1. Be sure the company file from which you created the Accountant's Copy is open.
2. Choose File | Accountant's Copy | Import Accountant's Changes From File (if the file is on removable media) or From Web (if your accountant is using Intuit's file transfer service).
3. Navigate to the location where you saved the file your accountant sent, and double- click the file listing; the file has the naming format <CompanyName> (Acct Changes).qby.
4. The Incorporate Accountant's Changes window opens so you can preview the changes that will be merged into your company data file and read any notes your accountant wrote. (Before you import the changes, you can save the report as a PDF file or print it.)
5. Click Incorporate Accountant's Changes. QuickBooks walks you through the process of backing up your current file before importing the changes and then merges the changes into your company data file.

If any transactions failed to merge with your company file, a message appears informing you of this. The window includes buttons you can click to save (as PDF) or print the information. QuickBooks, however, will automatically create a PDF and save it in the same location as your QuickBooks data file.

Click Close. QuickBooks displays a message asking if you'd like to set a closing date and password-protect the closed period as of the dividing date you set. If the dividing date on this Accountant's Copy was the last day of the previous fiscal year, this is a good idea, so click Yes; if not, use your own judgment. QuickBooks opens your company file, the text on the title bar changes back to its normal contents (instead of displaying a notice that an Accountant's Copy is outstanding), and you can work in the file with no restrictions.

After you're up and running again normally, you can delete the file your accountant sent you, and you can delete the Accountant's Copy file you created if you saved it instead of uploading it.

Cancel the Accountant's Copy

Sometimes, accountants report that they have no changes to make; or they send you an e-mail to notify you of a small change and ask you to enter the transaction manually; or sometimes, you decide you made the Accountant's Copy in error and don't want to wait for a file to come back (don't forget to tell the accountant about your decision). Whatever the reason, if you're not going to get a file back from your accountant, you can cancel the Accountant's Copy in order to work normally in your company file.

Another reason to cancel the Accountant's Copy is that you simply don't want to import the changes you saw in the Incorporate Accountant's Changes window. Call your accountant and discuss the problem. If the result is that you prefer not to import the changes, close the Incorporate Accountant's Changes window without importing the changes and cancel the Accountant's Copy.

To cancel the Accountant's Copy, choose File | Accountant's Copy | Remove Restrictions. QuickBooks asks you to confirm your decision. Select the Yes, I Want To Remove The Accountant's Copy Restrictions option, and click OK.

However, if you cancel the Accountant's Copy and then later decide you want to import and accept the changes, you cannot import the copy you've just canceled. You'll have to create a new Accountant's Copy, send it to your accountant again, and he or she, in turn, will need to redo whatever changes were made in the Accountant's Copy.

Fixing Common Problems

Chapter 18

I n this chapter:

- Understanding the various versions of QuickBooks

- Suggestions for entering your data into QuickBooks

- The various types of backups

- Working with your printers

- Banking issues and some general reconciliation tips

- Payroll ideas and comments

- Prepayments, undeposited funds, and other accounts receivable issues

- Using the Loan Manager to fix old paid bills

- Dealing with sales tax issues

- Using reports in QuickBooks

- Working with inventory

- Using a QuickBooks Advisor

Although QuickBooks is easy to set up and use, occasionally, mispostings or other computer misfortunes occur. This chapter discusses some of those misfortunes and explains how to avoid them—or fix them if they cannot be avoided. It also includes suggestions and tips that you may find useful for your company.

Version Comparisons

To choose the QuickBooks version that is best for your company, consider the following differences between the desktop versions. Table 18-1 does not include QuickBooks Online features. Remember that each computer must have a licensed copy of QuickBooks installed.

Data Entry Issues

Whether you are entering transactions manually or downloading them from your bank or credit card company, it is easy to mistype, transpose, miscode, or simply not see a transaction. Consider these tips when entering data:

- Enter data in batches and verify each 10 to 20 entries to find typos and/or transposition errors before they cause a problem. Enter all transactions for one income or expense account at one time to ensure you have coded each transaction correctly.

Feature	Pro	Premier	Enterprise
Number of simultaneous users	3	5	30
Can download both bank and credit card transactions	Yes	Yes	Yes
Operating system NOTE FOR ALL VERSIONS: At the time of this writing, Windows 10 is not mentioned as a supported system on any system requirements list. However, most Windows 10 users are not experiencing any issues using QuickBooks 2016 with Microsoft's new operating system.	Windows 8.1, Windows 7, Vista, Windows Server 2012 and 2008, Windows Small Business Server 2011 and 2008	Windows 8.1, Windows 7, Vista, Windows Server 2012 and 2008, Windows Small Business Server 2011 and 2008	Windows 8.1, Windows 7, Vista, Windows Server 2012 and 2008, Windows Small Business Server 2011 and 2008
Sales orders available	No	Yes	Yes
Ability to create a business plan	No	Yes	Yes
Inventory assembly	No	Yes	Yes
Balance Sheet report by class	No	Yes	Yes
Industry-specific reports	No	Yes	Yes
Change order option	No	Yes	Yes

TABLE 18-1   QuickBooks Version Comparisons

- Use the Multiple Entry option when possible, both to save time and to see each entry in the group.
- Use the Spell Checker preference to ensure that your spelling is correct. Click Edit | Preferences | Spelling and select Always Check Spelling.

List Entries

One of the most common problems with data entry is duplicate entries in lists. For example, you may have entered a vendor as "Smith, John," whereas another user has entered the vendor name as "John Smith." To eliminate such issues, first create a company-wide protocol for entering customer and vendor names and ensure that each user understands the process. This can be last names first or first names first, as long as everyone is consistent.

To solve this type of entry issue once it occurs, you can do the following:

- Delete a name if that name is not used in any transactions.
- Inactivate a name used in transactions if it will not be used again. To do so, double-click the name and check the (*Vendor/Customer/Job/Account*) Is Inactive check box.
- Merge the two names as explained in Chapter 2; remember that you cannot undo a merge.

Account Type Errors

If an account has been entered as the wrong type, such as Income instead of Expense, you can usually correct it by doing the following:

1. Right-click the account name and choose Edit Account Window.
2. Select the proper type from the Account Type drop-down list.
3. Click Save & Close to close the window.

You cannot change the type of a subaccount. Only parent account types can be changed. To change a subaccount type, you must first make it a parent account and then change the type. Then you can change it back to a subaccount.

Duplicate Name/Functions

QuickBooks does not allow duplicate names to be used for different functions. For example, if you have a customer with the name "John Smith" and purchase items from that customer, you should create a vendor name such as "John Smith-Vendor" to be used when you purchase goods. If you use the customer name "John Smith" when you purchase goods, your financial statements may be incorrect.

Understand Name Types in QuickBooks

Review the name types in QuickBooks to ensure that each name you add is properly classified. You can change the name type in the Other Name list into one of the other three types. If you need to change the name type for a customer, vendor, or employee, you will need to delete or inactivate the original name and create a new name in the appropriate list. Following are the four name types you can use:

- **Customer** These people pay your company after you have sold them either merchandise or services.
- **Employee** These folks receive a paycheck through QuickBooks payroll. If you reimburse an employee for merchandise purchased on behalf of your company, create a name in the Vendor section, adding a "V" to the name to make it different from the employee name. This will help avoid confusion that the reimbursement is part of payroll.
- **Vendor** Vendors are companies or people that you pay for providing goods or services, including utilities such as the telephone company. You could even create a vendor name to record draws made by owners or partners.
- **Other Name** These folks do not fit in any of the three main categories. Many companies enter officer names as "Other Names."

Small Business Tip In many lists, the Duplicate Item is immediately above the Delete Item option. Watch for this, as it is easy to choose Delete when you meant to choose Duplicate.

Keyboard Shortcuts

Table 18-2 shows some common QuickBooks keyboard shortcuts. You can see many more in QuickBooks Help by clicking Help | QuickBooks Help and typing **Keyboard Shortcuts** in the Search box.

First Key	Second Key	Action
ALT	B	Opens Banking menu
CTRL	J	Opens Customer Center
CTRL	A	Opens the chart of accounts
CTRL	C	Copies selected item to the Clipboard
CTRL	F	Opens the Find window
CTRL	I	Opens the Create Invoice window
CTRL	V	Pastes items selected by pressing CTRL-C
Right-click		Opens context menus through QuickBooks

TABLE 18-2 QuickBooks Keyboard Shortcuts

QuickBooks Maximum File Sizes

As discussed in earlier chapters, no hard-and-fast rule governs file sizes in QuickBooks. There is no built-in warning when you are approaching the maximum. You may, however, notice some of the following signs that indicate you are getting close:

- QuickBooks shuts down with a variety of error messages.
- You can't run a backup properly.
- The Rebuild or Verify utilities do not appear to be working.
- It takes forever to run a report or for a report to display.

To view the information about your file, press either the F2 key or CTRL-1 to open the screen shown in Figure 18-1.

Look at these three areas.

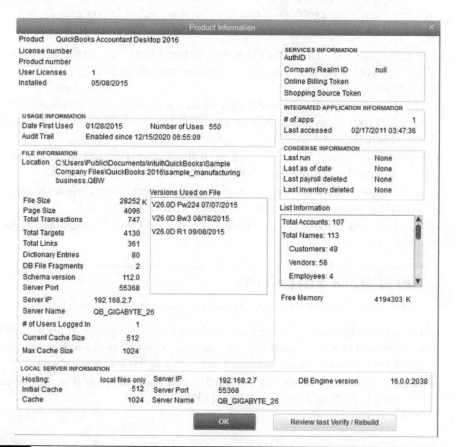

FIGURE 18-1   The Product Information screen provides information about your data.

File Size

According to QuickBooks, the file size should be less than 150MB. Again, according to Intuit's guidelines, the file size that QuickBooks will support depends on the amount of random access memory (RAM) on your computer.

List Information

According to QuickBooks guidelines, QuickBooks Pro and Premier can accommodate a total of 14,500 names in the Employee, Customers, Vendors, and Other Names lists. (The guidelines suggest a maximum of 10,500 entries in an individual list.) The same maximum exists for the Items list. If you upgrade to QuickBooks Enterprise, that number increases to 100,000 for both Names and Items lists.

DB File Fragments

In this case, DB stands for database. If your QuickBooks database field (shown in DB File Fragments) shows a number of 10 or less—then according to QuickBooks guidelines, there is no problem. If that number approaches 20, try to reduce the fragments using one of these steps:

- Rebuild your data. Click File | Utilities | Rebuild Data. This process requires a backup. Remember that you can never have enough backed up files. Follow the onscreen instructions.
- Use the Windows Defragmentation tool on the computer where your files are stored. If your file is stored on a server, work with your IT administrator before attempting this process.
- In Windows 10 and 8.1, open the Search application, type **defrag**, and select Defragment And Optimize Drive(s). Follow the directions on the screen.
- In Windows 7, click Start and type **defrag** in the search box. Select Defragment Your Hard Drive from the menu and follow the directions.
- Use the Condense Data utility (click File | Utilities | Condense Data), as discussed in Chapter 15.

General Data Entry Tips

Here are several tools and tips you can use when entering data into QuickBooks:

- *Use the QuickMath calculator.* Click inside a field (such as the Amount field on an invoice) and press the equal sign (=) on your keyboard to open the calculator. Or, when your cursor is in any field that contains a dollar amount, press +-* or press /.
- *Use a QuickBooks folder.* Create a QuickBooks folder on your desktop for file copies you want to copy to a flash drive or CD/DVD.

- *Keep your chart of accounts simple.* Use only the subaccounts you need to track so your reports are useful.
- *Close the QuickBooks windows.* Close all windows when quitting for the day. Click Window | Close All. This not only saves time but allows QuickBooks to load faster the next time.

Back Up, Back Up, Back Up

Backing up your data could be the most important way of saving your data and even your business. Back up your QuickBooks data to an external hard drive and take the drive home, and/or back up to an online storage service such as Dropbox or ShareFile. Back up your data at least daily.

You can choose from several types of backups:

- **Full backup**   This method backs up all selected files and folders. It takes time and storage space, but should be performed at least weekly.
- **Incremental backup**   This method backs up files and folders that have been added or changed since the last backup. For example, if you do a full backup on Wednesday evening and an incremental on Thursday evening, all changes since the Wednesday evening backup will be recorded. If you do another backup on Friday, only the files changed since the backup on Thursday are amended. Although this type of backup is faster, if you need to restore the data, you must restore the full backup first and then restore each incremental backup in the order that it was performed.
- **Differential backup**   This type backs up all files and folders that have been changed since the last full backup. For example, if you do a full backup on Wednesday and a differential backup on Thursday and Friday, Friday's backup will include all changes from both Thursday and Friday, essentially duplicating the differential backup from Thursday. To restore the data, you only need the full backup and the latest differential backup.

General Backup Tips

The following tips will help you create your company backup policies and procedures:

- Create a checklist to ensure the most important files are backed up first.
- Make sure the backup storage media has enough room for your QuickBooks file.
- Create at least two copies of your backed-up files on two different storage mediums.
- If you have problems, use another form of backup media.
- Use the Verify Data and Rebuild utilities if you continue to have problems.

- Double-check your media to ensure that the file exists. A QuickBooks backup filename has a .qbb extension.
- Create a backup schedule and vary the locations. Ensure that everyone using QuickBooks adheres to the same schedule.
- If you have only a few files to back up, consider copying them rather than using a backup procedure. Copying a file is much quicker than restoring it from a backup.

Printer Issues

Printer issues reported by QuickBooks users cover a wide range of concerns. Often, the problem is with the printer itself:

- Ensure that the printer has paper and that it has been loaded correctly.
- Make sure the printer is connected both to your computer and to an electric outlet and that the cables are seated securely.
- Test the printer outside of QuickBooks by printing from another program.
- If you encounter a problem, turn off the printer and then your computer. Restart your computer and then turn the printer back on.

The New Printer Won't Print

You have just installed a new printer and verified through Windows that it functions and prints a test page, but QuickBooks will not recognize it. Try the following first:

1. Click File | Printer Setup. From the Form Name drop-down list, choose the form that won't print.
2. Click the Printer Name drop-down list to select the appropriate printer for this form.
3. Click Options and choose the appropriate orientation and any other settings for the form.
4. Click OK to return to the Printer Setup window. Select Printer Type and any other options to complete your choices. Click OK to close the window and print your form. If that does not work, close and restart QuickBooks and try again.

If you still can't print to your new printer, close QuickBooks, and from Windows, search for a file named qbprint.qbp. Rename that file qbprint.qbp.old. Restart QuickBooks, and you should be able to print to the new printer.

Check Printing Isn't Working

Printing checks, especially payroll checks, can be frustrating. Consider the following if you encounter problems.

If the text (printing) looks odd, make sure you have aligned your check stock properly:

1. Click File | Printer Setup. Select Check/Paycheck.
2. Click the Align button.

If the checks printed in reverse order, follow these steps:

1. In Windows, open the Control Panel.
2. In Hardware And Sound, click View Devices And Printers. Right-click your printer's icon.
3. Look to see whether your printer prints the first or last page first. Make any necessary corrections and save.

Or, simply change the check numbers in your register!

Banking Issues

Banks make errors as well as people. When reviewing your bank statements, check for errors or additional charges before you start a reconciliation. Enter any necessary corrections or charges before reconciling your account. If you download your transactions, review each transaction rather than accepting them all at once.

Bank Reconciliation Issues and Tips

As you enter information into the Begin Reconciliation window, ensure that you have entered the appropriate ending date from the bank statement. Then, make sure that the beginning balance matches both your bank statement and your previous month's ending balance. If your beginning balance is not correct and you cannot locate the problem by clicking the Locate Discrepancies button, undo the last reconciliation. If that beginning balance does not match, go back to the point where the beginning balance matches the bank statement and redo all the reconciliations to solve the problem.

Double-check the balance you entered into the Ending Balance field to guard against transpositions. Hide any transactions after the bank statement's ending date and ensure that old, uncleared transactions are legitimate.

If you find problems when reconciling your bank account, click the Locate Discrepancies button to open the screen shown next. From here, you can run a Discrepancy Report, see previous reports, and click the link for other reconciliation tips from QuickBooks. The problem may be deleted transactions or items that have changed since you last reconciled.

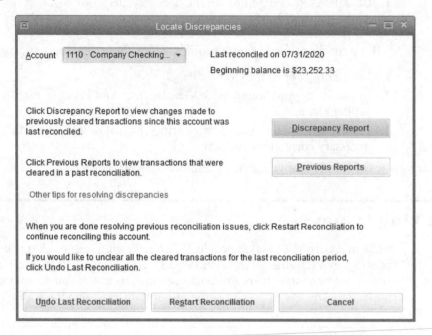

General Banking Tips

As you continue to work with QuickBooks, you may find that you want more detail about your bank accounts or you are having trouble during reconciliations. If so, consider the following:

- Consider creating a separate expense account for credit card fees and other bank charges so that you can track the cost. Over time, these fees can eat up profits, and many banks will waive them to keep your business.
- Watch for reversed transactions if you enter your data manually. For example, did you enter a deposit as a check or vice versa?
- Ensure that you are reconciling the correct bank account.

Payroll Issues

Payroll is one of the most sensitive areas in accounting. Chapters 9 and 10 have more detailed information, but the following tips may be useful. If you are unsure of how to set up payroll, work with your accountant to use the QuickBooks Payroll Setup Wizard. Here are two of the more common payroll issues:

- Payroll item types, including addition or deduction items, and company contributions
- Understanding when a payroll item is tax-exempt

After you have completed the setup, create a Payroll Item report for review.

Paying Payroll Tax Liabilities

When you create paychecks, QuickBooks adds the tax amounts due (your *payroll liabilities*) in special accounts. Do not pay payroll taxes with the Write Checks window. Instead, use the Pay Liabilities window:

> **Small Business Tip**   Failure to use the Pay Liabilities window often results in the overstatement of both your payroll tax liabilities and payroll tax expenses.

1. Click Employees | Payroll Center Or Employees | Payroll Taxes And Liabilities and choose Pay Scheduled Liabilities. You can also access this screen from your Home page. Click the Pay Liabilities icon in the Employees section shown here.

2. Select the liability you want to pay and click the View/Pay button at the bottom right of the Pay Taxes section as seen in Figure 18-2.
3. The payment appears in the Liability Payment window. If it does not already appear on the check memo, enter the payroll period this payment covers and the appropriate tax form. Then print the check.

> **Small Business Tip**   If your tax agency allows e-payments, the liability payment will show e-pay instead of a check number. Follow your taxing agency's directions to make the payment.

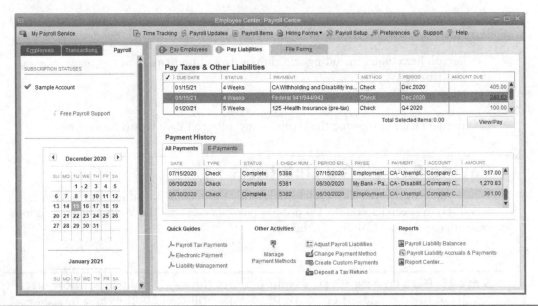

FIGURE 18-2 Use the Employee Payroll Center for information about many of your payroll-related activities, including some payroll reports.

Small Business Tip If you use QuickBooks Enhanced Payroll, the IRS, as well as a number of state taxing agencies, accept electronic payments. For most, including the IRS, you have to enroll in the program before your first payment. To learn more, select the Electronic Payment link in the Quick Guides section of your Payroll Center.

General Payroll Tips

Tracking employee and payroll information is important to every company. Follow these tips to ensure your records provide the information you need:

- Create item-specific expense and liability accounts, such as Medicare Expense and Medicare Withheld and Payable, rather than lumping everything into one expense and one liability account, such as Payroll Tax Expenses and Payroll Taxes Payable.
- Make sure you update your payroll data regularly. Do not ignore that message from QuickBooks.

- Consider creating a default employee template if many of your employees have similar jobs.
- Review the rules for employees versus independent contractors with your tax professional to ensure that your company is complying with current law.
- Ensure that tax deposits cover the appropriate payment period. The taxes are due based on the date the payroll is paid, not the period for which it was earned.

Account Receivable Issues

This section deals with some of the more common errors affecting your accounts receivable records and your financial statements.

Prepayments and Customer Deposits

When you receive a down payment or other prepaid funds, it becomes yours only when you perform the services or supply the goods. Therefore, the money you are holding is a liability until the transaction is complete. Enter the funds as shown here:

- **Memo** Down payment received from Smith
- **Debit** Bank Account
- **Credit** Unearned Revenue (Customer Funds Held)

Making Deposits to the Bank

When you go to the bank, you probably take several checks to deposit at the same time. That's the beauty of the Undeposited Funds account in QuickBooks: it keeps your deposits together so that you can tell QuickBooks which checks you deposited at the same time. Use this account so that QuickBooks recognizes that you deposited ten checks equaling $6259.50 instead of having to figure out which payments were included in that $6259.50 shown on the bank statement. To use the Undeposited Funds account properly when receiving a customer payment, follow these steps:

1. Click Customers | Receive Payments.
2. In the Receive Payments window, enter the information. Notice the Where Does This Payment Go? link in the middle of the screen. Click it to see the QuickBooks explanation of the Undeposited Funds account.
3. When you have completed entering the payment, click Save & Close, or, if you will be entering additional payments, click Save & New.

4. When you are ready to go to the bank, select Banking | Make Deposits to open the Payments To Deposit window. From this screen, shown next, select the checks to be included in this deposit and click OK. The Make Deposits window appears showing each of the selected checks.

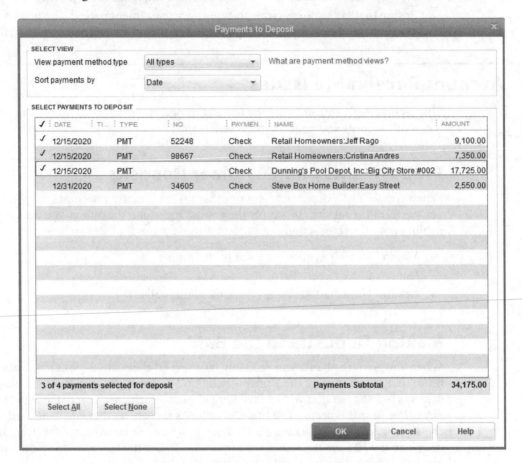

5. Add any other deposits you might be including and note the Deposit Total field. This shows the amount that will appear on your bank statement, as shown in Figure 18-3.

Undeposited Funds Balance Increases or Accounts Receivable Aging Shows Old, Paid Invoices

If your Undeposited Funds account seems to grow without ever shrinking, someone may be entering deposits directly into the check register instead of using the Receive Payments and Make Deposits windows. Two issues, each explained separately here, may be the cause. If the bank account has *not* been reconciled, try the following steps.

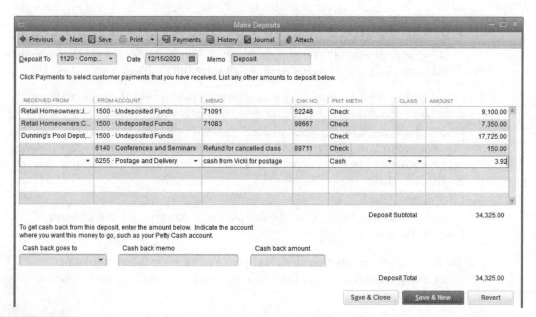

RECEIVED FROM	FROM ACCOUNT	MEMO	CHK NO.	PMT METH.	CLASS	AMOUNT
Retail Homeowners:J...	1500 · Undeposited Funds	71091	52248	Check		9,100.00
Retail Homeowners:C...	1500 · Undeposited Funds	71083	98667	Check		7,350.00
Dunning's Pool Depot,...	1500 · Undeposited Funds			Check		17,725.00
	6140 · Conferences and Seminars	Refund for cancelled class	89711	Check		150.00
	6255 · Postage and Delivery	cash from Vicki for postage		Cash		3.92

FIGURE 18-3   You can include both customer payments and other funds when making a deposit.

Undeposited Funds Account Has High Balance

If you see a high balance in the Undeposited Funds account, do the following:

1. Open your check register and delete the deposit made directly into the register.
2. Click Banking | Make Deposits | Payments To Deposit and select the appropriate checks for each group deposit.
3. Make the deposit and close the Make Deposit window.

Accounts Receivable Aging Shows Old, Paid Invoices

If you see old, paid invoices in the Accounts Receivable account, do the following:

1. Open your check register and delete the deposit made directly into the register.
2. Click Customers | Receive Payments and enter the appropriate customer payments.
3. Deposit these payments by clicking Banking | Make Deposits | Payments To Deposit and completing that process.

If the bank account *has* been reconciled, undo the reconciliation, delete the deposits that have been entered directly, enter the payments and deposits properly, and reconcile the statement again. If this has been going on for several months, you may have to undo the reconciliations for several months and start at the month in which this first happened.

Customer Balance Is Zero but Shows Open Invoices

This usually happens when the person entering the payment does not check the invoice being paid in the Receive Payments window. To solve the problem, follow these steps:

1. From the A/R Aging Summary, select either the payment or the negative amount and choose Payment to open the Receive Payments window for that payment.
2. Place a check mark by the invoice being paid with that check. Depending on what you selected in Edit | Preferences | Payments | Customer Preferences, QuickBooks may automatically apply the payments, starting with the oldest invoice and moving forward.
3. Click Save & Close.
4. To verify the transaction, rerun the A/R Aging Summary, and that customer's balance will show properly.

If there are open credits that should apply to payments, follow the same procedure, but select the open credits before you click Save & Close on the Receive Payments window.

General Accounts Receivable Tips

The following tips may help prevent accounts receivable issues:

- To ensure that deposits have been entered properly through the Receive Payments and Make Deposits windows, review both the Payments To Deposit windows and the A/R Aging Summary before reconciling each month's bank statement.
- Click Preferences | Sales & Customers | Company Preferences to ensure the Use Undeposited Funds As A Default Deposit To Account is checked for *all* users.
- If there are small amounts due, write them off. Consider using a separate account to see what effect, if any, write-offs have on your bottom line.
- Review your Customer/Jobs list to ensure there are no duplicate entries. Merge any that are duplicated.
- Ensure that your jobs are assigned properly.

Accounts Payable Issues

Paying bills is just as important as collecting the money from your customers. One source of confusion is understanding the difference between "cash" basis and "accrual" basis accounting for your vendor bills. If you record each vendor bill when it arrives and pay that bill from the Pay Bills window at a later date, you are using *accrual* accounting for that bill. If you simply write a check for a vendor's bill and record the expense at that time, you are using *cash* basis accounting for paying your bills.

Many companies have experienced difficulties when previously recorded bills are paid without using the Pay Bills window. If you see unusual numbers on your payable reports, check for unapplied vendor credits or bills paid with a regular written check instead of through the Pay Bills window.

Old Paid Bills Show in Bills To Pay

If your company enters bills, sometimes a bill is paid through the Write Checks window as a manually written check instead of creating the check through the Pay Bills window. In this case, the original bill continues to appear in your Bills To Pay list. Normally, when you try to pay a bill you've entered with a regular check, you'll see the warning message shown here:

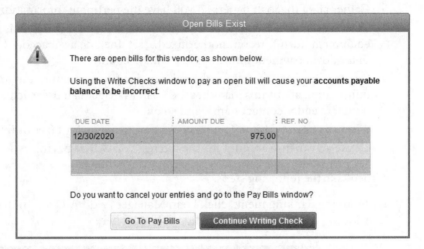

However, occasionally, if someone has written a check to pay a recorded bill, you can solve the issue when your books are kept on an accrual basis by following these steps:

1. Click Vendors | Pay Bills and select the bill that was paid.
2. In the Payment section, type the date of the original check.
3. In the Method section, select Check, Assign Check Number and choose the account from which you originally wrote the check.
4. Click Pay Selected Bills and insert the check number and the original date of the check.
5. Click OK.

If necessary, void the original check.

To solve the issue when you work on a cash basis, follow these steps:

1. Find the check and change the account to Accounts Payable. Include the vendor name in the Customer: Job field on the check.
2. A message will appear asking if you want to record your changes. Click Yes.

3. Link the check to the bill by opening the Pay Bills window. Select the appropriate bill and click Set Credits to open the Discount And Credits window.

4. Select the appropriate credit. That credit is applied to the bill and shows the Amount To Pay as zero, since you have now linked the payment and the bill.

5. Click Done to close the window and return to the Pay Bills window.

Using the Loan Manager to Fix Balance Sheet Issues

Many QuickBooks users enter their monthly loan payments as bills and in that way create problems with their Balance Sheet and other reports. QuickBooks helps solve that problem with the Loan Manager. Before you start, do the following:

- Gather all of the loan papers so you have the pertinent information at hand.
- Then create a fixed asset for the total cost of the item if this loan is for real property, equipment, furniture, or another fixed asset. Include a subaccount for depreciation. Enter down payment information to this account.
- Create a liability account for the balance due (loan amount) and include any information about this loan that the Loan Manager can use, such as account number, lender contact name, and so on.
- Create an asset account if you pay escrow payments for taxes or insurance.
- Create an expense account for the interest you will be paying.

Then take the following steps:

1. From the Banking menu, click Loan Manager | Add A Loan. In the Add Loan window, complete the information as shown here.

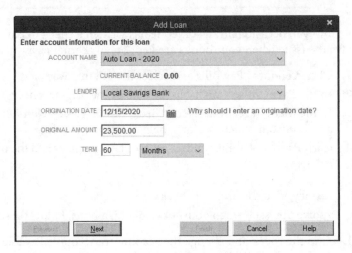

2. Click Next to enter the payment information.

3. Add any escrow payments if they apply and clear the Alert Me 10 Days Before A Payment Is Due check box if you do *not* want the alert.

4. If you have not entered the vendor information, including address and contact name, enter that now.

5. Click Next to enter interest information and indicate the accounts that are used to make these payments.

6. Click Finish, and from the Loan Manager screen, click Close to complete the process, as shown next.

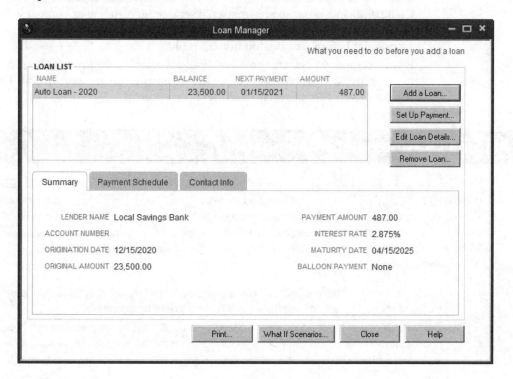

Small Business Tip You must enter all of the information described here in order to make Loan Manager information work for you. Pay special attention to the What You Need To Do Before You Add A Loan link at the top right of the Loan Manager window.

General Accounts Payable Tips

Following these suggestions can help you ensure that reports and financial statements reflect the proper amounts:

- Don't enter both a credit card charge *and* a bill in the Enter Bill section for the same expense. If it is a charge, use the Enter Credit Card Charge window rather than entering it in the Enter Bills window.

- Use subaccounts for tracking expenses. For example, rather than grouping all utilities together, consider using subaccounts such as Electricity, Propane, Waste Collection, and Water to see what each service is costing your company. Do be aware, however, that subaccounts can be an issue if there are too many. Talk to your accountant before creating too much detail.

- If your company pays vendors who should receive a 1099 form at the end of the year, work with your tax professional to ensure you are following all 1099 regulations and are properly tracking those vendors.

➡ Small Business Recommendation

You can use your QuickBooks data to create letters to mail using Microsoft Word 2007, 2010, and 2013 and Office 365 when it is installed on your computer (both 32-bit and 64-bit versions). The web edition of Office 365 is not recommended. At the time of this writing, Microsoft Word 2016 has not been officially addressed by Intuit. However, when using these features, the writer found Word 2016 works in the same manner as earlier versions of Microsoft Word.

Follow these steps:

1. Click Company | Prepare Letters With Envelopes. Select the type of letter you want to use from the menu. For this example, we're sending letters to customers.

2. Depending on the letter you chose in Step 1, you see a list of recipients from which to choose in the Letters And Envelopes window. You may see a message as shown next. If so, select Copy to complete the process.

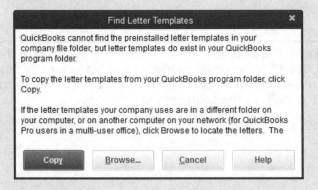

3. The Letters And Envelopes window appears showing your customer list. You may choose by both active and inactive customers, and you can create one letter for each customer or for each job. Select the names you want and click Next.

4. Choose a letter template from the list and click Next. You can create a new template or edit an existing template.

5. Enter a name and title for the person who will be signing the written letter. Click Next.

6. Microsoft Word creates the letter. To print each letter, click File | Print. You may also select File | Save to save it and print it later.

7. If you want to print an envelope at this time, return to the Print Letters And Envelopes window by closing the Word window and selecting Next. Otherwise, click Cancel to close the Letters And Envelopes window.

Sales Tax Issues

Chapter 6 discusses paying and reporting sales tax, but it is important to ensure your sales tax obligations are properly set up for each sales tax jurisdiction, as each has its own rules. Review that chapter again as well as these tips. You have two ways of reporting (and paying) your sales tax obligations: when you make a sale, even if you have not yet received payment (this is called paying on an *accrual basis*), or when you actually receive funds from your customer (the *cash basis*). You tell QuickBooks the appropriate method in Preferences. Follow these steps:

1. Click Edit | Preferences and choose the Sales Tax icon on the left side of your screen.

2. Select Company Preferences.

3. In the Owe Sales Tax area, choose either As Of Invoice Date or Upon Receipt Of Payment.

Once you've selected an option, QuickBooks shows the appropriate sales tax due on the Balance Sheet.

Sales Tax on Discounted Items

Depending on how you set them up, discount items affect sales tax calculations when they are applied. For example, you may find your sales tax is less than you expect if your discount item is a specific dollar amount and you have several line items on your invoice. In this case, the discount is distributed proportionally over each line item appearing above the discount item.

When you set a discount as a percentage of the sale, unless you add a subtotal item *before* you insert the discount item on your invoice, the sales tax is applied only to the item directly above the discount item.

When the Pay Sales Tax Window and the Sales Tax Liability Report Totals Don't Match

When you pay sales tax, the Pay Sales Tax and the Sales Tax Liability report totals should match. If they do not, here are some things to check:

- Check your Preferences to ensure all settings are correct.
- Check the ending dates for both reports to make sure those dates match.
- Compare your sales tax amounts. Double-click each amount in the Sales Tax Liability report Sales Tax Payable column to look for adjustments.
- Each item includes the proper sales tax *group* instead of a sales tax item.
- BILLPMT or CHK checks instead of TAXPMT checks are used to pay the sales taxes due.
- Check transaction dates to ensure this transaction is in the correct period.
- Check journal entries that may not affect sales taxes due.
- Check sales tax payments for previous periods.

Create Reports to Find Problems

Take the time to review both your Profit & Loss statement and your Balance Sheet regularly. The Profit & Loss statement can be a quick way of identifying problem areas or even incorrect coding. The Balance Sheet items should reconcile and be matched to the latest statements from your bank, credit card, and loan accounts. Tax and asset accounts can be reconciled as well. In addition, ensure that your credit card charges (and credits) are entered in the same way as any other bill, and review the expenses regularly.

Most companies print and review their monthly (and year-to-date) Profit & Loss and Balance Sheet reports regularly. However, QuickBooks provides other reports that offer more information and additional detail.

Multiyear Profit & Loss Comparison

To create a Profit & Loss comparison report for more than two years, follow these steps:

1. From the Reports menu, select Company & Financial | Profit & Loss Prev Year Comparison.
2. Click Customize Report.

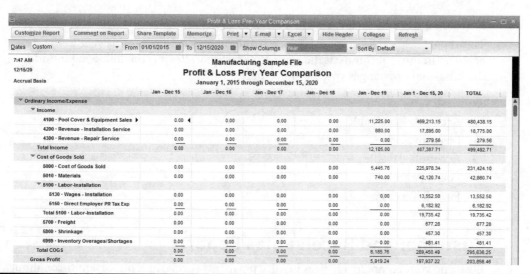

FIGURE 18-4   You can create reports for one, two, or more years.

3. Change the dates to the years you want to use. For example, 01/01/2016 through 12/31/2020.

4. In the Columns field, from the drop-down list, change the display to Year.

5. In the Add Subcolumns For area, clear the Previous Year check box.

6. Click OK to see your report, an example of which is shown in Figure 18-4.

Balance Sheet Reports

In addition to the standard Balance Sheet, each of the other Balance Sheet reports affords the reader a better understanding of the totals. All of the Balance Sheet reports can be accessed through the Report Center or from the Report menu. Click Report | Company & Financial | Balance Sheet *xxxxx*.

Balance Sheet Detail

If your Accounts Receivable total appears odd, run the Balance Sheet Detail report to see the individual transactions in the account for the last month. If there are too many transactions for the month, run the report by week or even by day, changing the dates at the top of the report.

Balance Sheet Prev Year Comparison

This report helps you compare your cash and other accounts for this year to the balances in those accounts at the same time last year. Review the following for odd discrepancies or changes you did not expect:

- Cash
- Accounts Receivable
- Inventory
- Accounts Payable
- Loans Payable
- Payroll Taxes Payable

Customer and Receivables Reports

Ensuring your company receives invoice payments regularly is important throughout the year. Consider using the following reports regularly to identify problems and collect overdue accounts. All of these reports are found in the Report Center and by selecting Reports | Customers & Receivables.

Collections Report

This report, shown here, shows unpaid, overdue invoices and includes the customer's telephone number. You can use this report to call or e-mail invoice copies to the customer.

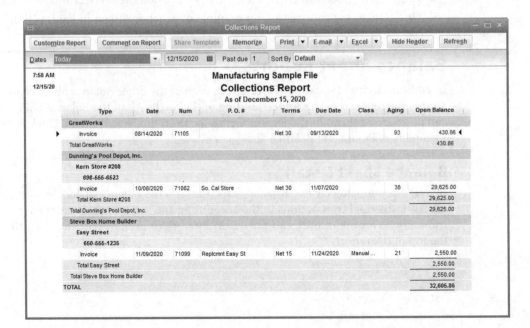

To send the overdue invoices via e-mail:

1. Double-click the amount to open the invoice and select Send at the top of the invoice.
2. Make the subject "Overdue Invoice" and add text to the e-mail.

Unbilled Costs by Job

This report lists any expenditures you have made that have not yet been billed to the customer. Consider running this report each month (or week) to ensure that all costs are billed promptly.

Accounts Payable Reports

Paying vendors promptly is just as important as collecting money from your customers. Although many smaller companies choose not to use the Enter Bills function and simply pay each bill with a check, during turbulent economic times, entering bills to ensure each bill is paid promptly can be useful. If your company chooses to do so, the A/P Aging Summary and Unpaid Bills Detail reports can be very useful. Consider running them monthly.

Using the Audit Trail

The Audit Trail report includes changes to any transaction in QuickBooks that affect the accounting process. You can identify each change easily because it appears in *bold italics*. The transaction itself is in boldface text, with a description of the type of transaction, followed by any applicable document number.

The following columns display content:

- **Num** This is the transaction number for each modified or deleted transaction. If this field is blank, the transaction may not yet have been assigned a number, such as a check ready to be printed.
- **Entered/Last Modified and Last Modified By** These columns show both the date on which the modification was made and the person making that change.
- **State** You will see either Latest or Prior in this column. Latest is the last time this particular transaction was changed, and Prior shows all the previous modifications.
- **Date** This is the original date of the transaction.
- **Name** The names shown here are the original names of vendors, customers, and/ or employees and the new names.
- **Memo** This column shows any memo attached to this transaction.

- **Account** This field shows both the original account numbers and any changes.
- **Split** This information comes from the original transaction.
- **Amount** The amount of the original transaction and any changes.

Track Inventory Issues

If you track inventory through QuickBooks, you may encounter some errors.

Negative Inventory

A negative inventory can occur when items have been received and sold but the stock has not been entered into QuickBooks. Although QuickBooks does warn you that you do not have enough stock on hand to fill an order, you can still create a sales receipt or invoice for these items. To solve the issue, ensure that all merchandise you receive for resale is posted into QuickBooks promptly, as your financial statements can be affected if there are negative inventory items.

Item Mistakes

Inventory errors can often be traced back to the Item list.

Item Is Used in Both Purchase and Sales Transactions

One of the most common issues is when an item is used in both purchase and sales transactions and someone forgot to click the This Item Is Used In Assemblies Or Is Performed By A Subcontractor Or Partner check box. When this happens, both the purchase information and the income information are posted to the income account. To solve the issue:

1. Click Lists | Item List.
2. Select the item, and in the Edit Item window, click the This *xxx* Is Used In *xxx* check box and select the appropriate expense account.

Item Is Assigned to the Wrong Account

You can change the assigned account for any item except a Sales Tax type item. If someone has assigned the wrong account, open the item and change the account to the correct one.

If you click Yes in response to the message that appears, all existing transactions will also be changed, and that will create a change in your financial statements. Check with your accountant before making such a change if there are many transactions in previous months or years.

QuickBooks Advisors

One of the main complaints about problem-solving tips is that the fix to *your* problem is not included. Consider connecting with a QuickBooks Advisor in your area to learn more about this great accounting resource!

Index